THE SEVEN CHAMPIONS OF CHRISTENDOM

Although Richard Johnson's chivalric romance *The Seven Champions of Christendom* is little known today, it was widely read for over three centuries after its first appearance in print in the 1590s, influencing the work of English writers from John Bunyan to G. K. Chesterton and profoundly affecting the representation of St George, England's patron saint, in folklore and popular culture.

In this volume, Jennifer Fellows offers, for the first time, a scholarly edition of *The Seven Champions of Christendom*. The text is based on the original printings of Parts I and II of the romance and is accompanied by explanatory notes and by an extensive introduction which places the work in its literary-historical context, traces its evolution through the centuries and presents what little is known of its author's life.

NON-CANONICAL EARLY MODERN
POPULAR TEXTS

Series Editor: John Simons

In recent years it has become broadly accepted that the central texts of English literature do not provide adequate materials for the critical study of the history of literary production and readership, a subject of growing interest. However, the availability of other texts, particularly from the early modern period, remains very limited. This series is designed to meet the demand for modern editions of non-canonical texts, concentrating on the period c.1580–c.1650.

The Seven Champions of Christendom (1596/7)

by Richard Johnson

Edited by
JENNIFER FELLOWS

ASHGATE

© Jennifer Fellows 2003

Published by
Ashgate Publishing Limited
Gower House
Croft Road
Aldershot
Hampshire GU11 3HR
England

Ashgate Publishing Company
Suite 420
101 Cherry Street
Burlington, VT 05401-4405
USA

Ashgate website: http//www.ashgate.com

British Library Cataloguing in Publication Data
Johnson, Richard, 1573-1659?
    The Seven champions of Christendom (1596-7) . -
    (Non-canonical early modern popular texts)
    1.Johnson, Richard, 1573-1659? . Seven champions of
    Christendom 2.Romances
    I.Title II.Fellows, Jennifer
    823.3 [F]

Library of Congress Cataloging-in-Publication Data
Johnson, Richard, 1573-1659?
    The seven champions of Christendom : 1596-7 / Richard Johnson ; [edited by] Jennifer Fellows.
        p. cm.-- (Non-canonical early modern popular texts)
    Includes bibliographical references (p.) and index.
    ISBN 0-7546-0198-6 (alk. paper)
    1. Christian saints--Legends I. Fellows, Jennifer, 1949- II. Title. III. Series.

PR2296.J6 S4 2004
823'.4--dc21   2002032997

ISBN 0 7546 0198 6

Printed and bound in Great Britain by MPG Books Ltd, Bodmin, Cornwall

For Eleanor

Contents

Acknowledgements

In the course of preparing this edition, I have benefited from the help of many people. I should like in particular to thank, in strictly alphabetical order, Jon Coe, Helen Cooper, James R. Kelly, Michael Langford, Katharine Martin, Helen Moore, Lynette Muir, Gillian Rogers, John Simons, Stephen Tabor (of the Henry E. Huntington Library), Suellen Towers (of the Folger Shakespeare Library) and Elizabeth Williams.

My greatest debt of gratitude, however, is owed to my daughter, Eleanor Fellows. She has helped me with every aspect of the preparation of this edition, from the textual to the technological; she has encouraged me in moments of despondency, when the task seemed endless; she has shared my pleasure in Richard Johnson's geographical solecisms; she has been a never-failing source of moral support. To her, therefore, this volume is dedicated with my love and thanks.

List of Abbreviations

7Ch	*The Seven Champions of Christendom*
BH	*Sir Bevis of Hampton*
DNB	*Dictionary of National Biography*, ed. Stephen et al.
EETS	Early English Text Society
ES	Extra Series
OS	Ordinary Series
FQ	Edmund Spenser, *The Faerie Queene*
ODEP	*Oxford Dictionary of English Proverbs*, ed. Wilson
OED	*Oxford English Dictionary*
STC	*Short-Title Catalogue ... 1475–1640*, ed. Jackson et al.
Wing	*Short-Title Catalogue ... 1641–1700*, ed. Wing

Introduction

Richard Johnson's life and works

Despite the enormous popularity of such works as *The Seven Champions of Christendom*[1] and *Tom a Lincolne*, very little is known of the life of their author. According to J. Payne Collier, Richard Johnson was baptized on 24 May 1573 and died in 1659;[2] but, as Richard S. M. Hirsch points out, 'Since Collier cited no authority, and is known to have been fond of fabricating, there is no good reason to accept [these dates].'[3] Johnson may have been born and bred in the Huntingdonshire area: he dedicated his romance *Tom a Lincolne* to 'THE RIGHT WORSHIPFVLL SIMON WORTEDG of *Okenberrie* [i.e. Alconbury] in the County of *Huntington*', being (he says) emboldened to do so by 'the great friendship which my parents haue heretofore found at the hands of your renowned Father'.[4] It may also be significant that the earliest work now attributed to Johnson, *Musarum Plangores* (1591), was written on the occasion of the death of Sir Christopher Hatton, who owned properties not far from Alconbury, in the neighbouring county of Northamptonshire.[5]

It is clear that Johnson spent the greater part of his life in London: the subject-matter of several of his works (such as *The Nine Worthies of London*, *The Pleasant Walkes of Moore-fields*, *Looke on Me London*) is London-related, and in many of his later writings he describes himself as a 'freeman of this Citty'.[6] It may well be also that his knowledge of the dramatic works of Marlowe and of Shakespeare, to which he makes several allusions in *7Ch*, was acquired in the London theatre.

In the dedication to *The Nine Worthies of London*, Johnson describes himself as 'a poore apprentice', though it is not known what his trade was. Given the phenomenal success of *7Ch*, however, it seems likely that he abandoned it and supported himself by his writings. The works attributed to him are as follows:

---

[1] Hereafter *7Ch*.

[2] J. Payne Collier, *A Bibliographical and Critical Account of the Rarest Books in the English Language* ..., vol. II (London: Lilly, 1865), p. 183.

[3] *The Most Pleasant History of Tom a Lincolne*, ed. Richard S. M. Hirsch (Columbia, SC: University of South Carolina Press, 1978), p. 20 n. 12.

[4] Ibid., p. 3.

[5] Hatton acquired Kirby Hall (near Corby) in the early 1580s and was also responsible for building Holdenby (six miles north-west of Northampton) in order to entertain Queen Elizabeth.

[6] *Tom a Lincolne*, ed. Hirsch, p. 20 n. 13. See also Naomi C. Liebler, 'Elizabethan pulp fiction: the example of Richard Johnson', *Critical Survey*, 12:2 (2000), 71–87 (p. 72).

1   *Musarum Plangores: vpon the death of the Right Honourable Sir Christopher Hatton, Knight, &c.* (1591). A competent, if undistinguished, verse elegy, first attributed to Johnson in 1963.[7] *STC* 14685.5.

2   *The Nine Worthies of London, explaining the honourable exercise of armes, the uertues of the valiant, and the memorable attempts of magnanimious minds* ... (1592). A work in verse and prose celebrating the martial exploits of nine Londoners 'whose vertues made them great, and whose renowne sprung not of the noblenes of their birth, but of the notable towardnesse of their well qualified mindes' (sig. B2ʳ).[8] Edited by Thomas Park in *The Harleian Miscellany*, vol. VIII (London: printed for White & Cochrane, John Harding and John Murray, 1811), pp. 437–61. *STC* 14685.7.

3   *The Most Famous History of the Seauen Champions of Christendome* (1596). See below.

4   *The Second Part of the Famous History of the Seauen Champions of Christendome* (1597). See below.

5   *The Most Pleasant History of Tom a Lincolne ... the Red Rose Knight* (1599–1607). An 'Arthurian' prose romance which, among Johnson's works, was second in popularity only to *7Ch*. Edited by Richard S. M. Hirsch as *The Most Pleasant History of Tom a Lincolne* (Columbia, SC: University of South Carolina Press, 1978). A dramatic version, which can probably be dated to the period 1611–1615, has been attributed to Thomas Heywood.[9] *STC* 14684.

6   *Anglorum Lacrimæ: in a sad passion complayning of the death of our late soueraigne lady Queene Elizabeth* (1603). A verse elegy shown to have been plagiarized from Thomas Rogers's *Celestiall Elegies of the Goddesses and the Muses* (1598).[10] *STC* 14671.

7   *A Lanterne-light for Loyall Subiects: or, A Terrour for Traytours* (1603). A prose tract 'describing many fayre examples of Traytours foule ends' (sig. A2ʳ) and, like Part I of *7Ch*, dedicated to Lord Thomas Howard. *STC* 14675.

8   *The Pleasant Walkes of Moore-fields* (1607). A tract on London life, in the form of a dialogue between a 'Countrey Gentleman, and a London Citizen' (sig. A3ʳ); mainly based on John Stow's *Chronicle*. *STC* 14690.

---

[7] See Jerry H. Bryant, 'Richard Johnson's *Musarum Plangores*', *Renaissance News*, 16:1 (1963), 94–8.
[8] Quoted in John Simons, 'Medievalism as cultural process in pre-industrial popular literature', *Studies in Medievalism*, 7 (1995), 5–21 (p. 10).
[9] See *Tom a Lincolne*, ed. Hirsch, pp. xxx–xxxi.
[10] Franklin B. Williams Jr, 'Richard Johnson's borrowed tears', *Studies in Philology*, 34 (1937), 186–90.

9 *The Pleasant Conceites of Old Hobson, the Merry Londoner* (1607). A collection of anecdotes which Johnson has associated with William Hobson, a well-known London haberdasher who died in 1581. Edited by W. Carew Hazlitt (London: Willis & Sotheran, 1866). *STC* 14688.

10 *A Crowne-Garland of Goulden Roses* (1612). A collection of twenty-six poems and historical ballads. Edited by W. Chappell as *The Crown Garland of Golden Roses: Consisting of Ballads and Songs*, Percy Society Publications 6, 15 (London: for the Percy Society, 1842–5). *STC* 14672.

11 *A Remembrance of the Honors Due to the Life and Death of Robert Earle of Salisbury, Lord Treasurer of England, &c.* (1612). A eulogistic prose biography. *STC* 14691.

12 *Looke on Me London* (1613). An exposé of abuses in London life, dedicated to the Lord Mayor, Sir Thomas Middleton, and shown to have been plagiarized from the work of George Whetstone.[11] Reprinted in *Illustrations of Early English Popular Literature*, ed. J. Payne Collier, vol. II (London: privately printed, 1864; repr. New York: Blom, 1966), no. 7. *STC* 14676.

13 *The Golden Garland of Princely Pleasures and Delicate Delights* (1620?). Another collection of ballads and poems, of which Johnson has been described as 'the compiler and reviser, rather than the author'.[12] Included among the twenty-nine items in this collection are 'A Princely Song of Richard Cordelion King of England', 'A Gallant Song of the Garter of England' and 'Titus Andronicus Complaint'. *STC* 14674.

14 *The History of Tom Thumbe* (1621). A version of the well-known nursery tale; perhaps largely the invention of Johnson, although references to the character Tom Thumb occur much earlier.[13] Edited by Curt F. Bühler as *R.I., The History of Tom Thumbe* (Evanston, IL: Northwestern University Press for the Renaissance English Text Society, 1965). *STC* 14056.

---

[11] Richard S. M. Hirsch, 'The source of Richard Johnson's *Look on Me London*', *English Language Notes*, 13 (1975), 107–13.

[12] Allan G. Chester, 'Richard Johnson's *Golden Garland*', *Modern Language Quarterly*, 10 (1949), 61–7. Given Johnson's plagiarism record, however, this may be to put too charitable a construction on the nature of his activities here.

[13] See *The Classic Fairy Tales*, ed. Iona and Peter Opie (London: Book Club Associates, 1974), pp. 30–1; *The History of Tom Thumbe*, ed. Bühler, pp. v–ix.

The Seven Champions of Christendom

Although he claims in the dedication of Part I of *7Ch* that the names of the Seven Champions 'to this day is [*sic*] held in great estimation through Europe',[14] Johnson actually seems to have invented the idea of this united band of Christian heroes himself, following a pattern established by, for example, the idea of the Nine Worthies or of the Fourteen Holy Helpers.[15] At first sight it might appear that *7Ch* belongs to a Spenserian tradition of Protestant hagiography; yet Johnson's protagonists (four from the British Isles, and one each from France, Spain and Italy)[16] are saints in name only. With the exception of some incidents relating to St George,[17] none of the adventures attributed to them here have any part in earlier, established versions of their legends;[18] even their deaths (described in the last seven chapters of the 1616 redaction of *7Ch*)[19] are, except in the case of St Denis, very different from those usually ascribed to them in more canonical hagiography. Johnson certainly knew *The Faerie Queene*,[20] borrowing from it many narrative motifs,[21] as well (probably) as the idea of making St George one of his heroes, but he shares none of Spenser's moral and religious preoccupations. For example, while Spenser (in accordance with established tradition)[22] allegorizes the fight between Redcrosse and the dragon (*FQ*, I.xi) in terms of the defence of the True Church and its deliverance from error, St George's encounter with the Egyptian dragon, though apparently influenced in some respects by *FQ*,[23] is merely the means by which he wins the love of the local princess, Sabra; nor is his deliverance of Egypt from the dragon used as an instrument of conversion, as in the *Legenda*

---

[14] See p. 3 below.

[15] The earliest instance of the phrase 'Seven Champions of Christendom' cited in *OED* is from the title of Johnson's work. He had earlier followed the same traditional pattern in *The Nine Worthies of London*. On the Fourteen Holy Helpers, see David Hugh Farmer, *The Oxford Dictionary of Saints* (Oxford: Clarendon Press, 1978), p. 156.

[16] Both St Denis (who, along with St George, was one of the Fourteen Holy Helpers) and St James the Great (whose shrine at Compostella was one of the principal places of pilgrimage in pre-Reformation Europe) were well known in England, with large numbers of churches dedicated to them. St Anthony has never been the patron saint of Italy – nor, indeed, was there any Italy as we know it in Johnson's time; but insofar as Johnson's Anthony relates to any recognized saint, it seems to be to St Antony of Padua.

[17] See notes to pp. 12–13, 16, 18–19.

[18] Indeed some of the protagonists' activities in *7Ch* are the very reverse of saintly – as in the distinctly unsavoury episode of St George's attempted seduction/rape of the Vestal Virgin Lucina (Part II, Chapter XIII).

[19] See pp. xxiii–xxiv below.

[20] Hereafter *FQ*.

[21] See the Notes (pp. 263–307 below), passim.

[22] Cf. Cornelia Steketee Hulst, *St George of Cappadocia in Legend and History* (London: Nutt, 1909), pp. 12, 39.

[23] See notes to p. 12.

aurea and its derivatives.[24] From time to time Johnson attributes to his heroes a specifically Christian motivation, or ascribes their success to their faith in God,[25] but not to the extent that this imparts to his work any real thematic unity – in *7Ch* the story is always paramount.

Where Spenser's narrative is directed by his allegorical purpose and informed by a high moral seriousness, the spirit of *7Ch* is, rather, that of a rather naive nationalism. The primary focus of attention is always the English champion, St George: he is the only one of the seven protagonists of whose *enfances* any account is given; he is always the one who rescues his fellow-champions from dangerous situations or exhorts them to new efforts; he sometimes brings to a satisfactory conclusion adventures begun by other champions.[26] Beyond their designations ('Saint *Andrew* of *Scotland*', etc.), there is no real association between the other champions and the countries of which they are patrons;[27] St George, on the other hand, is born in Coventry, the son of an English aristocrat, and the grandson of the king himself. The world outside England is a largely amorphous arena for the assertion of Christian, and specifically English Christian,[28] superiority; a region where one is as likely as not to find oneself in 'a Land as then inhabited with wild beasts' and to have to endure there 'pennurie & scarcitie of victualles'.[29] Part and parcel of Johnson's Anglocentrism is his cavalier disregard for (or ignorance of) geographical actualities: the Alps, we are told, 'deuide the countries of *Italie* and *Spaine*'; Hungary is apparently a pagan land in Asia; and Peru is in Greece, 'a myle from *Constantinople*'.[30]

The world of *7Ch* is, then, very much that of romance rather than hagiography, let alone reality; indeed, the influence of Middle English romance pervades Part I.[31] Undoubtedly the single most important influence on Johnson is the verse romance of *Sir Bevis of Hampton*,[32] which he ransacks for narrative motifs (usually in relation to St George) and often quotes verbatim.[33] *BH* was itself enormously popular: the manuscripts range in date from the period 1330–40 to the end of the fifteenth century, and the romance continued to be printed in metrical form,

---

[24] Cf. Jennifer Fellows, 'St George as romance hero', *Reading Medieval Studies*, 19 (1993), 27–54 (p. 33).

[25] E.g. pp. 50, 60, 63, 86, 88, etc.

[26] E.g. pp. 5–9, 62–3, 69, 140–1.

[27] We *are*, however, told that St Anthony was born in Seville (p. 36).

[28] It is St George who leads the Christian armies and wins three crowns (p. 92).

[29] Quotation from p. 25; cf. pp. 46, 52, etc.

[30] See pp. 33, 88, 261.

[31] Cf. notes to pp. 20, 34–5, 41, 115, etc.

[32] Hereafter *BH*.

[33] Cf. notes to pp. 13, 14, 61, 62, etc.

substantially unchanged, from the late 1490s until 1711;[34] probably only *7Ch* itself can lay claim to a longer shelf-life as a popular text.[35]

Johnson's debt to *BH* has long been recognized: in June 1762, the antiquarian Thomas Percy wrote to Richard Farmer:

> I am convinced you are right with regard to the Æra of the 7 Champions: but I have to-day made a discovery with regard to that book: which is that the principal Features of St George's story are from the Old Romance in rhyme of Bevis of Southampton: Almost everything of consequence relating to the single story of St George is very literally copied from Bevis.[36]

In fact, Percy has overestimated Johnson's dependence on *BH* and underestimated his facility in conflating narrative elements from a variety of sources. Johnson usually does this successfully, a particularly good example being his account of St George's dragon-fight and its aftermath, where motifs from two distinct episodes in *BH* are mixed with ones drawn from the Tristan story, from *FQ*, from bestiary lore and from the *Legenda aurea* tradition.[37] However, his 'magpie' habits sometimes betray him into narrative or thematic inconsistency. When St George escapes from a seven-year imprisonment, itself closely modelled on *BH*, he uses a trick borrowed from Bevis in order to induce the porter to open the gates for him, claiming that St George has killed his warders and escaped and that he has been sent in pursuit of him. Unlike Bevis, however, St George has *not* killed his warders. Later, he overhears Sabra's song, in which she makes it perfectly clear that she has been able to retain her virginity through seven years of marriage to Almidor, but only pages later shows, in a passage that echoes *BH* closely, that he is ignorant of the fact that she has managed to remain physically faithful to him.[38]

A slightly more complex example of Johnson's failure fully to integrate with one another motifs or ideas from disparate sources occurs in the episode of St Anthony, St Andrew and the swan princesses. When Rossalinde tells St Anthony how her sisters came to lose their human forms, she says that when they were faced with the prospect of rape by the giant Blanderon, 'their earnest praiers so preuailed in the sight of God, that he preserued their chasteties by a most straunge and woonderfull miracle, and turned their comely bodies into the shape of milke-white Swannes'.[39] In thus combining a Christianized version of an Ovidian metamorphosis with narrative elements borrowed from the Swan Knight legend, however, Johnson has got himself into a thematic muddle: God's 'woonderfull

---

[34] See Jennifer Fellows, '*Bevis redivivus*: the printed editions of *Sir Bevis of Hampton*', in *Romance Reading on the Book: Essays on Medieval Narrative presented to Maldwyn Mills*, ed. Jennifer Fellows, Rosalind Field, Gillian Rogers and Judith Weiss (Cardiff: University of Wales Press, 1996), pp. 251–68 (pp. 256–61).

[35] See pp. xxiii–xxviii below.

[36] *The Correspondence of Thomas Percy & Richard Farmer*, ed. Cleanth Brooks, The Percy Letters (Baton Rouge, LA: Louisiana State University Press, 1946), pp. 3–4.

[37] Cf. notes to p. 12.

[38] Cf. note to pp. 72–7.

[39] Quoted from p. 42.

miracle' later becomes the ladies' 'punishments', which can only be reversed by their father's conversion to belief in that same God.[40]

I have discussed elsewhere the way in which romance and hagiography interacted in the literary representation of St George as early as 1311.[41] Although the ascendancy of romance over hagiography in the treatment of George's legend might be said to have reached its apogee in *7Ch*, the process had in fact begun long before Johnson wrote. Many saints acquire a folklore of their own,[42] or come to have associated with them attributes or narrative motifs unrelated to their original legends,[43] but I am not aware that the stories of any of the other protagonists of *7Ch* underwent such radical transformation as did that of St George, or that any of these other six saints found themselves playing a leading role in a secular romance,[44] before they appeared as characters in Johnson's work. It is probably the introduction into St George's legend of the dragon-fight that is responsible for this difference:[45] whereas he had hitherto been venerated primarily as a martyr, George came increasingly (from the *Legenda aurea* onwards) to be celebrated above all for his victory over the dragon[46] – an achievement that he shares with many heroes of secular romance. Whatever the reasons for it, St George's legend had undergone a considerable degree of 'romanticization' before the era of *7Ch*, and it may even be that romances now lost to us influenced Johnson's treatment of the English champion in his work.[47]

Second only to medieval romance in their influence on *7Ch* are the classics. Much of Johnson's classical knowledge was probably derived from Virgil's *Aeneid* or from Ovid's *Metamorphoses*;[48] he may well have known also some of the Senecan tragedies current in English translation during the Elizabethan period.[49] His imagery is fraught with classical allusion, and he appears to feel no unease in the juxtaposition of classical deities and the Christian God.[50] He refers frequently to the Trojan War and its aftermath,[51] to the story of Jason and Medea,[52] and, above

---

[40] See p. 50.

[41] Fellows, 'St George', pp. 39–41.

[42] E.g. the tradition that St Patrick was responsible for expelling snakes from Ireland.

[43] St Cecilia, for example, was originally venerated as a martyr and only later came to be associated with music: see Richard Luckett, 'The Legend of St Cecilia in English Literature: a Study' (unpub. Ph.D. diss., University of Cambridge, 1972).

[44] See Fellows, 'St George', pp. 39–41, for St George's role in the *Roman d'Auberon*, an early fourteenth-century text attached to the *Huon de Bourdeaux* cycle, in which St George is the son of Julius Caesar and Morgan le Fay, and the twin brother of Auberon.

[45] The dragon-fight seems first to have been attributed to St George in the twelfth century: see John E. Matzke, 'The legend of Saint George: its development into a *roman d'aventure*', *PMLA*, 19 (1904), 449–78.

[46] See Fellows, 'St George', pp. 32–5.

[47] Cf. ibid., pp. 38, 41–2.

[48] See, e.g., notes to pp. 6, 21, 23, 58, 137, 165.

[49] See note to p. 7.

[50] Cf. pp. 21, 25, 28, 35, etc.

[51] Cf. pp. 5, 6, etc.

[52] Cf. pp. 34, 57, 128, etc.

all, to that of Tereus, Philomela and Procne. This last named is the only classical legend to have any significant *narrative* impact on *7Ch*; indeed, Johnson seems to take a salacious delight in tales of rape and violence against women, several such episodes in *7Ch* being influenced by this Ovidian story.[53]

On the whole, Johnson seems to have been rather less well-read in the work of his contemporaries or near-contemporaries than he was in older literature. He apparently knew some of the dramatic works of Shakespeare and Marlowe,[54] perhaps from visits to the theatre; but, although there is some evidence for his familiarity with such works of Elizabethan prose fiction as Lord Berners's translation of *Arthur of Little Britaine*, William Painter's *The Palace of Pleasure*, George Pettie's *A Petite Pallace of Pettie His Pleasure* and Thomas Lodge's *Rosalynde*,[55] there is surprisingly little for the specific influence of more sophisticated courtly romances such as Sir Philip Sidney's *Arcadia* or the chivalric narratives of Iberian provenance that came largely to supplant the older, native romances in popular favour during the course of the sixteenth century.[56] However, *7Ch* does show a certain amount of similarity to these works in the interweaving of the adventures of a number of different characters, and in the use from time to time of relatively high-flown imagery (often based on classical allusion) and other rhetorical devices.[57] Without influencing the narrative substance of Johnson's work to any great extent, then, the general tradition to which these romances belong does seem to have contributed something to the stylistic and structural diversity of *7Ch*.

In the introduction to his edition of Johnson's *Tom a Lincolne*, Hirsch remarks that 'the author employs both a plain and an ornamented style, varying their use according to the necessities of his narrative';[58] much the same might be said of *7Ch*, except that here the stylistic situation is further complicated by Johnson's dependence on a variety of sources in a variety of different genres, and by the introduction into his narrative of sometimes quite extended passages of verse.

By comparison to much of the fictional prose of the period, *7Ch* is fairly unelaborate in its general style. The diction is usually plain and non-Latinate, and the syntax straightforward. This is not to say, however, that Johnson's prose is altogether innocent of rhetorical ornament.[59] In more descriptive passages, his imagery (as noted above), tends to depend heavily on classical allusion;[60] quite often it is circumlocutory, and therefore more obfuscating than ekphrastic in its

---

[53] Cf. pp. 95, 106–7, 180–4.

[54] See, e.g., notes to pp. 41, 91, 98, 106.

[55] See notes to pp. 39, 44, 45, 102, 115, 116, 119, 124.

[56] See Ronald S. Crane, *The Vogue of Medieval Chivalric Romance during the English Renaissance* (Menasha, WI: University of Wisconsin Press, 1919), p. 7. Cf., however, notes to pp. 118, 193, 198, for the likely influence of one episode in *Amadis de Gaule*.

[57] Cf. John J. O'Connor, *'Amadis de Gaule' and Its Influence on Elizabethan Literature* (New Brunswick, NJ: Rutgers University Press, 1970), pp. 4, 98, 110.

[58] *Tom a Lincolne*, ed. Hirsch, p. xiv.

[59] Cf. Hans Werner Willkomm, *Über Richard Johnsons 'Seven Champions of Christendom' (1596)* (Berlin: Mayer & Müller, 1911), pp. 134–54, which provides a catalogue of the different rhetorical devices employed in *7Ch*.

[60] Cf. ibid., pp. 138–9.

effect: for example, 'Thus sorrow was his companion, and dispaire his chiefe soliciter, till *Hiperion* with his golden Coach had thirtie times rested in *Thetis* purple Pallace, & *Cinthia* thirtie times daunst vppon the Christall waues ...' is a rather long-winded way of telling us that St George's sufferings continued for a month.[61] More effective is Johnson's employment of homely images in a plain style, as when he describes how George and Sabra, having lost their way in the forest, 'were constrained to wander in the Wildernes like solitarie Pilgrims ... euen as a childe when hee hath lost himselfe in a populous Cittie, runneth vp and downe not knowing how to returne to his natiue dwelling'.[62]

A favourite stylistic device of Johnson's, particularly in set speeches, is the use of balance and antithesis in combination with repetition, as in Osmond's lament for the loss of his power:

> I that was wont to couer the Seas with Fleetes of ships, now stand amazed to heare the Christians Drums, that sound foorth dolefull Funerals for my souldiers: I that was wont with armed Legions to drinke vp riuers as wee marched, and made the earth to groane with bearing the number of our multitudes: I that was wont to make whole kingdomes tremble at my frownes, and force imperious Potentates to humble at my feete: I that haue made the streetes of many a Cittie run with bloud, and stoode reioycing when I saw their buildings burne: I that haue made the mothers wombs the Infants toombes, and caused Cradles for to swimme in streames of bloud, may nowe behold my Countries ruine, my kingdomes fall, & mine owne fatall ouerthrow.[63]

Sometimes Johnson's striving for effect results in downright absurdity: Lord Albert, bewailing the theft of his infant son, cries:

> O that the winde would be a messenger and bring me happie newes of his abode: if hee bee drenched in the deepest Seas, thether will I diue to fetch him vp: if hee bee hidden in the cauerns of the earth, thether will I digge to see my sonne: or if he like a feathered foule lye houering in the ayre, yet thether will I flie, and imbrace him that neuer yet my eyes behelde.[64]

Still more bathetic is the description of St Denis's distress on finding himself transformed into a hart:

> Thus discribed hee his owne miserie, till the watrie teares of calamitie gushed in such aboundance from the Conduits of his eyes, that they seemed to quench the burning thunder-bolts of heauen, & his scortching sighes so violently forced from his bleeding breast, that'they seemed to dim the brightnes of the sunne; whereat the vntamed Beares, & merciles Tygers relented at his mones, and like to harmeles Lambes sate bleating in the woods to heare his wofull exclamations.[65]

---

[61] Quoted from p. 20.
[62] Quoted from p. 124.
[63] Quoted from p. 137.
[64] Quoted from p. 7.
[65] Quoted from p. 26.

Another aspect of Johnson's rhetorical aspirations is the introduction into his prose narrative of passages of verse. Although these sometimes convey useful information to the reader or to other characters within the story,[66] they are on the whole more ornamental than functional: that is to say, they never carry any significant narrative weight. They tend to be either oracular and prophetic or elegiac and lyrical,[67] perhaps the most effective as verse being Rossalinde's 'swan song' and Sabra's 'sorrowfull Dittie' lamenting her prolonged separation from St George;[68] these themselves depend heavily upon such stylistic and rhetorical devices as apostrophe, alliteration and repetition.

One stylistic feature of *7Ch* that appears not to have been remarked hitherto is the contrast between Parts I and II. Part I is by far the more dependent on literary sources, which are sometimes quoted verbatim;[69] at times, indeed, Johnson appears to have inserted direct quotations of lines of verse into his prose: for example, '*Thetis* tripping on the siluer sandes'; 'the Doues did kisse when they beganne to sing ...'; 'Haue I had power to rend the vales of earth, and shake the mightie mountaines with my charmes?'.[70] Not only is Part II far less allusive than Part I, but it gives the impression of being a more careless composition altogether, as though Johnson was resting on the laurels of his success with Part I and was not always fully engaged with his own narrative. In the adventure of the golden fountain, for example, St James's encounter with the giant, and its outcome, are dealt with in a single sentence:

> Thus in this gallant manner departed he from the Iewes habitation, leauing the other Champions at their deuine contemplations for his happie successe, but his fortune chanced contrarie to his wishes, for at the Giants first encounter he was likewise born to the rock of stone, to accompany Saint *Denis*.[71]

Sometimes Johnson experiments with different rhetorical or stylistic devices but then, apparently, loses interest or confidence in them, so that they fall rather flat. An example of this occurs in the account of Rosana's combat with the magician:

> *Rosana* who saw his determination, did procure to defend her selfe, and offend her enemy.
>
> Oh my muse that I had such learned eloquence, for to set out and declare the noble incounters of these two gallant warriors: *Rosana* although shee was but a Feminin nature, yet was she as bolde in heroycall aduentures as any Knight in the world, except the Christian Champions.
>
> But now to returne we to our historie ...[72]

---

[66] See, e.g., George's appearance to Sabra in a dream (pp. 22–3), Eglantine's account of her own transformation into a mulberry tree (pp. 26–7), and Sabra's affirmation of her continued fidelity to St George (pp. 72–3).

[67] See, e.g., pp. 6–7, 57–8, 126–7, 208–9 (prophetic); pp. 39–40, 107–8, 225–6 (lyrical).

[68] See pp. 39–40, 72–3.

[69] See, e.g., notes to pp. 6, 7, 12–15, 41.

[70] See pp. 81, 142, 143.

[71] Quoted from p. 169.

[72] Quoted from p. 235.

Most striking of all is the anti-climactic ending of Part II, which fizzles out with the happy conclusion to the adventures of a distinctly secondary (if not tertiary) character, Pollemus. It is not until the 1616 redaction that Johnson brings his narrative to a proper close, with the deaths of the Seven Champions, and signs off with an appropriate peroration.[73]

One area in which Part II takes rather *more* care than Part I is in the use of embedded narrative. Both parts contain episodes in which subsidiary characters pour out their woes to one or more of the protagonists. In Part I, they tend to recount events which they cannot possibly have witnessed, and which only an omniscient narrator could know (as in Ormondine's account of '*the miserie of his children*' in Chapter X). In Part II, on the other hand, Johnson is more careful to ensure that he has in place some narrative device by means of which secret events can become more generally known – as in Chapter VI, where Leoger's gruesome rape and murder of the shepherd's younger daughter are revealed partly through the introduction of the character of the faithful squire, partly through the narrative device of the dream in which the unfortunate girl herself recounts her '*vnhappie fortunes*' to her father.[74]

Whatever the stylistic infelicities of *7Ch*, and the occasional absurdities of its plot, these features seem to have had no effect on the work's popular appeal. Johnson published Part II only a year after Part I, 'being thertoo incouraged by [the gentle reader's] greate curtesie in the kinde acceptation of my first part'.[75] The two parts were re-issued together, with only minor textual changes, in 1608; in 1616 they appeared again, this time with more substantial modification, including the addition of seven new chapters to the end of Part II:

CHAP. XVII
Of the renowned and praise-worthy death of Saint *Patricke*, how hee buryed his owne selfe: and for what cause the Irish-men to this day, doe weare their red Crosse vpon Saint *Patrickes* day.

CHAP. XVIII
Of the Honourable victory wonne by *S. Dauid* in *Wales*: of his death, and the cause why Leekes are by custome, of *Welsh-men* worne on *S. Dauids* day: with other things that hapned.

CHAP. XIX
How S. *Denis* was beheaded in his owne Country, and how by a miracle shewed at his death, the whole Kingdome of *France* receiued the Christian Faith.

CHAP. XX
Of the tyrannous death that the Spanish Champion was put vnto: and how God reuenged the same in a strange manner: and of other things that happened.

CHAP. XXI
Of the Honourable and worthy death of the *Italian* Champion, how in the height of his pleasure in his owne country, death by a Prophesie seazed vpon him.

---

[73] See p. xxiv below.
[74] See pp. 182–3, 185–6.
[75] Quoted from p. 149.

CHAP. XXII

Of the Martyrdome of *S. Andrew* the Scottish Champion, and how his death was reuenged by the King of that Countrey, and by what meanes *Scotland* was brought vnto the Christian Faith.

CHAP. XXIII

Of the aduenture performed by *S. George*: how he receiued his death by the sting of a venemous Dragon: and of the honours and royalties done vnto his name being entituled our English Patron of Knighthood.

The final chapter describes the honours and offices conferred on St George's three sons (it is here, for the first time, that an association is made between the eldest and Guy of Warwick)[76] and concludes with the focus firmly back on St George himself, always the first among equals of the original Seven Champions:

> [The King] likewise decreed by the consent of the whole Kingdome, that the Patron of the Land should be named S. *George*, our Christian Champion, in that he had fought so many battels in the honour of Christendome. All which we see (with many more honours) to this day here maintained in remembrance of this good Knight, who (no doubt) resteth in eternall peace with the other renowned Champions of Christendome: so God grant we may doe all. Amen.[77]

In this extended version, *7Ch* was reprinted steadily throughout the seventeenth century.[78] Indeed, with its lustful giants and deflowered virgins, not to mention the outlandish adventures associated with heroes who are nominally champions of Christendom, it is likely to have played a significant part in provoking the hostility towards popular romance that persisted throughout this period.

The most famous example of disapproval of this particular work is expressed by John Bunyan: in *Sighs from Hell* (1657), the condemned soul, looking back on its misspent youth, is made to say: 'The Scriptures, thought I, what are they? A dead letter, a little ink and paper … Give me a ballad, a news-book, *George on Horseback* or *Bevis of Southampton* …'.[79] Bunyan's attitude towards such works as *7Ch* and *BH* was, however, distinctly ambivalent: on the one hand, he inveighed against 'filthy ballads and romances';[80] on the other, these popular works clearly appealed to his imagination, furnishing him with the raw material for much of his allegory.[81]

---

[76] Guy is created Earl of Warwick; Alexander becomes 'Captaine generall of [the King's] Knights of Chiualrie'; David becomes the King's cupbearer (sig. Cc3^v).

[77] Ibid.

[78] STC and Wing between them list twenty-two editions between 1616 and 1700. See also Willkomm, *Über Richard Johnsons 'Seven Champions of Christendom' (1596)*, pp. 2–6.

[79] *The Entire Works of John Bunyan*, ed. Henry Stebbing, vol. I (London: Virtue, 1859), pp. 126–78 (p. 166ª).

[80] *'Life and Death of Mr Badman' and 'The Holy War'*, ed. John Brown, Cambridge English Classics (Cambridge: Cambridge University Press, 1905), p. 213.

[81] Harold Golder, 'Bunyan's Valley of the Shadow', *Modern Philology*, 27 (1929), 55–72 (pp. 59–64), and 'Bunyan and Spenser', *PMLA*, 45 (1930), 216–37 (p. 217), concludes that Bunyan undoubtedly knew *7Ch* and used it in *The Pilgrim's Progress*. Cf., however,

Johnson's romance also seems to have had some influence on variant versions of the Mummers' Play, though scholars disagree as to the extent of that influence.[82] The cast of characters often includes St George and 'the Morocco King', and St George's description of his own past exploits in, for example, the Minehead Mummers' Play is clearly influenced by *7Ch*'s version of events:

> I am a famous champion,
> Likewise a worthy knight,
> And from Britain did I spring
> And will uphold her might.
> I travelled countries far and near,
> As you may understand,
> Until at last I did arrive
> In the Egyptian land.
> Wherein that horrid fight
> With the fiery dragon bold,
> Did neither overcome, nor kill,
> Nor make my blood run cold.
> I fought the cursed dragon and brought him to the slaughter,
> And for that deed did win the King of Egypt's daughter.[83]

More directly based on *7Ch* is John Kirke's play *The Seven Champions of Christendome* (1638).[84] This five-act blank-verse drama retains the outline of certain episodes in Johnson's romance (notably those of Kalyb, the Egyptian dragon, Ormondine and Blanderon), but with substantial modifications. Some episodes, such as that of the dragon, are related by the Chorus; others are omitted altogether. Comic relief is introduced in the person of the clown Suckabus, one of many characters who have no counterpart in *7Ch*. The play ends with the marriage of Sts Anthony, Denis and Patrick to the transformed swan princesses (here reduced in number to three) and with dancing at their nuptials, before the departure of the champions abroad 'for fame of Christendome'.

Willkomm, *Über Richard Johnsons 'Seven Champions of Christendom' (1596)*, p. 158, where the influence of *7Ch* on Bunyan is minimized.

[82] See Sir Edmund Chambers, *The English Folk-Play* (Oxford: Clarendon Press, 1933), pp. 174–85; R. J. E. Tiddy, *The Mummers' Play* (1923; repr. Chicheley: Minet, 1972), passim; Alan Brody, *The English Mummers and Their Plays: Traces of Ancient Mystery* (London: Routledge & Kegan Paul, [1970]), pp. 46–52; Alex Helm, *The English Mummers' Play*, Mistletoe Series 14 (Woodbridge: Brewer for the Folklore Society, 1980), pp. 4–8. See also Fellows, '*Bevis redivivus*', p. 261, on the influence of *BH* (Johnson's single most significant source in *7Ch*) on the Mummers' Play.

[83] See Helm, *The English Mummers' Play*, p. 74.

[84] *The Seven Champions of Christendome. Acted at the Cocke-pit, and at the Red-Bull in St Johns Streete, with a generall liking. And never Printed till this Yeare 1638. Written by J.K.* (London: Printed by J. Okes, 1638). It has been suggested, on stylistic grounds, that Thomas Heywood may have had a part in the composition of this work: see Paul Merchant, 'Thomas Heywood's hand in *The Seven Champions of Christendom*', *Library*, 3rd series, 33:3 (1978), 226–30.

Towards the end of the seventeenth century, Johnson's romance was affected by two significant changes. One of these was the addition in 1686 of a third part, which recounts the adventures of the original Seven Champions' sons;[85] the other was the appearance of the first chapbook versions of *7Ch*.

Chapbooks, which had begun to appear by the 1670s,[86] are notoriously hard to date. The earliest chapbook of *7Ch* listed in Wing is tentatively dated to 1700,[87] though there is some evidence that chapbooks based on Johnson's romance may have been in circulation before that, even if they did not share its title: Samuel Pepys's collection includes one, *The Life and Death of the Famous Champion of England, St George*, which was advertised by its printer, W. Thackeray, in the 1680s and apparently based on parts of *7Ch*.[88] Certainly *7Ch*, or something like it, was available in a form suitable (one hopes!) for children (and therefore, probably, as a chapbook) by 1709, when it was described by Steele in the *Tatler* as being among the favourite books of Mr Bickerstaffe's little godson.[89]

Attention in the chapbooks is fairly equally divided between the original Seven Champions; there is no account of their sons (all the episodes included, with the exception of those of the champions' deaths, are from Part I), and very little of their lady loves – indeed, Sabra is barely mentioned. Verse is used where the

---

[85] *The Famous History of the Seven Champions of Christendom.The Third Part. Shewing The Valiant Acts and Renowned Atchievements of St George's Three Sons, Sir Guy, Sir Alexander, and Sir David. As ALSO The Warlike Exploits and Martial performances of Sir Turpin son to St Denis of France, Sir Pedro son to St James of Spain, Sir Orlando son to St Anthony of Italy, Sir Ewin son to St Andrew of Scotland, sir Phelim Son of St Patrick of Ireland, and Sir Owen son to St David of Wales. Their strange Fights and Combats with Gyants, Monsters, and Dragons, their Tilts and Turnaments in Honour of Ladies, their Battles with Miscreants and Tyrants in defence of the Christian Religion, and relief of distressed Knights and Ladies, their punishing of Negromancers, and putting to an end their inchantments, with other their knightly Prowess and Chevalry. As ALSO How St George's three Sons came all of them to be Kings, as the Fairy Queen had Prophesied of them. Licensed, May the 29th. 1685. R.L.S.* (London: printed by J.R. for Benj. Harris at the Anchor and Marriner in Thread-needle, [1686]). (Wing J806.) The work is attributed to William Winstanley in Heinrich F. Plett, 'An Elizabethan best seller: Richard Johnson's *The Seven Champions of Christendom* (1596)', in *Modes of Narrative: Approaches to American, Canadian and British Fiction presented to Helmut Bonheim*, ed. Reingard M. Nischik and Barbara Korte (Würzburg: Königshausen & Neumann, 1990), pp. 234–51 (p. 236), where, however, no reason for the attribution is offered and the date is given as 1696.

[86] See *'Guy of Warwick' and Other Chapbook Romances: Six Tales from the Popular Literature of Pre-Industrial England*, ed. John Simons (Exeter: University of Exeter Press, 1998), p. 16.

[87] Wing J809B.

[88] See Margaret Spufford, *Small Books and Pleasant Histories: Popular Fiction and Its Readership in Seventeenth-Century England* (London: Methuen, 1981), pp. 227–9; Chambers, *The English Folk-Play*, p. 179.

[89] Quoted in Arthur Johnston, *Enchanted Ground: the Study of Medieval Romance in the Eighteenth Century* (London: Athlone Press, 1964), p. 31; F. J. Harvey Darton, *Children's Books in England: Five Centuries of Social Life*, 3rd edn, rev. Brian Alderson (Cambridge: Cambridge University Press, 1982), p. 32.

original work uses it (and sometimes where it does not), but this is rewritten in a more modern idiom. Thus Kalyb's prophetic pronouncement to Alfred becomes:

> Sir Knight begone and mark me well,
> Within the lady's womb doth dwell,
> A son, who like a dragon fierce,
> His mother's tender womb shall pierce,
> A valiant champion he shall be,
> In noble acts and chivalry,
> Begone, I now bid you adieu:
> You'll find what I have told is true.[90]

The scenes of rape and violence that abound in Johnson's work are all omitted, and there is nothing that would have been unsuitable reading for the children who seem to have constituted the principal part of the chapbook's public during the eighteenth century.[91]

Chapbooks of *7Ch* continued to be printed throughout the eighteenth century, together with longer versions of Johnson's work. By the end of the century, the romance was being published on both sides of the Atlantic,[92] and (though the chapbook versions had largely died out by this time) it was steadily reprinted throughout the nineteenth and into the twentieth century.[93] Many of these later editions seem to have been designed specifically for children: an edition of 1816 was published in the New Juvenile Library series, and one of 1862 was 'especially adapted for the enlightenment, edification, and instruction of the rising generation'.[94] Naturally, any explicitly sexual content was much reduced in such versions: in an edition of 1861, for example, the following account is given of the transformation of the swan princesses:

> ... when the cruel giant Blanderon espied us, as he walked upon his battlements, he suddenly descended the mountain, and fetched us all under his arm up into the castle, where ever since we have lived in great slavery; and, for my six sisters, he turned their comely bodies into the shape of milk-white swans.[95]

---

[90] Quoted from *'Guy of Warwick' and Other Chapbook Romances*, ed. Simons, p. 82; cf. pp. 6–7 below. The *7Ch* chapbook edited by Simons was printed in Shrewsbury in the 1730s.

[91] See the passage from *Tristram Shandy*, ch. 20, quoted in Darton, *Children's Books in England*, p. 80; and cf. Gillian Avery, 'Books for the first enterers', *Signal*, 75 (1994), 194–208 (p. 202).

[92] An edition was published by Stewart & Cochran in Philadelphia in 1794, and another by Samuel Preston in Amherst, New Hampshire, in 1799.

[93] See Willkomm, *Über Richard Johnsons 'Seven Champions of Christendom' (1596)*, pp. 7–8.

[94] Quoted ibid., p. 8.

[95] *The Extraordinary Adventures of the Seven Champions of Christendom* (London: Griffin, Bohn, [1861]), p. 55. Cf. p. 42 below, from which a whole paragraph is here omitted. A still more highly sanitized version of this same episode occurs in a retelling of *7Ch* by Rose Yeatman Woolf, published by Raphael Tuck in the 1920s; here Blanderon transforms the

During the nineteenth century, two pantomimic stage adaptations of *7Ch* appeared: one (under the title *St George and the Dragon*), by Gilbert À Beckett and Mark Lemon, in the 1830s; the other, by the prolific author of such 'fairy extravaganzas' James Robinson Planché, in 1879. Neither of these works treats its subject-matter with any reverence, but both seem to assume their audience's familiarity with some version of Johnson's romance, depending on it for many of their humorous effects. That such familiarity *could* be assumed is evident from the many literary references to *7Ch* throughout the century.[96] A painting by Dante Gabriel Rossetti, *The Wedding of Saint George and the Princess Sabra* (now in the Tate Gallery, London), dates from 1854;[97] there was even a card game of the Seven Champions, produced in Manchester in 1858;[98] and in 1898 no lesser a literary luminary than G. K. Chesterton wrote a play for toy theatre based on the romance.[99]

A few illustrated, and mostly abridged, versions of *7Ch* appeared in the early years of the twentieth century, but the stream of editions which had been flowing steadily for over three hundred years was at last beginning to dwindle to a trickle. In our own time, the work has been little read and less studied. Histories of the prose fiction of the sixteenth and seventeenth centuries barely mention it,[100] and no extended study of it has been published since Willkomm's monograph in 1911; there has never been a scholarly edition of the work. Typical of the responses to it are that it is 'virtually unreadable' and the work of 'a writer for the illiterate'.[101] Perhaps it is time that it was reassessed: after all, generations of readers found it far from 'unreadable'. It may not be possible to hail it as a neglected literary masterpiece, but an informed understanding of its place in literary history might be expected to further our understanding of the popular culture of over three centuries.

---

princesses, who are depicted as young children, into swans because they are 'too small and thin to be worth eating' (p. 71).

[96] E.g. Washington Irving, *A History of New York ... by Diedrich Knickerbocker* (1809), vol. II, book VI, ch. 7; William Wordsworth, *The Prelude*, v.344; W. M. Thackeray, *The Memoirs of Barry Lyndon* (1856), ch. 19; Thomas Hardy, *The Return of the Native* (1878), ch. 5; John Ruskin, *Præterita*, vol. I (1885), ch. 1.

[97] I am grateful to Dr Gillian Rogers for drawing my attention to this painting.

[98] See Willkomm, *Über Richard Johnsons 'Seven Champions of Christendom' (1596)*, p. 8.

[99] See Peter Baldwin, *Toy Theatres of the World* (London: Zwemmer, 1992), pp. 145–7. A toy theatre version of *7Ch* was available as late as the 1970s: see *'Guy of Warwick' and Other Chapbook Romances*, ed. Simons, p. 26.

[100] Cf. Plett, 'An Elizabethan best seller', p. 235.

[101] Cf. Helm, *The English Mummers' Play*, p. 4; Ernest A. Baker, *The History of the English Novel: the Elizabethan Age and After* (London: Witherby, 1929), p. 197.

The Text

The editions consulted in the preparation of the text are as follows:

1 THE MOST / famous History of the / Seauen Champions of Christendome: Saint / *George* of England, Saint *Dennis* of Fraunce, / Saint *Iames* of Spaine, Saint *Anthonie* of / Italie, Saint *Andrew* of Scotland, Saint / *Pattricke* of Ireland, and Saint / *Dauid* of Wales. // Shewing their Honorable battailes / by Sea and Land: their Tilts, Iousts, and Tur- / naments for Ladies: their Combats with / *Giants, Monsters, and Dragons: their* / aduentures in forraine Nations: their / *Inchauntments in the holie Land: their* / Knighthoods, Prowesse, and Chiualrie, / in Europe, Affrica, and Asia, with / their victories against the ene- / mies of Christ. // [Printer's ornament.] // AT LONDON / Printed for Cuthbert Burbie, and are to be sold at his / shop, at the Royall Exchange. / 1596.

Quarto in 4s: A–Dd⁴; lacks end. Page and signature numbers. Errors in pagination: 21 for 31; 123 for 124; 124 for 125; 125–200 for 128–203; 200–4 for 204–8. Running heads: (verso) *The Honorable Historie of*; (recto) *the seuen* [or *seauen*] *Champions of Christendome*. Unique surviving copy in Henry E. Huntington Library, San Marino, California (imperfect). *STC* 14677.

2 The second Part of / the famous History of the sea- / uen Champions of Christen- / dome. / Likewise shewing the Princely prowesse of / *Saint Georges three Sonnes, the liuely* / Sparke of Nobilitie. // *With many other memoriall atchiuements* / worthy the golden spurres of / Knighthood. // [Printer's ornament.] // *LONDON,* / *Printed for Cuthbert Burbie, and are to* / be solde at his shop, vnder the / *Royall Exchange* / *1597*.

Quarto in 4s: A–Aa⁴; Bb³. No page numbers. Errors in signatures: A2 for B2; M2 followed by M, M2, M3, [M4]; Z3 occurs twice. Errors in chapter numbering: VI for VII; XII occurs twice. Running heads: (verso) *The second Part of*; (recto) *the seuen Champions*. Unique copy in British Library, London. *STC* 14678.

3 THE MOST FA- / MOVS HISTORY OF / the seuen Champions of Chri- / stendome: Saint *George* of Eng- / land, Saint *Denis* of Fraunce, Saint *Iames* / of Spayne, Saint *Anthony* of Italie, / Saint *Andrew* of Scotland, Saint / *Patricke* of Ireland, and / Saint *Dauid* of Wales; // Shewing their Honorable battailes by Sea / *and Land: their Tilts, Iousts and Turnaments* / *for Ladies: their Combats with Giants,* / Monsters, and Dragons: their aduentures / in forraine Nations: their inchaunt- / *ments in the holy Land: their Knight-* / hoods, Prowesse and Chiualtry [*sic*], in / Europe, Affrica, *and* Asia, / with their victories against / the enemies of Christ. // [Printer's ornament.] // LONDON / Printed for *Elizabeth Burbie*, and are to be sold at / *her shop in Pauls Church-yard.* / 1608.

Part II has a separate title-page:
The second part of / the famous Historie of the sea- / uen Champions of Christen- / dome. / Likewise shewing the Princely prowes of / *Saint Georges three Sonnes,* *the liuely* / Sparke of Nobilitie // With many other memorable atchiuements /

worthy the golden spurres of / Knighthood. // [Printer's ornament.] // LONDON, / Printed for *Elizabeth Burbie*, and are to / be solde at her shop, in Paules Church-yard / at the signe of the Swan   1608.

Quarto in 4s: A–Dd⁴, Ee³; A–Aa⁴, Bb³. Page numbers in Part I only. Errors in pagination: 31 for 30; 119 for 120; 102 for 121; 121–204 for 122–205; 203 for 206; 206–17 for 207–18. Running heads: (Part I, verso) *The Honorable Historie of the*; (Part I, recto) *seuen Champions of Christendome*; (Part II, verso) *The second Part* [or *part*] *of*; (Part II, recto) *the seuen Champions*. Copies in British Library, London; Folger Shakespeare Library, Washington, DC (imperfect); New York Public Library (imperfect). *STC* 14679.

4   THE / FAMOVS / HISTORIE OF / the Seauen Champions of / Christendome. // Saint GEORGE of *England*, Saint DENIS of *France*, / Saint IAMES of *Spaine*, Saint ANTHONY of *Italy*, / Saint ANDREW of *Scotland*, Saint PATRICKE / of *Ireland*, and Saint DAVID of *Wales*. / [Single rule.] / *The first Part*. [Single rule.] / Shewing their Honourable Battels by Sea / and Land: their Tilts, Iusts,Turnaments for Ladies: / their Combats with Giants, Monsters and Dragons: their aduentures in forraine Nations: their Inchantments / *in the Holy Land: their Knighthoods, Prowesse and* / Chiualry, in *Europe, Africa*, and *Asia*, with their / victories against the enemies of *Christ*. // *Whereunto is added by the first Author, the true manner* / of their deaths, being seauen famous Tragedies: and / how they came to be called the seauen Saints / of CHRISTENDOME. / [Double rule.] / *LONDON:* / Printed by THOMAS SNODHAM. [1616]¹⁰²

Part II has a separate title-page:

THE / FAMOVS / HISTORIE OF / the Seauen Champions of / Christendome. // [Single rule.] / *The second Part*. / [Single rule.] / *LIKEWISE* / Shewing the Princely Prowesse of Saint / GEORGES three Sonnes, the liuely / Sparkes of Nobilitie. / [Single rule.] / *Whereunto is added by the first Author, the true manner* / of their deaths, being seauen famous Tragedies : and / how they came to be called the seauen Saints / of CHRISTENDOME. / [Printer's ornament within single rules.] / *LONDON:* / Printed by THOMAS SNODHAM.

Quarto in 4s: A–Dd⁴, Ee³; A–Bb⁴, Cc³. Page numbers in Part I only. Errors in pagination: 33 for 29; 36 for 32; 29 for 33; 32 for 36; 131 followed by 132, 131, 132, 133; 131 for 139; 132 for 140; 123 for 141; 912 for 144; 129 for 145; 192 for 202. Errors in chapter numbering: (Part I) IIII for V; IIII for VI. Running heads: (Part I, verso) *The Honourable* [variously spelt] *History of the*; (Part I, recto) *seuen Champions of Christendome.*; (Part II, verso) *The second part of the*; (Part II, recto) *seauen Champions of Christendome*. Copies in British Library, London; Lincoln Cathedral Library; National Library of Scotland, Edinburgh; Queen's College, Oxford (imperfect). *STC* 14680.

The text of this edition is based on the first printing of each part (numbers **1** and **2** above). The last two chapters of Part I have been supplied from the 1608 edition

---

¹⁰² The date appears at the end of Part I (p. 216).

(number **3**), since they are lacking in the unique surviving copy of the first edition. Variants from later editions have been included only where they elucidate corrupt or obscure readings in the copy texts.

The transcription of the text is diplomatic except in the following respects: (1) patent errors that are clearly the compositor's have been corrected; except in the case of incorrect word-division, the unemended reading is shown in the footnotes; (2) *ée* has been transcribed as *ee*, and *vv* as *w*; (3) where a macron has been used to denote the suspension of a nasal (e.g. *vpō* for *vpon*), this has been silently expanded.

All the editions consulted are printed in black-letter, with proper nouns (usually) in roman type; I have represented the change of typeface by the use of italics (e.g. Saint *George* of *England*). The exception to this rule is in the transcription of the title-pages and preliminary matter, where black-letter is not used; here, therefore, italics represent the use of italic in the original.

THE MOST

famous History of the

Seauen Champions of Christendome: Saint

George of England, Saint *Dennis* of Fraunce,
Saint *Iames* of Spaine, Saint *Anthonie* of
Italie, Saint *Andrew* of Scotland, Saint
Pattricke of Ireland, and Saint
Dauid of Wales.

Shewing their Honorable battailes

by Sea and Land: their Tilts, Iousts, and Turnaments for Ladies: their Combats with
Giants, Monsters, and Dragons: *their*
aduentures in forraine Nations: their
Inchauntments in the holie Land: their
Knighthoods, Prowesse, and Chiualrie,
in Europe, Affrica, and Asia, with
their victories against the enemies of Christ.

AT LONDON

Printed for Cuthbert Burbie, and are to be sold at his
shop, at the Royall Exchange.
1596.

To the Right Hono-
rable Lord Thomas Howard, &c.
R. I. wisheth health, ho-
nor and happinesse.

HAuing heard (Right Honourable) by a general report of the laudable & vertuous qualities, wherewith your Honours minde is beautefied, and your fauourable acceptance of good will from the meanest, I haue attempted (though fearing to fall like *Phaiton*) to present into your Lordships handes this homely gift: which is a Historie of the seauen Champions of Christendome, whose names to this day is held in great estimation through Europe: where in steede of musicke, I bring you mislike: for a learned booke, an idle[1] discourse: thereby to beguile your ingenious Iudgements exercised in the best rudiments. Yet presuming vpon this, that as the Noblest mindes are euer the most curteous, so your Honour will vouchsafe to cast a smiling glaunce at this simple toy: if not for the workemanship, yet for the good will of the giuer: wherewith if I be fauoured (as I hope well) my labour hath his reward, and my desire his content: in which assured hope resting, I commit your Honour to the Almightie.

Your Honours in all humilitie most affectionate.
R. I.

---

[1] idle] ildle *1596*

To all curteous Readers, Richard
Iohnson wisheth increase of vertuous
knowledge.

GEntle Readers, in kindnes accept of my labours, and be not like the chattering Cranes nor Momus mates, that carps at euery thing: what the simple say I care not: what the spightfull speake I passe not: only the censure of the conceited I stand vnto, that is the marke I aime at: whose good likeinges if I obtaine, I haue wonne my race: if not, I faint in the first attempt, and so loose the quiet of my happie goale.

Yours in kindnes to command.
R. I.

The Authors Muse vpon the Historie.

The famous factes O Mars, deriu'd from thee,
By wearie pen, and paynefull Authors toyle:
Enroulde we finde, such feates of Chiualrie,
As hath beene seldome seene in any soyle.

Thy ensignes here we finde in field displaide,
The Trophies of thy victories erected:
Such deedes of Armes, as none could haue assaide,
But Knights, whose courage feare hath not detected.

Such Ladies sau'd, such monsters made to fall,
Such Gyants slaine, such hellish Furies queld:
That Humane forces few or none at all,
In such exploits, their liues could safely shield.

But vertue stirring vp their Noble mindes,
By valiant Conquests to inlarge their Fames:
Hath causde them seeke, aduentures forth to finde,
Which registreth their neuer dying names.
Then Fortune, Time, and Fame agree in this,
That Honours gaine the greatest glorie is.

Gentle Reader, beare with the faults ouerpast in correction, and they shall be amended God willing, in the next Impression.

The Honorable Hi-
storie of the Seauen Champions
of Christendome.

CHAP. I.

Of the wonderfull and straunge birth of Saint George of England: how he was cut out of his Mothers wombe, and after stole from his Nurses by Kalyb the Lady of the woods: Her loue to him, and her giftes, and how hee inclosed her in a rocke of stone, and redeemed sixe Christian Knights out of prison.

AFter the angrie Greekes had ruinated the chiefest Cittie in *Phrigia*, and turnd King *Priams* glorious buildinges to a waste and desolate wildernes, Duke *Æneas* exempted from his natiue habitation, with manie of his distressed countrimen (like Pilgrims) wandered the world to finde some happie region, where they might erect the Image of their late subuerted *Troy*, but before that labour could bee accomplished, *Aenæas* ended his dayes in the confines of *Italie*, and left his sonne *Askanius* to gouerne in his steede: *Askanius* dying, left *Siluius* to rule, *Siluius* deceasing, left the noble and aduenterous *Brutus*, which *Brute* (being the fourth decent from *Aenæas*) First made conquest of this land of *Brittaine*,[1] then inhabited with Monsters, Gyants, and a kinde of wilde people without gouernement, but by pollicie hee ouercame them, and established good and ciuell lawes: Here he laide the first foundation of newe *Troy*, & named it *Troynouant*, but since by processe of time called *London*: then began the Ile of *Brittaine* to flourish, not onlie with sumptious buildinges, but with valiant and couragious Knights, whose aduenterous and bolde attempts in Chiualrie, fame shall discribe what obliuion buried in obscuritie: After this the land was plentefied with Cities, & deuided into Sheires and Counties: Dukedomes, Earledoms, and Lordshippes was the patrimonie for high and noble mindes: wherein they liude not then like fearefull cowards in their Mothers bosome, but merrited renowne by martiall discipline: For the famous Cittie of *Couentrie* was the place wherein the first Christian Champion of *England* was borne, & the first that euer sought for forraine aduentures, whose name to this day al Europe highly hath in regard, and for his bold and magnanimious deedes at Armes gaue him this title, (*the valiant Knight Saint George of England*) whose golden garter is not onelie worne by Nobles, but by Kinges, and in memorie of his victories, all *England* fights euermore vnder his Banner: Therefore *Caliope* thou sacred sister of the Muses, guide so my pen that it may write the true discourse of this worthie Champion.

When nature by true consanguinitie had created him in his mothers wombe, shee dreamed to be conceaued of a Dragon which should bee the cause of her death: which dreame long she concealed and kept secret, vntill her painfull burthen

---

[1] *Brittaine*] *Brittanie 1596*

grew so heauie, that her wombe was scarce able to indure it, so finding
opportunitie to reueale it to her Lord and Husband beeing then the Lord high
steward of *England*, repeated her dreame after this manner. (My Honourable Lord)
you knowe I am by birth the King of *Englands* daughter, and for these one and
twenty yeares haue beene your true and lawfull wife, yet neuer was in any hope of
child till now, or that by me your name should suruiue: Therfore I coniure you by
the pleasures of your youth, and by the deare and naturall loue you beare to the
Infant conceaued in my wombe, that either by Arte, wisedome, or some celestiall
inspiration, you calculate vpon my troublesome dreames, and what they signifie.
For these thirtie nightes past my silent slumbers haue beene greatly hindered by a
grieuous dreame, for night by night no sooner could sweet sleep take possession of
my sences, but methought I was conceaued with a dreadfull Dragon which should
be the cause of his Parents deaths: euen as heauenly *Hecuba* the beautious Queene
of *Troy*, when *Paris* was in her wombe, dreamed to be conceaued with a firebrand,
which indeede was truely verified: for *Paris* having ravished the Parragon of
Greece, and brought *Hellena* into *Troy*: in reuenge thereof the *Grecians* turnde the
Towers of *Illium* into a blaze of fire: Therefore most deare and welbeloued Lord,
preuent the like daunger, that I be not the mother of a viperous sonne. These words
stroke such a terrour to his heart, that for a time hee stood speechles, but hauing
recouered his lost sences, answered her in this manner.

(My most deare and beloued Ladie) what Arte or Learning can performe with
all conuenient speed, shall bee accomplished, for neuer rest shall take possession in
my heart, nor sleepe close vp the closets of mine eyes, till I vnderstand the
signification of thy troublesome dreames: So leauing her in her Chamber in
company of other Ladies that came to comfort her in her melancholy sadnes, tooke
his iournie to the solitarie walkes of *Kalyb* the wise Lady of the woods, without
any company except another Knight, that bore vnder his arme a milke white Lamb,
which they intended to offer to the Inchantres: So trauailing for the space of two
daies, they came to a thicket beset about with old withered and hollow trees,
wherein they were entertained with such a dismall croking of night Rauens, hissing
of Serpents, bellowing of Bulles, and roaring of monsters, that it rather seemed a
wildernesse of furies, than any worldly habitation: by which they knew it to be the
inchanted vale of *Kalyb* the Lady of the woodes: So pacing to the middle of the
thicket, they came to a Caue whose gate and entrey was of Iron, whereon hung a
mightie brasen horne for them to winde that would speake with the Sorceresse, first
offering their Lambe with great humilitie before the posterne of the Caue, then
exempting all feare they winded the brasen horne, the sounde whereof seemed to
shake the foundation of the earth, after which they heard a loude and hollow voice
that vttered these wordes following.

> *Sir Knight from whence thou camst retorne,*
> *Thou hast a Sonne most strangely borne:*
> *A Dragon fell shall split in twaine,*
> *Thy Ladies wombe with extreame paine:*
> *A Champion bold from thence shall spring,*
> *And practise many a wondrous thing:*

Returne therefore make no delay,
For it is true what I doo say.

THis darke Riddle or rather misticall Oracle being thrice repeated in this order, so much amazed them that they stood in doubt whether it were best to returne, or to winde the brazen horne the second time: but being perswaded by the other knight not to mooue the impatience of *Kalyb*, hee rested satisfied with that answere.

Thus left he the inchaunted Caue to the gouernement of *Kalyb*, and with all speede dispatched his iourney to his natiue habitation, but in the meane time his Lady being ouercharged with extreame paine and bitter anguish of her laborsome wombe, was forced either to the spoyle of her Infant, or decay of her owne life: But regarding more the benefit of her countrie, than her own safetie, and for the preseruation of her childe, shee most willingly committed her tender wombe to be opened that her Infant might bee taken forth aliue.

Thus with the consent of many learned Chirurgions, this most Noble and Magnanimious Ladie was cast into a dead sleepe, her wombe cut vp with sharpe razers, and the Infant taken from the bed of his creation: Upon his brest nature had picturde the liuely forme of a Dragon, vpon his right hand a bloody Crosse, and on his left leg a golden garter, they named him *George*, and prouided him three nurses, one to giue him sucke, another to keepe him a sleep, and the third to prouide him foode. not many dayes after his natiuitie, the fell Inchantresse *Kalyb* beeing the vtter enemy to true Nobilitie, by charmes and witchcrafts stele the Infant from his careles Nurses: At which time (though all too late) her Noble Lord and Husband returned in good hope to heare a ioyfull deliuerie of his Lady, and a comfort of a Sonne: but his wished ioy, was turned into a lasting sorrow, for hee founde not onely his Lady dismembred of her wombe, but his yong Sonne wanting, without any newes of his abode; which wofull spectakle bereaued him of his wits, that for a time hee stood senceles, like weeping *Niobe*, but at last brake into these bitter exclamations.

O heauens! why couer you not earth with euerlasting night? or why doe these accursed eyes behold the sunne? O that the woes of *Oedipus* might end my dayes, or like an exile ioy in banishment,where I may warble forth my sorrowes to the whispering woods, that senceles trees may record my losse, & vntamed beasts grieue at my want. What monster hath bereaude me of my Childe? or what Tyrant hath beene glutted with his Tragedie? O that the winde would be a messenger and bring me happie newes of his abode: if hee bee drenched in the deepest Seas, thether will I diue to fetch him vp: if hee bee hidden in the cauerns of the earth, thether will I digge to see my sonne: or if he like a feathered foule lye houering in the ayre, yet thether will I flie, and imbrace him that neuer yet my eyes behelde: But why doe I thunder foorth my exclamations thus in vaine, when neyther heauen, nor earth, nor seas, nor any thing in heauen, in earth, nor seas will lend mee comfort for his recouerie?

Thus complayned he many months for the losse of his sonne, and sent messengers into euery Cyrcuite of the Land, but no man proude so fortunate as to returne him happie tydings: He then beeing frustrate of all good hopes, stored himselfe with Iewels, and so intended to trauaile the wide world, eyther to speed in his iournie, or to leaue his bones in some forraine region: Thus leauing his natiue Countrie, wandred from place to place, till the haires of his head were growne as white as siluer, and his beard like to the thistle downe, but at last he ended his trauaile in *Bohemia*, where what for age and excessiue griefe, laide him selfe downe vnder a ruinate Monasterie wall & dyed, the Commons of that countrie hauing knowledge of his name (by a Iewel he wore in his bosome) ingraued it in Marble stone right ouer his sepulchre, where we leaue him sleeping in peace, and returne to his sonne remayning with *Kalyb* the Lady of the woods in the inchaunted Caue.

Now twice seauen yeares were fully finished since *Kalyb* first had in keeping the Noble Knight *Saint George* of England, whose minde many times thirsted after honorable aduentures, and often attempted to set him selfe at libertie, but the fell inchantresse tendring him as the apple of her eye, appointed twelue sturdy Satiers to attend his person, so that neyther force nor pollicie could further hys intent: shee kept him not to triumph in his Tragedie, nor to spend his dayes in slauerie, but feeding his fancie with all the delightes and pleasures that Arte or Nature could afford: For in him she fixed her chiefest felicitie, and lusted after his beautie: But he seeking to aduance his name by Martiall Discipline and Knightly attempts, vtterly refused her proffered curtesies, and highly disdainde to affect so wicked a creature: who seeing her loue bestowed in vaine, vpon a time beeing in the secretst corner of her Caue, began to flatter him in this manner.

Thou knowest (Sir Knight) how worthily I haue deserued thy Loue, and how for thy sake I haue kept my Uirginity vnstainde, yet thou more cruell than the Tigers breed in *Libia*, reiecteth me. Deare Knight fulfill my desiers, and at thy pleasure my charmes shall practise woondrous thinges, as to mooue the heauens to rayne a shower of stones vpon thy enemies, to conuert the Sunne to fire, the Moone to blood, or make a desolation of the whole world.

The Noble Knight *Saint George* considered in his mind that Loue would make the wisest blind: Therefore by her faire promises he hoped to obtaine his liberty, the which mooude him to make her this answere.

Most wise and learned *Kalyb*, the woonder of the world, I condiscend to all thy desiers vpon this condition, that I may be sole Protector and Gouernour of this Inchaunted Caue, and that thou discribe to me my birth, my name, and Parentage, wherto she willingly consented, and began her discourse in this manner. Thou art by byrth, said shee, son to the Lord *Albert* high Steward of *England*, and to this day haue I kept thee as my child within these solitary woods: So taking him by the hand she led him to a Brasen Castel, wherin remayned as prisoners, sixe of the brauest knights in the world: These are sayd she, six of the worthiest champions of Christendome, the first is *Saint Dennis* of *France*, the second *Saint Iames* of *Spaine*, the third *Saint Anthonie*[2] of *Italie*, the fourth *Saint Andrew* of *Scotland*, the fift *Sa. Pattricke* of *Ireland*, the sixt *Saint Dauid* of *Wales* whereof thou art borne to bee the seauenth, and thy name *Saint George* of *England*, for so thou shalt bee

---

[2] *Anthonie*] *Anhonie 1596*

termde in time to come: Then leading hym a little further she brought him into a large faire roome where stood seauen of the goodliest Steedes that euer the world beheld, sixe of these (sayd shee) belong to the sixe Champions, and the seauenth will I bestowe on thee, whose name is *Bayard*: likewise shee lead him to another roome, where hung the richest Armour that euer eye beheld, so choosing out the strongest Corslet from her Armorie, shee with her owne handes buckled it on hys brest, laced on his Helme, and attyred him with rich Caparison, then fetching forth a mighty fauchion, shee put it likewise in hys hand, (now sayd shee) art thou Armed in richer furniture than was *Ninus* the first Monarke of the worlde: thy steed is of such force and inuincible power, that whilst thou art mounted on hys backe, there can be no Knight in all the world so hardy as to conquere thee: Thy Armour of the purest *Lidian* steele, that neyther weapon can pearce, nor Battailaxe bruse, thy sword which is called *Ascalon* is framed of such excellent mettle by the curious workmanship of the *Ciclops*, that it will seperate and cut the hardest flint, and hew in sunder the strongest steele, for in the pummell lies such pretious vertue, that neyther treason, witchcrafts, nor any violence can bee proffered thee, so long as thou wearest it.

Thus the lustfull *Kalyb* beeing so blinded in her owne conceit, that she not onely bestowed the riches of her Caue vpon him, but gaue him power and authoritie through a siluer wand which shee put in his hand to worke her owne destruction for comming by a huge great rocke of stone, this valiant minded Knight stroke his charming rod thereon, whereat it opened, and shewed apparantly before his eyes a number of sucking Babes which the Inchauntresse had murthered by her witchcrafts and sorceries: O said she this is a place of horror, where nought is heard but scrikes and rufull grones of dead mens soules, but if thy eares can indure to heare them, and thy eyes behold them, I will lead the way: So the Lady of the woodes boldly stepping in before, little mistrusting the pretended pollicie of *S. George*, was deceaued in her owne practises, for no sooner entred she the rocke, but he stroke his siluer wand thereupon, and immediatly it closed, where shee bellowed foorth exclamations to the senceles stones without al hope of deliuery.

Thus this Noble Knight deceaued the wicked Inchantresse *Kalyb*, and set the other sixe Champions likewise at libertie, who rendred him all Knightly curtesies, & gaue him thankes for their safe deliuerie, so storing themselues with all thinges according to their desiers, tooke their iournies from the Inchanted groue, whose proceeding fortunes and heroicall aduentures shall bee shewed in this Chapter following.

Kalybs Lamentation in the Rocke of stone, her Will & Testament, and how shee
was torne in peeces by Spirits: with other thinges that hapned in the Caue.

BUT after the departure of the seauen worthy Champions, *Kalyb* seeing her selfe
fast closed in the rocke of stone, by the pollicie of the English Knight, grew into
such extreame passion of minde, that shee cursed the houre of her creation, and
bitterly banned all motions of coniuration, the earth she wearied with her cries,
whereby the verie stones seemd to relent, and as it were, wept cristall teares, &
sweat with verie anguish of her griefe: the blasted Oakes that grewe about the
Inchaunted rocke, likewise seemde to rue at her exclamations, the blustering
windes were silent, the murmuring of Birds still, and a solitarie dumbnes tooke
possession of euery creature that abode within the cercuite of the woods, to heare
her wofull Lamentation, which she vttered in this manner.

O miserable *Kalyb*! accursed be thy desteny, for nowe thou art inclosed within a
desolate & darkesome den, where neyther sunne can lend thee comfort with his
bright beams, nor aire extend his breathing coolenes to thy wofull soule:[1] for in the
deepe foundations of the earth, thou art for euermore inclosed: I that haue beene
the woonder of my time for Magicke, I that by Arte haue made my iournie to the
deepest dungeons of hell, where multitudes of vglie blacke and fearefull spirits
hath trembled at my charmes: I that haue bound the furies vp in beds of steele, and
caused them to attend my pleasure like swarmes of hornets, that ouerspreads the
mountaines in *Egipt*, or the flies vpon the parched hills, where the tawnie tanned
Mores doo inhabite: am now constrained to languish in eternall darkenes: woe to
my soule: woe to my charmes, and woe to all my Magicke spels: for they haue
bound me in this hollowe rocke: pale bee the brightnes of the cleare sunne, and
couer earth with euerlasting darkenesse: skyes turne to pitch, the elements to
flaming fire, rore hell, quake earth, swell seas, blast earth, rockes rend in twaine,
all creatures mourne at my confusion, and sighe at *Kalybs* wofull and pittifull
exclamations.

Thus wearied she the time away, one while accusing Fortune of tirranny,
another while blaming the falsehood & trechery of the English Knight, sometimes
tearing her curled locks of bristled haire, that like a wreath of snakes hung dangling
downe her deformed necke, then beating her breasts, another while rending her
ornaments, whereby shee seemd more liker a fury than an earthly creature, so
impacient was this wicked inchantres *Kalyb* being frustrate of all hope of recouery,
began afresh to thunder forth these tearmes of coniuration: Come, come you
Princes of the elements, come, come and teare this rocke in peeces, and let me be
inclosed vp in the eternal languishment: appeare you shadowes of blacke mistie
night: *Magoll, Cumath, Helueza, Zontomo*: Come when I call, *venite festinate*
inquam: At which wordes the earth began to quake, and the verie elements to
tremble: for all the spirits both of aire, of earth, of water, and of fire were obedient

---

[1] soule:] soule,: *1596*

to her charmes, and by multitudes cam flocking at her call: some from the fire in the likenes of burning Dragons, breathing from their fearefull nostrels, sulphure and flaming Brimstone, some from the water in shape of Fishes, with other deformed creatures, that hath their abiding in the Seas, some from the aire the purest of the ellements, in the likenes of Angels and other bright shadowes, and other some from the grose earth most vglie, blacke and dreadfull to behold: So when the legions of spirits had incompast the wicked Inchantresse, hell began to rore such an infernall and harsh mellodie, that the Inchanted rocke burst in twaine, and then *Kalybs* charmes tooke no effect, for her Magick no longer indured, than the tearme of an hundred yeares, the which as then were fullie finished and brought to end: for the Obligation which shee subscribed with her dearest blood, and sealed with her own hands, was brought as a witnes against her, by which she knew and fullie perswaded her selfe that her life was fully come to end: therefore in this fearefull manner she began to make her Will & latest Testament.

First welcome (said shee) my sad Executors, welcome my graue and euerlasting toombe, for you haue digde it in the fierie lakes of *Phlegethon*, my winding sheet wherein to shrowde both my body and condemned soule, is a Calderne of boyling lead and brimstone, and the wormes that should consume my Carkasse, are the fiery forkes, which tosse burning firebrands from place to place, from furnace to furnace, and from calderne to calderne: therefore attend to *Kalybs* wofull testament, and ingraue the Legacies she giues in brasse rolles vpon the burning bankes of *Acheron*. First these eyes that now too late weepe helples teares I giue vnto the watrie spirits, for they haue rakt the treasures hidden in deepest Seas to satisfie their most insatiate lookes: next I bequeath these hands which did subscribe the bloody Obligation of my perpetuall banishment from ioy, vnto those spirits that houer in the Aire: my tongue that did conspire against the Maiestie of Heauen, I giue to those spirits which haue their beeing in the fire: my earthly hart I bequeath to those groce *Dæmons* that dwell in the dungeons of the earth: and the rest of my condemned body, to the torments due to my deseruings: which straunge and fearefull Testament, being no sooner ended, but all the spirits generally at one instance ceazed vpon the Inchantresse and dismembred her bodie to a thousand peeces, and deuided her limbes to the corners of the earth, one member to the Aire, another to the water, another to the fire, and another to the earth, which was carried away in a moment by the spirits, that departed with such a horror, that all things within the hearing thereof sodainely died, both Beastes, Byrds, and all creeping wormes which remayned within the compasse of those inchanted woodes, for the trees which before was wont to flourish with greene leaues, withered away and died, the blades of grasse perished for want of naturall moysture, which the watrie clouds denied to nourish in so wicked a place.

Thus by the iudgments of the heauens, sensles things perished for the wickednes of *Kalyb*, whom wee leaue to her endles torments both of body and soule, and returne to the seauen worthy Champions of Christendome, whose laudable aduentures fame hath inrold in the bookes of memorie.

CHAP. III.

How Saint George slewe the burning Dragon in Egipt, and redeemed Sabra the Kinges Daughter from death: How hee was betraied by Almidor the blacke King of Moroco, and sent to the Soldan of Persia, where hee slew two Lyons and remained seauen yeares in prison.

AFter the seauen Champions departed from the Inchaunted Caue of *Kalib,* they made their abode in the Cittie of *Couentrie,* for the space of nine monthes, in which time they erected vp a sumptuous & costly monument ouer the herse of *Saint Georges* Mother, and so in that time of the yeare, when the spring had ouerspred the earth, with the mantles of *Flora,* they Armed themselues like wandring Knights, and tooke their iournie to seeke for forraine aduentures, accounting no dishonour so great, as to spend their dayes in idlenes atchiuing no memorable accident: So trauailing for the space of thirtie dayes without any aduenture worthie the noting, at length came to a large broad Plaine, whereon stood a brasen piller, whereat seauen seuerall waies deuided, which caused the seauen Knights to forsake each others companie, and to take euery one a contrary way, where we leaue sixe of the Champions to their contented trauailes, and wholly discourse vpon the fortunate successe of our worthy English knight, who after some few months trauaile, happily ariued within the teretories of *Egipt,* which countrie as then was greatly annoyed with a dangerous Dragon but before hee had iournied fullie the distance of a mile, the silent night approched, and solitary stilnes tooke possession of all liuing thinges, at last he espied an old poore Hermitage, wherein he purposed to rest his horse, and to take some repast after his wearie iournie, til the sunne had renewed his mornings light that he might fall to his trauaile againe: but entring the Cottage, hee found an aged Hermit ouerworne with yeares, and almost consumed with griefe: to whome hee began in this manner to conferre.

Father (said hee) for so you seeme by your grauety, may a trauailer for this night craue entertainment within your Cottage, not onely for himselfe but his horse, or is there some Cittie neare at hande, whetherto I may take my iournie without daunger: The oldman starting at the sodaine approch of *Saint George,* replyed vnto him in this order.

Sir Knight (quoth hee) of thy countrie I neede not demaund, for I know it by thy Burgonet, (for indeed thereon was grauen the Armes of England,) but I sorrow for thy hard fortune that it is thy destenie to ariue in this our countrie of *Egipt:* Wherein is not left sufficient aliue to burie the dead, such is the distresse of this land, through a dangerous and tirrible Dragon now ranging vp and downe the countrie, which if hee bee not euery day appeased with a pure and true virgin, which he deuoureth downe his venemous bowels, but that day so neglected will he breath such a stench from his nostrels, whereof will grow a most grieuous plague and mortallity of all thinges, which vse hath beene obserued for these foure and twentie yeares, but now there is not left one true virgin but the Kings only daughter throughout *Egipt,* which Damsell to morrow must bee offered vp in Sacrifice to the

Dragon: Therefore the King hath made Proclamation, that if any Knight dare proue so aduenterous as to combat with the Dragon, and preserue his daughters life, shall in reward haue her to his wife, and the Crowne of *Egipt* after his discease.

This large proffer so incouraged the English Knight, that hee vowde eyther to redeeme the Kinges Daughter, or els to loose his life in that honourable enterprise: So taking his repose and nightly rest in the olde mans Hermitage, till the chearefull Cocke beeing the true messenger of day, gaue him warning of the Sunnes vp-rise, which causd him to buckle on his Armour, and to furnish his Steed with strong habilliments of war, the which being done he tooke his iournie guided onely by the olde Hermit to the valley where the kinges Daughter should bee offered vp in Sacrifice: But when he approched the sight of the valley, he espied a far off a most fair and beautifull Damsell, attired in pure *Arabian* silke going to sacrifice, guarded to the place of death onlie by sage & modest Matrons, which wofull sight so encouraged the English Knight to such a forwardnesse, that he thoght euery minnute a day til he had redeemed the Damsell from the Dragons tyrannie: So approching the Lady, gaue her comfort of deliuerie, and returnde her back to her Fathers Pallace againe.

After this the Noble Knight like a bold aduenterous Champion entred the valley, where the Dragon had his residence, who no sooner had a sight of him, but hee gaue such a tirrable yell as though it had thundered in the ellements, the bignes of the Dragon was fearefull to behold, for betwixt his shoulders and his tayle were fiftie foote in distance, his scales glistered brighter than siluer, but farre more harder than brasse, his belly of the coloure of gold, but more bigger than a Tun. Thus weltred he from his hideous denne, and fiercely assailed the sturdie Champion with his burning winges, that at the first encounter, hee had almost felled him to the ground, but the Knight nimbly recouering him selfe, gaue the Dragon such a thrust with his speare, that it shiuerd in a thousand peeces, whereat the furious Dragon so fiercely smote him with his venemous tayle, that downe fell man and horse, in which fall two of *Saint Georges* ribs were sore brused, but yet stepping backward, it was his chaunce to leape vnder an Orringe tree, which tree had such pretious vertue, that no venemous worme durst come within the compasse of the braunches, nor within seauen foote thereof, where this valiant Knight rested himselfe vntill hee had recouered his former strength: who no sooner feeling his spirits reuiued, but with an eger courage smote the burning Dragon vnder his yellow burnisht bellie with his trustie sworde *Askalon*, whereout came such abundance of venome, that it sprinkled vpon the Champions Armour, whereby immediatly through the impoysoned strength of the venome his Armour burst in twaine, and the good Knight fell into a greeuous and dead sound, that for a time he lay breathles: but yet hauing that good memorie remayning, that he tumbled vnder the branches of the Orringe tree; in which place the Dragon could proffer him no further violence. The fruit of the tree was of such an excellent vertue, that whosoeuer tasted thereof should presently bee cured of all manner of diseases and infirmities whatsoeuer: So it was the Noble Champions good and happie fortune, a little to recouer through the vertue of the tree, and to espie an Orringe which a little before had dropped downe wherwith he so refreshed himself, that hee was in short time as sound as when hee first began the incounter: Then kneeled hee downe and

made his diuine supplication to heauen, that God would send him (for his deare
sonnes sake) such strength and agillity of body as to slay the furious and tirrable
monster, which beeing done, with a bold and couragious heart, hee smote the
Dragon vnder the wing, where it was tender without scale, wherby his good sworde
Askalon with an easie passage went to the verie hilts through both the Dragons
heart, liuer, bone and blood, whereout issued such aboundance of purple gore, that
it turned the grasse which grewe in the valley into a crimson colour, & the ground
which before partched through the burning stinch of the Dragon, was now
drenched with ouermuch moysture which voyded from his venemous bowels,
where at last through want of blood, and long continuance in fight, the Dragon
yeelded his vitall spirits to the mercy of the conquering Champion. The which
beeing happely performed, the Noble Knight *Saint George* of *England*, first
yeelding due honour to Almighty God for the victorie, then with his good sword
Askalon he cut off the Dragons head and pitcht it vpon the trunchion of a speare,
which at the beginning of the battaile hee shiuered against the Dragons scalie
backe: During this long and dangerous Combat, his trustie Steede lay altogether in
a sounde without any moouing, which caused the English Champion with all speed
to crush the ioyce of an Orringe into hys cold mouth: the vertue whereof presently
expelled the venemous poysons, and recoured his former strength againe.

There was as then remayning in the Egiptian Court, one *Almidor* the blacke
King of *Moroco*, who long had prosecuted (in the way of marriage) the Loue of
Sabra the Kinges daughter, but by no pollicie, meanes, nor manhood, could hee
accomplish what his hart desired: But now finding opportunitie to expresse his
trecherous minde, intended to robbe and spoyle *Saint George* of his victorie,
whereby he thought to attaine the gratious fauour, and singuler good liking of his
Lady and Mistresse, who lothed his companie like the detested Crokadiles, but
euen as the Wolfe though all in vaine barkes at the Moone: So this fantasticall and
cowardly *Almidor*, through many rich gifts and faire promises, hired twelue
Egiptian Knights to beset the valley where *Saint George* slue the burning Dragon,
& by force bereaue him of his conquest: But when this magnanimious Champion
of *England* came ryding in triumph from the valley, espected to haue beene
entertained like a Conquerour with Drums and Trumpets, or to haue heard the
belles of *Egipt* rung a ioyfull sound of victorie, or to haue[1] seene the streetes
beautified with bonefires: but contrary to his imagination was he met with Troupes
of Armed Knights, not to conduct him peacefullie to the *Egiptian* Court, but by
falshood and trechery to dispoyle him of his life and honour: For no sooner had he
ridden past the entry of the valley, but he espied how the *Egiptian* Knights
brandished their weapons, and deuided themselues to intercept him in his iournie to
the Court: By which he knew them to be no faithfull friendes, but vowed enemies:
So tying his Horse to a Hathorne tree, he intended to try his fortune on foote for
feare of disaduantage, they beeing twelue to one, but in the skirmish *Saint George*
so valiantly behaued himselfe with his trustie sword *Askalon*, that at one stroke he
slue three of the *Egiptian* Knights, and before the golden Diamond of heauen had

---

[1] haue] haue haue *1596*

wandred the zodiack the compasse of an houre: but some he dismembred of their
heads: some had their limbes lopt off: some their bodies cut in twaine, & some
their intrayles trayling downe, so that not one was left aliue to carrie news to
Almidor the black King, which stood (during all the time of skirmish) a far off
vpon a mountaine toppe, to behold the successe of his hired Champions: But when
he saw the *Egiptians* bloodie Tragedies, & howe the happie fortune of the English
Knight had wonne the honour of the day: hee accursed his destenie, and accused
the Queene of chaunce with crueltie, for disapointing hys pretended enterprise, but
hauing a heart fraught with all wicked motions, secretlie vowed in his soule, to
practise by some other trechery *S. Georges* vtter confusion: So running before to
the Court of King *Ptolomie*, not reuealing what had hapned to the twelue *Egiptian*
Knights, but crying in euery place as he went, *Victoria, Victoria*, the enemie of
Egipt is slaine. Then *Ptolomie* commaunded euerie street of the Citty to be hung
with rich Arras & imbrothered Tapestry, and likewise prouided a sumptuous
Charriot of gold, the wheeles and other timber worke of the purest Ebonie, the
couering thereof was made of purple silke, crosse barde with staues of gold:
Likewise a hundred of the Noblest Peeres of *Egipt*, attired in Crimson Veluet and
white, mounted on milke white Coursers with rich Caparison attended the coming
of *S. George*: Thus were[2] all things appointed[3] for his Honourable intertainement,
which they performed in such solemne order, that I lacke memorie to discribe it:
For when he first entred the gates of the Cittie, he heard such a mellodious
harmonie of heauenly sounding Musicke, that it seemed in his conceite to surpasse
the sweetnes of the Cherubins, or the holy company of Angels: Then they most
Royally presented him with a sumptuous and costly Pale of gold, and after inuested
him in that Iuorie Charriot, wherein he was conducted to the Pallace of King
Ptolomie, where this Noble and Princelie minded Champion, surrendred vp his
conquest and victorie to the seemelie handes of the beautious *Sabra*: where shee
with like curtesie and more humillity requited his bountie: For, at the first sight of
the English Knight, she was so rauished with his Princely countenance, that for a
time shee was not able to speake: Yet at last taking him by the hand she led him to
a rich pauillion, where she vnarmed him, and with most precious salues imbalmed
his woundes, & with her teares washed away the blood, which being done she
furnished a table with all manner of dillicates for his repast, where her Father was
present, who demaunded his Country, Parentage & name: after the banquet was
ended, he instauld him with the honour of Knighthood, and put vpon his feete a
paire of golden spurres: But *Sabra* who feeding vpon the banquet of his loue,
conducted him to hys nightes repose, where she sate vpon hys bed and warbled
forth most heauenly melody vppon her Lute, till his sences were ouercome with a
sweet and silent sleepe, where she left hym for that night after hys dangerous
battaile: But no sooner did *Auroraes* radiant blush, distaine the beauty of the East,
and the sun shew his morning countenance, but *Sabra* repayred to the English
Champions lodging, and at his first vprising presented him with a Diamond of most
rare and excellent vertue, the which he wore vpon his finger: The next that entered

---

[2] were] *om. 1596*
[3] appointed] apopinted *1596*

his lodging, was the Trecherous *Almidor* the blacke King of *Moroco*, hauing in his hand a boule of Greekish Wine, which hee offered to the Noble Champion *Saint George of England*: but at the receaite thereof, the Diamond the Lady gaue him which he wore vpon his finger waxed pale, and from his nose fell three droppes of blood, whereat he started: which sodaine accident caused the kings daughter to suspect some secret poyson compounded in the Wine, and thereupon so vehemently scriked, that a sodaine vprore presently ouerspread the whole Court, whereby it came to the Kinges intelligence of the proffered Trecherie of *Almidor* against the English Champion: But so deare was the loue of the *Egiptian* King, to the blacke King of *Moroco*, that no beliefe of Trecherie could enter into hys minde.

Thus *Almidor* the second time was preuented of hys practise, whereat in minde he grew more inraged than the chafed Bore: yet thinking the third should pay for all: So[4] spying a time wherein to worke his wicked purpose, which he brought to passe in this manner.

Many a day remained *Saint George* in the Egiptian Court, sometimes reuelling amongst Gentlemen, dancing and sporting with Ladies, other some in Tilts and Turniments, with other Honourable exercises: Likewise long and extreame was the loue that beautious *Sabra* bore to the English Champion, of the which this Trecherous *Almidor* had intelligence by many secret practises, and manie times his eares were witnes of their discourses: So vpon an Euening, when the gorgious Sunne lay leuell with the ground, it was his fortune to walke vnder a Garden wall, to take the coolenes of the Euenings aire, where vnseene of the two Louers, hee heard their amorous discourses as they sate dallying in the bower of Roses, Courting one another in this manner.

My soules delight, my hearts cheefe comfort, sweete *George* of *England*, saide the loue-sicke *Sabra*! Why art thou more obdurate than the Flint: which the teares of my true heart can neuer mollifie? How many thousand sighes haue I breathde for thy sweete sake, which I haue sent to thee as true messengers of loue, yet neuer wouldst thou requite mee with a smiling countenance. Refuse not her, deare Lord of England, that for thy loue will forsake hir Parents, Countrie and Inheritance, which is the Crowne of *Egipt*, and like a Pilgrime followe thee throughout the wide world. O therefore knit that gordion knot of wedlocke, that none but death can afterwards vnty, that I may say the Sunne shall loose his brightnesse, the Moone her splendant beames, the Sea her tides, and all thinges vnder the cope of heauen grow contrarie to kinde, before *Sabra* the Heire of *Egipt* prooue vnconstant to her deare *S. George* of *England*.

These wordes so fiered the Champions heart, that hee was almost intangled in the snares of loue, which before time onlie affected Martiall discipline: But yet to trie patience, a little more, made her this answere. Ladie of *Egipt*, canst thou not bee content that I haue ventured my life to set thee free from death, but that I should sinke my future fortunes in a womans lappe, and so burie all my honours in Obliuion? No, no *Sabra George* of *England* is a Knight borne in a Countrie where true Chiualrie is nourisht, and hath sworne to search the world so far as euer the

---

[4] So] So so *1596*

Lampe of Heauen doth lend his light, before he tie himselfe to the troublesome state of marriage, therefore attempt me no more, that am a stranger and a wanderer from place to place, but seek to aime at higher States, as the King of *Moroco*, who will attempt to climbe the heauens to gayne thy loue and good liking: at which speeches shee sodainely replyed in this manner.

The King of *Moroco* is as bloody minded as a Serpent, but thou more gentle than a Lamb, his tongue as ominous as the scriking night Owle, but thine more sweeter than the morninges Larke, his kind imbracinges like the stinging Snakes, but thine more pleasant than the creeping vine: What if thou beest a Knight of a strange countrie? thy body is more precious to myne eyes than Kingdomes in my heart. There stay (replyed the English Champion,) I am a Christian, thou a Pagan: I honour God in heauen, thou earthly shadowes below: therefore if thou wilt obtaine my loue and liking, thou must forsake thy *Mahomet*, and bee christned in our Christian faith. With al my soule (answered the *Egiptian* Lady) will I forsake my country Gods, & for thy loue become a Christian, and therewithall she burst a ring in twaine, the one halfe she gaue to him in pledge of Loue, & kept the other halfe her selfe: and so for that time departed the Garden.

But during all the time of their discourses, the Trecherous minded *Almidor* stood listning to their speeches, & fretted inwardly to the verie gall to heare the Mistresse of hys hart, reiect hys former curtesies: Therfore intending now or neuer to infringe their plighted band, went in all hast to the *Egiptian* King, and in this maner made his suplication.

Know great Monarcke of the East, that I haue a secret to vnfold, which toucheth nerely the sauegard of your countrey: It was my chance this Euening at shutting vp of *Titons* golden gates, to take the comfort of the Westerne breathing aire vnder your priuate Garden walkes, where I heard (though all vnseene) a deepe pretended Treason betwixt your Daughter and the English Knight, where shee hath vowde to forsake her God and beleeue as the Christians doo, and likewise shee intendes to flye from her natiue Countrie, and to goe with this wandring trauailer, which hath beene so highly honoured in your Court.

Now by *Mahomet*, *Apollo*, and *Termagaunt*, three Gods we *Egiptians* commonly adore (sayde the King) this damned Christian shal not gaine the conquest of my daughters loue, for hee shall loose hys head, though not by violence in our *Egiptian* Court: Therefore *Almidor* bee secret in my intent, for I will send him to my cosen the *Persian* Soldan, from whence he neuer shall returne to *Egipt* againe, except hys Ghost bring newes of bad successe vnto my Daughter, and thereuppon they presentlye contriued this Letter.

The Letter to the Soldan of Persia.

I *Ptolomie* King of *Egipt* & the Easterne territories sendeth Greeting to thee the mightie Soldan of *Persia*, great Emperour of the Prouinces of bigger *Asia*. This is to request thee vpon the league of friendship betwixt vs, to shewe the bearer hereof thy seruant death, for he is an vtter enemie to all *Asia* and *Affrica*, and a proude contemner of our Religion: Therefore faile me not in my request, as thou wilt answere on thine oath, and so in hast farewell.

> *Thy kinseman Ptolomie the King of Egipt.*

Which Letter beeing no sooner subscribed & sealed with the great Seale of *Egipt*, but *Saint George* was dispatched with Embassage for *Persia*, with the bloody sentence of hys owne destruction: to the true deliuery whereof, he was sworne by the honour of his Knighthood, and for hys pawne he left behinde hym his good Steede, and hys trusty sword *Askalon* in the keeping of *Ptolomie* the *Egiptian* King, only taking for hys puruay & easie trauayle one of the Kinges horses.

Thus the Innocent Lambe betrayed by the willie Foxe was sent to the hungerstarued Lyons den, beeing suffered not once to giue his Lady and Mistris vnderstanding of hys sodaine departure, but trauailde day and night through many a long and solitarie Wildernes without any aduenture worthy the memorie, but that hee heard the dismall crie of Night-Rauens thundring in his eares, and the fearefull sound of Crickets in the creueses of the earth, and such like messengers of mischance, which foretelled some fatall accident to be at hand: yet no feare could daunt his noble minde, nor danger hinder his intended trauaile, till he had a sight of the Soldans[5] Pallace, which seemed more liker a Paradice than any earthly habitation for as the Historie reports the walles and towers of the Pallace was of the purest Marble stone, the windowes of carued[6] siluer worke, inamiled with *Indian* Pearle, beset with lattine and christall glas, the outward walles and buildings painted with gold, the pillers and gates were all of brasse, about the Pallace was a mighty ditch of a woonderfull bredth and depth, ouer the ditch stoode a stately bridge, erected vp with sumptuous workemanship of grauen Images, vnder the bridge a hundred siluer Belles were hung by Arte, so that no creature might passe into the Pallace, but they gaue warning to the Soldans Guard, at the end of the bridge was built an Alablaster Tower, whereon stoode an Eagle of goold, hys eyes of the richest precious stones, the brightnesse whereof glisterd so much, that al the Pallace did shine with the light thereof.

Uppon the day (*Saint George* entered the Soldans[7] Court) when the *Persians* solemnelie sacrificed to their Gods *Mahomet, Apollo, Tirmigaunt*, which vnchristian Procession so mooued the impatience of the English Champion, that he tooke the ensignes and streamers whereon the *Persian* Gods were pictured, and trampled them vnder hys feete: whereupon the Pagans presently fled to the Soldan for succour, and shewed him how a straunge Knight had despised their *Mahomet* and trampled their banners in the dust, then presently he sent a hundred of his Armed knights, to know the cause of that sodaine vprore, and to bring the Christian Champion bound vnto his Maiestie: but the *Persian* Knights, were intertainde[8] with

---

[5] Soldans] Soldians *1596*
[6] carued] caued *1596*
[7] Soldans] Soldians *1596*
[8] intertainde] intainde *1596*

such a bloody banquet, that some of their heads run tumbling in the streetes, and the Channels ouerflowde with streames of blood: the Pauements of the Pallace were ouerspred with slaughtered men and the walles besprinkled with purple gore: so victoriously he behaude himselfe agaynst the enemies of Christ, that ere the Sun had declined in the West, he brought to ground a hundred of the Soldans Souldiers, and inforced the rest like flockes of sheepe to flye to the Soldan for ayde and succour, which as then remained in his Pallace with the guard of three thousand souldiers: Who at the report of this vnspected vprore, furnished hys Souldiers with habilliments of warre, and came marching from hys Pallace with such a mightie power as though the strength of Christendome had beene come to inuade the terretories of *Asia*: But such was the inuincible courage of *Saint George*, that he encountred with them all, and made such a Massaker in the Soldans Court, that the Pauements were ouerspread with slaughtered *Persians*, and the Pallace gates stuffed with heapes of murdered Pagans: At the last the larum bels was caused to be rung and the Beacons set on fire, wherat the commons of the Countrie rose in Armes, and came flocking about the English Champion like swarmes of Bees, where at last through his long encounter, and the multitude of his enemies, his neuer daunted courage was forced to yeelde, & hys restles Arme wearied with fight, constrayned to let hys weapens fall to the ground.

Thus he whose fortitude sent thousandes to wander on the bankes of *Acharon*, stood now obedient to the mercies of ten thousands, which with their brandishing weapons, and sharpe edged fauchions inuironed him about.

Now bloody minded monster (said the Soldan) what country man so euer thou art, Iew, Pagan, or misbeleeuing Christian: looke for a sentence of seuere punishment for euery droppe of blood thy vnhappie hande hath shed. First, thy skin with sharpe razers shall bee pared from thy fleshe aliue: Nexte thy flesh with burning Irons seared from thy bones, & lastly thy accursed limbes drawne in peeces ioynt from ioynt with vntamed horses. This bloody Iudgement pronounced by the Soldan not a little mooued *S. George* to reply in this maner. Great Potentate of *Asia*, I craue the liberty & law of Armes, whereto all the kings of the earth by oath are bound: First my discent in my natiue Country is of Royall blood, and therefore challenge I a combat: secondly an Embassador I am from Ptolomie[9] the King of *Egipt*, & therefore no violence must be proffered me, lastlie, the lawes of *Asia* graunts me safe conduct back to *Egipt*: therefore what I haue done *Ptolomie* must answere, and thereuppon hee deliuered the Letter seeled with the great Seale of *Egipt*, the which was no sooner broken vp and read, but the Soldans eyes sparkled like vnto fire, and vpon his countenance appeared the Image of wrath and discontent.

Thou art by the report of *Ptolomie* (said the Soldan) a great contemner of our Gods, & a despiser of our Lawes: Therefore his pleasure is that I should ende thy daies by some inhumane death: the which I sweare by *Mahomet*, *Apollo*, and *Termigaunt* to accomplish, and thereupon he gaue him in keeping to a hunderd of his Ianasaries till the day of execution, which was appointed within thirtie dayes

---

[9] Ptolomie] Ptolmoie *1596*

following: So they disrobde him of his apparrell and attired him in simple and bace array: His armes that late was imployed to welde the mighty Target, and tosse the waighty Battaileaxe, they strongly fettered vp in iron bolts, and those handes which were wont to bee garnished with steely Gauntlets, they bound vp fast in hempen bands, that the purple blood trickled downe from his fingers ends, and so beeing dispoylde of all Knightly dignitie, they conuaide him to a deepe, darke and desolate dungeon: wherein the golden Sunne did neuer shewe his splendant beames, nor neuer could the comfortable light of heauen be seene: betwixt the day and night no difference could bee made, the[10] summers partching heat & winters freezing cold were both alike, his chiefest comfort was to number the *Persians* he had slaine in the conflict, one while pondering in his restles thoughtes the ingratitude of *Ptolomie* the Egiptian King another while remembring his loue, his vow, & deepe affection that he bore to the Egiptians daughter, and howe vnkindlie shee tooke his departure, caruing her picture with the nayles of his fingers vpon the walles of the dungeon: to which sensles substance he many times would thus complaine.

O cruell destenies! Why is this grieuous punishment allotted to my penaunce? Haue I conspired against the maiestie of heauen, that they haue throwne this vengeance on my head? shall I neuer recouer my former libertie, that I may be reuenged vpon the causers of my imprisonment? frowne angry heauens vpon these bloody minded Pagans, those daring miscreants, & professed enemies of Christ, and may the plagues of *Pharo* light vpon their countries, & the miserie of *Oedipus* vpon their Princes: that they may bee eye witnesses of their daughters rauishments, and beholde their Citties flaming like the burning battailementes of *Troy*. Thus lamented he the losse of his libertie, accursing his birth day, and houre of his creation, wishing that it neuer might be numbred in the yeare, but counted ominous to all insuing ages: His sighes exceeded the number of the Ocian sandes, and his teares the water bubbles in a raynie day, and as one deminished, another presently appearde.

Thus sorrow was his companion, and dispaire his chiefe soliciter, till *Hiperion* with his golden Coach had thirtie times rested in *Thetis* purple Pallace, & *Cinthia* thirtie times daunst vppon the Christall waues: which was the verie time his compleat mones should ende, according to the seuere and cruell Iudgment of the Soldan of *Persia*: But by what extraordenary meanes he knew not: So looking euery minnute of an houre to entertaine the wished messenger of death, he heard a farre off the tirrable roring of two hunger starued Lyons, which for the space of fourteene dayes had beene restrayned from their foode, and naturall sustinance, onely to deuoure and staunch their hunger starued bowels with the bodie of this thrice renowned Champion: which crie of the Lyons so terrified hys minde that the haire of his head grew stiffe, & hys browes sweat blood through anguish of hys soule, so extreamely hee feared the remorceles stroke of death: that by violence hee burst the chaines in sunder wherewith he was bound, and rent the curled tresses from hys head, that was of the colour of Amber, the which hee wrapped about hys

---

[10] the] the the *1596*

armes against the Assault of the Lyons, for he greatly suspected them to be the ministers of hys Tragedie, which indeede so fell out, for at that same instant they descended the dungeon, being brought thither by the Guard of Ianasaries, onely to make a ful period of the Champions life: But such was the inuincible fortitude of *Saint George*, and so polliticke hys defence, that when the starued Lyons came running on him with open Iawes, he valiantly thrust hys sinnewed Armes into their throats (beeing wrapped about with the haire of hys head) whereby they presently choaked, and so he pulled out their bloody harts.

Which spectakle the Soldans Ianasaries beholding, wer so amazed with feare, that they ran in all haste to the Pallace, and certified the Soldan what had hapned, who commaunded euery part of the Court to be strongly guarded with Armed Souldiers, supposing the English Knight rather to be some monster ascended from the Sea, than any creature of humane substaunce, or els one possessed with some diuine inspiration, that by force of Armes had[11] accomplished so manie aduenterous stratagems: such a terrour assayled the Soldans heart, seeing hee had slaine two Lyons, and slaughtered two thousand *Persians* with hys owne hands, and likewise had intelligence how he slewe a burning Dragon in *Egipt*: caused the dungeon to be closed vp with bars of Iron, lest he should by pollicie or fortitude recouer his libertie, and so indanger the whole countrie of *Persia*: where he remayned in want, pennury, and great necessitie, for the tearme of seauen winters, feeding onelie vpon rats and mice, with other creeping wormes which he caught in the dungeon.

During which time hee neuer tasted of the bread of Corne, but of wheate branne and Channell water, which daylie was serued him through the Iron grates, where now we leaue *Saint George*, languishing in great misery, and returne againe into *Egipt*, where wee left *Sabra* the Champions betrothed Lady, lamenting the want of hys companie, whome she loued dearer than any Knight in all the world.

Sabra that was the fairest maide that euer mortall eye beheld, in whom both Arte and nature seemed to excell in curious workemanship, her body beeing comlier than the stately Ceder, and her beautie purer then the *Paphian* Queenes: the one with ouerburthened griefe was quite altered, and the other stayned with flouds of brackish teares, that daylie trickled downe her christall cheekes: wherby she found the very Image of discontent, the map[12] of woe, and the only mirrour of sorrow, she accounted all companie loathsome to her sight, and excluded the fellowship of all Ladyes, onely betaking her selfe to a solitarie Cabbinet, where shee sate sowing many a wofull storie vpon a crimson Sampler: whereon sometimes bathing a wounded heart with luke warme teares, that fell from the Conduits of her eyes, then presently with her crisped lockes of haire which dangled downe her Iuorie necke, dry vp the moysture of her sorrowfull teares: then thinking vpon the plighted promises of her deare beloued Knight, fell into these passionate and pittifull complaints.

O Loue (said shee) more sharper than the pricking Brier! with what vnequallity dost thou torment my wounded heart, not lincking my deare Lorde in the like

---

[11] had] hath *1596*
[12] map] nap *1596*

affection of minde? O *Venus*! if thou be imperious in thy Deitie, to whom both
Gods and men obay, commaund my wandred Lorde to returne againe, or that my
soule may flee into the clowds, that by the winds it may be blowne into his sweet
bosome, where liues my bleeding hart: But foolish fondling that I am, he hath
reiected me, and shuns my company like the *Syrens*, else had hee not refused the
Court of *Egipt* where hee was honoured like a king, and wandered the world to
seeke another loue: No, no it cannot be: he beares no such inconstant minde, for I
greatly feare some treacherie hath bereaude me of his sight, or els some stonny
prison includes my *George* from me: If it be so sweet *Morpheus* thou God of
golden dreames, reueale to me my loues abiding, that in my sleepe his shaddow
may appeare and report the cause of his departure. After this passion was breathed
from the mansion of her soule, she committed her watchfull eyes to the
gouernement of sweete sleepe, which being no sooner closed, but there appeared as
she thought, the shadow and very shape of her dearely beloued Lord Saint *George*
of *England*, not as hee was wont to bee, flourishing in his grauen Burgonet of
steele, or mounted on a stately Genet, deckt with a watchet Plume of spangled
feathers, but in ouerworne and simple attyre, with pale looks and leane body, like
to a Ghoast risen from some hollow graue, breathing as it were these sad and
wofull passions:

> *Sabra, I am betraide for loue of thee,*
> *And logde in hollow Caues of dismall night:*
> *From whence I neuer more shall come to see,*
> *Thy louing countenance and beautie bright.*
> > *Remaine thou true and constant for my sake,*
> > *That of thy loue, they may no conquest make.*

> *Let tyrants thinke if euer I obtaine,*
> *What now is lost by treasons cursed guile:*
> *False Egipts scourge I surelie will remaine,*
> *And turne to streaming blood Morocos smile.*
> > *The damned dogge of Barbarie shall rue,*
> > *The balefull stratagems that will insue.*

> *The Persian towers shall smoke with fire,*
> *And loftie Babilon be tumbled downe:*
> *The Crosse of Christendome shall then aspire,*
> *To weare the proud Egiptian triple Crowne.*
> > *Ierusalem and Iuda shall behold,*
> > *The fall of Kinges by Christian Champions bold.*

> *Thou maide of Egipt still continue chaste,*
> *A Tyger seekes thy virgins name to spill:*
> *Whilst George of England is in prison plast,*
> *Thou shalt be forst to wed against thy will.*

But after this shall happen wondrous thinges,
For from thy womb shal spring three mighty kings.

This strange and tragicall discourse being no sooner ended, but she awaked from her sleepe, and presently reached forth her seemely handes thinking to embrace him, but shee catched nothing but the brittle ayre, which caused her to renew her former complaints; O wherefore died I not in this my troublesome dreame (saide the sorrowfull Lady) that my Ghost might haue haunted those inhumane monsters which falsely betrayed the brauest Champion vnder the cope of heauen? yet for his sake will I exclaime against the ingratitude of *Egypt*, and like the rauisht *Philomele* fill euery corner of the land with ecchoes of his wrong: my woes shall exceede the sorrows of *Dido* queene of *Carthage*, mourning for the ingratiude of *Aeneas*: with such like passions wearied she the time away, till twelue months were fully finished: at last her father vnderstanding what feruent affection she bore to the English Champion, began in this manner to dilate.

Daughter (saide the Egiptian King) I charge thee by the bands of nature, and the true obedience thou oughtest to beare my age, to banish and exclude all fond affections from thy minde, & not to settle thy loue vpon a wandring Knight that is vnconstant, and without habitation: thou seest heehath forsaken thee, and returnde into hys owne Countrie, where hee hath wedded a wife of that Land and Nation: Therefore I charge thee vpon my displeasure, to affect and loue the blacke King of *Moroco*, that rightfully hath deserued thy loue, which shall bee Honourably holden to the Honour of *Egipt*, and so departed without any answere at all: By which *Sabra* knew hee would notbee crost in hys will and pleasure: therefore shee sighed out these lamentable wordes.

O vnkinde Father to crosse the affection of hys childe! and to force loue where no liking is: Yet shall my minde continue true vnto my deare betrothed Lord, although my body be forst against nature to obay, and *Almidor* haue the honour of my marriage bed: Yet English *George* shall enioy my true Uirginity, if euer he returne againe to *Egipt*. and therewithall she pulled forth a chaine of gold, and wrapt it seauen times about her Iuorie necke. This (said shee) hath seauen dayes beene steept in Tygers blood, and seauen nights in Dragons milke, whereby it hath obtainde such excellent vertue, that so long as I weare it about my necke, no man on earth can enioy my virginitie: though I bee forced to the state of marriage, and lie seauen yeares in wedlocks bed: yet by the vertue of this chaine I shall continue a true virgin.

Which wordes being no sooner ended, but *Almidor* entered her sorrowfull Cabbinet, and presented her with a wedding garment, which was of the pure vnspotted silke, imbost with Pearle, and rich refined gold, perfumed with sweete Sirrian powders. it was of the colour of the Lillie when *Flora* had bedeckt the field in May with natures orniments, so glorious and costly her vestures seemed, and so stately were her Nuptiall rights solemnized, that *Egipt* admired the bountie of her wedding: which for seauen dayes was holden in the Court of King *Ptolomie*, and then remoqued to *Tripolie*, the chiefe Cittie in *Barbarie*, where *Almidors* forced Bride was Crowned Queene of *Moroco*: at which Coronation the Conduits ranne with *Greekish* Wines, and the streets of *Tripolie* were beautified with Pageants and delightfull showes. The Court resounded such melodious Harmonie as though *Apollo* with his siluer Harpe had descended from the heauens. such Tilts and Turniments were performed betwixt the *Egiptia*n Knights, and the Knights of *Barbarie*, that they exceeded the Nuptials of *Heccuba*, the beautious Queene of *Troy*: which Honourable proceedings, wee leaue for this time to their owne contentments: some masking: some dancing: some reuelling: some Tilting, and some banqueting: Also leauing the Champion of *England Saint George*, mourning in the Dungeon in *Persia* as you heard before, and returne to the other six Champions of Christendome, which departed from the brazen piller, euery one his seueral way, whose Knightly and Noble aduentures, if the Muses graunt mee the bountie of faier *Castalian* springes, I will most amply discouer, to the honour of Christendome.

CHAP. IIII.

How Saint Dennis the Champion of France, liued seauen yeares in the shape of a Hart, and howe proud Eglantine the Kings Daughter of Thessalie, was transformed into a Mulberie Tree, and how they both recouered their former shapes by the meanes of Saint Dennis his horse.

CAlling now to memorie the long & weary trauailes *S. Dennis* the Champion of *Fraunce* indured after his departure from the other sixe Champions at the brazen piller, as you heard in the beginning of the former Chapter, from which he wandred through many a desolate groue and wildernes, without any aduenture worthy the noting, till he arriued vppon the borders of *Thessalie*, (beeing a Land as then inhabited with wilde beasts): wherein he indured such a pennurie & scarcitie of victualles: that hee was forced for the space of seauen yeares to feede vpon the hearbes of the fields, & the fruits of trees, till the haires of his head were like to Egles feathers, and the nayles of his fingers to birds clawes: his drink the dew of heauen, the which hee licked from the flowers in the meadows, the attire he cloathed his bodie withall, bay leaues and broad dockes, that grew in the woodes: his shooes the barke of trees, whereon hee trauailde through many a thornie brake: But at last it was his fortune and cruell destinie, (beeing ouerpressed with the extreamitie of hunger) to taste & feede vpon the berries of a Mulberie tree, whereby he lost the liuely forme and Image of hys humane substance, and was transformed into the shape and likenes of a wilde Hart: Which strange & sodaine transformation, this Noble Champion little mistrusted, till he espied his misshapen forme in a cleare fountaine, which nature had erected in a coole and shadie valley: but when he behelde the shadow of his deformed substaunce, and howe hys heade late Honoured with a Burgonet of steele, now dishonoured with a paire of siluaine hornes: his face whereon the countenance of true Nobilitie late caractred, now couered with a beastlike similitude, and his body late the true Image of magnanimity, now ouerspread with a hearie hide, in colour like to the fallow fieldes: which strange alteration not a little perplexed the minde of *S. Dennis*, that it caused him with all speed (hauing the naturall reason of man still remaining) to repaire backe to the Mulberie tree againe, supposing the berries he had eaten to be the cause of his transformation, vnder which tree the distressed Knight laid his deformed limbs vpon the bare ground, and thus wofully began to complaine.

What Magicke charmes (said hee) or rather bewitching spels, remaynes within this accursed tree? whose wicked fruite hath confounded my future fortunes, & conuerted mee to the tipe of miserie? O thou celestiall directer of the world! & all you pitteous powers of heauen: Looke downe with kindely lookes vpon my haplesse transformation, and bende your browes to heare my wofull lamentation; I was of late a man but now a horned beast: I was a souldier & my Countries Champion: but now a loathsome creature and a pray for dogs; my glistring Armour is exchaunged into a hide of haire: my braue array more baser than the lowlye earth: henceforth in steed of Princely Pallaces, these shadie woods must serue to shrowde me in: wherein my Bedde of downe must bee a heape of sunburnde mosse: my sweete recording Musicke the blustering of the windes, that with Tempestious gustes doo make the Wildernes to tremble: the companye I dayly keepe must bee the Siluane Satiers, Driades, and Faire Nimphes, which neuer appeare to worldly eyes, but in twilights, or at the prime of noone: the Starres that beautifie the Christall vale of heauen, shall henceforth serue as Torches to light me to my wofull bed: the scouling cloudes shall be my Cannopie: my Clocke to count how time runs stealing on, the sound of hissing snakes or els the croking of toads.

Thus discribed hee his owne miserie, till the watrie teares of calamitie gushed in such aboundance from the Conduits of his eyes, that they seemed to quench the burning thunder-bolts of heauen, & his scortching sighes so violently forced from his bleeding breast, that they seemed to dim the brightnes of the sunne; whereat the vntamed Beares, & merciles Tygers relented at his mones, and like to harmeles Lambes sate bleating in the woods to heare his wofull exclamations.

Long and manye dayes continued this Champion of *Fraunce* in the shape of a Hart, in more distressed miserie than the vnfortunate English Champion in *Persia*, not knowing how to recouer his former likenes, and humane substance. So vpon a time, as he lamented the losse of natures ornaments vnder the branches of that Mulbery tree, which was the cause of his transformation, he heard a moost grieuous and tyrrible groane, which he supposed to bee the induction of some admirable accident that would insue: So taking truce for a time with his sorrowes, hee heard a hollow voice breath from the trunke of that Mulberie tree, these words following.

The voyce in the Mulberie tree.

Cease to lament thou famous man of Fraunce,
With gentle eares come listen to my mone:
In former times it was my fatall chaunce
To be the proudest maide that ere was knowne.
By birth I was the Daughter of a King,
Though now a breathles tree and sensles thing.

My pride was such that heauen confounded me,
A Goddesse in mine owne conceit I was:
What nature lent too bace I thought to be,
But deamd[1] my selfe all earthly things to passe:
And therefore Nectar and Ambrosia sweet,
The food of heauen for me I counted meete.

My pride contemned still the bread of wheate,
But pure foode I daylie sought to finde,
Refined gold was boiled in my meate,
Such selfe conceit my fancies fond did blinde:

---

[1] deamd] dead *1596*

For which the Gods aboue transported me,
From humane substance to this sensles tree.

Seauen yeares in shape of Hart thou must remaine,
And then the purple Rose by heauens decree;
Shall bring thee to thy former shape againe,
And end at last thy wofull miserie:
When this is done be sure thou cut in twaine,
This fatall tree wherein I doo remaine.

After the voice had breathed these speeches from the Mulberie tree, he stood so much amazed at the straungnes of the words, that for a time his sorrowes bereaued him of his speech, and his long appointed punishment constrayned hys thoughts to loose their naturall vnderstanding: But yet at last recouering his senses, though not hys humane likenes, bitterly complayned hys hard misfortunes.

O vnhappy creature (said the wofull Champion) more miserable than *Progne*, in her transformation, and more distressed than *Acteon* was, whose perfect imitation I am made: His miserie continued but a short season, for hys owne dogges the same day tore him in a thousand peeces, & buried his transformed carkasse in their hungrie bowels: mine is appointed by the angry destenies, till seauen times the summers sun hath replenisht his radient brightnesse, and seauen times the winters rayne hath washt mee with the showers of heauen. Thus complained the transformed Knight of *Fraunce*: sometimes remembring hys former fortunes, and how he had spent hys dayes in the Honour of hys countrey: sometimes thinking vpon the place of hys Natiuity, renowned *Fraunce* the Nurse and Mother of his life: sometimes treading with his feete (as for hands hee had none) in sandy ground, the print of the wordes the which the Mulberie tree had repeated, and many times numbering the minnutes of hys long appointed punishment, with the Flowers of the field. Ten thousand sighes hee dayly breathed from hys breast, and when the blacke and pitchy mantles of darke nyght had ouerspred the azurde firmamentes, and drawne her sable Curtaines before the brightsome windowes of the heauens, all creatures tooke their sweet reposed rest, and committed their tyred eyes to quiet sleepes: All thinges were silent except the murmering of the running waters: which sounding musicke was the chiefest comfort this distressed Champion enioyed: the glistering Queene of night clad in her christall robes, three Hundred times a yeare, was witnes of his nightly lamentations: the wondring Howlat, that neuer singes but in thenight, sate yelling ouer his head: the rufull weeping Nightingale with mournefull mellodie, chearefully attending on hys person: for during the limitation of his seauen yeares miserie, his trustie Steede neuer forsoke him, but with all diligence and true loue attended vpon him day and night, neuer wandring away, but euer keeping him companie: If the extreame heate of Summer were intollerable, or the pinching colde of Winter violent, his Horse woulde bee a shelter to defend him.

Thus when the tearme of seauen yeares were fully finished, and that hee should recouer his former substaunce, and humane shape, his good Horse which he tendred as the Apple of hys eye, clambered a high and steepy Mountaine, which nature had beautified with al kinde of fragrant flowers, as odorifferous as the garden of *Hesperides*: from whence he pulled a braunch, of purple Roses and brought them betwixt his teeth to hys distressed Master, beeing in hys former passions of discontent, vnder the Mulberie Tree: The which the Champion of *Fraunce* no sooner beheld, but he remembred that by a purple Rose hee should recouer hys former similitude; and so ioyfully receaued the Roses from hys trustie Steede: then casting hys eyes vp to the celestial throne of heauen, hee conuayed these consecrated flowers into his emptie stomacke.

After which he laid him downe vpon the bosome of his mother[2] earth, where he fell into such a sound sleep, that all his senses and vitall spirits were without moouing, for the space of foure and twenty houres: In which time the windowes and the doores of heauen were opened, from whence descended such a shower of rayne, that it washed away his hairie forme and beastlike shape: his horned head and long visage, was turned againe into a liuely countenance, and al the rest of his members, both armes, legges, handes, feete, fingers, toes, with all the rest of natures giftes, receaued their former shapes.

But when the good Champion awaked from hys sleepe, & perceauing the wonderfull workmanship of the Heauens, in transforming him to hys humane likenes: First gaue honour to Almightie God: next kissing the ground whereon he had liued so long in miserie: then beholding hys Armour which stoode hard by hym bestainde and almost spoild with rust, his Burgonet and kene[3] edged Curtle-axe besmeered ouer with dust: then lastlie pondring in his minde of the faithfull seruice his trustie Steed had done him during the time of his calamitie, whose sable coloured mane hung frisling downe his brauny neck, which before was wont to be pleyted curiously with artificiall knots, and his foreheade which was wont to bee beautified with a tawnie plume of feathers: now disfigured with ouergrowne haire, whereat the good Champion *Saint Dennis* of *Fraunce* so much grieued, that he stroaked downe his Iettie backe, till the haire of his body lay as smooth as *Arabian* silke, then pulled he out his trustie Fauchion, which in many fierce assaults and dangerous Combats, had beene bathed in the blood of hys enemies, which by the long continuance of idle time was almost consumed with cankered rust, but by his labour and industrious paines, he recouered the former beauty and brightnes againe.

Thus both his sword his horse, his Martiall furniture, & other habilliments of warre, beeing brought to their first and proper quallities, the Noble Champion intended to perseuer and goe forwarde in the aduenture in cutting downe the vnhappie Mulberie tree: So taking his sworde which was of the purest Spanish steele, gaue such a stroake at the roote therof, that at one blow he cut it quite in sunder, wherout presently flashed such a mightie flame of fire, that the mane from his horse necke was burned, and likewise the haire of his owne head had beene fiered, if hys Helmet had not preserued him: for no sooner was the flame extinguished, but there ascended from the hollow tree, a naked Uirgin, in shape

---

[2] mother] mothers *1596*
[3] kene] kine *1596*

like *Daphnie* which *Apollo* turnde to Bay: fairer then *Pigmalions* Iuorie Image, or the Northen driuen snow, her eyes more clearer than the Isie mountains, her cheekes like Roses dipt in milke, her lips more louelier than the Turkish Rubies, her Alablaster teeth like Indian Pearles, her seemely necke an Iuorie Tower, her daintie breasts a Parradice[4] where milke white Doues may sit and sing, the rest of natures liniaments, a staine to *Iuno* Queene of heauen: at whose most excellent beautie this valiant & vndaunted Champion more admired, then at her woonderfull transformation: For his eyes were so rauished with such exceeding pleasure, that his tongue could indure no longer silent, but was forced to vnfold the secrets of his heart, and in these tearmes began to vtter his[5] minde.

Thou most diuine and singuler ornament of nature, (said hee) fairer than the feathers of the siluer Swannes, that swim vpon *Mœanders* Christall streame & farre more beautifull than *Auroraes* morning countenance, to thee the fairest of all faiers, most humblie therefore to thy beautie doe I onelie submit my affections: Also I sweare by the Honour of my Knighthood, and by the loue of my Countrie *Fraunce*: which vow I will not violate for all the Treasures of rich *America*,[6] nor the golden Mines of higher *India*: Whether thou beest an Angell descended from the Heauens, or a Furie ascended from the dominions of *Proserpine*: whether thou beest some Fayrie or siluaine Nimph; which inhabits in these fatall woodes, or els an earthly creature for thy sin transformed into this Mulberie tree, I may not iudge: Therefore sweete Saint in whome my heart must pay his deuotion, vnfold to me thy Birth, Parentage, and name, that I may the bolder presume vppon thy curtesies: At which demaunde this newe borne Uirgin with a shamefaste looke, modest gesture, sober grace and blushing countenance, began thus to reply.

Sir Knight by whome my life, my loue, and fortunes, are to be commanded, and by whome my humane shape & naturall forme is recouered: First know thou Magnanimious Champion, that I am by birth the King of *Thessalies* Daughter, and my name was called for my beauty, proude *Eglantine*: For which contemptuous pride, I was transformed into this Mulberie tree: in which greene substance I haue continued fourteene yeares; as for my loue thou hast deserued it before all other Knights in the world, and to thee doo I plight that true promise before the Omnipotent Iudger of all thinges, & before that secret promise shall be infringed, the Sun shal cease to shine by day, & the Moone by night, & all the Planets forsake their proper natures.[7]

At which wordes the Champion gaue her the courtesie of his countrie, and sealed her promises with a louing kisse: After which the beautifull *Eglantine* being ashamed of her nakednes, weaued her such a garment of greene rushes intermixed with such varietie of sondry flowers; that it surpassed for workmanship the *Indian* maidens curious webs: her crisped lockes of haire continued still of the colour of the Mulberie tree: whereby shee seemde like *Flora* in her greatest royaltie, when the fields were bedeckt with natures tapestrie.

---

[4] Parradice] Palladice *1596*
[5] his] hir *1596*
[6] *America*] *Ameria 1596*
[7] natures] natares *1596*

After which she washed her Lillie handes, and Rosy coloured face in the dewes of heauen, which she gathered from a bed of violets. Thus in her greene vestments, shee intendes in companie of her true Louer (the valiant Knight of *Fraunce*) to take her iournie to her Fathers Court, beeing as then the King of that countrie: where after some fewe dayes[8] trauaile, they arriued safely in the Court of *Thessalie*: whose welcomes were to their owne wishes, & their entertainements most Honourable: for no sooner did the King behold his Daughters safe approch, of whose strange transformation he was euer ignorant, fell into such a dead sound through the exceeding ioy of her presence, that for a time his sences were without vitall moouing, and his hart imbraced so kindly her dainty body, and proffered such curtesie to the straunge Knight, that *Saint Dennis* accounted him the mirrour of all curtesie, and the patterne of true Nobilitie.

After the Champion was vnarmed, his stiffe and weary limbes were bathed in new milke and white wines, he was conuaied to a sweet smelling fire made of Ginniper, and the faire *Eglantine* conducted by the Maidens of Honour to a priuate chamber, where she was disrobed of her Siluaine attire, & apparelled in a Pall of[9] purple silke: In which Court of *Thessalie* we will leaue this our Champion of *Fraunce* with his Ladie, and goe forward in the discourses of the other Champions, discouering what aduentures hapned to them during the time of seauen yeares: But firste howe *Saint Iames* the Champion of *Spaine* fell in loue with a faire *Iew*, and how for her sake he continued seauen yeares dumb, and after if *Apollo* graunt my Muse the gift of *Scolorisme*, and dip my pen in the inke of Arte: I will not rest my wearie hand, till I haue explainde the Honourable proceedings of the Knights, of *England*, *Fraunce*, *Spaine*, *Italie*, *Scotland*, *Wales*, and *Ierland*, to the Honour of Christendome, and the dishonour of all the professed enemies of Christ.

---

[8] dayes] dayee *1596*
[9] of] *om. 1596*

CHAP. V.

How Saint Iames[1] the Champion of Spaine, continued seauen yeares dumb for the loue of a faire Iew, and howe he should haue beene shot to death by the Maidens of Ierusalem, with other thinges which chaunced in his trauailes.

NOw must my Muse speake of the strange aduentures of *Saint Iames* of *Spaine*, the third Champion and renowmed Knight of Christendome, and what hapned vnto him in his seauen yeares trauailes through manie a straunge countrie, both by Sea and land, where hys Honourable actes were so dangerous and full of wonder, that I want memorie to expresse, and Arte to subscribe, also I am forced for breuities sake, to passe ouer his fearefull and dangerous battaile with the burning Drake vpon the flaming mount in *Sicill*, which terrible Combat continued for the space of seauen dayes and seauen nights: Likewise omitting his trauell in *Capadocia* thorough a wildernes of Monsters, with his passage ouer the red seas, where his ship was deuoured with wormes, his Marriners drowned, and himselfe his horse and furniture safely brought to land by seanymphs and Meremaids, where after his long trauels, passed perrils, and dangerous tempests, amongst the boysterous billowes of the raging seas, arriued in the vnhappy dominions of *Iuda*; vnhappy by reason of the long and troublesome misery hee indured for the loue of a fayre Iew: For comming to the rich and beautifull Citty of *Ierusalem*, (being in that age the woonder of the world for braue buildings, Princely Pallaces, gorgeous Monuments, and time woondering Temples) hee so admired the glorious scituation thereof, (being the richest place that euer his eyes beheld) that he stoode before the walles of *Ierusalem* one while gazing vppon her golden gates glistering against the Suns bright countenance, another while beholding her stately Pinnacles, whose lofty peering tops seemde to touch the Clouds; another while woondring at her towers of Iasper, Iett, and Ebony, her strong and fortefied walles three times doubled about the Citty, the glistering Spires of the Temples of *Sion* built in the fashion and similitude of two Piramides the auncient monument of *Greece*, whose battlements were couered with steele, the walles burnished with siluer, and the ground paued with tinne. Thus as this inobled and famoused knight at Armes stood beholding the scituation of *Ierusalem*, there sodainely thundred such a peale of Ordinance within the Citty, that it seemed in his rauished conceit, to shake the vales of heauen and to mooue the deepe foundations of the fastned earth, whereat his horse gaue such a sodaine start, that he lept forty foote from the place whereon he stood: After this he heard the chearefull sound of Drums, and the ecchoes of brazen Trumpets, by which the good Champion expected some honorable pastime, or some great turnament to be at hand, which indeede so fell out, for no sooner did he cast his vigilant eyes toward the East side of the City, but he beheld a troope of well appointed horse come marching through the Gates, after them twelue Armed Knights mounted on Warlike Coursers, bearing in their handes twelue blood red streamers, whereon was wrought in silke, the picture of *Adonis* wounded with a

---

[1] Iames] Dennis *1596*

Bore, after them the King drawne in a Charriot by Spanish Genets, (which be a certaine kind of Steeds engendred by the winde.) The Kings Guard were a hundred naked Moores, with Turkish Bowes and Darts feathered with Rauens quilles, after them marched *Celestine* the King of *Ierusalems* faire Daughter, mounted on a tame Vnicorne, in her hand a Iauelin of siluer, & Armed with a breast plate of gold, artificially wrought like the skales of a Porcupine, her Guard were a hundred *Amazonian* Dames clad in greene silk, after them followed a number of Squiers & Gentlemen, some vpon *Barbarian* Steeds, some vpon *Arabian* Palfrayes, and some on foote, in pace more nimbler than the tripping Deare, & more swifter then the tameles Harts vpon the mountaines of *Thessalie*.

Thus *Nabuzaradan*, great King of *Ierusalem* (for so was he called,) solemnely hunted in the Wildernes of *Iuda*, beeing a countrie verie much anoyed with wilde beasts, as the Lyon, the Leopard, the Bore and such like: In which exercise the King apointed as it was proclaimed by his chiefe Harrold at Armes: (the which he heard repeated by a sheepheard in the fieldes,) that whosoeuer slewe the first wilde beast in the Forrest, shuld haue in reward a Corslet of steele so richlie ingraued, that it shuld be worth a thousand sickles of siluer. Of which Honorable enterprise when the Champion had vnderstanding, & with what liberall bountie the aduenterus Knights should bee rewarded, his heart was fraughted with inuincible courage, thirsting after glorious attempts, not onely for hope of gaine, but for the desire of Honour: At which hys illustrious and vndaunted minde aymed at to eternize[2] his deedes in the memorable records of Fame, and to shine as a Christall mirrour to all insuing times: So closing downe his Beuer, and locking on his furniture, scoured ouer the plaines before the Hunters of *Ierusalem*, in pace more swifter than the winged windes, till he aproched an olde solitarie and vnfrequented Forrest, wherein he espied a huge and mighty wilde Bore lying before his mossie den, gnawing vpon the mangled ioynts of some passenger which hee had murthered as hee trauailed through the Forrest.

This Bore was of a wonderfull length and bignes, & so tyrrable to behold, that at the first sight, hee almost daunted the courage of this *Spanish* Knight: for his monstrous head seemed vgly and deformed, hys eyes sparkeled like a firie furnace, hys tuskes more sharper than picks of steele, and from hys nostrels fumed such a violent breath, that it seemed like a tempestious whirle winde, his brissels were more harder than seauen times milted brasse, and his tayle more loathsome than a wreath of Snakes: Nere whome when *Saint Iames* approched, and beheld how he drank the blood of humane creatures, and deuoured their fleshe, hee blew hys siluer horne, which as then hung at the pummell of hys saddle in a scarfe of greene silke: whereat the furious monster roused himselfe, and most fiercely assailed the Noble Champion, which most nimbly leaped from his horse, & with his speare stroke such a violent blow against the brest of the Bore, that it shiuered into twentie peeces: Then drawing his good Fauchion from hys side, gaue him a second incounter: but all in vaine, for hee stroke as it were on a Rocke of stone, or a piller of Iron nothing hurtfull to the Bore: but at last with staring eies (which sparkled

---

[2] eternize] internize *1596*

like burning steele,) and with open Iawes the greedy monster assailed the Champion, intending to swallow him aliue, but the nimble Knight as then trusted more vpon pollicie than to fortitude, and so for aduantage skipped from place to place, till on a sodaine he thrust his keene edged Curtle-axe downe his intestine throate, and so most valiantly split his hart in sunder: The which being accomplished to his owne desiers he cut off the Bores head, and so presented the Honour of his Combat to the King of *Ierusalem*, (who as then with his mightie traine of Knights, were but now entered the Forrest: but hauing gratiously accepted the gift and bountifullie fulfilled his promises, demaunding the Champions Countrie, his Religion & place of Natiuitie: who no sooner had intelligence how he was a Christian Knight, and borne in the territories of *Spaine*: but presently his patience exchaunged into extreame furie, and by these wordes hee expressed his cankered stomacke towardes the Christian Champion.

Knowst thou not bold Knight (said the King of *Ierusalem*) that it is the law of *Iuda*, to harbour no vncircumsiced man, but eyther bannish him the land, or end his dayes by some vntimely death: Thou art a Christian and therefore shalt thou die, not all thy countries treasure, the wealthie *Spanish* mines, nor if all the Alphes which deuide the countries of *Italie* and *Spaine* were turned to hilles of burnisht gold, and made my lawfull heritage, they shuld not redeeme thy life: Yet for the Honour thou haste done in *Iuda*, I grant thee this loue by the law of Armes to choose thy death, els hadst thou suffered a timmerous torment: which seuere Iudgment so[3] amazed the Champion, that desperately he would haue gorgde him selfe vppon his owne sworde, but that he thought it an honour to hys countrie, to die in the defence of Christendome: So like a true innobled Knight fearing neyther the threates of the Iewes, nor the impartiall stroake of the fatall sisters gaue this sentence of his own death: First he requested to bee bounde to a pine tree with his breast laid open naked against the Sun: then to haue an howers respite to make his suplication to his Creator, and afterwardes to be shot to death by a pure Uirgin.

Which wordes were no sooner pronounced, but they disarmed him of hys furniture, bound him to a Pine tree, and laide his breast open readie to entertaine the bloody stroke of some vnrelenting maiden: but such pittie, meeke mercy, and kinde lenity lodged in the heart of euerie maiden, that none would take in hand to be the bloody Executioner of so braue a Knight: At last the tyrranous *Nabuzaradan* gaue strickt commandement vpon paine of death, that lots shuld be cast amongst the maidens of *Iuda* that were there present, and to whome the lot did fall should be the fatall executioner of the condemned Champion: But by fortune the chaunce fell to *Celestine* the Kinges own Daughter, beeing the Parragon of beautie, and the fairest Maide then liuing in *Ierusalem*, in whose heart no such deede of crueltie coulde be harboured, nor in whose hand no bloody weapon could be entertained. In steede of deathes fatall Instrument, shee shot towards his breast, a deepe strained sigh the true messenger of loue, and afterward to heauen she thus made her humble supplication.

---

[3] so] *om. 1596*

Thou great commaunder of celestiall moouing powers, conuert the cruell motions of my Fathers minde, into a spring of pittifull teares, that they may wash away the blood of this innocent Knight from the habitation of his stained purple soule. O *Iuda* and *Ierusalem*! within whose bosomes liues a wildernes of Tygers, degenerate from natures kinde, more cruell than the hungry Canibals, and more obdurate than vntamed Lyons: what merciles Tyger can vnrip that breast, where liues the Image of true Nobilitie, the verie patterne of Knighthood, and the map of a Noble minde? No, no, before my handes shall bee stained with Christians blood, I will like *Scilla* against all nature sell my countries safetie, or like *Mœdea* wander with the golden Fleece to vnknowne Nations.

Thus, and in such manner complained the beautious *Celestine* the Kings Daughter of *Ierusalem*, till her sighes stopped the passage of her speech, and her teares stained the naturall beautie of her Rosie Cheekes, her haires which glistered like to golden wiers, she besmerde in dust, and disrobed her selfe from her costly garments, and then with a traine of her *Amazonian* Ladies, went to the King her Father, where after a long sute, she not onely obtainde his life, but libertie, yet therwithall his perpetuall banishment from *Ierusalem*, and from all the borders of *Iuda*, the want of whose sight more grieued her hart, than the losse of her owne life: So this Noble & praise worthie *Celestine* returned to the Christian Champion, that expected euerie minnute to entertaine the sentence of death, but his expectation fell out contrarie: for the good Ladie, after shee had sealed two or three kisses vpon his pale lips, beeing exchaunged through the feare of death, cut the bandes that bound hys body to the tree in a hundred peeces, & then with a floud of sault teares, the motions of true loue, she thus reuealed her minde.

Most Noble Knight and true Champion of Christendome, thy life and libertie I haue gainde, but therewithall thy banishment from *Iuda*, which is a hell of horror to my soule: for in thy bosome haue I built my happines, and in thy hart I account the Paradice of my true loue: thy first sight and louely countenance did so rauish mee, when these eyes beheld thee mounted on thy Princely Palfray, that euer since my hart hath burnde in affection: therefore deare Knight in reward of my loue, be thou my Champion, and for my sake weare this ring with this posie ingrauen in it, *Ardeo*[4] *affectione*: and so giuing him a ring from her finger, and therewithall a kisse from her mouth, shee departed with a sorrowfull sigh, in companie of her Father and the rest of his Honourable traine, backe to the Citty of *Ierusalem*, beeing as then neere the setting of the Sunne: But now *Saint Iames* the Champion of *Spaine*, hauing passed the danger of death, and at full libertie to depart from that vnhappie Nation, hee fell into a hundred cogitations, one while thinking vpon the true loue of *Celestine*, (whose name as yet he was ignorant of,) another while vpon the crueltie of her father: then intending to depart into his[5] owne countrie, but looking backe to the Towers of Ierusalem his minde sodainely altered, for thither hee purposed to goe, hoping to haue a sight of hys Lady and Mistresse, and to liue in some disguised sort in her presence, and bee her loues true Champion against all commers: So gathering certaine blackberies from the trees, he coloured his body all

---

[4] *Ardeo*] *Ardio 1596*
[5] his] hys his *1596*

ouer like a Blackamoore: But yet considering that hys speech would discouer him, intended likewise to continue dumbe all the time of his residence in *Ierusalem*: So all thinges ordered according to his desier, he tooke his iournie to the Cittie, where with signes and other motions of dumbnes, he declared his intent: which was to bee entertained in the Court, and to spend his time in the seruice of the King: But when the King behelde his countenance, which seemed of the naturall colour of the Moore, hee[6] little mistrusted him to be the Christian Champion whome before he greatly enuied, but accounted him one of the brauest *Iudean* Knights that euer his eye behelde: therefore hee instauld him with the honour of Knighthood, and appointed him to bee one of his Guard; and likewise his Daughters onlie Champion: But when *Saint Iames* of *Spaine* sawe himselfe inuested in that honoured place, his soule was rauished with such exceeding ioy, that he thought no pleasure comparable to hys, no place of *Elisium* but the Court of *Ierusalem*, and no Goddesse but hys beloued *Celestine*.

Long continued he dumb, casting foorth manie a louing sigh in the presence of his Ladie and Mistresse, not knowing how to reueale the secrets of his minde.

So vppon a time there ariued in the Court of *Nabuzaradan* the King of *Arabia*, with the Admirall of *Babilon*, both presuming vpon the loue of *Celestine*, and crauing her in the way of marriage: but shee exempted all motions of loue from her chaste minde, onlie building her thoughtes vpon the *Spanish* Knight, which shee supposed to bee in hys owne Countrie.

At whose melancholie passions her importunate sutors the King of *Arabia*, and the Admirall of *Babilon* meruailed: and therefore intended vppon an Euening to present her with some rare deuised Maske: So choosing out fit consorts for their Courtly pastimes: Of which number the King of *Arabia* was chiefe and first leader of the traine, the great Admirall of *Babilon* was the second, and her owne Champion *Saint Iames* the third, who was called in the Court by the name of the dumb Knight, and in this manner the Maske was performed.

First entered a most excellent Consort of Musicke, after them the aforesaid Maskers in cloth of gold, most curiously imbrothered, and danced a course about the hall, at the ende whereof, the King of *Arabia* presented *Celestine* with a costly sword, at the hilt whereof hung a siluer Globe, and vpon the point was erected a golden Crowne: then the Musicke sounded another course, of which the Admirall of *Babilon* was leader, who presented her with a vesture of purple silke, of the colour of the rainebow; brought in by *Diana*, *Venus*, and *Iuno*: which being done the Musicke sounded the third time, in which course *Saint Iames* (though vnknowne) was the leader of the daunce, who at the ende whereof likewise presented *Celestine* with a garland of Flowers, which was brought in by the three Graces, and put vpon her head: Afterwarde the Christian Champion intending to discouer himselfe to his Ladie and Mistresse, tooke her by the seemely hand and led her a stately Morisco daunce: which beeing no sooner finished, but hee offered her the Diamond ring which she gaue him at his departure in the woodes, the which shee presently knew by the posie, and shortly after had intelligence of his long

---

[6] hee] *om. 1596*

continued dumbnesse, his counterfet colour, his chaunging of nature, and the great daunger that hee put himselfe in for her sake, which caused her with all the speede shee coulde possiblie make, to breake off companie, and to retire into a Cabbinet which shee had hard by, where the same Euening she had a long conference with her true and faithfull louer and aduenterous Champion; and to conclude, they made such agreement betwixt them: that the same night vnknowne to anie in the Court, she bad *Ierusalem* adue, & by the light of *Cinthias* glistering beames, stole from her Fathers Pallace, where in companie of none but *S. Iames* shee tooke her iournie toward the countrie of *Spaine*: But this noble Knight by pollicie preuented all insuing daungers, for he shodde his horse backewards, whereby when they were missed in the Court that they might be followed the contrarie waie.

By this meanes escaped the two Louers from the furie of the Iewes, and ariued safely in *Spaine* in the Cittie of *Ciuill*, wherin the good Champion *Saint Iames* was borne: where as now we leaue them for a time to their owne contented mindes: Also passing ouer the hurly burly in *Ierusalem* for the losse of *Celestine*, the vaine pursutes of aduenterous Knights, in stopping the Ports and Hauens, the preparing of fresh horses to follow them, and the mustering of souldiers to pursue them, the franticke passions of the King for hys daughter, the melanchollie mones of the Admirall of *Babilon* for his Mistris, and the wofull lamentations of the *Arabian* King for his Ladie and Loue, and returne to the aduentures of the other Christian Champions.

CHAP. VI.

The tyrrible battaile betwixt S. Anthonie the Champion of Italie, and the Giant Blanderon, and afterward of his strange entertainment in the Giants Castell, by a Thrasian Ladie, and what hapned to him in the same Castell.

IT was at that time of the yeare, when the earth was newly deckt with a summers liuerie, when the Noble and Heroicall minded Champion *Saint Anthonie* of *Italie* ariued in *Thrasia*, where hee spent his seauen yeares trauailes to the honor of his countrie, the glory of God, and to hys owne lasting memorie: For after he had wandred through many a weariesome waie both by Sea and Land, through woods and wildernesses, by hilles and dales, by caues and dens, and other vnknowne passages, he ariued at last vpon the top of a high and steepie mountaine, wheron stood a wonderfull huge and strong Castell, which was kept by the most mightiest Giant vnder the cope of heauen, whose puissant force all *Thrasia* could not ouercome, nor once attempt to withstand, but with the danger of their whole countrie. The Giants name was *Blanderon*, hys Castell of the purest Marble stone, his gates of yellowe Brasse, and ouer the principall gate was graued in Letters of gold these verses following.

> *Within this Castell, liues the scourge of Kinges,*
> *A furious Giant, whose vnconquered power:*
> *The Thracian Monarke to subiection bringes,*
> *And keepes his Daughters prisoners in his Tower.*
> *Seauen Damsels faire the monstrous Giant keepes,*
> *That singes him Musicke while he nightly sleepes.*

> *His bats of steele a thousand Knights hath felt,*
> *Which for these virgins sakes haue lost their liues:*
> *For all the Champions bold that with him dealt,*
> *This most intestine[1] Giant still suruiues,*
> *Let simple passengers take heede in time,*
> *When vp this steepie mountaine they do clime.*

> *But Knights of worth, and men of Noble minde,*
> *If any chaunce to trauaile by this Tower:*
> *That for these Maidens sakes will be so kinde,*
> *To trie their strengthes against the Giants power:*
> *Shall haue a virgins praier both day and night,*
> *To prosper them with good successefull fight.*

After he had read what was written ouer the gate, desire of Fame so incouraged him, and the thirst of honour so imboldned his valiant minde, that he eyther vowed

---

[1] *intestine*] intestiue *1596*

to redeeme the Ladies from their seruitude, or die with honour by the furie of the Giant: So going to the Castell gate, he stroke so vehemently thereon with the pummell of hys sword, that it sounded like a mightie thunder clap: Wherat *Blanderon* sodainely started vp, beeing fast a sleepe close by a Fountaines side, and came pacing foorth at the Gate with a mightie Oake vppon his necke: which at the sight of the *Italian* Champion, so lightly flourished it about hys head, as though it had beene but a light Dimmilaunce, and with these wordes gaue the Noble Champion entertainement

What Furie hath incenst thy ouer boldned mind (proude Princockes) thus to aduenture thy feeble force against the violence of my strong arme: I tell thee haddest thou the strength of *Hercules*, who bore the mountaine *Atlas* on his shoulders, or the pollicie of *Vlisses*, by which the Cittie of Troy was ruinated, or the might of *Xerxes*, whose multitudes drunke huge riuers as they passed: yet all too feeble, weake, and impudent, to encounter with the mightie Giant *Blanderon*: thy force I esteeme like a blast of winde, and thy strokes as light as a few drops of water: Therefore betake thee to thy weapon, which I compare vnto a bulrush, for on this ground will I measure out thy graue, and after cast thy feeble Palfray in one of my handes headlong downe this steepie mountaine.

Thus boasted the vaine glorious Gyant vpon his owne strength: During which time, the valerous and hardie Champion had alighted from his horse: where after hee had made hys humble supplication to the heauens for hys good speede, and committed his Fortune to the impartiall Queene of destenie, hee approached within the compasse of the Giants reach, who with his great Oake so nimbly besturde him with such vehement blowes, that they seemed to shake the earth, and to rattle against the walles of the Castell like mighty thunder claps, and had not the polliticke Knight continually skipped from the furie of his blow, hee had beene brused as small as flesh vnto the potte, for euerie stroke that the Giant gaue, the roote of hys Oake entered at the least two or three foote deepe into the ground: But such was the wisedome and pollicie of the worthie Champion, not to withstand the force of his weapon, till the Giant grew breathles, and not able through his long labour to lift the Oake aboue his heade, and likewise the heate of the Sunne was so intollerable, (by reason of the extreame haight of the Mountaine, and the mightie waight of hys Iron coate) that the sweat of the Gyants browes ran into hys eyes, and by the reason that hee was so extreame fat, hee grewe blinde, that hee coulde not see to indure Combat with him any longer, and as farre as hee coulde perceiue, woulde haue retired or runne backe againe into hys Castell; but that the *Italian* Champion with a bold courage assailed the Giant so fiercely, that he was forced to let his Oake fall, and stand gasping for breath, which when the noble Knight beheld, with a fresh supplie hee redoubled his blowes so couragiously, that they battered on the Giants Armour like a storme of winters haile: whereby at last *Blanderon* was compelled to aske the Champion mercie, and to craue at his hands some respite of breathing, but his demaunde was in vaine, for the valiant Knight supposed now or neuer to obtaine the honour of the day, & therefore neuer resting his wearie arme, but redoubling blow after blow, till the Gyant for want of breath, and through the anguish of his deepe gashed woundes, was forced to giue the world a farewell, and to yeelde the riches of his Castell to the most renowned

Conquerour *S. Anthonie* the Champion of *Italie*: But by that time the long and
dangerous encounter was finished, and the Giant *Blanderons* head disseuered from
his bodie, the Sunne sate mounted on the highest part of the Elements, which
caused the day to be extreame hote and sultrie, whereby the Champions Armour so
extreamely scalded him, that hee was constrained to vnbrace his Corslet, and to lay
aside his Burgonet, and to cast his body on the cold earth, onely to mittigate his
ouerburthened heate: But such was the vnnaturall coolenes of the earth, and so
vnkindely to his ouerlabored heart, that the melted grease of his inward parts was
ouercooled sodainely, whereby his bodie receiued such vnnaturall distemperature,
that the vapors of the cold earth stroke presently to hys heart, by which hys vitall
aire of life was excluded, and hys body without sence or moouing: where[2] in the
mercie of pale death he lay bereaued of feeling for the space of an houre.

During which time faire *Rossalinde* (one of the Daughters of the *Thracian*
Kinges, beeing as then Prisoner in the Castell,) by chaunce looked ouer the walles,
and espied the bodie of the Giant headles, vnder whose subiection shee had
continued in great seruitude for the time of seauen monthes, likewise by him a
Knight vnarmed, as she thought panting for breath, the which the Ladie Iudged to
bee the Knight that had slaine the Giant *Blanderon*, & the man by whome her
deliuerie should be recouered, she presently descended the walles of the Castell,
and ran with all speed to the aduenterous Champion, whome she found dead: But
yet beeing nothing discouraged of his recouerie, feeling as yet a warme blood in
euerie member, retired backe with all speede to the Castell, and fetcht a box of
pretious Balme, the which the Giant was wont to poure into hys woundes after his
encounter with any knight: with which Balme this curteous Ladie chafed euerie
part of the breathles Champions bodie, one while washing his stiffe limbes with her
salt teares, the which like pearles fell from her eyes, another while drying them
with the tresses of her golden haire, which hung dangling in the winde, then
chafing hys liueles bodie againe with a Balme of a contrarie nature, but yet no
signe of life could she espie in the dead Knight: which caused her to growe
desperate of all hope of his recouerie: Therefore like a louing, meeke, and kinde
Lady, considering he had lost his life for her sake, shee intended to beare him
companie in death, and with her owne handes to finish vp her dayes, and to die
vpon his breast, as *Thisbe* died vpon the breast of her true *Pyrramus*: therfore as
the Swanne singes a while before her death, so this sorrowfull Ladie warbled
foorth this Swan-like song ouer the bodie of the Noble Champion.

> *Muses come mourne with dolefull mellodie,*
> *Kinde Siluane Nimphes that sit in Rosie bowers:*
> *With brackish teares commix your harmonie,*
> *To waile with me both minutes, monthes and houres:*
> *A heauie, sad, and Swan-like song sing I,*
> *To ease my hart a while before I die.*

---

[2] where] wheres *1596*

Dead is the Knight, for whome I liue and die,
Dead is the Knight which for my sake is slaine:
Dead is the Knight, for whome my carefull crie,
With wounded soules, for euer shall complaine:
A heauie, sad, and Swan-like song sing I,
To ease my hart a while before I die.

Ile set my breast vpon a siluer streame,
And swim vnto Elisium lillie fields:
There in Ambrosian trees Ile write a Theame,
Of all the wofull sighes my sorrow yeelds:
A heauie sad and Swan-like song sing I,
To ease my hart a while before I die.

Farewell faire woods where singes the Nightingales,
Farewell faire fields, where feeds the light foote Does,
Farewell you groues, you hilles and flourish dales,
But fare thou ill the cause of all my woes:
A heauie, sad, and Swanlike song sing I,
To ease my hart a while before I die.

Ring out my ruth you hollow Caues of stone,
Both birds, and beasts, with all things on the ground:
You sencsles trees be all assistant to my mone,
That up to heauen my sorrowes may resound:
A heauie, sad and swanlike song sing I,
To ease my hart a while before I die.

Let all the Townes of Thrace ring out my knell,
And write in leaues of brasse what I haue said:
That after ages may remember well,
How Rosalinde, both liude and dide a Maid:
A heauie, sad, and Swanlike song sing I,
To ease my hart a while before I die.

This wofull Dittie beeing no sooner ended but the desperate Ladie unsheathed the Champions sword, which as yet was all besprinkled with the Gyants blood, and beeing at the verie point to execute her intended Tragedie, and the bloody weapon directly placed against her Iuorie breast, but shee heard the distressed Knight give a grieuous & tyrrible grone: whereat she stopped her remorceles hand, & with more discreation tendered her owne safetie, for by this time the Balme wherewith she anoynted hys bodie, by wonderfull operation recouered the dead Champion, insomuch that after some few gaspes and earnest sighes, hee raised vp hys stiffe limbes from the cold earth, where like one cast into a trance, for a time gazed vp and downe the Mountaine: but at the last hauing recouered hys lost senses, espied the *Thracian* Damsell standing by, not able to speake one word her ioy so abounded: But after some continuance of time, hee reuealed to her the manner of hys dangerous Encounter, and successefull victorie, and she the cause of his recouerie, & her intended Tragedie: Where after manie kinde salutations, she curteously tooke him by the hand & led him into the Castell, where for that night he lodged hys wery limbs in an easie bed stuffed with Turtles feathers, & softest thistle downe, the chamber had as manie windowes where he lay, as there were dayes in the yeare, and as many dores as there were minutes in a day, and to discribe the curious architecture and the artificiall[3] workmanship of the place, were too tedious and a worke without end.[4]

But to be short, the Noble minded Knight slept soundlie after his dangerous battaile, without mistrust of Treason, or such Rebellious cogitations, till golden *Phœbus* bad him good morrow, then rising from his slouthfull bed, hee attired himselfe, not in his wonted habilliments of warre, but in purple garments according to the time of peace, and so intended to ouerview the Nobilities of the Castell: But the Ladie *Rossalinde* all the night was busied in looking to hys Horse, preparing dilicates for hys repast, and in making a fire against his vprising, where after he had refreshed hys wearie spirites with a daintie banket, & caroused downe two or three bowles of Greekish Wines, hee after by the counsell of *Rossalinde*, stripped the Giant from hys Iron furniture, and left his naked bodie vpon a craggie Rocke to bee deuoured of hungrie Rauens: which beeing done, the *Thracian* Uirgin discouered all the secrets of the Castell to the aduenterous Champion: First shee led him to a leaden Tower, where hung a hundred well approoued Corslets, with other Martiall furniture, which were the spoyles of such Knights as he had violently slaine, after that shee brought him to a stable, wherein stoode a hundred pampered Iades, which daily fed vpon nothing but humane flesh: Against it was directly placed the Gyants owne lodging, his bed was of Iron, corded with mightie bars of steele, the testerne and couering of carued brasse, the curtaines were of leaues of gold, and the rest of a straunge and wonderfull substance of the colour of the Elements: after this shee led him to a broad pond of water, more clearer than quicksiluer, the streames wherof lay continually as smooth as Christall Ice, whereon swam six milke white Swans with Crownes of gold about their neckes.

O here saide the *Thracian* Lady, begins the hell of al my griefe! At which wordes a pearled shower of teares ran from the Conduits of her eyes, that for a time they staide the passage of her tongue, but hauing discharged her heart from a few sorrowfull sighes, she began in this manner to tell her passed fortunes.

These sixe milke-white Swans most honoured Knight, you behold swimming in this riuer (quoth the Ladie *Rossalinde*) be my naturall sisters, both by birth and blood, and all Daughters to the King of *Thrace*, beeing now Gouernour of this vnhappie Countrie, and the beginning of our imprisonment befell in this vnfortunate manner.

The King my Father ordayned a solemne hunting to be holden through the land, in which Honourable pastime, my selfe in companie of my sixe sisters were

---

[3] artificiall] arificiall *1596*
[4] end.] end, *1596*

present: So in the middle of our sportes, when the Lords and Barrons of *Thracia* were in chace after a mightie shee Lyon, the heauens sodainely began to lower, the firmaments ouer cast, and a generall darkenesse ouerspread the face of the whole earth, then presently rose such a storme of lightning and thunder, as though heauen and earth had met together: by which our mightie troupes of Knights and Barrons were seperated one from another, and we poore Ladies forced by misfortune to seeke for shelter vnder the bottome of this high and steepie mountaine: where when this cruell Gyant *Blanderon* espied vs as hee walked vpon his Battailements, sodainely descended the mountaine, and fetcht vs all vnder hys Arme vp into his Castell, where euer since we haue liued in great seruitude, and for the woonderfull transformation of my sixe sisters, thus it came to passe as followeth.

Upon a time the Gyant beeing ouercharged with wine, grewe innamored vpon our beauties, and desired much to enioy the pleasures of our virginities, our excellent gifts of nature so inflamed hys minde with lust, that he would haue forced vs euerie one to satisfie hys sinfull desires: but as he tooke my sisters one by one into hys lodging thinking to deflowre them, their earnest praiers[5] so preuailed in the sight of God, that he preserued their chasteties by a most straunge and woonderfull miracle, and turned their comely bodies into the shape of milke-white Swannes, euen in the same forme as heere you see them swimming: So when this monstrous Gyant sawe that hys intent was crost, and howe there was none left behinde to supplie hys want, but my vnfortunate selfe, hee restrained hys filthie lust, not violating my Honour with any staine of infamie, but kept mee euer since a most pure Uirgin, onlie with sweet inspiring musicke[6] to bring him to his sleepe.

Thus haue you heard (most Noble Knight) the true discourse of my most vnhappy fortunes, and the wonderfull transformation of my sixe sisters, whose losse to this day is greatly lamented throughout all *Thrace*, and with that word she made an end of her Tragicall discourse, not able to vtter the rest for weeping: whereat the Knight being oppressed then with like sorrow, imbraced her about the slender waste, and thus kindely began to comfort her.

My most deare and kinde Ladie, within whose countenance, I see how vertue is inthronized, and in whose minde liues true Magnanimitie, let these few wordes suffice to comfort thy sorrowfull cogitations: First thinke that the Heauens are most beneficiall vnto thee in preseruing thy chastity from the Giants insatiate desires, then for thy deliuerie by my meanes from thy slauish seruitude: Thirdly and lastly, that thou remaining in thy naturall shape & likenes, mayest liue to bee the meanes of thy sisters transformations: Therefore drie vp those Cristall pearled teares and bid thy long continued sorrowes adue: for griefe is companion with dispaire, and dispaire a procurer of an infamous death.

Thus the wofull *Thracian* Ladie was comforted by the Noble Christian Champion: where after a fewe kinde greetings they intended to trauaile to her Fathers Court, there to relate what had hapned to her sisters in the Castel, likewise the Gyants confusion, and her owne safe deliuery by the illustrious prowesse of the

---

Christian Knight: So taking the keyes of the Castell, which was of a wonderful waight, they locked vp the gates and paced hand in hand downe the steepie mountaine, till they aproached the *Thracian* Court, which was distant from the Castell some tenne miles: but by that time they had a sight of the Pallace the Sunne was wandred to the vnder world, and the light of heauen sate muffled vp in cloudes of pitch, the which not a little discontented the wearie trauailers: but at last comming to her Fathers Gates, they heard a solemne sound of belles, ringing the funerall knell of some Noble estate: the cause of which solemne ringing they demaunded of the Porter, who in this manner expressed the truth of the matter vnto them.

Faire Ladie, and most renowned Knight, (said the Porter) for so you seeme both by your speeches and Honourable demaundes, the cause of this ringing is for the losse of the Kinges seauen daughters, the number of which Belles be seauen, called after the name of the seauen Princes, which neuer yet hath ceased their dolefull melodie, since the departure of the vnhappie Ladies, nor neuer must vntill ioyfull newes be heard of their safe returne.

Then now their taskes be ended, (said the Noble minded *Rossalinde*) for wee bring happie newes of the seauen Princes abidings: At which wordes the Porter beeing rauished with ioy, in all hast ranne to the steeple, and caused the Belles to cease: whereat the King of *Thrace* beeing at hys Royall supper, and hearing the Belles to cease their wonted melodie, sodainely started vp from hys Princelie seate, and like a man amazed ran to the Pallace gate, where as he founde his Daughter *Rossalinde* in companie of a strange Knight, which when he beheld hys ioy so exceeded, that hee sounded in his daughters bosome, but beeing recouered to his former sence, he brought them both vp into his Princely Hall, where their entertainements were so honorable, and so gratious in the eyes of the whole Court, that it were too tedious and ouerlong to describe, but their ioy continued but a short season, for it was presently dasht with *Rosalindes* tragicall discourse: for the good old King when he heard of his daughters transformations, and how they liued in the shapes of milke-white Swans, hee rent his lockes of siluer haire, which time had died with the pledge of wisdome, his rich and imbrothered garments he tore into a thousand peeces, and clad hys aged limbes in a dismall blacke, and sable mantle, more discontented than the woful King of *Troy*, when he beheld hys owne Sonnes by the haire of the heads dragged vp and downe the streetes, also he commaunded that his Knights and aduenterous Champions, in steede of glistring Armour should weare the weeds of death, more blacke in hew than winters darkest nights, and all the Courtly Ladies and gallant Thracian maydens in steede of silken vestments he commaunded to weare both heauy sad and melancholly ornaments, and euen as vnto a solemne funerall, so to attend him to the Giants Castell, & there obsequiously to offer vp vnto the angry Destenies, many a bitter sigh and teare in remembrance of his transformed daughters: Which decree of the sorrowfull Thracian King was performed with all conuenient speede, for the next morning no sooner had *Phœbus* cast his beauty vnto the Kinges bed-chamber, but hee apparrelled himselfe in mourning garments, and in company of his melancholly trayne set forward to his wofull Pilgrimage: But now we must not forget the Princely minded Champion of *Italie*, nor the Noble Lady *Rossalinde* who at the

Kinges departure towardes the Castell craued leaue to stay behinde, and not so sodainely to beginne a newe trauell, whereunto the King quickly condiscended, considering their late iourney the euening before, so taking the Castell keyes from the Champion, he bid his Pallace adew, and committed his fortune to his sorrowfull iourney: where wee leaue him in a world of discontented passions, and a while discourse what hapned to the Christian Champion and his beloued Lady, for by that time the Sunne had thrice measured the world with his restles steedes, and thrice his sister *Luna* wandred to the west, the Noble Italian Knight grewe weary of his long continued rest, and thought it a great dishonour & a scandall to his valiant minde, to remayne where naught but Chamber sportes were resident, desired rather to abide in a Court that entertaynde the dolefull murmuring of tragedyes, where the ioyfull sound of Drums and Trumpets shoulde bee heard, therefore taking *Rossalinde* by the hand, being then in a dumpe for the want of her father, to whome the good Knight in this manner expressed his secrete intent: My most deuoted Lady and Mistris (sayd the Champion) a second *Dido* for thy loue, a staine to *Venus* for thy beautie, *Penelopes* compare for constancie, and for chastetie the wonder of all maides: the faithfull loue that hitherto I haue found since my arriuall, for euer shall be shrined in my hart, and before all Ladies vnder the cope of heauen, thou shalt liue and die my loues true gouernesse, and for thy sake Ile stand as Champion against all Knights in the worlde: But to impaire the honour of my Knighthood, and to liue like a carpet dancer in the laps of Ladies I willnot, though I can tune a Lute in a Princes Chamber, I can sounde as well a fierce alarum in the field: honour calles mee foorth deare *Rossalinde*, and fame intendes to buckle on my Armour, which now lies rusting in the idle Court of *Thrace*: Therefore I am constrained (though most vnwilling) to leaue the comfortable sight of thy beautie, and commit my fortune to a longer trauaile, but I protest wheresoeuer I become, or in what Region soeuer I be harboured, there will I mainetaine to the losse of my life, that both thy loue, constancie, beautie, and Chastetie, surpasseth all Dames aliue, and with this promise my most diuine *Rossalinde*, I bid thee farewell: But before the honorable minded Champion could finish what he had purposed to vtter, the Ladie beeing wounded inwardly with extreame griefe, not able to indure to keepe silent any longer, but with teares falling from her eyes, brake off his speeches in this manner.

Sir Knight (said shee) by whome my libertie hath bin obtained: Therefore the name of Ladie & Mistresse wherwith you intitle me, is to high and proude a name, but rather call me handmaid, or seruile slaue, for on thy Noble person will I euermore attend: It is not *Thrace* can harbour me when thou art absent, and before I doo forsake thy companie and kinde fellowship, the heauen shall be no heauen, the sea no sea, nor the earth no earth: but if thou prouest vnconstant, as *Ninus* did to *Scilla*, who for hys sake stole her Fathers purple haire, whereon depended the safetie of his countrie, or like wandring *Aenæas* flie from the Queene of *Carthage*: yet shall these tender handes of mine which neuer shal vnclaspe, but hang vpon thy horse bridle, till my bodie like *Thesius* sonnes be dasht in sunder against hard flintie stones: Therefore forsake me not deare knight of Christendome. If euer *Camma* was true to her *Sinatus*, or euer *Alsione* to her *Ceyx*, so *Rossalinde* will bee to thee, & with this plighted promise shee caught him fast about the necke, from whence shee would not vnclose[7] her handes, till he had vowde by the Honor of true Chiualrie, to make her sole companion, and onely partner in hys trauailes, and so after this order it was accomplished.

Thus beeing both agreed, shee was most trimlye attired like a Page in greene sarcenet, her haire bounde vp most cunningly with a silken list, & so artificially wrought with curious knots, that she might trauaile without suspition or blemmish of her honour, her Rapier was a Turkish blade, and her Poniarde of the finest fashion, the which shee wore at her backe tyed with an Orringe tawnie coloured scarfe, beautefied with tassels of vnwouen silke, her Buskins of the smoothest Kiddes skinnes, her Spurres of the purest *Lidian* steele: In which when the Noble and beautifull Lady was attired, she seemed in stature like the God of loue, when he sate dandled vpon *Didos* lap, or rather *Ganemede, Ioues* minnion, or *Adonis* when *Venus* shewde her siluer skin, to intrappe hys eyes to her vnchaste desires: But to bee briefe, all thinges beeing got in readines for their departure from *Thrace*, this famous worthie Knight mounted vppon hys eger Steede, and the magnanimious *Rossalinde* on her gentle Palfray, in pace more easier than the winged windes, or a Cockbote floting vpon the Christall streames, they both bid adue to the Countrie of *Thracia*, and committed their iournie to the Queene of chaunce: Therefore smile heauens and guide them with a most happie starre, vntill they ariue where their soules doe most desire. The brauest and boldest Knight that euer wandred by the way, and the most loueliest Ladie that euer anye eye beheld: In whose trauailes my Muse must leaue them for a season, and speake of the *Thracian* mourners, which by this time had watered the earth with abundance of their ceremonious teares, and made the elements true witnesses of their sad laments, as hereafter followeth in thys next Chapter.

---

[7] vnclose] vnclase *1596*

CHAP. VII.

How Saint Andrew the Champion of Scotland trauailed into a vale of walking Spirites, and how hee was set at libertie, by a going fire. After his iournie into Thracia, where he recouered the six Ladies to their naturall shapes, that had liued seauen yeares in the likenes of milk-white Swannes, with other accidents that befell the most Noble Champion.

NOW of the Honourable aduentures of *Saint Andrew* the famous Champion of *Scotland* must I discourse, whose seauen yeares trauailes were as straunge as any of the other Champions: For after hee had departed from the Brazen Piller, as you heard in the beginning of the Historie. He trauailed through many a strange and vnknowne Nation, beyond the cercuit of the sunne, where but one time in the yere she shews her brightsome beames, but continually darkenes ouerspreads the countrie, & there is a kind of people that haue heads like dogs, & in the extreamity of hunger doe deuoure one another: from which people this Noble Champion was woonderfull strangelie deliuered, for after he had wandred some certain dayes, neither seeing the gladsome brightnes of the Sunne, nor the comfortable countenance of the Moone, but only guided by duskie palenes of the elements, he hapned to a vale of walking spirits: which he supposed to bee the verie dungeon of burning *Acharon*: For there he heard blowing of vnseene fiers, boyling of furnases, ratling of Armour, trampling of horses, gingling of chaines, lumbring of tubbes, roring of spirits, and such like horrible hearinges, that it made the Scottish Champion almost at hys wits end: But yet hauing an vndaunted courage, exempting all feare, he humblie made his supplication to heauen, that God woulde deliuer him from that discontented place of terrour: and so presently as the Champion kneeled vpon the barren ground (wheron grew neyther hearbe, flower, grasse, nor any other greene thing,) he beheld a certaine flame of fire walking vp and downe before him, whereat he grew vnto such an extasie of feare, that he stood for a time amazed whether it were best to goe forward, or to stand still: But yet recalling his sences, he remembred himselfe, how hee had read in passed times of a going fire called *Ignis fatuus*,[1] the fire of destenie, or some Will with the wispe, or Will with the lanthorne, & likewise by some simple countrie people, the faire maide of Ireland, which commonly vsed to lead wandring trauailers out of their wayes. The like imagination entered the Champions minde: So encouraging himselfe with hys owne conceits, and chearing vp his dull sences late oppressed with extreame feare, he directly followed the going fire which so iustly went before him, that by the time the guider of the night had climbed twelue degrees in the zodiacke, hee was safelie deliuered from the vale of walking spirits, by the direction of the going fire.

Now began the Sunne to daunce about the firmament, which he had not seene in many monthes before: whereat hys dull sences so much reioyced, beeing so long

---

[1] *fatuus*] *fatuis 1596*

couered before with darkenes, that euerie step he troad was as pleasurable, as though he had walked in a garden bedeckt with all kinde of fragrant flowers.

At last without any further molestation he ariued within the territories of *Thracia*, a countrie as you heard in the former Chapter, adorned with the beautie of many faire Woodes and Forrestes, through which hee trauailed with small rest, but lesse sleepe, till hee came to the foote of the mountaine, wherevpon stoode the Castell wherein the wofull King of *Thrace* in companie of hys sorrowfull subiects, still lamented the vnhappie destenies of hys six daughters turnde into Swannes, with Crownes of gold about their neckes: But when the valiant Champion *Saint Andrew* beheld the loftie scituation of the Castell, and the inuincible strength it seemed to be of, he² expected some straunge aduenture to befall him in the said Castell: So preparing his sword in readines, and buckling close hys Armour, which was a shirt of siluer maile for lightnesse in trauaile: Hee climbed the Mountaine, wherevpon he espied the Giant lying vpon a craggie Rocke, with limbes and members all to be rent and torne, by the furie of hunger starued foules: which loathsome spectakle was no little woonder to the worthie Champion, considering the mightie stature & bignes of the Giant: So leauing his putrified bodie to the windes, he approached the gates: where after he had read the superscription ouer the same, without any interruption entred the Castle where hee expected a fierce encounter by some Knight that should haue defended the same, but all things fell out contrary to his imagination, for after he had found many a straunge nouelty and hidden secrete closed in the same, he³ chaunced at last to come where the Thracians duly obserued their ceremonious mournings, which in this order was dayly performed: for vppon sondayes which in that Country is the first day in the weeke, all the Thracians attyred themselues after the manner of *Bacchus* Priestes, and burned perfumed incence, and sweete *Arabian* francuinsence vpon a religious shrine which they offered to the Sun as chiefe gouernour of that day, thinking thereby to appease the angrie destenies, and so recouer the vnhappie Ladies to their former shapes: vpon Mundaies clad in garments after the manner of Syluanes, & colour like to the waues of the sea, they offered vp their wofull teares to the Moone, beeing the guider and mistresse of that day: vpon Teusdayes like Souldiers trayling their Banners on the dust, and Drums sounding sad and dolefull melody in signe of discontent, they committed their proceedings to the pleasure of *Mars*, being ruler and guider of that day: vppon Wensday like schollers vnto *Mercurie*: vppon Thursday like Potentates to *Ioue*: vpon Fridayes like louers with sweet sounding Musicke to *Venus*: and vpon Saterdaies like Manuall professors to the angry and discontented *Saturne*.

Thus the wofull *Thracian* King with his sorowful subiects, consumed seauen months away, one while accusing fortune of dispite, another while the heauens of iniustice: the one for Childrens transformations, the other for their long limited punishments: But at last when the Scottish Champion heard what bitter mone the *Thracians* made about the riuer, he demaunded the cause, and to what purpose they obserued such vaine ceremonies, contemning the Maiestie of high *Iehoua*, and only

---

² *he*] om. *1596*
³ *he*] om. *1596*

worshipping but outward & vaine Gods: to whome the King after a fewe sadde teares strained from the Conduits of his aged eies replied in this manner.

Most noble Knight for so you seeme, both by your gesture and other outward appearance, (quoth the King,) if you desire to know the cause of our continuall griefe, prepare your eares to heare a tragicke and wofull tale, whereat I see the elements begin to mourne, and couer their azurde countenance, with sable cloudes. These milk-white Swannes you see, whose neckes be beautified with golden Crownes, are my sixe naturall Daughters, transformed into thys Swan-like substance, by the appointment of the Gods: for of late this Castell was kept by a cruell Giant named *Blanderon*, who by violence would haue rauished them: But the heauens to preserue their chasteties, preuented his lustfull desires, and transformed their beautifull features to those milk-white Swannes: And nowe seauen times the chearefull spring hath renewed the earth with a Sommers liuerie, and seauen times the nipping Winters frostes, hath bereaued the trees of leafe and bud, since first my Daughters lost their Uirgins shapes: Seauen sommers haue they swamme vpon this Christall streame: where in steede of rich attire, and imbrothered Uestments, the smooth siluer coloured feathers adornes their comelie bodies: Princelie Pallaces wherein they were wont like vnto tripping Sea-nimphes daunce their measures vp and downe, are now exchanged into cold streames of water: wherein their chiefest melodie, is the murmuring of the liquid bubbles, and their ioyfullest pleasure, to heare the harmonie of humming Bees, which the Poets call the Muses birds.

Thus haue you heard most worthie Knight the rufull Tragedies of my Daughters, for whose sakes I will spend the remnant of my dayes, chearefully complaining of their long appointed punishments, about the Bankes of thys vnhappie riuer. Which sad discourse beeing no sooner ended, but the Scottish Knight (hauing a minde furnished with all Princely thoughts, & a tongue washt in the Fountaine of Eloquence), thus replied to the comfort and great reioycing of all the companie.

Most noble King (quoth the Champion) your heauie and dolorous discourse, hath constrained my heart to a wonderfull passion, and compelled my very soule to rue your Daughters miseries: But yet a greater griefe and a deeper sorrow then that, hath taken possession in my brest, wherof my eies hath bin witnes, and my eares vnhappy hearers of your misbeliefe, I meane your vnchristian faith: For I haue seene since my first ariuall into this same Castell your prophane & vaine worshipping of straunge and false Gods, as to *Phœbus, Luna, Mars, Mercurie,* and such like Poeticall names, which the Maiestie of high *Iehoua* vtterly contemnes: but magnificent gouernour of *Thracia*, if you seeke to recouer your Daughters happinesse by humble praiers, and to obtaine your soules content by true teares, you must adandon all such vaine Ceremonies, and with true humillity beleeue in the Christians God, which is the God of wonders, and chiefe commaunder of the rouling Elements, in whose quarrell this vndaunted arme, and this vnconquered hart of mine shall fight: and now be it known to thee great King of *Thrace*, that I am a Christian Champion, and by byrth a Knight of Scotland, bearing my countries Armes upon my breast (for indeede thereon he bore a siluer Crosse set in blue silke) and therefore in the honour of Christendome I challenge forth thy prowdest

Knight at Armes, against whom I will mayntaine that our God is the true God, and the rest fantasticall and vayne ceremonies.

Which sodaine and unexpected challenge so daunted the Thracian Champions that they stoode amazed for a time; gazing one vpon another, like men dropt from the cloudes: but at last consulting together, howe the challenge of the strange Knight, was to the dishonour of their Countrie, & vtter scandall of all Knightly dignitie: therefore with a generall consent they craued leave of the King that the challenge might bee taken, who as willingly condiscended as they demaunded: So the time and place was appoynted which was the next morning following by the Kings commandement upon a large and playne meadowe close by the riuer side, whereon the sixe Swans were swimming, and so after the Christian Champion had cast downe his steely Gauntlet and the Thracian Knights accepted thereof, euery one departed for that night, the Challenger to the East side of the Castell to his lodging, and the Defendants to the west, where they slept quietly till the next morning, who by the breake of day were wakened by a Harrold at armes, but all the passed night our Scottish Champion neuer intertaynde one motion of rest, but busied himselfe in trimming his horse, buckling on his Armour, lacing on his Burgonet, and making his prayers to the Diuine Maiesty of God for the conquest and victory, till the mornings beauty chaced away the darkenes of the night, but no sooner was the windowes of the day fully opened, but the valiant and Noble minded Champion of Christendome entred the List, where the King in company of the Thracian Lordes were present to beholde the Combat: and so after saint *Andrew* had twice or thrice traced his horse vp & downe the Listes brauely florishing his Launce, at the toppe whereof hung a pendant of golde, whose Posie was thus written in siluer letters: *This day a Martyr or a Conquerour.* Then entered a Knight in exceeding bright Armor, mounted vpon a Courser as white as the northerne snow whose caparison was of the colour of the elements, betwixt whom was a firce encounter, but the *Thracian* had the foyle, and with disgrace departed the Listes: Then secondly entred another Knight in Armor varnished with greene varnish, his Steede of the colour of an Iron gray, who likewise had the repulse by the worthie Christian: Thirdly entred a knight in a blacke corslet, mounted vpon a big bonde Palfray, couered with a vale of sable silk, in his hand he bore a Lance nailed round about with plates of steele: which Knight amongst the *Thracians* was accounted the strongest in the world, except it were those Giants that discended from a monstrous linnage: But no sooner encountred these hardy Champions, but their Launces shiuered in sunder, and flew so violently into the Aire, that it much amazed the beholders: Then they alighted from their Steedes, and so valiantly besturd them with their keene edged Fauchions, that the fierie sparkles flew as fiercely from their Noble Champions steelie Helmets, as from an Iron Anuill: But the Combat indured not verie long before the most hardie *Scottish* Knight espied an aduantage, wherein he might shew hys matchles fortitude: then he stroke such a violent blow vpon the *Thracians* Burgonet, that it cleaued hys head iustly downe to the shoulders: whereat the King sodainely started from hys seate, and with a wrathfull countenance, threatned the Champions death in this manner.

Proude Christian (said the King) thou shalt repent hys death, and curse the time that euer thou camst to *Thracia*: hys blood we will reuenge vpon thy head, and quit thy committed crueltie with a sodaine death: and so in company of a hundred Armed Knights, he incompassed the Scottish Champion, intending by multitudes to murder him: But when the valiant Knight *Saint Andrew* saw how hee was supprest by trecherie, and inuironed with mightie Troups, he called to heauen for succour, and annimated him selfe by these wordes of incouragement: Now for the Honour of Christendome, *this day a Martyr or a Conquerour*, and therewithall he so valiantly behaued himselfe with his trustie Curtleaxe, that he made Lanes of murthered men, and feld them downe by multitudes, like as the haruest man doth mowe downe eares of ripened corne: whereby they fell before his face like leaues from trees, when the Sommers pride declines her glorie: So at the last after much blood shed, the Thracian King was compelled to yeeld to the Scottish Champions mercie, who swore him for the sauegarde of hys life, to forsake his prophaned religion and become a Christian, whose liuing true God the Thracian king vowde for euermore to worship, and thereupon hee kist the Champions sword.

This conuersion of the Pagan King, so pleased the Maiestie of God, that he presently gaue end to his Daughters punishments, & turned the Ladies to their former shapes: But when the King behelde their smooth feathers, which were whiter than the Lilly, exchanged to a naturall fairenes, & that their blacke bils and slender necks were conuerted to their first created beauties, (where for excellent fairenes, the Queene of loue might builde her Parradice,) hee bad adue to hys griefe and long continued sorrowes, protesting euer hereafter to continue a true Christian for the Scottish Champions sake: by whome and by whose diuine Orrizons hys Daughters obtained their former features: So taking the Christian Knight in company of the six Ladies, to an excellent rich Chamber, prepared with al thinges according to their wishes: where first the Christian Knight was vnarmed, then his woundes washed with white Wine, new Milke, and Rose-water, and so after some daintie repast, conuayed to hys nights repose. The Ladies beeing the ioyfullest creatures vnder heauen, neuer entertainde one thought of sleepe, but passed the night in their Fathers companie, (whose minde was rauished with vnspeakable pleasure,) till the mornings messengers bad them good morrow.

Thus all thinges being prepared in a readines, they departed the Castell, not like mourners to a heauie Funerall: but in triumphing manner marching backe to the *Thracian* Pallace, with streaming Banners in the winde. Drums and Trumpets sounding ioyfull melodie, and with sweet inspiring musicke, causing the aire to resound with harmony: But no sooner were they entred the Pallace, (which was in distance from the Giants Castell, some ten miles) but their triumphes turned to exceeding sorrow, for *Rossalinde* with the Champion of *Italie* as you heard before was departed the Court: which vnexpected newes so daunted the whole companie, but especially the King, that the triumphes for that time were deferred, and messengers dispatcht in pursute of the aduenturous *Italian*, and the louely *Rossalinde*.

But when *Saint Andrew* of Scotland had intelligence, how it was one of the Knights that was imprisoned with him vnder the subiection of the wicked Inchauntresse *Kalyb*, as you heard first of all in the beginning of the Historie, his heart thirsted for hys most Honourable companie, and hys eyes neuer closed quietly, nor tooke any rest at all vntill hee was likewise departed in the pursute of hys sworne friend, which was the next night following, without making any acquainted with his intent: likewise when the six Ladies vnderstood the secret departure of the Scottish Champion, whome they affected dearer than any Knight in all the world, stored themselues with sufficient treasure, and by stealth tooke their iournie from their Fathers Pallace: intending eyther to finde out the victorious and approoued Knight of *Scotland*, or to end their liues in some forraine Region.

The rumor of whose departure, no sooner came to the Kinges eares, but he purposed the like trauaile, eyther to obtaine the sight of his Daughters againe, or to make his toombe in a countrie beyond the cercuite of the Sunne: So attyring himselfe in a homely russet, like a Pilgrime with an Ebon staffe in his hand tipt with siluer, tooke his iournie all vnknowne from hys Pallace, whose sodaine and secret departure, stroke such an extreame & intollerable heauines in the Court, that the Pallace gates were sealed vp with sorrow, and the walles be-hung with sable mourning cloth. The *Thracian* Lordes exempted all pleasure, and like a flocke of sheepe strayed vp and downe without a shepheard, the Ladies and Courtly gentles, sate sighing in their priuate chambers: where we leaue them for this time, & speake of the successe of the other Champions, and howe Fortune smiled on their aduenterous proceedinges.

CHAP. VIII.

How Saint Pattricke the Champion of Irelande, redeemed the six Thracian Ladies out of the handes of thirtie bloodie minded Satiers, and of their purposed trauaile in the pursute after the Champion of Scotland.

BUT now of the valiant & hardie Knight at Armes, *Saint Pattrick* the Champion of *Ireland* must I speake, whose aduenterous accidents were so Noblie performed, that if my pen were made of steele, yet should I weare it to the stumpes, sufficiently to declare hys prowesse and worthie aduentures. When he departed from the brazen Piller, from the other Champions, the heauens smiled with a kinde aspect, and sent him such a happie starre to bee hys guide, that it lead him to no Courtly pleasures, nor to vaine delights of Ladies beauties, but to the throne of fame, where honour sate instauld vpon a seat of gold: Thether trauailed the warlike Champion of *Ireland*, whose illustrious battailes the northen Iles hath Chronicled in leaues of brasse: therefore *Ireland* be proude, for from thy bowels did spring a Champion, whose prowesse made the enemies of Christ to tremble, and watered the earth with streames of Pagans blood: witnes whereof the Ile of *Rhodes*, the key & strength of Christendome was recouered from the Turkes, by hys Martiall and inuincible prowesse: where hys dangerous battailes, fierce encounters, bloodie skirmishes, and long assaults, woulde serue to fill a mightie volume, all which I passe ouer, & wholly discourse of things appertaining to this History: for after the warres at *Rhodes* were fully ended, which continued some two yeares the worthy Champion saint *Pattricke* (accounting idle ease the nurse of cowardise) bad *Rhodes* farewell, being then strongly fortefied with Christian Souldiers, and tooke his iourney thorough many an vnknowne Countrey, where at last it pleased so the Queene of chance to direct his steppes into a solitary wildernesse, inhabited onely by wilde Satyrs, and a people of inhumane quallities, giuing theyr wicked mindes onely to murther, lust and rape, wherein the noble Champion trauelled vp and downe many a weary steppe, not knowing how to sustaine his hunger, but by his owne industry in killing of wild venison, and pressing out the blood betwixt two mighty stones, dayly rosted it by the heate of the Sunne, his lodging was in the hollow truncke of a blasted tree, which nightly preserude him from the dropping showres of heauen, his chiefe companion was the sweete resounding eccho, which commonly reanswered the Champions wordes: In this manner liued saint *Pattrick* the Irish Knight in the woods, not knowing how to set him selfe at liberty, but wandring vp and downe as it were in a maze wrought by the curious workemanship of some excellent Gardner, it was his chaunce at last to come into a dismall shady thicket beset about with balefull misselto, a place of horror wherein he heard the cryes of some distressed Ladies, whose bitter lamentations seemd to pierce the clowds, and to craue succour at the hands of God, which vnexspected cryes not a little daunted the Irish Knight: so that it causde him to prepare his weapon in readines, against some sodain incounter: So couching himselfe close vnder the roote of an olde withered Oake, (which had not flourished with greene leaues in many a yeare) hee espied a farre off a crew of bloody minded Satyrs, hauling by the hayre the sixe vnhappy Ladies thorough many a thorny brake and bryer, whereby the beauty of theyr crimson cheekes, was all to besprent with purple gore, and theyr eyes (within whose cleare glasses one might behold the God of loue dancing) all to be rent & torne by the fury of the bryers, whereby they could not see the light of heauen, nor the place of theyr vnfortunate abyding: which wofull spectacle forced such a terror in the heart of the Irish Knight, that he presently made out for the rescue of the Ladies, against the bloody fury of the mercilesse Satyrs which were in number about some thirty, euery one hauing a mighty clubbe vpon his necke, which they had made with roots of yong Oakes and Pine trees, yet this aduenterous Champion being nothing discouraged, but with a bold and resolute minde he let driue at the sturdiest Satyr, whose Armour of defence was made of a Buls hide, which was dryed so hard against the Sunne, that the Champions Curtle-axe little preuayled: after which the fell Satyrs incompassed the Christian Knight round about, and so mightely opprest him with downe right blowes, that had he not by good fortune leapt vnder the boughes of a mighty tree, his life had beene forst to giue the world a speedy farewell: But such was his nimblenes and actiue pollicy, that ere long he sheathed his sharpe pointed Fauchion in one of the Satyrs breasts, which wofull sight caused all the rest to fly from his presence, and left the sixe Ladyes to the pleasure & disposition of the most Noble and couragious Christian Champion.

Who after he had sufficiently breathed and cooled himself in the chill Ayre (being almost windles through the long incounter and bloody Skirmish,) he demaunded the cause of the Ladyes trauels, and by what meanes they hapned into the handes of those mercilesse Satyrs, who most cruelly and tyrannically attempted the vtter ruine and endlesse spoyle of their vnspotted virginity: To which curteous demand one of the Ladies after a deepe fetcht sigh or two (being constrained from the bottome of her most sorrowfull hart) in the behalfe of her selfe and the other distressed Ladies, replied in this order. Most redeemed vs distressed Ladies from a double death: the one in preseruing our chasteties from the lustfull desires of the Satiers, the other in sauing our liues from the threatning furies of the monsters.[1]

Know, braue minded Knight, that wee are the vnfortunate Daughters of the King of *Thrace*, whose liues hath beene vnhappie euer since our creations: For first wee did indure a long imprisonment vnder the handes of a cruell Giant, and after the heauens to preserue our Chasteties from the wicked desires of the said Gyant, transformed vs into the shape of Swans, in which likenes we remayned seauen yeares, but at last recouered by a worthy Christian Knight, named *S. Andrew*, the Champion of *Scotland*, after whom we haue trauailed many a wery step, neuer crost by any violence, vntill it was our angry fates to ariue in this vnhappy Wildernes, where your eyes haue beene true witnesses of our wofull misfortunes: Which sad discourse beeing no sooner finished, but the worthy Champion began thus to comfort the distressed Ladyes.

The Christian Champion after whom you take in hand this wearie trauaile (said the Irish Champion) is my approoued friend, for whose companie and wished sight,

---

[1] Most ... monsters] *om. 1608; 1616*

I wil goe more weary miles, than there be trees in this accursed Wildernes, and number my steppes with the multitude of sands hidden in the seas: therefore most excellent Ladies, true ornaments of beautie, bee sad companions in my trauailes, for I will neuer cease til I haue found our honorable friende the Champion of *Scotland*, or some of those braue Knightes whome I haue not seene these seauen Sommers.

These wordes so contented the sorrowfull Ladies, that without any exception they agreed, and with as much willingnes consented, as the Champion demaunded: So after they had recouered their sights, eased their wearines, and cured their woundes: which was by the secret vertues of certaine hearbes growing in the same woodes, tooke their iournies anew, vnder the conduct of this worthie Champion *Saint Pattrick*, where after some dayes trauaile, obtained the sight of a broade beaten way, where committing their fortunes to the fatall sisters, and setting their faces toward the east, merrilie iournied together: In whose fortunate trauailes we leaue, and speake of the seauenth Christian Champion, whose aduenturous exployts and Knightly Honours, deserues a golden pen, dipt in the inke of true Fame to discourse at large.

CHAP. IX.

How Saint Dauid the Champion of Wales slewe the Countie Palatine in the Tartarian Court, and after howe hee was sent to the Inchaunted Garden of Ormondine, wherein by Magicke Arte he slept seauen yeares.

SAint Dauid the most Noble Champion of Wales, after his departure from the brazen piller where as the other Champions of Christendome deuided themselues seuerally, to seeke for forraine aduentures, he atchiued many memorable thinges, as well in Christendome, as in those Nations that acknowledge no true God: which for this time I omit, and only discourse what hapned vnto him amongst the *Tartarians*: For beeing in the Emperour of *Tartaries* Court (a place very much honoured with valerous Knights, and highlie gracte with a trayne of beauteous Ladies) where the Emperour vpon a time ordayned a solemne Ioust and Turnament to be holden in the honour of hys birth day: whether resorted at the time appointed, (from all the borders of Tartarie) the best and hardiest Knights there remayning: In which honorable and Princely exercise, the Noble Knight *Saint Dauid* was appointed Champion for the Emperour, who was mounted vppon a *Moroco* Steede, betrapped in a rich Caparison, wrought by the curious workmanship of the Indian women, vppon whose shield was set a golden Griffon rampant in a fielde of blew.

Against him came the Countie *Palatine*, Sonne & heire aparant to the Tartarian Emperour, brought in by twelue Knights, richly furnished with all habilliments of honour, and paced three times about the Lists, before the Emperor and many Ladies that were present to behold the honourable Turnament: The which beeing done, the twelue Knights departed the Lists, and the Countie *Palatine* prepared himselfe to encounter with the Christian Knight: being then appointed chiefe Champion for the day: who likewise locked downe his Beuer, and at the Trumpets sound by the Harrolds appointment, ran so fiercely one against the other, that the ground seemed to thunder vnder them, & the skies to resounde ecchoes of their mighty strokes.

At the second race the Champions ran, *Saint Dauid* had the worse, & was constrained through the forcible strength of the Countie *Palatine*, to fall backwarde almost beside hys saddle: whereat the Trumpets began to sound in signe of victorie: but yet the valiant Christian nothing dismayed, but with a courage (within whose eyes sate Knightlie reuenge) ran the third time against the County *Palatine*, and by the violent force of hys strength, he ouerthrew both horse & man, wherby the Counties body was so exstreamly brused with the fall of hys horse, that hys heart blood issued foorth from hys nostrels, and hys vitall spirits pressed from the mancion of hys breast, that he was forced to giue the world a timeles farewell.

This fatall ouerthrow of the Countie *Palatine*, abashed the whole company: but especially the Tartarian Emperour, who hauing no more sonnes but him, caused the Lists to be broken vp, the Knights to be vnarmed, and the murthered Countie to bee brought by foure Squiers into hys Pallace: where after he was dispoyled of hys furniture, & the Christian Knight receaued it in the honour of hys victorie. The wofull Emperour bathed the Tartarians bodie with teares which dropped like

Christall Pearles vpon his congealed blood, where after many sadde sighs hee breathed forth this wofull lamentation.

Now are my triumphs turnd to euerlasting woes, from a commicall pastime, to a dierefull and bloody tragedy: O most vnkinde fortune, neuer constant but in change! Why is my life deferde to see the downefall of my deare Son, the Noble County *Palatine*? why rends not this accursed earth whereon I stand, and presently swallow vp my body into her hungrie bowels: Is this the vse of Christians for true Honour, to repay dishonour, could no bace blood serue to staine hys deadly handes withall, but with the precious blood of my deare Sonne, in whose reuenge the face of the heauens is stained with blood, and cryes for vengeaunce to the Maiesty of high eternall *Ioue*, the dreadfull furies, the direfull daughters of darke night, and all the balefull companie of burning *Acharon*, whose loynes be girt with Serpents, and haire behangde with wreathes of Snakes, shall haunt, pursue and followe that accursed Christian Champion, that hath bereaued my Countrie *Tartarie*, of so precious a Iewell as my deare Sonne the Countie *Palatine* was, whose magnanimious prowesse, did surpasse all the Knights of our Countrie.

Thus sorrowed the wofull Emperour for the death of his Noble sonne: sometimes making the ecchoes of his lamentations pearce the elements: another while forcing his bitter curses to sinke to the deepe foundation of *Acharon*: one while intending to bee reuenged vpon *Saint Dauid* the Christian Champion, then presently his intent was crost with a contrary imagination, that it was against the Lawe of Armes, and a great dishonour to his Country, by violence to oppresse a strange Knight, whose actions hath euer beene guided by true honour, but yet at last this firme resolution entred into his minde.

There was adioyning vppon the borders of *Tartary*, an inchaunted garden kept by Magicke art, from whence neuer any returned that attempted to enter, the Gouernour of which garden was a notable and famous Nigromancer named *Ormondine*, to which Magitian the *Tartarian* Emperour intended to send the aduenterous Champion saint *Dauid*, thereby to reuenge the County *Pallatines* death: So the Emperour after some fewe dayes passed, and the Obsequies of his sonne being no sooner perfourmed, but he caused the Christian Knight to be brought into his presence, to whom he committed this heauy taske and weary labour. Proude Knight (sayd the angry Emperour) thou knowest since thy ariuall into our Territories howe highly I haue honoured thee, not onely in graunting liberty of life, but making thee chiefe Champion of *Tartarie*, which high honour thou haste repaide with great ingratitude, and blemished true Nobilitie, in acting of my deare sonnes Tragedy: For which vnhappie deede thou rightly haste deserued death: But yet know accursed Christian, that mercie harboureth in a Princely minde, and where honour sits inthronized, there Iustice is not too seuere. Although thou hast deserued death: yet if thou wilt aduenture to the Inchaunted garden, and bring hether the Magitians head, I graunt thee not only thy life, but therewithall the Crowne of *Tartarie* after my discease: because I see thou haste a minde furnished with all Princely thoughtes, and adornde with true Magnanimitie.

This heauie taske, and strange aduenture, not a little pleased the Noble Champion of Wales, whose minde euer thirsted after straunge aduentures: and so after some considerate thoughts, in this manner he replied.

Most high and magnificent Emperour (said the Champion) were this taske which you inioyne me to, as woonderfull as the labors of *Hercules*, or as fearefull as the enterprise which *Iason* made for the golden Fleece: yet would I attempt to finish and returne with more triumph to *Tartarie*, than the *Macedonian* Monarke did to *Babilon*, when he had conquered the Angels of the world: Which words beeing no sooner ended, but the Emperour bounde him by hys oath of Knighthood, and by the loue he beares vnto hys natiue countrie, neuer to follow any other aduenture, till he had performed hys promise, which was to bring the Magitian *Ormondines* head into *Tartarie*: And so the Emperour departed from the Noble Knight *Saint Dauid*, hoping neuer to see him returne, but rather heare his vtter confusion, or euerlasting imprisonment.

Thus this valiant Christian Champion, being bounde to a heauie taske, within three dayes prepared all necessaries in readines for hys departure: and so trauailed westward, till he approached the sight of the Inchaunted Garden, the scittuation whereof somewhat daunted his valiant courage: for it was incompassed with a hedge of withered thornes and briers, which seemed continually to burne: vpon the toppe thereof, sate a number of straunge and deformed thinges, some in the likenes of night Owles, that woondered at the presence of *Saint Dauid*: some in the shape of *Prognes*[1] transformation, foretelling hys infortunate successe, and some like Rauens, that with their harsh throats ring foorth a balefull knell of some wofull Tragedie: the elements which couered the Inchaunted Garden, seemed to bee ouerspread with mistie cloudes, from whence continually shot flames of fire, as though the skies had bin filled with blazing Commets: which fearefull spectakle, or rather the very patterne of hell, stroke such a terror into the Champions hart, that twice he was in minde to returne without performing the aduenture; but for hys oath and Honor of Knighthood, which he had pawnde for the accomplishment thereof: So laying hys body on the bare earth, beeing the first nurse and mother of his life, hee made hys humble petition to God, that hys minde might be neuer opprest with cowardize, nor his heart daunted with any faint feare, till he had performed what the *Tartarian* Emperour had bound him to, the Champion rose from the ground, and with chearefull lookes beheld the elements, which seemed at hys conceit to smile at the enterprise, and to foreshew a luckie euent.

So the Noble Knight *Saint Dauid* with a valiant courage went to the Garden gate, by which stoode a Rocke of stone, ouerspread with mosse: In which Rock by Magicke Art was inclosed a sworde, nothing outwardly appearing but the hilt, which was the richest to hys iudgement that euer hys eyes beheld, for the steele worke was ingraued very curiously, beset with Iasper and Saphier stones, the pummell was in the fashion of a Globe, of the purest siluer that euer the mines of rich *America* brought foorth: about the pummell was ingrauen in Letters of gold these verses following.

> *My Magicke spels, remaines most firmely bound,*
> *The worlds straunge woonder vnknowne by any one:*

---

[1] *Prognes*] *Progines 1596*

> *Till that a Knight within the North be founde,*
> *To pull this sword from out this Rocke of stone:*
> *Then ends my charmes, my Magicke Arts and all,*
> *By whose strong hand, wise Ormondine must fall.*

These verses draue such a conceited Imagination into the Champions minde, that hee supposed himselfe to bee the Northen Knight, by whome the Nigromancer should bee conquered: Therefore without anye further aduisement he put hys hand into the hilt of the rich sworde, thinking presently to pull it out from the Inchaunted Rocke of *Ormondine*: But no sooner did hee attempt that vaine enterprise, but hys valiant courage and inuincible fortitude fayled him, & all hys sences was ouer taken with a sodayne & heauie sleepe, whereby he was forced to let goe hys hold, and to fall flatte vppon the barraine ground, where hys eyes were so fast locked vp by Magicke Arte, and hys waking sences drowned in such a dead slumber, that it was as much impossible to recouer himselfe from hys sleepe, as to pull the Sunne out of the firmament: For through the secret misterie of the Nigromancers skill, hee had intelligence of the Champions vnfortunate successe: who sent from the Inchaunted garden foure spirits, in the similitude and likenes of foure beautifull Damsels, which wrapped the drousie Champion in a sheete of the finest *Arabian* silke, and conuayed him into a Caue, directly placed in the middle of the Garden, where they laide him vpon a soft bed, more softer than the downe of Culuers: where these beautifull Ladies through the Artes of wicked *Ormondine*, continually kept him sleeping for the tearme of seauen yeares: one while singing with sugered songes, more sweeter and delightfuller than the Syrens mellodie: another while with rare conceited Musicke, surpassing the sweetnes of *Arions* Harpe, which made the mightie Dolphins in the Seas, to daunce at the sounde of hys sweete inspiring Melodie: or like the Harmonie of *Orpheus* when he iournied downe into hell, where the diuelles reioyst to heare hys admired notes, and on earth both trees and stones did leep when he did but touch the siluer stringes of hys Iuorie Harpe.

Thus was *Saint Dauids* aduenture crost with a woonderfull bad success, whose dayes trauailes was turned into a nights repose: whose nights repose, was made a heauy sleepe, which indured vntill seauen yeares were fullie finished: where wee leaue *Saint Dauid* to the mercie of the Nigromancer *Ormondine* sleeping, and returne now to the most Noble and magnanimious Champion *S. George*, where we left him imprisoned in the Soldans[2] Court: But now gentle Reader thou wilt thinke it straunge, that all these Christian Champions should meete together agayne, seeing that they bee seperated into so many borders of the world: For *Saint Dennis* the Champion of Fraunce, remaineth now in the Court of *Thessalie*, with hys Ladie *Eglantine*: *Saint Iames* the Champion of Spaine, in the Citty of *Ciuell* with *Celestine*, the faire Lady of Jerusalem: *Saint Anthonie* the Champion of Italie, trauailling the world, in the companie of a Thracian maiden, attired in a Pages apparrell: *Saint Andrew* the Champion of Scotland, seeking after the Italian: *Saint Pattricke* the Champion of Ireland, after the Champion of Scotland, *Saint Dauid* of

---

[2] Soldans] Seldans *1596*

Wales, sleeping in the Inchaunted garden adioyning to the Kingdome of Tartarie, and *Saint George* the famous Champion of England, imprisoned in Persia: of whome, and of whose noble aduentures, I must a while discourse, till the honoured Fame of the other Champions, compelles mee to report their Noble and Princelie atchiuementes.

How Saint George escaped out of prison at Persia, and how he redeemed the Champion of Wales from his Inchauntment, with other thinges that hapned to the English Knight, with the Tragicall tale of the Nigromancer Ormondine.

NOW seauen times had frosty bearded winter couered both hearbes and flowers with snow, & behung the trees with Christall Isickles, seauen times had Ladie *Ver*[1] beautified euerie field with natures ornaments, and seauen times had withered *Autum* robbed the earth of springing flowers, since the vnfortunate *Saint George* beheld the chearefull light of heauen, but obscurely liued in a dismall dungeon, by the Soldan of *Persias* commaundement, as you heard before in the beginning of the Historie: His vnhappy fortune so discontented hys restles thoughtes, that a thousand times a yeare he wisht an end of his life, & a thousand times he cursed the day of his creation, his sighs in number did counteruaile a heape of sand, whose toppe might seeme to reach the skies, the which he vainely breathed forth against the walles of the Prison: Many times making his humble supplication to the heauens, to redeeme him from that vale of miserie, and many times seeking occasion desperatly to abridge hys dayes, whereby to triumph in hys owne Tragedie.

But at last when seauen yeares were fully ended, it was the Champions luckie fortune to finde in a secret corner of the dungeon, a certaine Iron Engin, which time had almost consumed with rust: wherwith by long labor, he digged himselfe a passage vnder the ground, till he ascended iust in the middle of the Soldans Court, which was at that time of the night when all thinges were silent: the heauens hee then beheld beautified with stars, & bright *Cinthia*, whose glistering beames he had not seene in many a hundred nights before seemed to smile at hys safe deliuerie, and to stay her wandring course till the noble English Champion founde meanes to get without the compasse of the *Persian* Court, where danger might no longer attend him, nor the stronge Gates of the Cittie hinder hys flight, which in this manner was performed: For the Noble Knight beeing as fearefull as the Birde newlie escaped from the Fowlers nets, gazed round about, and listned where he might heare the voice of people: At last he heard the Groomes of the Soldans stable, furnishing forth Horses against the next morning for some Noble atchiuement: then the valiant Champion *S. George* taking the Iron Engin, wherewith hee redeemed himself out of prison & burst open the dores, where he slew all the Groomes in the Soldans stable, which beeing done hee tooke the strongest Palfray, and the richest furniture, with other necessaries appertayning to a Knight at Armes, & so rode in great maiestie to one of the City Gates, where hee saluted the Porter in this manner.

Porter, open thy Gates, for *S. George* of England is escaped, & hath murdered his warders, in whose pursute the Citty is in Armes: which wordes the simple *Persian* beleeued for a truth, and so with all speede opened the Gates, whereat the

---

[1] *Ver*] *Vir 1596*

Champion of England departed and left the Soldan in hys dead sleepe, little mistrusting hys sodaine escape.

But by that time the purple spotted morning had parted with her gray, and the Suns bright countenaunce appeared on the mountaine toppes, *Saint George* had ridden twentie leagues from the *Persian* Court, and before hys departure was bruted in the Soldans Pallace, the English Champion had recouered the sight of *Grecia*, past all danger of the *Persian* Knights, that followed him with a swift pursute: By which time the extreamity of hunger so sharpely tormented him, that he could trauaile no further, but was constrained to suffise himselfe with certaine wilde Chesnuts in stead of bread, and sower oringes in stead of drinke, & such fainte food that grew by the wayes as he trauelled, where the necessity and want of victualles compelled the Noble Knight *Saint George* to breath forth this pittifull complaint.

O hunger, hunger, (said the Champion) thou art more sharper than the stroake of death, and the extreamest punishment that euer man indured: if I were now King of *Armenia*, & cheife Potentate of *Asia*, yet would I giue my Diadem my Scepter with al my prouinces for one shiuer of browne bread oh that the earth would be so kind, as to rippe hir bowells, and to cast vp some food, to sustaine my want, or that the ayre might bee choakt with mistes, whereby the fethered foules for want of breath might fall and yeald me some succour in this my famishment, and extreame penurye, or that the *Oceans* would outspread their braunched armes and couer these sunburnd vallyes with their treasures, that I might suffice my hunger: but now I see both heauen and earth, the hilles and dales, the skyes and seas, the fish and foules, the birdes and Siluane beastes, & all things vnder the cope of heauen, conspires my vtter ouerthrow: better had it beene if I had ended my dayes in *Persia*, than to bee famished in the broade worlde, where all things by natures appointment is ordained for mans vse: now in steed of Courtly dillicates, I am forced to eat the fruit of trees, and in steed of Greekish wines, I am compelled to quench my thirst with the mornings dew, that nightly falles vpon the blades of grasse.

Thus complained *Saint George*, vntill glistering *Phœbus* had mounted the top of heauen, and drawen the mistie vapors from the ground, where hee might behold the prospects of *Grecia*, and which way to trauaile for most safetie, he espied directly before his face a Tower standing vpon a chalkie clift, in distance from him some three miles, whether the Champion intended to goe, not to seeke for any aduenture, but to rest himselfe after hys long iournie, & to get such victuals as therein hee could finde to suffice his want.

So setting forward with an easie pace, the heauens seemed to smile, and the birds to ring such a cherping peale of mellodie, as though they did prognosticate a fortunate euent: The way he found so plaine, and the ioumie so easie, that within halfe an houre hee approached before the saide Tower: where vpon the wall stoode a most beautifull woman, her attire after the manner of a distressed Ladie, and her lookes as heauie as the Queenes of *Troy*, when she beheld her Pallace set on fire. The valiant Knight *S. George*, after he had alighted from his horse, he gaue her this curteous salutation.

Lady (said the Knight) for so you seeme by your outward appearance, if euer you pittied a trauailer, or graunted succour to a Christian Knight, giue to mee one meales meate, now almost famished: To whome the Lady after a curst frowne or two, answered him in this order.

Sir Knight (quoth shee) I aduise thee with all speede to depart, for here thou gets a cold dinner: my Lord is a mightie Giant, and beleeueth in *Mahomet*, & *Termagaunt*, and if he once vnderstand how thou art a Christian Knight: it is not all the gold of higher *India*, nor the riches of wealthy *Babilon* that can preserue thy life. Now by the honour of my Knighthood, (replied *Saint George*) and by the God that Christendome adores: were thy Lord more stronger than was mightie *Hercules*, that bore a mountaine on hys backe: here will I either obtaine my dinner, or die by hys accursed hands.

These wordes so abashed the Lady, that shee went with all speed from the Tower, and told the Gyant how a Christian Knight remayned at hys Gate, that had sworne to suffice hys hunger in dispite of hys will: whereat the furious Gyant sodainely started vp, beeing as then in a sound sleepe, for it was at the middle of the day: who tooke a bat of Iron in hys hand, and came downe to the Tower Gate: his stature was in haight fiue yeardes: hys heade brisled like a Bores, a foote there was betwixt each brow, his eies hollow, hys mouth wide, hys lippes were like two flaps of steele, in all proportion more like a diuell than a man: Which deformed monster so daunted the courage of *Saint George*, that he prepared himselfe to death: not through feare of the monstrous Gyant, but for hunger and feeblenes of body: but God so prouided for him, and so restored the Champions decayed strength, that hee indured battaile till the closing vp of the Euening, by which time the Gyant was almost blinde, through the sweate that ran downe from hys monstrous browes, whereby *Saint George* had the aduantage, and wounded the Giant so cruelly vnder the short ribs, that hee was compelled to fall to the ground, and to giue end to hys life.

After which happie euent of the Gyants slaughter, the inuincible Champion *Saint George*: first gaue the honour of hys victorie to God, in whose power all hys fortune consisted: Then entering the Tower, whereas the Lady presented him with all manner of dillicates, and pure wines: but the English Knight suspecting some trecherie to be hidden in her proffered curtesie, caused the Ladie first to taste of euerie daintie dish: Likewise of his wine, lest some violent poyson shoulde bee therein commixt: So finding all thinges pure and holsome as nature required, hee suffized hys hunger, rested hys wearie body, and refreshed his horse: And so leauing the Tower in keeping of the Ladie, he committed hys fortune to a new trauaile: where hys reuiued spirits neuer entertained longer rest, but to the refreshing of himselfe and hys horse: So trauailed he through the parts of *Grecia*, the confines of *Phrigia*, and so into the borders of *Tartarie*, within whose Territories he had not long iournied, but he approached the sight of the Inchaunted Garden of *Ormondine*, where *S. Dauid* the Champion of Wales had so long slept by Magicke Art. No sooner did he behold the woonderfull scituation thereof, but hee espied Ormondines sword inclosed in the Inchaunted Rocke: where after he had read the superscription written about the pummell, he assaied to pull it out by strength: where he no sooner put hys hand into the hilt, but he drew it forth with much ease, as though it had beene hung but by a thred of vntwisted silke: but when hee beheld the glistring brightnesse of the blade, and the wonderfull richnes of the pummell, hee accounted ye prize more worth than the Armour of *Achilles*, which caused *Aiax* to runne mad, and more richer then *Medeas* golden Fleece: But by that time *Saint George* had circumspectly lookt into euerie secret of the sword, he heard a straunge and dismall voice thunder in the skyes, a tyrrible & mighty lumbring in the earth, whereat both hils & mountaines shooke, Rockes remooued, and huge Oakes rent into peeces: After this the Gates of the Inchaunted Garden flew open, whereat incontinently came foorth *Ormondine* the Magitian, with hys haire staring on hys head, hys eyes sparckling, hys cheekes blushing, hys hands quiuering, hys legs trembling, and all the rest of hys body distempered, as though legions of spirits had incompast him about: he came directly to the worthy English knight that remayned still by the Inchaunted Rocke, from whence hee had pulled the Magitians sword, where after the Nigromancer had sufficiently beheld hys Princely countenance, whereon true honour sate inthronized, and viewed hys portly personage, the Image of true Knighthood, the which seemed in the Magitians eyes, to be the rarest work that euer nature framed: First taking the most valiant and magnanimious Champion *Saint George* of England by the steelie Gauntlet, and with great humilitie kissed it, then proffering him the curtesies due vnto strangers, which was perfourmed verie graciously: hee after conducted him into the Inchaunted Garden, to the Caue where the Champion of Wales was kept sleeping by the foure virgins delightfull songes, and after setting him in a chaire of Ebonie, *Ormondine* thus began to relate of wonderfull things.

Renowned Knight at Armes (saide the Nigromancer) Fames worthiest Champion, whose straunge aduentures, all Christendome in time to come shall applaude: therfore be silent till I haue told my Tragicke tale, for neuer after this my tongue shall speake againe: The Knight which thou seest here wrapped in this sheete of gold, is a Christian Champion as thou art, sprung from the auncient seede of *Troian* warriours, who likewise attempted to drawe this Inchaunted sword, but my Magicke spels so preuailed, that he was intercepted in the enterprise, and forced euer since to remaine sleeping in this Caue: but now the houre is almost come of hys recouery, which by thee must be accomplished: thou art that aduenterous Champion, whose inuincible hand must finish vp my detested life, and send my fleeting soule to draw the fatall Charriot vppon the banckes of burning *Acharon*: for my time was limited to remaine no longer in this Inchaunted Garden, but vntill that from the North should come a Knight that shuld pull this sword from the Inchaunted Rocke, which thou happilie hast now perfourmed: therefore I know my time is short, & my houre of destenie is at hand: what I report write it vp in brazen lines, for the time will come when thys discourse shall highly benefit thee. Take heed thou obserue three thinges: first that thou take to wife a pure maide: next that thou erect a Monument ouer thy Fathers graue, and lastly that thou continue a professed foe to the enemies of Christe Iesus, bearing Armes in the Honour and praise of thy Countrie. These thinges beeing truely and iustly obserued, thou shalt attaine to such honour, that all the kingdomes of Christendome shall admire thy dignitie: What I speake is vppon no vaine imagination sprung from a franticke braine, but pronounced by the misticall and deepe Art of Nigromancie.

These words being no sooner ended, but the most honoured and fortunate Champion of England requested the Magitian to describe his passed fortunes, & by what meanes he came first to be gouernour of that inchaunted garden.

To tell the discourse of mine owne life (replied *Ormandine*) will breede a newe sorrowe in my heart, the remembrance whereof will rend my very soule: but yet (most Noble[2] Knight) to fulfill thy request, I will force my tongue to declare what my hart denies to vtter: therefore prepare thy eares to entertayne the wofulst tale, that euer any tongue deliuered, and so, after saint *George* had a while sate silent expecting his discourse, the Magitian spake as followeth.

The wofull and tragicall discourse pronounced by the Nigromancer Ormondine, of the misery of his children.

I Was in former times, (so long as fortune smiled vpon me) the King and onely commaunder of *Scythia*, my name *Ormondine*: gracte in my youth, with two fayre daughters, whome nature had not onely made beautifull, but replenisht them with all the gifts that Art could deuise, the elder whose name was *Castria*, the fayrest mayde that euer *Scythia* brought forth, her eyes like flaming torches so dazeled the gazers, that like attractiue Adamants, they coniured all eyes to admire her beauty, amongst a number of knights that were insnared with her loue: there was one *Floridon* sonne to the King of *Armenia*: equail to her in all excellent ornaments of nature, a louelier couple neuer trod on earth, nor gracte any Princes[3] Court in the whole world.

This *Floridon* so feruently burned in affection, with the admired *Castria*, that he lusted after virginitie, and practised both by pollicie and faire promises to enioy that precious pleasure, which after fell to his owne destruction: For vppon a time when the mantles of darke night had closed in the light of heauen, and the whole Court had entertained a silent rest: this lustfull *Floridon* entered *Castrias* lodging furthered by her chamber maide, where to hys hard hap he cropped[4] the bud of sweet virginity, and left such a pawne with in her wombe, that before many dayes were expired, her shame began to appeare, and the deceaued Ladie was constrained to reueale her griefe to *Floridon*: Who in the meane time had betrothed himselfe to my yonger daughter, whose name was *Marcilla*, no lesse beautified with natures gifts, than her elder sister: But when this vnconstant *Floridon* perceaued that her belly began to growe big with the burden of his vnhappy seed, he vpbraided her with shame, laying dishonour in her dish, calling her strumpet, with many ignominious words, forswearing himself, neuer to haue committed any such infamous deede, protesting that hee euer scornde to linke in womans bandes, and

---

[2] (most Noble] most (Noble *1596*
[3] Princes] Princesse *1596*
[4] cropped] crapped *1596*

counted chamberloue a deadlie sting, and a deepe infection to the honour of Knighthood.[5]

These vnkinde speeches droue *Castria* into such extreame passion of minde, that she with a shamefast looke, and blushing cheekes, after this manner reuealed her secrecie vnto him.

What knowes not *Floridon* (quoth the Lady) her whom hys lust hath stained with dishonour? See see vnconstant Knight the pledge of faithles vowes, beholde the wombe where springes thy liuely image, behold the marke which staines my Fathers auncient house, and sets a shamefaste blush vpon my cheekes. When I behold the companie of chaste virgins, deare *Floridon* shadow this my shame with marriage rightes, that I be not accounted a by word to the world, nor that my Babe in time to come, bee tearmed a base borne childe, remember what plighted promises, what vowes and protestations past betwixt vs, remember the place and time of my dishonour, & bee not like the furious Tyger, to repay loue with dispite.

At which wordes *Floridon* with a wrathfull countenance, replyed in these wordes. Egregious and shameles creature (quoth he) with what brazen face darest thou out braue mee thus: I tell thee *Castria*, my loue was euer yet to follow Armes, to heare the sound of Drummes, to ride vppon a nimble Steede, and not to trace a carpet daunce, like *Priams* sonne before the lustfull eyes of *Mænalaus* wife: Therefore begone disturbing strumpet, goe sing thy harsh melodie in company of nightly birdes, for I tell thee the day will blushe to couer thy monstrous shame.

Which reprochfull speeches beeing no sooner ended, but *Floridon* departed her presence, leauing not behinde him so much as a kinde looke: whereat the distressed Lady, beeing oppressed with intollerable griefe suncke downe dead, not able to speak for a time, but at last recouering her sences she began a new to complaine.

I that was wont (quoth shee) to walke with Troupes of maides, must nowe abandon and vtterly forsake all companies and seeke some secret Caue, wherein I may sit for euermore and bewaile my lost Uirginitie: If I returne vnto my Father, hee will refuse mee: if to my friends they will bee ashamed of mee: if to strangers, they will scorne mee: if to my *Floridon*, oh he denieth mee, and accounts my sight as ominous as the baleful Crokadiles. Oh that I might in the shape of a birde, or like the rauisht *Philomele* fill euery wood and wildernes with my dishonour, for now am I neyther chaste virgin, nor honest wife, but shameles strumpet, and the worldes chiefe scorne: whereat me thinkes I see howe vertuous and chaste maidens point, and tearmes me a viscious dame. Oh vnconstant *Floridon*! thou diddest promise to shadowe this my fault with marriage, but vowes I see are vaine: Thou haste forsaken mee, and tyed thy faith vnto my sister *Marcilla*, who must enioy thy loue, because shee continues chaste without any spot of dishonour. Oh woe to thee vnconstant knight, thy flattering eyes deceaued me, and thy golden tongue enticed mee to commit that sin, which all the *Ocean* streames can neuer wash away: But why stand I relating thus in vaine, the deede is done, and *Floridon* will triumph in the spoile of my virginitie, while he lyes dallying in my sisters Armes: Nay first the fatall lights of Funeralles shall maske about hys marriage bed, and hys bridall

---

[5] Knighthood.] Knighthood, *1596*

blaze, Ile quench with blood: for I will goe vnto their marriage Chamber, where as these handes of mine shall rende my sisters wombe, before she shall enioy the interest of my bed: rage heart, in steede of loue delight in murther, let vengeance be euer in thy thoughtes, vntill thou haste quencht with blood, the furies of disloyall loue.

Thus complayned the wofull *Castria*, vp and downe the Court of *Scythia*, vntill the mistresse of the night had spent fiue months: at the end of which time, the appointed marriage of *Floridon* and *Marcilla* drewe nigh: the thought whereof, was an endles terrour to her heart, and of a more intollerable burden, than the paynes of her wombe: the which she girded in so extreamely for feare of suspition, and partly vnder colour to bring about her intended Tragedie, which was in this bloody maner accomplished and brought about.

The day at last came, whereon *Floridon* and *Marcilla* should tye that sacred knot of marriage, and the Princes & Potentates of *Scythia* were al present as witnesses to *Hymens* holy rites: In which Honourable assembly, none were more busier than *Castria* to beautifie her sisters wedding. The Ceremonies beeing no sooner performed, and the day spent in all pleasures fitting the Honour of so great and mighty a traine, but *Castria* requested the vse of the Countrie, which was this, that ye first night of euerie maydens marriage, a pure virgin should lye with the Bride, which honourable taske was committed to *Castria*: who prouided against the houre appointed, a siluer bodkin and hid it secretly in the trammels of her haire, wherewith she intended to prosecute reuenge. The Brides lodging chamber was appointed farre from the hearing of any one, lest the noyse of people should hinder their quiet sleepe.

But at last when the houre of her wishes approached, that the Bride should take leaue of the Ladies and maidens that attended her to her Chamber, the new married *Floridon* in company of many *Scythian* knights, committed *Marcilla* to her quiet rest, little mistrusting the bloody intent of her sisters minde.

But now behold howe euery thing fell out according to her desires. The Ladies and gentle women beeing no sooner departed, & silence taken possession of the whole Court, But *Castria* with her own handes locked the chamber dore, and secretly conuaide the keyes vnder the beds heade, not perceaued by the betrayed *Marcilla*: which pore Ladie after some few speeches departed to bed: wherein she was no sooner layed, but a heauie sleep ouer mastered her sences, wherby her tongue was forced to give her Sister good night, who as then sate discontented by her bed side, watching the time wherein shee might conueniently inact the bloody Tragedy: vppon a Court table stoode two burning Tapers that gaue light to the whole Chamber, which in her conceit seemed to burne blew: which fatall spectakle incouraged her to a speedy performance, and by the light of the two lamps shee vnbraced her vestures, and stripped her selfe into her milke-white smock, hauing not so much vpon her head as a Caule to hold vp her golden haire: After this she tooke her siluer bodkin that before shee had secretly hidden in her haire, and with a wrathfull countenance (vpon whose browes sate the image of pale death) shee came to her newe married sister, beeing then ouercome with a heauie slumber, and with her Bodkin perced her tender breast: who immediatly at the stroke thereof, started from her sleepe, and gaue such a pittifull scrike, that it would haue wakened the whole Court, but that the Chamber stoode farre from the hearing of all company, except her bloody minded sister, whose hand was ready to redouble her furie with a second stroke.

But when *Marcilla* beheld the sheetes and ornaments of her bed bestained with purple gore, and from her breast ran streames of Crimson blood, which like to a fountaine trickled from her Iuorie bosome, shee breathed foorth thys earnest exclamation against the crueltie of *Castria*.

O sister (said she) hath nature harboured in thy breast a bloody minde! What Furie hath incenst thee thus to commit my Tragedy? In what haue I misdone, or wherein hath my tongue offended thee? What cause hath beene occasion that thy remorceles hand, against true natiuity hath conuerted my ioyfull Nuptials, to a wofull Funerall. This is the cause (replyed *Castria*, and therewithall shewed her wombe growne big through the burden of her Childe) that I haue bathed my handes in thy detested blood.

See, see, *Marcilla* (said shee) the vnhappie bed wherin thy accursed husband hath sowen his seed, by which my virgins honour is for euer stainde: this is the spot which thy heart blood must wash away, and this is the shame that nothing but death shall finish: Therefore a sweet reuenge, and a present murther will I likewise committ vppon my selfe, whereby my loathed soule, in company of my vnborne babe shall wander with thy Ghost along the *Stygian* lakes.

Which wordes beeing no sooner finished, but she violently pierced her owne breast: whereby the two sisters bloods were equally mingled together: but now *Marcilla* beeing the first wounded, and the nearer drawing towards death, she wofully complained this dying Lamentation.

Draw nere (said shee) you blazing starres, you earthlie Angels and imbrothered Girls, you louely Ladies & flourishing Dames of *Scythia*, behold hir wofull end, whose glories mounted higher than the elements, behold my marriage bed which is beautified with Tapestrie, now conuerted to deaths bloody habitation, my braue attire to earthly mould, and my Princely Pallaces, to *Elizium* shades, being a place appointed for those Dames that liude and dide true virgins: for now I feele the paines of death closing my liues windowes, and my heart readie to entertaine the stroke of destenie: Come *Floridon* come, in steed of armes get Eagles wings, that in thy bosome I may breath my murthered Ghost: world fare thou well, I was too proud of thy inticing pleasures: thy Princely pompe, and all thy glistering ornaments I must for euer bid adue. Father farewell with all thy masking Traine of Courtly Ladies, Knights & Gentlewomen: my death I know will make thy Pallace deaths gloomie regiment, and last of all farewell my Noble *Floridon*, for thy sweete sake *Marcilla* nowe is murthered.

At the end of which words, the dying Ladie beeing faint with the abundance of blood that issued from her wounded breast, gaue vp the Ghost: No sooner had pale death ceazed vpon her liueles body, but *Castria* likewise through the extreamitie of her wound was readie to entertaine the stroke of the fatall sisters who likewise complained in this manner. Harken you louing Girles (saide shee) to you I speake, that knowes what endles griefe, disloyall and false loue breedes in constant mindes, the thought whereof is so intollerable to my soule, that it exceeds the torments of *Danaus* daughters, that continually filles water into the bottomles tubs in hell. Oh that my eares had neuer listned to his sugered speeches, or neuer knowne what Courtly pleasures meant, where beautie is a baite for euery lustfull eye: but rather to haue liude a Countrie Lasse, where sweete content is harboured, and beauty shrowded vnder true humility! then had not *Floridon* bereaued me of my sweet virginity: nor had not this accursed hand committed this cruell murder: but oh I feele my soule passing to *Elizium* shades, where *Crusas* shadow, and *Didos* Ghost hath their abiding. thither doth my spirit flye, to bee entertained amongst those vnhappy Ladies that vnconstant loue hath murdered: thus *Castria* not beeing able to speake any longer, gaue a verie grieuous sigh, and so bad adue to the world.

But when the morninges sun had chast away the darksome night, *Floridon* who little mistrusted the tragedy of the two sisters, repayred to the chamber dore with a Consort of skillfull Musitians, where their conspiring harmonye sounded to the walls: and *Floridons* morninges salutations were spente in vayne: for death so stopt the two Princes eares that no resound of thankes at all reanswered his wordes, which caused *Floridon* to departe thinking them to be a sleepe, and to returne with in an hower after, who without any company came to the chamber dore where he again found all silent: at which suspecting some further euent burst open the dore, where being no sooner entred, but he found the two Ladies weltring in purple gore: which wofull spectackle presently so bereaued him of his wits, that like a franticke man he raged vp and downe, and in this maner bitterly complained. Oh you immortal powers! open the wrathfull gates of heauen, & in your Iustice punish me, for my vnconstant loue hath murthered two of the brauest Ladies that euer nature framed: reuiue sweete Dames of *Scythia* & heare mee speake, that am the wofullest wretch that euer spake with tongue: If Ghost may here be giuen for Ghost, deare Ladies take my soule and liue, or if my hart might dwell within your breasts, this hand shal equally deuide it: What are wordes vaine? although my proffer cannot purchase life, nor recouer your breathing spirits againe, yet vengeaunce shall you haue: This hand shall vntwine my fatall twist, and bereaue my bloody brest of soule, whereby my vnhappie Ghost shall followe you, through Tartar gulfes, through burning lakes, & through the lowring shades of dreadfull *Cossitus*: gape, gape, sweete earth, & in thy wombe make all our toombes together.

Which wofull lamentation being no sooner breathed from hys sorrowfull brest but he finished his dayes, by the stroke of that same accursed bodkin, that was the bloody instrument of the two sisters deathes, the which he found still remayning in the remorceles hand of *Castria*.

Thus haue you heard (most worthie Knight) the true Tragedy of three of the goodliest personages, that euer nature framed: but now with dilligent eares listen to the vnfortunate discourse of mine owne miserie, which in this vnhappy manner fell out: For no sooner came the flying musicke of the murthered Princes to my eares, but I grewe into such a discontented passion, that I abandoned my selfe from company of people, and sate for seauen monthes in a solitarie passion lamenting the losse of my Children, like weeping *Niobe*, which was the sorrowfullest Lady that euer liued.

During which time the report of *Floridons* vnhappie Tragedy, was bruted to hys fathers eares, beeing the sole King of *Armenia*: whose griefes so exceeded the bounds of reason, that with all conuenient speede,[6] the greatest strength. *Armenia* could make, and in reuenge of his sonnes vnhappy murther, entered our Territories, and with hys wel approued warriours subdued our Prouinces, slaughtered our Souldiers, conquered our Captaines, slew our Commons, burnt our Citties, and left our Country villages desolate: whereby when I beheld my Countrey ouerspread with famine, fire and sworde, three intestine plagues wherewith heauen scourgeth the sinnes of the wicked, I was forced for safegard of my life to forsake my natiue habitation and Kingly gouernement, onely committing my fortune (like a bannisht Exile) to wander vnknown passages, where care was my chiefe companion, and discontent my onely soliciter: At last it was my desteny to ariue in this vnhappy place which I supposed to be the walks of dispayre, where I had not remayned many dayes in my melancholly passions, but mee thought the warie iawes of deepe *Auerna* opened from whence ascended a most fearefull diuell, that inticed mee to bequeath my fortune to hys disposing, and he would defend me from the furie of the whole world: to which I presently condescended vpon some assurance: Then presently hee placed before my face, this Inchaunted sword, so surely closed in stone, that should neuer be pulled out but by the hands of a Christian Knight, and till that taske were performed I should liue exempt from all danger, although all the Kingdomes of the earth assailed me: which taske (most aduenterous Champion) thou now haste performed, whereby I knowe the houre of my death approacheth, and my time of confusion to be at hand.

This discourse pronounced by the Nigromancer *Ormondine* was no sooner finished, but the worthie Champion *Saint George* heard such a tyrrible ratling in the skyes, & such a lumbring in the earth, that he expected some strange euent to follow: then casting his eies aside, he saw the Inchaunted Garden to vanish, and the Champion of Wales to awake from hys dead sleepe, wherein hee had remayned seauen yeares: who like one newly risen from a sounde, for a time stood speechles, not able to vtter one word, till he beheld the Noble Champion of England, that stedfastly gazed vpon the Nigromancer: who at the vanishing of the Inchauntment, presently gaue a most tyrrible grone & died.

The two Champions after many curteous imbrasinges and kinde greetings reuealed each to other the straunge aduentures they had passed, and how *Saint Dauid* was bound by the oath of his Knighthood to performe the aduenture of *Ormondine*: to which *Saint George* presently condescended, who deliuered the Inchaunted sword, with the Nigromancers head into the handes of *Saint Dauid* the which he presently disceuered from hys dead body: Here must my wearie Muse leaue *Saint Dauid* trauailing with *Ormondines* head to the *Tartarian* Emperour, and speake of the following aduentures that hapned to *Saint George*, after his departure from the Inchaunted Garden.

---

[6] speede,] speede *1596*

CHAP. XI.

How Saint George ariued at Tripolie in Barbarie, where he stole away Sabra the Kinges Daughter of Egipt from the Blackamore King, and how shee was knowne to bee a pure virgin by the meanes of a Lyon, and what hapned to him in the same aduenture.

SAint George after the recouerie of *Saint Dauid*, as you heard in the former Chapter, dispatched his iourny towards Christendome, whose pleasant banks he long desired to behold, and thought euerie day a yeare till hys eyes enioyed a sweete sight of hys Natiue Countrie England, vpon whose Chalkey cliffes he had not treade in many a wearie Sommers day: therefore committing his iournie to a fortunate successe, he[1] trauailde through many a dangerous countrie: where the people were not only of a bloody disposition giuen to all manner of wickednes, but the soyle greatly anoyed with wilde Beasts, through which he could not well trauaile without danger: therefore hee carried continually in one of hys handes, a weapon readye charged to encounter with the Heathen people if occasion should serue, and in the other hande a bright burning blaze of fire, to defend him from the furie of the wilde Beasts, if by violence they assayled him.

Thus in extreame daunger trauailed the Noble and aduenterous Champion *Saint George*, till hee ariued in the Territories of[2] *Barbarie*, in which Countrie he purposed for a time to remaine, and to seeke for some noble atchiuement, whereby hys fame might be increased and hys honored name ring through all the Kingdomes of the world: and beeing incouraged with this Princely cogitation, the Noble Champion of England, climbed to the top of a huge mountaine, where he vnlocked hys Beuer, which before had not beene lifted vp in many a day, and beheld the wide and spacious Countrie how it was beautified with loftie Pines, & adornde[3] with many good Pallaces: But amongst the number of the Townes & Cities which the English Champion beheld, there was one which seemed to exceede the rest, both in scituation and braue buildinges, which he supposed to be the chiefest Cittie in all the Countrie, and the place where the King vsually kept hys Court: to which place *S. George* intended to trauaile, not to furnish himselfe with any needfull thinge, but to accomplish some Honorable aduenture, whereby hys worthy deedes might bee eternized[4] in the Bookes of memorie: So after he had descended from the top of the steepy mountaine, and had trauailed in a low valley about some two or three miles, he approched an olde and almost ruinated Hermitage ouergrowne with mosse, & other withered weedes: before the entrie of which Hermitage sate an auncient Father vpon a rounde stone, taking the heate of the warme Sun, which cast such a comfortable brightnes vpon the Hermits face, that hys white beard seemed to glister like siluer, and hys head to exceed the

---

[1] he] *om. 1596*
[2] of] of of *1596*
[3] adornde] adernde *1596*
[4] eternized] enternized *1596*

whitenes of the Northen Isickles: Of whom after *Saint George* had giuen the due reuerence that belonged vnto age, he[5] demaunded the name of the Countrie, and the Cittie hee trauailed to, & vnder what King the Countrie was gouerned: to whom the curteous Hermit thus replyed.

Most Noble Knight, for so I gesse you are by your furniture and outward appearance (said the Hermit) you are now in the confines of *Barbarie*, the Cittie opposite before your eyes is called *Tripolie*, now vnder the gouernement of *Almidor* the blacke King of *Moroco*: in which Cittie he now keepeth hys Court, attended on by as many valiant Knights, as any King vnder the cope of heauen.

At which wordes the Noble Champion of England sodainely started, as though hee had intelligence of some balefull newes, which deepely discontented hys Princely mind; hys heart was presently incenst with a speedy reuenge, and his minde so extreamely thirsted after *Almidors* Tragedy, that hee could scarce make answere againe to the Hermits wordes: But yet brideling hys furie, the angry Champion spake in this manner.

Graue father (said he) through the trechery of that accursed King, I indured seauen yeares imprisonment in *Persia*, where I suffered both hunger, cold, and extreame misery: but if I had my good sword *Askalon*,[6] and my trustie Palfray which I left in the *Egiptian* Court, where remaines my betrothed Loue, the Kinges Daughter of *Egipt*, I would bee reuenged vppon the head of proude *Almidor*, were his Guard more stronger than the Armie of *Xerxes*, whose multitudes dranke Riuers drie: Why said the Hermit, *Sabra* the Kinges Daughter of *Egipt* is now Queene of *Barbarie*, and since her Nuptials were solemnely performed in *Tripolie*, are seauen Sommers fullie finished.

Now by the Honour of my Countrie England (replied *Saint George*) the place of my Natiuitie, and as I am true Christian Knight, these eyes of mine shall neuer close, nor this vndaunted hart neuer entertain one thought of peace, nor this vnconquered hand receaue one minutes rest, vntill I haue obtained a sight of that sweet Princesse, for whose sake I haue indured so long imprisonment: therefore deare Father bee thus kinde to a trauailer, as to exchaunge thy clothing, for this my rich furniture and lustie Steede which I brought from the Soldan of *Persia*: for in the Habit of a Palmer I may enioy the fruition of her sight without suspicion: otherwise I must needs be constrained by violence, with my trustie Fauchion to make way into her Princelie Pallace: where I knowe shee is attended on most carefully by many valiant and couragious Champions: therefore curteously deliuer me thy Hermits gowne, and I will giue the in boote with my Horse and Armour, this Boxe of precious Iewels: which when the graue Hermit beheld,[7] he humbly thanked the Noble Champion, and so with all the speede they could possiblie make, exchaunged apparell, and in this manner departed.

The Palmer being glad, repaired to his Hermitage with *Saint Georges* furniture, and *Saint George* in the Palmers apparell trauailed towards the Cittie of *Tripolie*: who no sooner came neare to the sumptuous buildinges of the Court, but he espied

---

[5] he] *om. 1596*
[6] *Askalon*] *Aaskalon 1596*
[7] beheld] behold *1596*

a hundred pore Palmers kneeling at the Gate, to whome *Saint George* spake in this manner, not with loftie and Heroicall speeches, beseeming a Princely Champion: but with meeke and humble words like to an aged Palmer.

My deare brethren (said the Champion) for what intent remaine you heare, or what exspect you from this Honorable Court.

Wee abide here (answered the Palmers) for an almes which the Queene once a day hath giuen this seauen yeares, for the sake of an English Knight, named *Saint George*, whome shee affecteth aboue all the Knights in the worlde. But when will this be giuen (said *Saint George*?)

In the after-noone (replied the Palmers) vntill which time vppon our bended knees wee hourely pray for the good Fortune of that most Noble English Knight: which speeches so highlie pleased the valiant minded Champion *Saint George*, that hee thought euery minute a whole yeare, till the Golden Sonne had past away the middle part of Heauen: for it was but newlie risen from *Auroraes* bed, whose light as yet with a shamefast radiant blush distained the Easterne skie.

During which time the most valiant and Magnanimious Champion *Saint George* of England, one while remembring of the extreame miserie hee endured in *Persia* for her sake, wherat hee let fall many Christall teares from hys eyes: another while thinking vpon the tyrrible Battaile he had with the burning Dragon in *Egipt*, where hee redeemed her from the fatall Iawes of death: But at last it was hys chance to walke about the Court, beholding the sumptuous buildings, and the curious ingrauen works by the atchiuement of man bestowed vpon the glistering windowes: where he heard to hys exceeding pleasure the heauenly voice of hys beloued *Sabra* descending from a window vpon the West side of the Pallace, where she warbled forth this sorrowfull Dittie vpon her Iuorie Lute.

> *Dye all desires of ioy and Courtly pleasures,*
> *Dye all desires of Princely Royaltie:*
> *Dye all desires of wealth and worldly treasures,*
> *Dye all desires of stately Maiestie:*
> *Sith he is gone that pleased most mine eye,*
> *For whome I wish ten thousand times to dye.*
>
> *O that mine eyes might neuer cease to weepe,*
> *O that my tongue might euermore complaine:*
> *O that my soule might in his bosome sleepe,*
> *For whose sweete sake my heart doth liue in paine:*
> *In woe I sing, with brinish teares besprent,*
> *Outworne with griefe consumde with discontent.*
>
> *In time my sighes will dim the heauen faire light,*
> *Which hourely flyes from my tormented brest,*
> *Except Saint George that noble English Knight,*
> *With safe returne abandon my vnrest:*

Then carefull cryes shall end with deepe annoy,
Exchaunging weeping teares for smiling ioy.

Before the face of heauen, this vow I make,
Though vnkinde friends hath wed me to their will:
And Crownde me Queene my ardent flames to slake,
That in despight of them shall flourish still.
Beare witnes heauen and earth what I haue said,
For Georges sake I liue and die a maide.

Which sorrowfull Dittie beeing no sooner ended, but she departed the window, quite from the hearing of the English Champion that stoode gazing vp to the casements, preparing his eares to entertaine her sweete tuned mellody the second time, but his expectation was in vaine: whereat he grew into more perplexed passions, than *Aeneas* when hee had lost hys beloued *Crusa* amongst the Armie of the *Græcians*: sometimes wishing the day to vanish in a moment, that the houre of hys beneuolence might approch, other times comforting his sad cogitations with the remembrance of her true chastetie and long continued constancy for hys sake: comparing her loue vnto *Thisbes*, her chastetie to *Dianaes*, and her constancie to *Penelopes*.

Thus spent he the time away, till the gorgious Sunne began to decline to the westerne parts of the earth, and the Palmers should receaue[8] her wonted beneuolence; against which time the English Champion placed himselfe in middest of the Palmers, that expected the wished houre of her comming, who at the time appointed came to the Pallace Gate attired in mourning vesture, like *Polixena* King *Priams* Daughter when she went to sacrifice: her haire after a careles maner hung wauering in the winde, ouerchanged almost from yellow burnisht brightnes, to the colour of siluer, through her long continued sorrow and griefe of hart: her eyes seeming to haue wept a sea of teares, and her wonted beautie (to whose excellent fairenes all the Ladies in the world did sometimes yeelde obeysaunce) was now stayned with the Pearled dew that trickled downe her cheekes: where after the sorrowfull Queene had iustly numbred the Palmers, and with vigilant eies beheld the Princely countenance of saint *George,* her colour beganne to exchange from red to white, and from white to redde, as though the Lilly and the Rose had stroue for superiority, but yet colouring her cogitations vnder a smooth browe, first deliuered her almes to the Palmers, then taking saint *George* aside, to whom shee thus kindly began to confer: Palmer (sayde shee) thou resemblest both in Princely countenance, and curteous behauiour, that thrice honoured Champion of England, for whose sake I haue daily bestowed my beneuolence for this seauen yeares, his name saint *George*, his fame I know thou hast heard reported in many a country, to bee the brauest Knight that euer buckled steeled Helme, therefore for his sake will I grace thee with the chiefest honour in this Court: In steede of thy russet

---

[8] receaue] recaue *1596*

gaberdine, I will cloth thee in purple silke; and in steede of thy Ebon staffe, thy hande shall wielde the richest sworde that euer Princely eye behelde, to whom the Noble Champion saint *George*, replied in this curteous manner.

I haue heard (quoth he) the Princely atchieuements and magnanimious aduentures of that honoured English Knight which you so dearely affect, bruted through many a Princes Court: and how for the loue of a Lady he hath indured a long imprisonment, from whence he neuer looketh to returne, but to spend the remnant of his dayes in lasting misery: At which wordes the Queene let fall from her eyes such a showre of Pearled teares, and sent such a number of strained sighes from her grieued hart, that her sorrow seemed to exceede the Queenes of Carthage, when shee had for euer lost the sight of her beloued Lorde: But the braue minded Champion saint *George,* purposed no longer to continue secrete, but with his discouery to conuert her sorrowfull moanes to smiling ioy: And so casting off his Palmers weede, acknowledged himselfe to the Queene, and therewithall shewed the halfe Ring, whereon was ingrauen this Posie, *ardeo affectione*: which Ring in former time (as you may reade before) they had most equally deuided betwixt them, to be kept in remembraunce of their plighted faithes: which vnsuspected sight highly pleased the beauteous *Sabra*, and her ioy so exceeded the bounds of reason, that she could not speake one word, but was constrained through the new conceaued pleasure, to breathe a sad sigh or two into the Champions bosome: who like a true innobled Knight, entertained her with a louing kisse: But after these two louers had fullie discoursed each to other the secrets of their soules: *Sabra* how shee continued for his loue a pure Uirgin, through the secret nature of a golden chaine steept in Tygers blood, the which shee wore seauen times doubled about her Iuorie necke: tooke him by the portly hand, and led him to her husbands stable, where stood hys approued Palfray, which shee for seauen yeares had fed with her owne handes: who no sooner espyed the returne of his master, but hee grewe more prouder of his presence, than *Bucephalus* of the *Macedonian* Monarckes, when he had most ioyfully returned in triumph from any victorious Conquest.

Now is the time (said the excellent Princesse *Sabra*) that thou mayest seale vp the quittance of our former loues: therefore with all conuenient speed, take thy approued Palfray, with thy trustie sword *Askalon*, which I will presently deliuer into thy handes, and with all celeritie conuay mee from this vnhappy countrie, for the King my husband, with all his aduenterous Champions, are nowe rode forth on hunting, whose absence wil further our flight: But if thou stay till his returne, it is not a hundred of the hardiest Knights in the worlde can beare mee from this accursed Pallace. At which words *Saint George* hauing a minde gracte with all excellent vertues, replyed in this manner.

Thou knowest my diuine Mistresse, that for thy loue I would indure as many dangers, as *Iason* suffered in the Ile of *Calcos*, so I might at last enioy the pleasures of true Uirginitie: But howe canst thou remayne a pure maide, when thou haste beene a Crowned Queene for these seauen yeares, and euerie night haste entertained a King into thy bed? If thou findest me not a true mayde in all that thou canst say or doo, send me backe againe hither vnto my foe, whose bed I account more loathsome, than a den of snakes, and his sight more ominous than the

Crocodiles: As for the *Moroco* Crowne, which by force of friendes was set vpon my head, I wish that it might be turnd into a blaze of quenchles fier, so it might not indanger my body, and for the name of Queene, I account it a vayne Tytle, for I had rather be thy English Lady, than the greatest Empresse in the world.

At which speeches (saint *George*) willingly condiscended, and with all speede purposed to goe into England: and therewithall sealed an assurance with as sweete a kisse, as *Paris* gaue to louely *Hellena* when shee consented to forsake her natiue country, and to trauell from her husband *Menelaus* into Troy: So loosing no time lest delay might breede danger: *Sabra* furnished her selfe with sufficient treasure, and speedily deliuered to saint *George* his trusty sworde, which she had kept seauen yeares for his sake, with all the furniture belonging to his approoued Steede, who no sooner receaued her proffered gifts, which hee accounted dearer than the *Asian* Monarchy, but presently sadled his horse, and beautified his strong limbes with rich caparison. In the meane time *Sabra* through fayre speeches and large promises, obtained the good will of an Euenuke, that was appoynted for her guard in the Kings absence, to accompany them in theyr intended trauailes, and to serue as a trusty guide if occasion required: which with the Lady stoode ready at the Champions commandement: who no sooner had furnished himselfe with sufficient habilliments of warre, belonging to so dangerous a iourney, but he plaste his beloued Mistris vpon a gentle Palfray, which alwaies kneeled downe vntill shee had ascended the saddle: And likewise her Euenuke was mounted vpon another Steede, whereon all their rich furniture with costly Iewels and other treasure was borne:

So these three worthy Personages committed their trauels to the guide of fortune, who preserued them from the dangers of pursuing enemies, which at the Kinges returne from hunting, followed amayne to euery Port and Hauon that deuided the kingdome of *Barbarie* from the Confines of Christendome: But kind destenie so guided their steps that they trauailed another way, contrarie to their exspectations: for when they looked to ariue vpon the Territories of Europe, they were cast vppon the fruitfull bankes of *Græcia*: in which Countrie we must tell what hapned to the three trauailers, and omit the vaine pursute of the *Moroco* Knights: the wrathfull melancholy of the King, and the bruted rumour that was amongst the Commons of the Queenes departure: who caused the Larum-belles to bee rung out, and the Beacons to be set on fire, as though the enemie had entred their Countrie.

But now *Melpomine*, thou Tragicke Sister of the Muses, report what vnluckie crosses hapned to these three trauailers in the Confines of *Græcia*, and howe theyr smiling Comedie was by ill fortune turned into a weeping Tragedie: For when they had iournied some three or foure Leagues ouer many a loftie hill, they approached into a mightie and fearefull Wildernes: through which the waies seemed so long, and the Sunne beames so exceedingly glowed, that *Sabra* what for wearines in trauaile, and the extreame heate of the day, was constrained to rest vnder the shelter of a mightie Oake, whose braunches had not beene lopt in many a yeare: where shee had not long remayned, but her heart began to faint for hunger, and her colour that was but a little before as faire as any Ladies in the world, beganne to chaunge for want of some drinke: whereat the famous Champion *Saint George* halfe dead with griefe, comforted her as well as hee could after this manner.

Faint not my deare Lady (said the Champion) here is that good sword, that once preserued thee from the burning Dragon, and before thou die for want of sustenance, it shall make way to euery corner of this wildernes: where I will eyther kill some venison to refreshe thy hungry stomacke, or make my toomb in the bowels of some monstrous beast: therefore abide thou here vnder this tree in company of thy faithfull Euenuke, till I returne eyther with the fleshe of some wilde Deare, or els some flying Birde to refreshe thy spirits to a new trauaile.

Thus left he hys beloued Lady with the Euenuke to the mercy of the woods, and trauailed vp and downe the Wildernes, till he espyed a Heard of fatted Deare, from which company he singled out the fayrest, and like a tripping Satire coursed her to death: then with hys keene edged sword cut out the goodlyest haunch of venison, that euer Hunters eye beheld: which gift he supposed to bee most welcome to his beloued Lady. But marke what hapned in his absence to the two wearie trauailers abiding vnder the tree: where after *Saint Georges* departure, they had not long sitten discoursing, one while of their long iournies, another while of their safe deliuerie from the Blackamoore King, spending the stealing time away with many an auncient storie: but there appeared out of a thicket two huge and monstrous Lyons, which came directly pacing towardes the two trauailers: which fearefull spectakle when *Sabra* beheld, hauing a hart ouercharged with the extreame feare of death, wholy committed her soule into the hands of God, and her body almost famished for foode, to suffice the hunger of the two furious Lyons: who by the appointment of heauen, proffered not so much as to lay their wrathfull pawes vpon the smallest part of the Ladies garment: but with eger moode assailed the Euenuke till they had buried hys body in the emptie vaults of their hungry bowels: then with their teeth lately imbrued in blood, rent the Euenukes Steed to a thousand peeces: which beeing done they came to the Lady which sate quaking halfe dead with feare, & like two Lambs couched their heads vpon her lap: where with her handes she stroked downe their brisled haire, not daring almost to breath, till a heauie sleepe had ouer-mastered their refreshed sences: by which time the Princely minded Champion *Saint George* returned with a peece of venison vppon the point of hys sword: who at that vnexpected sight, stood in a maze whether it were best to flye for sauegard of hys life, or to venture hys fortune against the furious Lions: But at last the loue of hys Lady so incouragde him to a forwardnes, which he beheld quaking before the dismal gates of death: So laying downe hys venison, he presently like a victorious Champion, sheathed hys approued Fauchion most furiously into the bowels of one of the Lyons. *Sabra* kept the other sleeping in her lappe till hys prosperous hand like wise dispatched him: which aduenture beeing performed, he first thanked heauen for the victorie, and then in this kinde manner saluted his Lady.

Now *Sabra* (said he) I haue by this sufficiently proued thy true virginitie: for it is the nature of euerie Lyon, be he neuer so furious, not to harme the vnspotted virgin, but humbly to lay his brisled heade vppon a maidens lappe. Therefore divine Paragon; thou art the worlds chiefe woonder for loue and chastetie, whose honoured vertues shall ring as farre as euer *Phœbus* lends hys light, & whose constancie I will mainetaine in euery Land where as I come, to be the truest vnder the cercuit of the Sunne: At which word he cast hys eye aside, and beheld the bloody spectakle of the Euenukes Tragedy, which by *Sabra* was wofully discoursed, to the great griefe of *Saint George*: whose sad sighes serued for a dolefull knell to bewaile hys vntimelie⁹ death: but hauing a Noble minde not subiect to vaine sorrow, where al hope of life is past, ceased his griefe, and prepared the venison in readines for hys Ladies repast: which in this order was dressed.

He had in hys pocket, a fire-locke, wherewith he stroke fire, and kindled it with sun-burnde mosse, and increased the flame with other drie wood which hee gathered in the Wildernes: against which they rosted the venison and suffized themselues to their owne contentments. After which ioyfull repast, these two Princely persons set forward to their wonted trauailes, whereby the happie guide of heauen so conducted their steppes, that before manie dayes passed, they ariued in the *Grœcian* Court, euen vpon that day when the marriage of the *Grœcian* Emperour should bee solemnely holden: which Royall Nuptials in former times had bin bruted into euery Nation in the world, as well into Europe as *Affrica* and *Asia*: At which Honorable marriage the brauest Knights that euer liude on earth were present: for golden fame had bruted the report thereof to the eares of the seauen Champions: into *Theslie* to saint *Dennis* the Champion of Fraunce, there remaining with hys beauteous *Eglantine*: into *Ciuillia* to saint *Iames* the Champion of Spaine, where he remained with hys louelie *Celestine*: to saint *Anthonie* the Champion of Italie then trauailing in the borders of *Scythia* with hys Lady *Rossalinde*: likewise to saint *Andrew* the Champion of Scotland: to saint *Pattricke* the Champion of Ireland: and to saint *Dauid* the Champion of Wales: who atchieued many memorable aduentures in the Kingdome of *Tartarie* as you haue heard before discoursed at large.

But nowe Fame and smiling Fortune consented to make their Knightlie atchiuements to shine in the eyes of the whole world: therefore by the conduction of Heauen, they generally ariued in the *Grœcian* Emperours Court: Of whose Tilts and Turnaments there in performed, to the honour of hys Nuptials, my weary Muse is bounde to discourse.

---

⁹ vntimelie] vntimeles *1596*

CHAP. XII.

How the seuen Champions ariued in Grœcia at the Emperours Nuptials, where they performed many Noble atchiuements, and how after open Warres was proclaimed against Christendome by the discouerie of many Knights, and how euerie Champion departed into hys own Countrie.

To speake of the number of Knights that assembled in the *Grœcian* Court together, were a labour ouer tedious, requiring the pen of a second *Homer*: Therfore will I omit the Honorable traine of Knights and Ladies that attended him to the Church: their costly garmentes and glistring ornaments, exceeding the Royaltie of *Heccuba* the beauteous Queene of *Troy*: Also I passe ouer the beauteous[1] banquets: the Honourable seruices and delicious cheare that beautified the Emperours Nuptials: with the statelye Maskes and Courtly daunces, performed by many Noble personages, and chiefely discourse of the Knightly atchiuements of the seauen Champions of Christendome, whose honourable proceedings, and magnanimious Encounters hath deserued a golden penne to relate: for after some few dayes spent in Chamber sports, to the great pleasure of the *Grœcian* Princes: the Emperour presently proclaimed a solemne Iousting to bee holden for the space of seauen daies in the honour of his marriage, and appointed for hys chiefe Champions the seauen Christian Knights: whose names as then were not knowne by any one except their owne attendants.

Against the appointed day the Turnaments should begin, the Emperour caused a woonderfull large frame of timber worke to bee erected: whereon the Empresse & her Ladies might stand for the better view of the Tilters, and at pleasure behould the Champions Encounters most Nobly performed in the Honour of their Mistresses: likewise in the compasse of the Listes were pitcht seuen Tentes of seuen seuerall colours, wherein the seuen Champions might remayne till the sound of siluer Trumpets summoned them to appeare.

Thus euery thing prepared in readines fitting so great a Royaltie: the Princes and Ladies placed in theyr seates: the Emperour with his new married Empresse inuested on theyr loftie throanes strongly garded with a hundred Armed Knights, the Kings Harrolds solemely proclaimed the Turnaments, which in this most Royall manner began.

The first day Saint *Dennis* of Fraunce was appointed chiefe Champion against all commers, who was called by the title of the golden Knight, who at the sounde of the Trumpet entered the Lists: hys Tent was of the colour of the Marigold, vpon the top an artificiall Sunne framed, that seemed to beautefie the whole assemblie: hys Horse of an Iron Gray, gracte with a spangled plume of feathers: before him rode a Page in purple silke, bearing vpon hys crest three golden *Flure-de-luces*, which did signifie hys Armes: Thus in this Royall maner entered Saint *Dennis* the Listes: where after he had traced twice or thrice vp and downe to the open view of the whole company, he prepared himselfe in readines to begin the Tournament:

---

[1] beauteous] sumptuous *1608*; *1616*

against whome ranne many *Grœcian* Knights, which were foyled by the French Champion, to the wonderfull admiration of all the beholders: but to be briefe, he so worthelie behaued himselfe, and with such fortitude, that the Emperour applauded him for the brauest Knight in all the world.

Thus in great Royaltie to the exceeding pleasure of the Emperour, was the first day spent, till the darke Euening caused the Knights to breake off company, and repaire to their nights repose: But the next Morning no sooner did *Phœbus* shewe his splendant brightnesse, but the King of Harrolds vnder the Emperour, with a noyse of Trumpets awaked the Champions from their silent sleepe, who with all speede prepared for the second dayes exercise. The chiefe Champion appointed for that day, was the victorious Knight Saint *Iames* of Spaine: which (after the Emperor with hys Empresse had seated themselues with a statelie traine of beautifull Ladies) entred the Listes vpon a Spanish Gennet betrapt with rich Caparison, his Tent was pitcht directly ouer against the Emperors Throane, which was of the colour of quick-siluer, whereon was portrayed many excellent deuices: before the Tent attended foure Squiers, bearing foure seuerall scutchions in their hands, whereon were curiously paynted the foure Elements: likewise he had the tytle of the siluer Knight, who behaued himselfe no lesse worthy of all Princely commendations, than the French Champion the day before: The third day saint *Anthony* of Italy was chiefe challenger in the Turnament, whose Tent was of the colour of the Skyes, his Steede furnished with costly Habilliments: his Armour after the Barbarian manner, his shield plated round about with steele, whereon was paynted a golden Eagle in a field of blew: which signified the auncient Armes of Rome: likewise hee had the Tytle of the Azurde Knight, whose matchlesse Chiualrie for that day, wan the Prize from all the *Grœcian* Knights, to the great reioysing[2] of his Lady *Rossalinde*, the King of Sycils Daughter, that still remained in Pages attyre, wherein (for the deare loue shee bore saint *Anthonie*) disguisedly stole from the Court, whose discouerie shall hereafter be expressed: The fourth day by the Emperours appointment, the valiant and worthie Knight saint *Andrew* of *Scotland* obtained that Honour, as to be chiefe challenger for the Turnament: hys Tent was framed in the manner of a ship swimming vppon the waues of the Sea, inuironed about with Dolphins Tritons, and many strange contriued Mearemaides: vppon the toppe stoode the picture of *Neptune*, the God of the Seas, bearing in hys hand a Streamer, where on was wrought in crimson silke a corner Crosse, which seemed to bee hys countries Armes, hee was called the red Knight, because his horse was couered with a bloody vale: hys worthie atchiuements obtained such fauour in the Emperours eyes, that hee threw him his siluer Gauntlet which was prized at a thousand Portegues, and with hys owne hands conducted him to a rich Pauilion, where after his noble encounters hee enioyed a sweete repose: The fift day saint *Pattricke* of *Ireland*, as chiefe Champion entred the Lists, vpon an Irish Hobbie, couered with a vale of greene, attended on by six siluane Knights: euery one bearing vpon his shoulder a blooming tree: hys Tent resembled a sommers bower, at the entrie whereof stoode the picture of *Flora*, beautefied with a wreath

---

[2] reioysing] reoysing *1596*

of sweet smelling Roses: he was named the greene Knight, whose worthie prowesse so daunted the defendants, that before the Turnament began they gaue him the honour of the day: vppon the sixt day the Heroicall and Noble minded Champion of *Wales* obtained such fauour at the Emperours handes, that hee was likewise chiefe challenger, who entred the Lists vpon a *Tartarian* Palfray, couered with a vale of blacke, to signifie a blacke and Tragicall day should befall to those *Græcian* Knights that durst approue his inuincible fortitude: hys Tent was pitcht in the manner and forme of a Castell in the west side of the Listes: before the entrie whereof, hung a golden shield: whereon was liuelie portraied a siluer Griffon rampant vppon a golden Helmet, which signified the auncient Armes of *Brittaine*: hys Princelye atchiuements, not onely obtained due commendations at the Emperours handes, but of the whole assemblie of *Græcian* Ladies, whereby they applauded him to bee the most Noblest Knight that euer shiuered Launce, and the most fortunate[3] Champion that euer entred into the *Græcian* Court: vppon the seauenth and last day of these Honourable Turnaments and most Noble proceedinges, the famous and valiant Knight at Armes saint *George* of *England* as chiefe challenger entred the Listes, vppon a sable coloured Steed, betrapt with barres of burnisht gold, hys forehead beautefied with a gorgeous plume of purple feathers, from whence hung many pendants of gold, his Armour of the purest Lidian steele, nayled fast together with siluer plates, hys Helmet ingrauen verie curiouslie, beset with *Indian* Pearle, and Iasper stones: before hys breast plate hung a siluer Table in a dammaske scarfe, whereon was pictured a Lyon rampant in a bloody fielde, bearing three golden Crownes vppon hys head, before hys Tent stood an Iuorie Charriot guarded by twelue coleblacke Negars, wherein hys beloued Lady and Mistresse *Sabra*, sate inuested vppon a siluer Globe to beholde the Heroicall Encounters of her most Noble and Magnanimious champion saint *George* of *England*: his Tent was as white as the Swannes feathers, glistring against the Sun, supported by foure ioyntles Elephants framed of the purest brasse, about his Helmet he tied a wreath of Uirgins haire, where hung his Ladies gloue, which he wore to maintaine her excellent gifts of nature to exceede all Ladies on the earth. These costlie habilliments rauished the beholders with such vnspeakeable pleasure, that they stood gazing at hys furniture, not able to withdrawe their eyes from so heauenlie a sight: But when they beheld his victorious Encounters against the *Graecian* Knightes, they supposed him to be the inuincible tamer of that seauen headed monster that clambred to the elements, offring to pull *Iupiter* from hys throne. His Steede neuer gaue Encounter with any Knight, but hee tumbled horse and man to the ground, where they lay for a time bereaft of sence. The Turnament endured for that day, from the Suns rising, till the cole blacke Euenings Star appeared: in which time he conquered fiue hundred of the hardiest Knights then liuing in *Asia*, and shiuered a thousand Launces, to the woonderfull admiration of the beholders.

Thus were the seauen dayes brought to ende by the seauen worthy Champions of Christendome, in rewarde of whose Noble atchieuements the *Græcian*

---

[3] fortunate] fortunates *1596*

Emperour (being a man that highly fauored knightly proceedinges)[4] gaue them a golden tree with seauen branches to be deuided equally amongst them. Which Honourable Prize they conuayed to saint *Georges* Pauilion, where in deuiding the braunches, the seauen Champions discouered themselues each to other, and by what good fortune they ariued in the *Grœcian* Court, whose long wished sights so reioyced theyr harts, whereby they accounted that happy day of meeting, the ioyfullest day that euer they beheld: But now after the Turnaments were fully ended, & the Knights rested themselues some few dayes, recouering their wonted agillitie of body, they fell to a new exercise of pleasure: not appearing in glistring Armour before the Tilt, nor following the loud sounding Drums & siluer Trumpets, but spending away the time in Courtly daunces amongst their beloued Ladies and Mistresses, in more Royaltie than the *Phrigian* Knights, when they presented the Paragon of *Asia* with an Inchanted Maske. There wanted no inspiring Musicke to delight their eares, no heauenly Sonets to rauish their sences, nor no curious daunces to please their eyes. *Sabra* she was the Mistresse of the Reuels: who gracte the whole Court with her excellent beautie, which seemed to exceede the rest of the Ladies, as farre as the Moone surpasseth her attending Stars in a frostie night: & when shee daunst, shee seemde like *Thetis* tripping on the siluer sandes, with whom the Sun did fall in loue: and if shee chaunst to smile, the cloudy elements woulde cleare & drop downe heauenly dew, as though they mournde for loue. There likewise remayned in the Court, the six *Scythian* Uirgins, that in former times liued in the shape of Swans, which were as beautifull Ladies as euer eye beheld: also many other Laidies attended the Empresse, in whose companies the seauen Champions daylie delighted: sometimes discoursing of amorous conceits: other times delighting themselues with sweete tuned Musicke: then spending the day in banqueting, reuelling, dancing, & such like pastimes, not once iniuring their true betrothed Ladies. But their Courtly pleasures continued not long, for they were sodainely dashed with a present newes of open Warres proclaymed against Christendome, which fell out contrarie to the expectations of the Christian Knights. There ariued in the *Grœcian* Emperours Pallace, a hundred Harrolds of a hundred seuerall Prouinces, which proclaimed vtter defiance to all Christian Kingdomes, by these words.

Wee the high and mightie Emperours of *Asia* and *Affrica*, great commaunders both of land & seas, proclaime by generall consent of all the Easterne Potentates, vtter ruine and destruction to the Kingdomes of Christendome, & to all those Nations where any Christian Knights are harboured: First the Soldan of *Persia* in reuenge of a bloody slaughter done in hys Pallace, by an English Champion: *Ptolomie* the Egiptian King in reuenge of his daughter violently taken away by the sayd knight: *Almidor* the blacke King of *Moroco* in reuenge of his Queene likewise taken away by the sayde English Champion: The great Gouernour of *Thessaly* in reuenge of his daughter taken away by a French Knight: The King of Ierusalem in reuenge of his daughter taken away by a Spanish Knight: The Tartarian Emperour in reuenge of his Sonne the Countie *Palatine*, slaine by the vnhappy hand of the

---

[4] proceedinges)] proceedinges, *1596*

Champion of Wales: The *Sicillian* Monarke in reuenge of hys vaine trauaile after his seauen daughters, now in the keeping of certaine Christian Knights: in reuenge of which iniuries, all the Kingdomes from the furthest part of *Prester Iohns* Dominions to the borders of the red Seas, hath set downe their handes and seales to be ayders in this bloodie Warre.

This Proclamation[5] beeing no sooner ended, but the *Grœcian* Emperour likewise consented to their bloody determination, and thereupon gaue speedy commandement to muster vp the greatest strength that *Grœcia* could afforde, to ioyne with the Pagans, to the vtter ruine and confusion of Christendome: which bloody edict, or rather inhumane Iudgement pronounced by the accursed Infidels, compelled the Christian Champions to a speedy departure, and euerie one to haste into his owne countrie, there to prouide for the Pagans entertainment: So after due considerations the seauen Champions departed from *Grœcia* in companie of their betrothed Ladies: who chose rather to liue in the bosoms of their husbands, than in the armes of their misbeleeuing Parents: where after some few dayes they ariued in the spacious bay of *Portingale*, in which Hauen they vowed by the Honour of true Knighthood, to meete againe within six monthes insuing: there to conioyne all their Christian Armies into one Legion: vpon which plighted resolution the worthie Champions departed one from another: Saint *George* into *England*: Saint *Dennis* into *Fraunce*: Saint *Iames* into *Spaine*: Saint *Anthonie* into *Italie*: Saint *Andrew* into *Scotland*: Saint *Pattrick* into *Ireland*: Saint *Dauid* into *Wales*: whose pleasant bankes they had not beheld in many a yeare before: where their entertainments were as Honorable as their harts desired: But to speake of the mustring vp of Souldiers in euerie Christian Kingdome, and what strength ariued at the appointed time in the bay of *Portingale*, shall be discoursed in the sequell of this Historie, and how troublesome warres ouerspread the whole earth, where the Heroicall deedes of these Noble Champions shall at large be discribed: Also of the ouerthrow of many Kings, and Kingdomes, ruines of Townes, and Citties, and the decay of many flourishing Commonweales: Likewise of the bloody Tragedies of many vnchristian Princes: whereat the heauens will mourne to see the effusion of blood trickle from the breasts of murthered Infants, the heapes of slaughtered Damsels trampled to peeces by souldiers horses, and the streetes of manye a Cittie sprinckled with the blood of reuerent age: Therefore gentle Reader accept of this my labour with a smooth brow & a kinde countenance, and my wearie Muse shall neuer rest, till I haue finished the true Historie of these Heroicall Champions.

---

[5] Proclamation] Prolamation *1596*

CHAP. XIII.

How the seauen Champions of Christendome ariued with their Troupes in the bay of Portingale, the number of the Christian Armies, and how Saint George made an Oration to his Souldiers.

AFter the seauen Champions of Christendome ariued in their Natiue Countries, and by true reportes had blazed abroade to euerie Princes eare the bloody resolution of the Pagans, & how the Prouinces of *Affrica* and *Asia*, had mustered vp their forces to the inuasion of *Europe*. All Christian Kinges then at the intreatie of the Champions, appointed mighty Armies of wel approued soldiers both by sea & land, to intercept the Infidels wicked intention: likewise by the whole consent of Christendome, the Noble and Fortunate Champion of England saint *George*, was appointed chiefe Generall, and principall leader of the Armies, and the other sixe Champions elected for hys Councell, and chiefe assistants in all attempts that appertained either to the benefit of Christendome, or the furtherance of their fortunate proceedings. This Honorable warre so fired the hearts of many youthfull Gentlemen, and so incouraged the mindes of euery common Souldier, that some morgagde their lands, and at their owne proper charges furnished themselues: Some sold their Patrimonies to serue in this Honorable warres: and other some forsooke Parents, Kindred, Wife, Children, friends and acquaintance, and without constraint of pressing, offered themselues to follow so Noble a Generall, as the renowned Champion of England, and to spend their blood in the iust quarrell of their Natiue Countrie. To be briefe, one might beholde the streetes of euerie Towne and Cittie throughout all the Dominions of Europe, beautefied with Troupes of Souldiers, which thirsted after nothing but Fame and Honour. Then the ioyfull sound of thundring Drums, and the ecchoes of siluer Trumpets summoned them to Armes, that followed with as much willingnes, as the *Grœcians* followed *Agamemnon* to the wofull ouerthrow of Troy: for by that time the Christian Champions had sported themselues in the bosomes of their kinde Mistresses, the forward Captaines taken leaue of their Courtly pastimes, and the willing Souldiers bidden adue to their friendes & acquaintance, the spring had couered the earth with a newe liuerie: which was the appointed time, the Christian Armies should meete in *Portingale*, there to conioyne their seuerall Troupes into one Legion: which promise caused the Champions to bid adue to their Natiue Countries, and with all speed to buckle on their furnitures, and to hoyst vp sayles: where after a short time, the winde with a calme and prosperous gale, cast them happely into the bay of *Portingale*. The first that ariued into that spacious Hauen, was the Noble Champion saint *George*, with a hundred thousand of couragious English Souldiers, whose forwardnes betokened a fortunate successe, and their willing mindes a ioyfull victorie. Hys Armie beeing set in Battaile ray, seemed to counteruaile the number of the *Macedonian* Souldiers, wherewith worthy *Alexander* conquered the Westerne world: hys Horsemen being in number twenty thousand, were Armed all in blacke Corslets: their Launces bound about with plates of steele: their Steedes couered with Maile three times doubled: their colours were the sanguine Crosse, supported by a golden Lyon: hys sturdy bowmen, whose conquering Gray-goose wing in former times hath terrified the cercled earth: beeing in number likewise twentie thousand, clad all in red Mandillians, with Caps of the same colour, bearing thereon likewise a sanguine Crosse, beeing the true badge and honor of England: their Bowes of the strongest Ewe, and their Arrowes of the soundest Ash, with forked heads of steele, and their feathers bound on with greene wax, and twisted silke: his Musketters being in number ten thousand, their Muskets of the widest bore, with firelocks wrought by curious workemanship, yet of such woonderfull lightnes, that they required no rest at all, to ease their headdy ayming armes, his Caliuer shotte likewise ten thousand of the smaller timbred men, but yet of as couragious a minde as the tallest souldier in his Army, his Pikes and Bills, to guard the wauing Aunsients thirty thousand strong, clad all in glistering bright Armour, likewise followed ten thousand labouring Pioners, if occasion serued to vndermine any towne or castell, to intrench Forts or Sconses, or to make a passage thorough hilles and mountaines, as worthy *Hanniball* did when as he made a way[1] for hys souldiers through the loftie Alphes, that deuide the Countries of *Italie* and *Spaine*: The next that ariued within the bay of *Portingale*, was the Princelie minded Champion saint *Dauid* of *Wales*, with an Armie of fiftie thousand of true borne *Brittaines*, furnished with all habilliments of Warre to so Noble and valiant a seruice, to the high renowne of his countrie and true Honour of hys Progenie: their Armour in richnes nothing inferiour to the Englishmens: their colours were a golden Crosse, supported by a siluer Griffon: which Scutchion signified the auncient Armes of Wales: For no sooner had saint *George* a sight of the valiant *Brittaines*, but hee caused his Musketters presently to entertaine them with a vollue of shotte, to expresse their happie and ioyfull welcome to shore, which speedely they performed so couragiously with such a ratling noyse as though the firmaments had burst in sunder, and the earth made eccho to their thundring mellodie.

But no sooner were the skeyes cleared from the smoake of the reaking powder, and that saint *George* might at pleasure deserne the Noble and Magnanimious Champion of Wales: who as then rode vppon a milke-white Hobbie in siluer Armour, guarded with a traine of Knights in purple vestures, but hee greeted saint *Dauid* with kinde curtesies, and accompanied him to the English Tent, which they had erected close by the Port side, where for that night these two Champions remayned spending the time with vnspeakeable pleasure, and so vppon the next day after saint *Dauid* departed to hys owne Tent, which he had caused to be pitcht, a quarter of a League, from the English Armie: The next that ariued on the fruitfull bankes of *Portingale*, was saint *Pattrick* the Noble Champion of *Ireland*, with an Armie likewise of fiftie thousand, attired after a straunge and woonderfull manner: their furnitures were of the skynnes of wilde Beasts: but yet more vnpearceable than the strongest Armour of proofe: they bore in their handes mightie Dartes, tipt at the end with pricking steele, which the couragious and valiant Irish Souldiers by the agillitie of their armes could throw a quarter of a mile, and with such a forcible

---

[1] a way] away *1596*

strength, that they woulde strike three or foure inches into an Oake, and with such a certaine ayme that they would not misse the bredth of a foote.

These aduenterous and hardie Souldiers no sooner ariued on the shore, but the English Musketters gaue them a Princely entertainement, and presently conducted the Noble minded Champion saint *Pattrick* to the English Tent: where the three Champions of *England*, *Wales*, and *Ireland* passed away the time with exceeding great Royaltie: laying downe plots how to pitch their Campes to the most disaduantage of the misbeleeuing enemie, and setting downe perfect directions which way they were best to martch, and such like deuicies for their owne safeties and the benefit of Christendome: The next that landed on the banckes of *Portingale*, was saint *Andrew* the worthie Champion of *Scotland*, with threescore thousand of well approued Souldiers, hys horsemen the bolde aduenterous Gallowayes, clad all in quilted Iackets, with lances of the Turkish fashion, thicke and short, bearing vpon their Beauers the Armes of *Scotland*, which was a corner Crosse supported by a naked Uirgin: his Pikemen the stiffe and hardie men of *Orcadie*, which continually vse to[2] lye vpon the freezing Mountaines, the Isie Rocks, & the Snowie Vallyes: hys shot the light footed *Callidonians*, that if occasion serue, can climbe the highest hill, and for nimblenes in running, ouergoe the swift footed Stag.

These bold aduenterous Scottishmen in al forwardnes, deserued as much honor at the English Champions hands, as any of the other Nations before: therefore he commanded hys shot at the first entrie on land to giue them a Noble entertainement: which they performed most Royally, & also conducted saint *Andrew* to the English Tent: where after he had giued *S. George* the courtesie of his countrie, departed to his Tent, which was distant from the English Tent a mile: The next that ariued was *S. Anthonie* the Champion of Italie with a band of foure score thousand braue Italian Souldiers mounted on warlike Coursers, euerie Horseman attended on by a naked Neger, bearing in hys hand a Streamer of watchet silke, with the Armes of *Italie* thereon set in gold, euery footeman furnished with approoued furniture, in as stately a manner as the Englishmen: who at their landing receaued as Royall an entertainment, as the other Nations, and likewise saint *Anthonie* was as highly honoured by the English Champion, as any of the other Christian Knights: The next that ariued was saint *Dennis* the victorious Champion of *Fraunce*, with a band of foure score thousand: After him marched twelue Dukes, of twelue seuerall Dukedomes, beeing then vnder the gouernement of the French King, euery one at hys owne proper cost and charges, mainetaining two thousand souldiers in these Christian warres: their entertainments were as glorious as the rest: The last of all the Christian Champions that ariued vppon the fruitfull bankes of *Portingale*, was the Magnanimious Knight saint *Iames* of *Spaine*, with a bande likewise of foure score thousand: with him he brought from the Spanish Mines ten tunne of refined gold, onely to mainetaine Souldiers in the defence of Christendome: who no sooner landed with his Troups, but the other sixe Champions gaue him the Honourable welcome of a Souldier, and ordained a

---

[2] to] to to *1596*

solemne banket for the generall Armies, whose number iustly surmounted to fiue hundred thousand: which Legions they conioyned into one Campe Royall, and after placed their winges and squadrons Battaile wise, chiefely by the direction of saint *George*, beeing then chiefe Generall by the consent of the Christian Kinges: who after hee had ouerviewd the Christian Armies, his countenance seemed to prognosticate³ a Crowned victorie, and to foretell a fatall ouerthrow to the misbeleeuing Potentates: Therefore to incourage hys Princely followers to perseuer in their wonted willingnes, pronounced this Princely Oration.

You men of *Europe* (said he) & my country men, whose Conquering fortunes neuer yet hath feared the enemies of Christ: you see we haue forsooke our Natiue Lands, and committed our destenies to the Queene of chaunce, not to fight in any vniust quarrell, but in the true cause of Israels annoynted, not against nature to climbe the heauens as *Nemrod* and the Gyants proffered in former times: but to preuent the inuasion of Christendome, the ruines of Europe, and the intended ouerthrow of all Christian Prouinces: the bloody minded Infidels, haue mustred vp Legions in numbers like the blades of grasse, that growe vppon the flourishing Downes of Italy, or the starres of heauen in the coldest winters night, protesting to fill our Countryes with seas of blood, to scatter our streets with mangled limbs and conuert our glorious Citties into flames of quenchles fier: Therefore deare Countrimen liue not to see our Christian Uirgins spoyld by lustfull Rape, nor dragde along our streetes like guiltles Lambes to a bloody slaughter: Liue not to see our harmeles Babes with brused braynes dasht against hard flinty stones, nor liue to see our vnlusty age, whose hayres resemble siluer Mynes, lye bleeding on the Marble pauements: But like true Christian souldiers fight in the quarrell of your Countries: What though the Pagans be in number ten to one: yet heauen I knowe will fight for Christendome, and cast them downe before our faces, like drops of Aprill showers. Bee not dismaied to see their men in ordered rankes, nor feare not when you behold the streamers houering in the wauing winde, when as their steeled Pikes like to a thornie Forrest will ouerspread whole Countries: thousands of them I know will haue no hearts to fight, but flye with cowardly feare like flockes of sheepe before the greedie Wolfe. I am the leader of your Noble mindes, that neuer fought in vaine, nor neuer entered battaile but returnde with Conquest. Then euery one with me build vpon this Princely resolution: for Christendome fight, for Christendome we liue and die.

This Souldierlike Oration being no sooner finished, but the whole Armie with a generall voice cried, to Armes, to Armes with the victorious *George* of *England*: which Noble resolution of the Souldiers, so reioyced the English Champion, and likewise incouraged the other Christian Champions with such a forwardnes of minde, that they gaue speedy commandement to remoue their Tents and to martch with easie iournies towards *Tripolie* in *Barberie*, where *Almidor* the blacke King of *Moroco* had hys residence: In which trauaile wee must leaue for a while the Christian Armie, and speake of the innumerable Troups of Pagan Knights that ariued at one instant in the Kingdome of *Hungarie*, and how they fell at varience in

---

³ prognosticate] pognosticate *1596*

the election of a Generall: which ciuell mutenie caused much effucion of blood, to the great hurt both of *Affrica* and *Asia*, as here after followeth.

CHAP. XIIII.

Of the dessention and discord that hapned amongst the Armie of the Pagans in Hungarie: the battlle betwixe the Christians and the Moores in Barberie, and howe Almidor the blacke King of Moroco was sodden to death in a cauldrone of boyling leade and brimstone.

THE irefull Pagans after they had leuied their Martiall forces both by Sea and Land, repaired to their generall place of meeting, there to conclude of the vtter confusion of Christendome: for no sooner could Winter withdrawe his chill frosts from the earth, and *Flora* tooke possession of hys place: but the Kingdome of *Hungarie* suffered excessiue pennurie through the numberles Armies of the accursed Infidels, beeing their appointed place of meeting: For though *Hungarie* of all other Countries both in *Affrica* and *Asia*, then was the richest, and plentifullest of victuals to mainetaine a Campe of men: yet was it mightely ouerprest & greatly burthened with multitudes: not onely with want of necessaries to releeue souldiers, but with extreame crueltie of those bloody minded miscreants, that through a ciuell discorde which hapned amongst them, about the election of a Generall, they conuerted their vnitie to[1] a most inhumane slaughter, and their triumphant victorie to a dismall bloody Tragedy: For no sooner ariued their Legions vpon the plaines of *Algernos* beeing in length and breadth one and twentie Leagues: but the King of *Hungarie* caused their muster Rolles to bee publikely read, & iustly numbred in the hearing of the Pagan Knights, which in this maner was proclaimed through the Campe.

First be it knowne vnto all Nations that fights in the quarrell of *Affrica* and *Asia* vnder the conduct of our three great Gods, *Mahomet, Termigaunt,* and *Apollo*: what inuincible forces be now ariued in this renowned Kingdome of *Hungarie*, a Land Honoured through the worlde, not only for Armes: but curious buildings, and plentified with all manner of riches. First we haue from the Emperour of *Constantinople* two hundred thousand Turkes. From the Emperour of *Græcia* two hundred and fiftie thousand. From the Emperour of *Tartarie* a hundred threescore and three thousand. From the Soldan of *Persia* two hundred thousand. From the king of *Ierusalem* foure hundred thousand. Of *Moores* one hundred & twenty thousand. Of coleblacke *Negars* one hundred and fortie thousand. Of *Arabians* one hundred and sixtie thousand. Of *Babilonians* one hundred thirtie thousand and odde. Of *Armenians* one Hundred and fiftie Thousande. Of *Macedonians* two hundred and ten thousand. Of *Siracusians*[2] fifteene thousand six hundred. Of *Hungarians* three hundred and sixe thousand. Of *Sissillians* seauenteene thousand three hundred. Of *Scythians* one hundred and fiue thousand. Of *Parthians* ten thousand and three hundred. Of *Phrigians* seauen thousand and two hundred. Of *Ethiopians* sixtie thousand. Of *Thracians* eleauen[3] thousand: Likewise from the

---

[1] to] to, *1596*
[2] *Siracusians*] Saracusians *1596*
[3] eleauen] a eleauen *1596*

Prouinces of *Prester Iohn* three hundred thousand of vnconquered Knights, with manye other pettie Dominions and Dukedomes: whose numbers I omit for this time, lest that I shoulde seeme ouer tedious to the reader: But to conclude, such a Campe of Armed souldiers ariued in *Hungarie*, that might in one month haue destroyed Christendome, had not God defended them from those barbarous nations,[4] and by his inuincible power confounded the Pagans in their owne practises: For no sooner had the Harrolds proclaimed through the Campe what number of Nations ioyned their bandes together, but the souldiers fell at discention one with another about the election of a Generall: some vowed to follow none but the king of *Ierusalem*: some *Ptolomie* the Egiptian King: and some the Soldan of *Persia*, euerie one protesting either to perseuer in their own willes or to loose their liues in the same quarrell.

Thus in this manner parties were taken on all sides, not only by the meaner sort, but by leaders and commaunders of bandes: whereby the Kings[5] and Potentates, were forced to commit their willes to the souldiers pleasure. This ciuell broyle so discouraged the whole Armie, that manye with drew their forces, and presently marched homewards: As the King of *Moroco* with hys tawnie Moores and cole-blacke Negers: Likewise the Soldan of *Persia*: *Ptolomie* the Egiptian King: The Kinges of *Arabia* and *Ierusalem* euery one departed into their owne countries, cursing the time they attempted first so vaine an enterprize: The rest not minding to pocket vp abuse, fell from brauing boastes, to downe right blows, wherby grew such a sharp and bloody war, that it cost more souldiers liues, than the ciuell mutenie at the destruction of *Ierusalem*: which battaile by the irefull Pagans, continued without ceasing for the space of three monthes: In which Encounters: the murthered Infidels like scattered corne ouerspred the fields of *Hungarie*: the fruitfull valleyes lay drowned in purple gore: the fieldes of Corne consumed with flames of fire: their Townes and Citties ruinated with wasting warre: wherein the Fathers were sad witnesses of their Childrens slaughters, and the Sonnes beheld their Parents reuerent haires, more whiter than tryed siluer, besmeered with clodded blood: there might the Mothers see their harmelesse Babes borne vp and downe the streets vpon souldiers Lances: there might they see their silken ornamentes and riche attire in pooles of blood lye swimming vp and downe: there might they see the braines of honest Dames and pure Uirgins dasht against hard flintie stones: there might they see their Courts & Pallaces by souldiers burned to the ground: there might they see howe Councellers in their Scarlet gownes lay burning in the fire: there might they see how Kings & Queenes were arme in arme consumed to ashes: there might they beholde[6] and see howe melted gold in choaked sinkes lay euerie where: there might they see the bloodiest tragedies that euer eye beheld, and the wofulst newes that euer Christians eare heard tolde: In this long and bloody warre, one sucking child was not left aliue to report the story to insuing ages: No not a souldier to carry Armes throughout the Kingdome of *Hungaria*, so iustly was the vengeance of God throwne vpon the heads of these

---

[4] nations] nation *1596*
[5] Kings] Kingsis *1596*
[6] beholde] behode *1596*

misbeleeuing miscreants, that durst attempt to lift their handes against hys true
anoynted Nations: for no doubt but the inuincible Armie of the Pagans, had
ruinated the borders of *Europe,* had not the mightie hand of God with hys
vnspeakeable mercie, beene Christendomes defence, and confounded the Infidels
in their owne ciuell warres: which bloody and strange ouerthrow of those
vnchristian people, let vs for euer burie in the lake of obliuion, and perseuer in the
fortunate proceedinges of the seauen Champions of Christendome, who had entred
the borders of *Barberie,* before *Almidor* the blacke king of *Moroco* with hys
scattered Troupes of Moores and Negars returned from *Hungarie,* and by fire and
sword, had wasted many of his chiefest Townes and Fortes, whereby the Countrie
was much weakned, and the Commons compelled to sue for mercie to the
Champions hands: who bearing true Christian minds,[7] within their hearts continuall
pittie harboured, vouchsafed to graunt mercie to those that yeelded their liues to the
pleasure of the Christian Knights: But when *S. George* had intelligence of
Almidors approach with his weakned Troupes, presently prepared hys Souldiers in
readines to giue the Moores a bloody banquet: which was the next morning by
breake of day perfourmed to the high honour of Christendome: but the night before
the Moores knowing the countrie better than the Christians, got the aduantage both
of winde and Sunne: whereat Saint *George* being something displeased, but yet
nothing discouraged, imboldned hys souldiers[8] with many Heroicall speeches,
proffering them franklie the enemies spoyles, and so with the Sunnes vprising
entred battell, where the Moores fell before the Christians swords, as eares of corne
before the reapers sickle: During this conflict, the seauen Champions still in the
forefrunt of the battell, so aduenturously behaued themselues, that they slew more
Negars than a hundred of the brauest Knights in the Christian Armies: At last
Fortune intending to make saint *Georges* prowesse to shine brighter than the rest,
singled out the *Moroco* King, betwixt whom and the English Champion, was a
long & dangerous fight: But saint *George* so couragiouslye behaued him with his
trustie sword, that *Almidor* was constrained to yeeld to his mercie. The Armie of
the Moores seeing their King taken prisoner, presently would haue fled: but that
the Christians beeing the lighter of foote, ouertooke them, and made the greatest
slaughter that euer hapned in *Barberie.*

    Thus after the battell ended, and the ioyfull sound of victorie rung through the
Christian Armie, the souldiers furnished themselues with the enemies spoyles, and
martched by saint *Georges* direction to the Cittie of *Tripolie,* being then almost
vnpeopled through the late slaughter: In which Cittie after they had rested some
few dayes, and refreshed themselues with holsome food, the English Champion in
reuenge of his former proffered iniuries by the *Moroco* King, gaue hys seuere
sentence of death: First hee commaunded a brazen cauldron to bee filled with
boyling Lead and Brimstone: then *Almidor* to be brought to the place of death by
twelue of the Noblest Pieres in *Barberie,* therein to be consumed, flesh, blood, and
bone: which was duelie performed within seauen dayes following, the brazen
cauldron was erected by the appointment of saint *George,* directlie in the middle of

---

[7] minds,] minds *1596*
[8] souldiers] souldies *1596*

the chiefest Market place, vnder which a mightie hot fire continually burned, for the space of eight and fortie houres: whereby the boyling Lead and Brimstone seemed to sparckle like the fierie furnaces in hell, and the heate to exceede the burning Ouen at *Babilon*. Thus all thinges beeing no sooner prepared in a readines, & the Christian Champions present to behold the wofull spectakle; but the condemned Blackamore King came to the place of Execution, in a shirt of the finest *Indian* silk, his hands pinniond together with a chaine of gold, & his face couered with a Damske Scarfe, his attendants, & chiefe conducters, twelue *Moroco* Pieres, clad in Sable gownes of Taffetie, carrying[9] before him the wheele of fortune, with the picture of a Usurper climbing vp, with this Motto on his breast: *I will be king in spite of Fortune*: vpon the top of the wheele, the picture of a Monarke vaunting with this Motto on his breast: *I am a King in spite of Fortune*: Lastly on the other side of the Wheele, the picture or perfect image of a deposed Potentate, falling with hys head downewards, with this Motto on hys breast: *I haue beene a King so pleaseth Fortune*: which plainelie signified the chaunce of warre, and the constancie of destenie: hys guard was a thousand Christian souldiers, holding fortune in disdaine: after them attended a hundred of *Moroco* virgins in blacke ornaments, their haire bounde vp with siluer wiers, and couered with vales of black silke, signifiing the sorrow of their countrie for the losse of their Soueraigne. In this mournefull manner came the vnfortunate *Almidor* to the boyling Caulderne: which when he beheld, hys heart waxed cold, and his tongue deuoide of vtterance for a time: yet at last he brake foorth into these earnest protestations, proffering more for his life than the whole Kingdome of *Barberie* can performe.

Most mightie & inuincible Champion of Christendome (quoth he) let my life be ransomed, and thou shalt yearely receaue ten tunnes of tried gold, a hundred webs of wouen silke, the which our *Indian* maides shall sit and spinne with siluer wheeles: a hundred Argases of spices and refined suger, shal be yearely paid thee by our *Barberie* Marchants: a hundred waggons likewise richly laden with Pearle and Iasper stones, which by our cunning Lapidistes shall be yearelie chosen foorth and brought thee home to *England*, to make that blessed countrie the richest land within the Dominions of *Europe*: Likewise I will deliuer vp my Diadem, with all my Princely dignities, and in companie of these *Moroco* Lordes, like bridled Horses drawe thee daylie in a siluer Charriot vp and downe the sercled earth, til death giues end to our liues Pilgrimage: Therefore most admired Knight at Armes, let these salt teares that trickle from the Conduits of my eyes, obtaine one graunt of comfort at thy handes, for on my bended knees I beg for life, that neuer before this time did kneele to any mortall man.

Thou speakst in vaine (replyed saint *George*) it is not the treasures hidden in the deepest seas, nor all the golden mines of rich *America* that can redeeme thy life: thou knowest accursed Homicide, thy wicked practises in the Egyptian Court, where thou profferedst wrongfully to bereaue me of my life: Likewise through thy treachery, I endured a long imprisonment in *Persia*: where for seauen yeares I

---

[9] carrying] carring *1596*

dranke the Channell water, and suffizde my hunger with the breade of branne meale: My foode the loathsome fleshe of Rats and Mice, and my resting place a dismall dungeon, where neither sunne nor the chearefull light of heauen lent me comfort during my long continued misery: For which inhumane dealing and proffered iniuries, the heauens inforceth me to a speedy reuenge, which in this manner shall be accomplished. Thou seest the Engine prepared for thy death, this brazen Caldron fild with boyling lead and brimstone, wherein thy cursed body shall be speedily cast, and boyled till thy detested limbs bee consumed, to a watry substance, by this sparkling lickour: therefore prepare thy selfe to entertaine the violent stroake of death, and willingly byd all thy kingly dignities farewell: But yet I let thee vnderstand, that mercy harboreth in a Christians hart, and where mercy dwels there faults are forgiuen vppon some humble penetence, though thy trespasse deserues no pitty, but seuere punishment, yet vpon these considerations I will graunt thee liberty of life: First that thou wilt forsake thy false Gods *Termagaunt*, *Mahomet*, and *Apollo*: which be but the vayne imaginations of man: and beleeue in our true and euerliuing God, vnder whose banner we Christians haue taken in hande this long warre: Secondly thou shalt giue commandement, that all thy barbarous Nations be christened in the faith of Christ: Thirdly and lastly, that thy three Kingdomes of *Barbary*, *Moroco* & *India*, sweare true alleagance to all Christian Kings, and neuer to beare Armes, but in the true quarrell of Christ and his annoynted Nations. These things duly obserued, thy life shall be preserued, and thy liberty obtayned, otherwise looke for no mercy, but a speedy and most tyrrible death.

These wordes more displeased the vnchristian King of *Moroco*, than the sentence of his condemnation, and in these briefe speeches set downe his resolution.

Great Potentate of *Europe* (replied *Almidor*) by whose mightines fortune sits fettered in the chaines of power, my golden Diadem and regall Scepter by constraint I must deliuer vp: but before I forsake my countrie Gods, I will indure a hundred deathes, and before my conscience be reformed to a new faith, the earth shall be no earth, the sea no sea, nor the heauen no heauen. Thinkest thou now proud Christian, by thy threatned tormentes to make mee forget my creator, and beleeue in thy false God, which was but the sonne of a Carpenter, and bacely borne vnder an Oxe stall: No, no, accursed Christians, you ofspringes of *Cayne*, you generations of *Iesmaell*, you seede of Uipers, and accursed through the world, looke for a speedie shower of vengeance to raine from heauen vppon your wicked Nations, your bloodie practises hath pearst the Battlements of *Ioue*, and your tyrranies beaten open the gates of mightie *Mahomet*, who hath prouided whips of burning wier to scourge you for your cruelties, proffered against his blessed worshippers, and now with this deadlie curse I bid you all farewell: the plagues of *Egipt* light vpon your kingdomes: the curse of *Cayne* vpon your children the famine of *Ierusalem* vpon your friends, and the miserie of *Oedipus* vppon your selues.

This wicked resolution and balefull curse beeing no sooner ended by the desperate minded *Almidor*, but the impatience of saint *George* was so highly mooued, that he gaue present commandement to the appointed Executioners, to cast him into the boyling cauldron, which incontinentlie they performed to the terror of all the beholders: to behold this wofull spectakle the Battlements of Temples were so thronged with people, the houses couered with women & children, and the streetes filled with Armed Souldiers, that it was a woonder to beholde: amongst which multitudes there were some perticular persons, that at the sight of *Almidors* death fell downe and broake their neckes: But the generall number, as well of Pagans as Christians, cryed with chearefull voyces, Honour and victory followe saint *George* of England, for he hath redeemed Barbary from a miserable seruitude. Which ioyfull hearing so delighted the seauen Champions of Christendome, that they caused the Conduits to runne with wine, the streets to be beautefied with bonefiers, and a sumptuous banquet to be proclaimed through the Citty, which after continued for the space of seauen dayes, in more magnificent Royaltie, than the banquet at Babilon, when the Macedonian Monarke returned from the worlds Conquest

The Champions liberality procured such faithfull loue in the harts of the *Moroco* Pieres, that with a generall consent, they chose saint *George* for theyr lawfull King: where after they had inuested him in the Princely seate of the *Moroco* Potentates, they set the Crown vpon his head, and after presented him with an imperious Pall which the Kings of Barbary vsually wore vppon their Coronation day, protesting to forsake theyr prophane Religion, and bee christened in the fayth of Christ.

This promised conuertion of the Infidels, more delighted the English Champion, than to haue the whole worlds honour at commaund, for it was the chiefeest poynt of his Knightly oath to aduaunce the faith of Christe and to inlarge the boundes of Christendome: after his Coronation was solemlie performed, the other six Champions conducted him to a Princely Pallace, where he tooke the true alegance of the *Moroco* Lordes by plighted oath to bee true to hys Crowne: after this he established Christian lawes, to the benefit of the whole countrie: then he commaunded al the ceremonious rites of *Mahomet* to be trodden vnder foote, & the true Gospell of Christ to be preached: likewise he caused all that did remaine in *Barberie* to be Christned in the new faith: But these obseruations continued but a time as[10] hereafter shall be discoursed at large: For fame not intending to let the worthie Champions long to remaine in the idle bowers of peace: but summoned them to perseuer in their Noble atchiuements; and to muster vp a new their souldiers, whose Armour, canckered ease had almost staind with rust: therefore saint *George* committed the gouernment of hys countrie, to foure of the principall Peares of *Moroco*, and martched towardes the Countrie of *Egipt*, where liued trecherous *Ptolomie*, the Father of hys beloued Lady *Sabra*, whome hee had left in the Kingdome of *England*: In which iournie and happie ariuall in *Egipt*, we will leaue the seauen Champions for a time, and speake of the faithles Infidels in *Barberie*, after the departure of the Christians, whose former Honours they slightly regarded: For no sooner had saint *George* with hys martiall Troupes bidden their countrie adue, but the faithles Moores reconciled themselues to their former Gods,

---

[10] as] as shall *1596*

and purposed a speedie reuenge for the death of *Almidor*, against all Christians that remained within the limmets of that Heathen Nation: For there were many souldiers wounded in the late battaile: Likewise a number oppressed with sicknes, had the Christian Champions left behinde for their better recoueries: vppon whome the barberous Moores committed their first tyrranie: for they caused the distressed souldiers to be drawen vpon slids to the outermost part of the Cittie, and there put them into a large and old Monestarie, which they presently set on fire, and most inhumanely burned the Christian souldiers, and after conuerted the place into a filthie leastall: many women and succourles children they dragged vp and downe the streetes, till their braines were dasht against the stones, and the blood had couered the earth with a purple hue: Many other cruelties were committed by the wicked Infidels against the distressed Christians, which I purpose to passe ouer, and wholie discourse of the wofull and bloody murther of an English Marchant and hys wife in the same Cittie of *Tripolie*, the report whereof may force the merciles Tygers to relent, and those eyes to shed a spring of teares that neuer wept before. The bloodie minded Negars violating both oath and promise before plighted to saint *George*: by violence set vppon the Marchants house, where first they made a massaker of his seruants, and before hys face cast their dead bodies to hunger starued Dogges: then comming to the Marchant, they bound him fast with hempen cordes to the strongest post in his house, and after tooke hys children, beeing seauen of the goodliest boyes, that euer nature framed, and likewise tied round about him: Then one of the Moores beeing crueller than the rest, proffered to deflowre the Marchants wife before hys face: but she in chastetie like *Camma*, chose rather an honourable death than an infamous life, spit in the Negars face, and most bitterly reuiled him, yeelding neyther to hys force, nor hys bloodie threates: but snatching a knife from hys girdle, vowed to sheath it in her bosome before she would loose that precious Gemme of honour, that once beeing gone cannot bee recouered for all the worldes treasure.

This resolution of the English Marchants wife, caused the sterne Negars to exceede in crueltie: but the principall of that wicked companie, beeing a bloody and merciles Tyrant, stabbed one of the sillie Children before the mothers face.

Now stubborne Dame (quoth he) wilt thou yeeld to my desires, and preserue the liues of thy other sixe Children, otherwise shalt thou beholde them butchered in the same manner. To sell my honour for the liues of my Children (replied shee) will be an offence to God, and a continuall corrasiue to my husbands heart if we liue together: Therefore accursed monsters prosecute your tyrranie: It is not all your threates and bloodie dealinges shall conuert my chaste minde, nor once inforce my thoughtes to giue any consent thereunto.

These wordes beeing no sooner ended, but the lustfull Moore tooke an other of her children and stabed before hir husbands face, thincking therby to force the Marchant to intreate his wife to consent to the wicked Negars determinations, but he beeing as resolute as his vertuous wife spake[11] in this manner.

---

[11] spake] (spake *1596*

O you cursed blacke Dogges of *Barberie*! more worse in quallitie than the bloody Tygers, and more merciles then the wicked Cannibals: thinke you that the murther of our children shall inforce our hearts to yeelde to your lustful desiers: No no, perseuer in your tyrranies: if I had a hundred children, twice the number of King *Priams*, yet would I loose them all, before I will indure to see my wiues dishonor: children may be gotten agayne but hir honor neuer recoured.

These words pricked the Negars to the gall and caused them to commit the wickedst deede that euer was practised vnder the celestiall Globe of heauen: First they sheathed there Poniards in the breastes of all the Marchantes children, whose guiltles blood staynd all the chamber with a crimson colour, then with there Fauchions did they cut there bodies all in sunder, and caused seauen Pies to be made of there flesh, and after serued in a banquet to there wofull Parents, whome the merciles Moores set at a square table, the Marchant placed directly opposite against his wife, wher they were constrained either to feede vpon there owne children, or starue for want of other sustenance.

This wofull spectakle stroke such a griefe into the English Marchants heart, that hee could scarce indure to speake for weeping: hys wife when shee beheld the heades of her louelie sonnes lying vpon the table, as it were looking to heauen for reuenge, breathed forth this woful dying lamentation.

O sillie Babes, I would you had beene strangled in my wombe at your first conception: then should not these accursed Infidels haue triumpht thus in your vnhappie Tragedies: Nor your vnfortunate Parentes beheld this luckles day: whereon I pray that neuer Sunne may shine againe, but bee accounted an ominous day throughout the whole earth, for heauen I hope (poore Babes) will raigne a showre of vengeance on their heades that hath caused this your vntimelie death, and with this praier I bid the worlde farewell.

At which wordes her griefe so exceeded the boundes of reason, that it stayed the passage of her speech: whereby she was forced to yeeld her soule to the Paradice of peace. Shee beeing no sooner dead but the sorrowfull Marchant likewise biterly exclaimed against the iniustice of Fortune, and the tyrranie of the barbarous Moores, accounting his destenie more haples than the Thracian Kinges, that buried his children in hys owne Bowels: and the cruelties of the Infidels to exceed the tyrranie of *Nero*, that caused hys Mothers wombe to be opened, that hee might beholde the place of hys creation: but when the Marchant had sufficiently bewailed the murther of hys children, the death of his wife, and hys owne miserie, he yeelded hys soule likewise to the furious stroke of death: The end of whose long languishments when the wicked Moores had intelligence, they caused their dead bodies to be carried to the top of a high mountaine, and there left for the pray of hungrie Rauens: But God most miraculously preserued them both from the furie of Foules, and the violence of rauenous beasts, for the sun consumed their bodies like the morninges dew, and by the wonderfull workemanship of heauen, in the same place sprung a bower of Roses, to signifie the vnspotted honour of the Marchant and his vertuous wife: which miracle wee leaue to the woonder of the Moores, and speake of the Christian Champions proceedinges, that by this time were ariued in the Kingdome of Egipt.

CHAP. XV.

How the Christians ariued in Egipt, and what hapned to them there: the Tragedie of the lustfull Earle of Couentrie: how Sabra was bound to a stake to be burned, & how Saint George redeemed her: lastly how the Egiptian king cast himselfe from the toppe of a Tower and broake hys necke.

DUring the time of the bloodie murther wrought by the barbarous Moores vpon the English Marchant and hys Wife, with his seauen Children as you hearde in the former Chapter, the Champions of Christendome ariued vppon the Territories of *Egipt*, where they supposed to haue met with Legions of Armed Souldiers, and to haue aduentured their liues vpon the chaunce of Warre: but all things fell out contrarie to their expectations, for they founde the Gates of euerie Cittie set open, and euerie Uillage and Towne vnpeopled: for the Commons[1] at the report of the Christians ariuall, secretly hid their treasure in the Caues of the earth, in deepe Welles, and such like obscure places, and a generall feare and extreame terrour assailed the Egiptians: as well the Pieres of the Land, as the simple countrie people: Many fled into woods and wildernesses, & closelie hid themselues in hollow trees: Many digged caues in the ground, where they thought best to remaine in safetie, and many fled to high mountaines, where they long time liued in great extreamity, feeding vppon the grasse of the ground: So greatly the Egiptians feared the Armie of Christians, that they expected nothing but the ruine of their owne countrie, with the losse of their owne liues, and the murther of their wiues and Children.

But to speake of the Christian Champions: who finding the countrie desolate of people, suspected some deepe pollicie of the Egiptians, thinking them to haue mustered their generall forces to bid them battaile: therefore Saint *George* gaue commaundement through the whole Campe, that not a man vpon paine of death should breake his ranke, but martch aduisedlie with three weapons ready prest to enter battaile, as though the enemie had directly plast themselues opposite against them: which speciall charge the Christian Souldiers dulie obserued, looking neyther after the wealth of Citties, nor the spoyle of Uillages, but circumspectly martched according to their leaders directions, along the Countrie of *Egipt*, till they approached the sight of King *Ptolomies* Court: which when the noble Champion of *England* beheld, in this manner incouraged hee hys followers.

Behold (saide hee) you inuincible Captaines of Christendome yonder cursed Towers where wicked *Ptolomie* keepes hys Court, those Battlements I say, were they as richlie built as great Piramides of *Greece*, yet shoulde they be subuerted and laid as leuell with the ground, as the Cittie of *Carthage*: there hath that accursed *Ptolomie* hys residence, that for preseruing his Daughter from the burning Dragon, trecherouslie sent me into *Persia*, where for seauen yeares I liued in great extreamitie[2] in a dismall dungeon, where the Sunne did neuer lend me light, nor the

---

[1] Commons] Commos *1596*

[2] extreamitie] extreamie *1596*

companie of people comfort: In reuenge wherof, my hart shall neuer rest in quiet till I see the buildinges of his Pallace set on fire, and conuerted into a place of desolation, like to the glorious Cittie in *Phrigia*, nowe ouerspread with stincking weedes and loathsome puddles: Therefore let all[3] Christian Souldiers, that fights vnder the banner of Christendome, and all that loues *George* of *England* your chosen Generall, draw forth their warlike weapons, and like the angry *Greekes* ouerturne these glistring Battlements, leaue not one stone vpon another, but lay it as leuell with the ground, as the haruest reapers doe the fields of ripened corne: let your wrathfull furies fall vppon these Towers like droppes of Aprill showers, or like a storme of winters haile, that it may be bruted through the world, what lustful vengeance did light vpon the pride of *Egipt*: Leaue not (I say) as you loue your Generall, when you haue subuerted the Pallace not one man aliue, no not a sucking babe, but let them suffer vengeance for the wickednes of their King. This is my decree braue Knights of Christendome: therefore march forward, Heauen and Fortune bee your good speede.

At which wordes the souldiers gaue a generall shoute in signe of their willing mindes. Then began the silken streamers to flourish in the aire, the Drums chearefully to sound forward, the siluer Trumpets recorded ecchoes of victorie, the barbed Steedes grew proude of this attempt, & would stand vpon no ground, but leapt and daunst with as much courage as did *Bucephalus* the horse of Macedonian *Alexander* alwaies before any notable victorie, yea euery thinge gaue an euident signe of good successe, as well sensles things as liuing creatures.

With this resolution martched the Christians, purposing the vtter confusion of the Egiptians, and the wofull ruine and destruction of *Ptolomies* sumptuous Pallace: but when the Souldiers approached the gates with wrathfull weapons, ready to assault, there came pacing out thereat the Egiptian King, with all the chiefest of his Nobles attired in blacke and mournefull ornaments, bearing in their hands Oliue branches: next them the brauest souldiers in *Egipt*, bearing in their handes breken weapons, shiuered Launces, and torne Auncients: Likewise followed thousands of women & children, with Lawrell wreathes about their heads, & in their handes Oliue braunches crying for mercie to the Christians, that they would not vtterlie destroy their declining countrie, but shew mercie to vnhappie *Egipt*. This vnexpected sight, or rather admirable woonder, caused saint *George* to sound retreate, and gaue commandement through the Christian Armie, to withhold their former vowed vengeance from the Egiptians, till hee vnderstoode what they required: which charge being giuen and duely[4] obserued, saint *George* with the other six Champions came together, and admitted the Egiptian King with their powers to their presence, who in this manner began to speake for hys countrie.

You vnconquered Knights of Christendome, whose worthie victories & Noble atchiuements, the whole worlde admires, let him that neuer kneeled to any man till nowe, and in former times disdained to humble himselfe to the greatest Potentate on the earth: Let him I say, the most vnfortunate wretch aliue craue mercie, not for my selfe, but for my countrie: my Commons blood wil be required at my hands:

---

[3] all] a- *(at end of line) 1596*
[4] duely] suely *1596*

our murthered Infants will call to heauen for reuenge, and our slaughtered Widdowes cryes senke downe to hel for reuenge: so will the vengeaunce of heauen light vppon my soule, and the curse of hel vpon my head: renowned Champions of *England*, vnder whose custodie my deare daughter is kept, euen for the loue of her be mercifull to *Egipt*: The former wronges I proffered thee, when I sent thee like a guiltles Lamb into *Persia* was contrarie to my will: For I was incenst by the flatterie of that accursed Blackamoore King: whose soule for euermore bee scourged with whips of wier, and plagued with the punishment of *Tantalus* in hell: If my life will serue for a iust reuenge, here is my naked breast: let my hart blood staine some Christians sword, that you may beare the bloody witnes of my death into Christendome or let me be torne into a thousand pieces, by mad vntamed Steeds, as was *Hippolitus* the Son of *Theseus* in hys charmed Charriot.

Most mightie controulers of the worlde, commaund the dearest thinges in *Egipt*, they be at your pleasures, we will forsake our Gods, and beleeue in that God which you commonly adore, for he is the true and liuing God, ours false & hatefull in the sight of heauen.

This penitent lamentation of the Egiptian King caused the Christian Champions to relent, but especially Saint *George*: who hauing a hart beautified with the welspring of pittie, not onely graunted mercie to the whole Country, but vouchsafed *Ptolomie* libertie of life, vppon condition that he would performe what he had promised: which was to forsake hys false gods, & beleeue in our true God, Christ Iesus.

This kindenes of saint *George* almost rauished *Ptolomie* with ioy, and the whole land, both Pieres and Commons more reioyced at the friendshippe of the Christians, than if they had beene made Lordes of the westerne world. The newes of this happie vnitie, was bruted into all the partes of *Egipt*: whereby the commons that before fled for feare into woods and wildernesses, dens and caues, hils and mountaines, returned ioyfully to their own dwellings, and caused bonefires to be made in euerie Cittie, Towne, & Village, the Bels of *Egipt* rung day and night, for the space of three monthes: in euerie place was seene banquetting, dauncing and masking, sorrow was banished, warres forgotten, and peace proclaimed.

The King at his owne charges ordained a sumptuous & costlie banquet for the Christian Champions, wherein for bountie it exceeded that which the *Troianes* made when *Paris* returned from *Greece* with the conquest of *Menalaus* Queene. The banquetting house was built with Cipresse wood, couered with the purest Adamant stone: so that neither steele nor bace Iron could come therein, but it was presently drawen to the top of the rooffe: as for the varietie of seruices, which graced forth the banquet, it were too tedious to repeate: but to be briefe, what both the Land & Sea could afford were there present. The seruittors that attended the Champions at the banquet, were attired in dammaske vestments wrought with the purest silke the *Indian* virgins spin vpon their siluer wheeles: at euerie course the seruitors brought in, a Consort of Egiptian Ladies vppon their Iuorie Lutes, strayned forth such admired Harmonie, that it surpassed *Arions* musicke, which when hee was cast into the Sea, caused the Dolphins to bring him safe on the shore: or the sweetnes of *Orpheus* siluer Harpe, which made both stones and trees to daunce, or the mellodie of *Apollos* inspiring musicke, when he descended from heauen for the loue of *Daphne*.

These pleasures so rauished the Christian Champions, that they forgot the sound of warlike Drummes that were wont to call them forth to bloody battailes: But these delightes continued but a short time, for there ariued a knight from *England* that brought such vnexspected newes to saint *George*, which chaunged his ioyes into extreame sorrowe, for after this manner began the messenger to tell hys woful tale.

Faire *Englands* Champion (said he) in steede of Armes get Swallowes winges and flye to *England*, if euer thou wilt see thy beloued Lady, for she is iudged to bee burned at a stake for murthering the Earle of *Couentrie*: whose lustfull desires would haue stayned her honour with infamie, and made her the scorne of vertuous women: Yet this mercie is graunted by the King of *England*, that if within foure and twenty months a Champion may be found, that for her sake will venture his life, and if it be his happie fortune to ouercome the challenger of her death, she shall liue: But if it be his fatall destenie to be conquered, then must she suffer the heauie iudgement before pronounced: therefore as you loue the life of your chaste and beloued Ladie, haste into *England*, delay no time, for delay is dangerous, & her life in hazard to be lost.

This wofull discourse[5] stroke such a terror to *S. Georges* hart, likewise to the Egyptian King her father, that for a time they stood gazing one in anothers face, as though they had bin distraught of their wits, not able to speak one word, but at last saint *George* recouered his former sences, and breathed forth this sorrowfull lamentation.

O England, vnkinde England, haue I aduentured my life in thy defence, and for thy safety haue layne in the fields of *Mars* buckled in my Armour, in many a partching summers day, and many a freezing winters night, when you haue taken your quiet sleepes in beds of Downe: and will you repay me with this discurtesie, or rather vndeserued wrong, to adiudge her spotles body to consuming fier: whose blood if it be spilt before I come, I vowe neuer to draw my trusty sword in *Englands* quarrell more, nor neuer account my selfe her Champion, but I will rend my warlike colours into a thousand peeces, the which I weare vpon my Burgonet (I meane the crimson Crosse of England) and wander vnknowne Countries, obscurely from the sight of any Christians eye: Is it possible that England is so ingratefull to her friend? Can that renowned Country harbour such a lustfull monster, to seeke to dishonour her, within whose hart the fountaine of vertue springes? Or can that Noble Citty, the Nurse and Mother of my life, entertayne so vile an Homeside, that will offer violence to her, whose chastety and true honour hath caused tamelesse Lyons to sleepe in her lap?

In this sorrowfull manner wearied saint *George* the time away, vntill the Egiptian King, whose sorrowes being as great as his, put him from his complaintes, and requested the English Knight to tell the true discourse of *Sabraes* proffered

---

[5] discourse] disourse *1596*

violence, and how she murthered the lustfull Earle of Couentry, to whom after a
bitter sigh or two, the wofull messenger replyed in this manner.

Most Noble Princes and Potentates of the earth, prepare your eares to entertaine
the wofulst tale, that euer English Knight discourst, and your eyes to weepe a sea
of brackish teares: I would I had no tongue to tell it, nor hart to remember it. But
seeing I am compelled through the loue and duty I owe to the Noble Champions of
Christendome to expresse it, then thus it was.

It was the fortune, nay I may say vnhappie destenie of your beloued Lady:
vppon an Euening when the Sunne had almost lodged in the West, to walke
without the wals of *Couentrie* to take the pleasures of the sweet fields, and
flowring meadowes, which *Flora* had beautefied in a Sommers liuerie: but as she
walked vp and downe, sometimes taking pleasure to heare the mellodie of chirping
Birdes, how they strained their siluer notes: other times taking delight to see howe
nature had couered both hilles and dales with sundrie sortes of Flowers: then
walking to see the Christal running Riuers, the murmuring Musicke of whose
streames exceeded the rest for pleasure: But she (kinde Ladie) delighting her selfe
by the Riuers side, a sodaine and strange alteration troubled her minde: for the
Chayne of gold that shee did weare about her necke presently chaunged colour,
from a yellow burnisht brightnes to a dimme palenes: her Ringes flew from her
fingers, and from her nose fell three drops of blood: whereat her hart began to
throb, her eares to glow, and euerie ioynt to tremble with feare. This strange
accident caused her speedilie to haste homeward: but by the way she met the noble
Earle of *Couentrie*, walking at that time to take the pleasure of the Eueninges Ayre,
with such a traine of worthie Gentlemen, as though he had beene the greatest Piere
in all England: whose sight when shee behelde a farre off, her heart beganne to
misgiue, thinking that Fortune had alotted those Gentlemen to proffer her some
iniurie: So that vppon her cheekes feare had set a vermillion dye, whereby her
beautie grew admirable: which when the Earle beheld hee was rauished therewith,
and deemed her the excellentst[6] creature that euer nature had framed: their meeting
was silent, shee shewed the humilitie of a vertuous Lady and he the curtesie of a
kinde Gentleman, shee departed homewardes, and he into the fields, shee thinking
all danger past, but he practised in his mind her vtter ruine & downefall: for the
dart of loue had shot from her beauteous cheekes into his heart, not true loue, but
lust: so that nothing might quench his desire, but the conquest of her chastetie, such
extreame passion bewitched his minde, that hee caused hys seruants euery one to
depart, and then like a discontented man he wandred vp and downe the fieldes,
beating in hys minde a thousand sundrie waies how to obtaine hys desire, for
without he inioyed her loue, he was likelie to liue in endles languishment: but at
last hee sighed out this passion of loue.

O you immortall powers, why haue you transported her from an earthly Lady, to
a heauenly Angell: *Sabra* is no worldly creature, but a diuine substance, her
beautie is a staine vnto the Queene of loue, and her countenance of more maiestie
than *Iunos* grace: her twinckling eyes, that glister like to flaming starres, and her

---

[6] excellentst] excellents *1596*

beauteous cheekes more pleasant than Roses dipt in milke, hath pearst my hart with the prickes of loue, and her loue I will enioy or loose my life: O but there is a barre which thwartes kinde affections, and hinders my desires: Saint *George* I meane her true and lawfull husband, the honour of whose bed she will not violate for all the Kingdomes in the world: Tush faint harted foole that I am, *Sabra* is beautefull, and therefore to be tempted: shee is wise, and therefore easie to bee woone: Her husband he is sporting in the fields of *Mars*, then why may not shee take pleasure in the Chamber of *Venus*: I wil vse many flattering gloses, many kind speeches, & many sweete embrases, but I will croppe that budde, which but to taste, I would giue my whole landes and reuenewes: I will tell her saint *George* is a wanderer, and one that neuer will returne: where as I am a mighty Piere in England, and one that can accomplish what so euer shee desiers: Many other circumstances this lustfull Earle vsed, to flatter himselfe in his vayne conceite. At last the scouling night with pitchy clowdes beganne to ouerspread the brightsome heauens, wherby he was forced to repayre homewards, and to smother vp his loue in silence, no quiete sleepe that night could enter in his eye, but fond and restles dreames, sometimes he thought hee had his louely Mistresse in his Armes, dallying like the *Paphian* Queene vpon her Minnions knee, but presently awaking, he found it but a glyding shadowe, which added newe griefe to his louesicke passions: then by and by hee thought he sawe howe the wrathfull Champion with dreadfull bloody Fauchion, came to reuenge his Ladies rauishment, whereat the troubled Earle started from his bed, and with lowde voyce cryed to his Chamberlayne for helpe, and howe saint *George* was come to murther him: which sodaine outcry not onely awaked the Chamberlayne but the whole house: which generally came to beare him company, they set vp Camphire Tapors to giue light, and made him Musicke to comfort him, and to driue all fonde fancies from his minde: but no sooner ceased the Musicke, but he fell into his former cogitations, pondering in his minde, which way he might obtaine his purpose, whereat a dismall night Rauen beat her winges against his Chamber window, and with a harsh voyce, gaue him warning of a bad successe: then presently began the Tapors to burne blue as though a troope of ghastly spirits did encompasse his lodging, which was an euident signe, that some straunge and vnhappy murther would shortly follow: All which coulde nothing withdrawe the lustfull Earle from his wicked enterprise, nor conuert his minde from the spoyle of so sweete a Lady. In this manner spent he the night away, till the Sunnes bright countenance summoned him from his restlesse bed, from whence beeing no sooner risen, but he sent for the Steward of his house, and gaue him a charge to prouide a most sumptuous and costly banquet, for he intended to inuite thereunto all the principall Ladyes in Couentry: what bountefull cheare was prouided, I thinke it needles to repeat, but to be short, at the time and houre appoynted the inuited Ladies repayred: the banquet was brought in by the Earles seruants, and placed vppon the table by the Earle himselfe: who after manie welcomes giuen, began thus to moue the Ladies delight.

I thinke my house most highlie honoured (said hee) that you haue vouchsafed to grace it with your presence: for mee thinkes you beautefie my hall, as the twinckling starres beautefie the vale of heauen: but amongst the number of you all you haue a *Cinthia*, a glistring siluer Moone, that for brightnes exceedeth all the rest: for she is fairer than the Queene of *Cipresse*: louelier than *Dido* when *Cupid* sate vppon her knee, wiser than the Prophetesse of *Troy*: Of personage more comlier than the *Græcian* Dame, and of more Maiestie than the Queene of heauen: so that all the Muses with their Iuorie pens, may write eternallie, and yet not sufficiently discribe her excellent ornaments of nature. This commendation caused a generall smile of the Ladies, & made them looke one vpon another whome it should bee: Many other Courtlike discourses pronounced the Earle, to moue the Ladies delight, till the banquet ended: which beeing finished, there came in certaine Gentlemen, by the Earles appointment with most excellent Musicke: other some that daunced most curiously, with as much Maiestie as *Paris* in the *Græcian* Court: At last the Earle requested one of them to choose out hys beloued Mistris, and lead her some stately Caranta: likewise requesting that none would be offended what Lady soeuer hee did affect to grace with that Courtly pastime: at which request all of them were silent, and silence is commonly a signe of consentment: therefore hee imboldned himselfe the more, to make his desires knowne to the beholders: then with exceeding curtesie and great humilitie, he kissed the beauteous hand of *Sabra*, who with a blushing countenance and bashfull looke accepted his curtesie, and like a kinde Lady disdained not to daunce with him: So when the Musicians strained forth their inspiring mellodie, the lustfull Earle lead her the first course about the Hall, in as great Maiestie as *Mauors* did the Queene of *Paphos* to gayne her loue, and shee followed with as much grace, as if the Queene of pleasure had beene present to behold their Courtly delights: and so when the first course was ended, he found a fit opportunitie to vnfold hys secret loue, and reueale vnto the Lady his exstreame passion of minde, which were in these speeches expressed.

Most Diuine and Piereles Paragon (said he) thou onlie wonder of the world, for beautie and excellent ornaments of nature: know that thy two twinckling eyes that shine more brighter than the lightnes of heauen, beeing the true Darts of loue, hath pearced to my heart, and those thy Crimson cheekes as louely as *Auroraes* countenance, when shee drawes the Curtaines of her purple bed to entertaine her wandring Louer: those cheekes I say hath wounded me with loue, therefore except thou graunt mee kinde comfort, I am like to spend the remnant of my life in sorrowe, care, and discontent: I blush to speake what I desire, because I haue setled my loue where it is vnlawfull, in a bosome where Kings may sleepe and surfet with delight: thy breast I meane my most diuine Mistres, for there my heart is kept a prisoner, beautie is the keeper, and loue the key, my ransome is a constant minde: thou art my *Venus*, I will be thy *Mars*: thou art my *Hellen*, and I wil be thy *Paris*: thou art my *Hyren*, I will be thy *Mahomet*: thou art my *Cressida*, I will be thy *Troylus*: thou art my loue, and I will be thy Parramour: Admit thy Lord and Husband be a liue, yet hath he most vnkindely left thee to spend thy young yeares in sollitarie widdowhood: he is vnconstant like *Aeneas*, and thou more haples than *Dido*: hee martcheth vp & downe the world in his glistring Armour, & neuer doth intend to returne: he abandoneth thy presence, & lieth sporting in strange Ladies laps: therefore deare *Sabra* liue not to consume thy youth in singlenes, for age will ouertake thee too soone and conuert thy beautie to wrinckled frownes.

To which wordes *Sabra* woulde haue presently made answere, but that the musicke called them to daunce the second course, which being ended she replied in this manner.

My Noble Lord (said she) for our bounteous banquet & curteous entertainment, I giue the humble thankes of a poore Ladie: but for your sute and vnlawfull desire, I doo detest as much as the sight of a Crokadile, and your flattering glozes I esteeme as much, as doth the *Ocean* of a drisling shower of raine: your Sirens songes shall neuer intice me to listen to your fond requests: but I will like *Vlisses* stop my eares, & burie all your flattering inticementes in the lakes of forgetfulnes: Thinke you that I will staine his marriage bed with the least spot of infamie, that wil not proffer me one thought of wrong for all the treasures of the wealthie seas: therefore the gorgeous sunne shall loose his light by day, the siluer Moone by night, the skyes shall fall, the earth shall sinke, and euerie thing shall chaunge from his kinde and nature, before I falsefie my faith, or prooue disloyall to my beloued *George*: attempt no more my Noble Lord to batter the fortresse of my good name, with the Gunshot of your flatterie, nor seeke to staine my honour with your lustfull desires. What if my Lord and Husband proue disloyal, and choose out other loues in forraine Lands: yet will I proue as constant to him, as did *Penelope* to her *Vlisses*: and if it bee hys pleasure neuer to returne, but spend hys dayes amongst straunge Ladies, then will I liue in single solitarines like to the Turtle Doue, when shee hath lost her mate, abandoning all companie, or as the mournefull Swan that swimmes vpon *Mœanders* siluer streames, where she recordes her dying tunes to raging billowes:[7] so will I spend away my lingring dayes in griefe and die.

This resolution of the vertuous Ladie daunted so the Earle, that he stoode like a sensles image gazing at the Sun, not knowing how to replie, but yet when they had daunced the third course, he began a new to assault her vnspotted chastetie in these tearmes.

Why my deare mistresse, haue you a heart more harde than Flint, that the teares of my true loue can neuer molefie? can you behold him plead for grace that hath beene sude vnto by many worthie Dames? I am a man that can commaund whole countries: yet can I not command thy stubburne heart to yeeld. Diuine *Sabra* if thou wilt graunt me loue, and yeelde to my desier: Ile haue thee clad in silken Robes and damaske Uestures, imbost with *Indian* Pearles and rich refined gold, perfumed with Camphier,[8] Bisse, and *Syrrian* sweete perfumes: by day a hundred Uirgins like to *Thetis* tripping on the siluer sands, shall euermore attend thy person: by night a hundred Euenukes with their strained Instruments shall bring thy sences in a golden slumber: If this suffizeth not thy sweet content, I will prepare a sumptuous Charriot made of gold, wherein thou shalt be drawne by Sable spotted Steedes along the fieldes and gallant pastures adioyning to our Cittie walles, wheras the Euening ayre shall breath a coolenes far more sweeter than Balme vpon thy cheekes, and make thy beautie glister like the purple Pallace of *Hiperion*, when he leaues *Aurora* blushing in her bed, whereby the heauens and all the powers therein shall stand and woonder at thy beautie, and quite forget theyr vsuall

---

[7] billowes] bellowes *1596*
[8] Camphier,] Camphier *1596*

courses: All this my deare, diuine and daintie Mistresse, is at thy commaund, and more, so that I may enioy thy loue and fauour: which if I haue not, I will discontentedly end my life in woodes and desert places, Tygers and vntamed beasts shall be my chiefe companions.

These vaine promises and flattering inticements caused *Sabra* to blush with bashfulness, and to giue him this sharpe answere. Thinke you my Lorde with golden promises, to obtaine that precious Gem, the which I will not loose for *Europes* treasurie: henceforth be silent in that enterprise and neuer after this attempt to practise my dishonor: which if you doe, I vowe by heauen to make it knowne to euery one within the Cittie, and fill all places with rumors of thy wilfull lust: A Troupe of modest maidens I will procure to haunt thee vp and downe the streetes, and woonder at thee like an Owle, that neuer comes abroade but in the darkest nights: this I am resolued to doe and so farewell.

Thus departed *Sabra* with a frowning countenance, whereby the rest of the Ladies suspected that the Earle had attempted her dishonour by secret conference, but they all assuredly knew that she was as farre from yeelding to hys desires as is the aged man to become young againe, or the azurde firmament to be a place for siluaine beastes to inhabit: In such like imaginations they spent awaie the day, till the darke night caused them to breake off companie. The Earle smothering his griefe vnder a smiling countenance, till the Ladies were euerie one departed, whome hee courteously caused his seruants to conduct homewards with Torch lightes, because it began to be verie darke: After their departure he accursed his owne Fortune, and like a Lyon wanting foode, raged vp and downe his Chamber, filling euerie corner with bitter exclamations, rending hys garments from his backe, tearing his haire, beating hys breast, and vsing all the violence he could deuise against himselfe.

In this manner spent hee away the night, suffering no sleepe to close the windowes of his body: such a melancholy and extreame passion discontented his minde, that hee purposed to giue an end to hys sorrowes by some vntimelie death: So when the morning appeared hee made hys repaire to an Orcharde, where *Sabra* commonlie once a daie walked to take the Ayre. The place was verie melancholy, and farre from the noyse of people: where after hee had spent some certaine time in exclaiming against the vnkindnes of *Sabra*, he pulled his Poyniard from his backe, & prepared hys breast to entertaine the stroke of death: but before the pretended Tragedie, with his dagger hee ingraued these verses following vpon the barke of a walnut tree.

> *O hart more hard than bloody Tyger fell,*
> *O eares more deafe, than senceles troubled seas:*
> *O cruell foe, thy rigor doth excell,*
> *For thee I dye, thy anger to appease:*
> *But time will come when thou shalt finde me slaine,*
> *That thy repentance will increase thy payne.*

I here ingraue my will and testament,
That my sad griefe thou mayst behold and see:
How that my wofull heart is torne and rent,
And gorg'd with blooddy blade for loue of thee:
Whome thou disdayndst as now the end doth try,
That thus distrest doth suffer me to dye.

Oh Gods of loue if so there anie be,
And you of loue that feeles the deadly payne:
O Sabra thou that thus afflictest me,
Heare these my wordes, which from my hart I straine:
Ere that my corpes be quite bereaud of breath,
Let me declare the cause of this my death.

You mountaine Nimphes which in the desarts raigne,
Cease off your chase from sauage beasts a while:
Prepare to see a hart opprest with paine,
Addresse your eares to heare my dolefull stile:
No strength nor Arte, can worke me any weale,
Sith she vnkind and Tyrantlike doth deale.

You Fayrie Nimphes of louers much adorde,
And gracious Damsels which in Eueninges faire:
Your Closets leaue, with heauenlie beautie storde,
And on your shoulders spread your golden haire:
Record with me, that Sabra is vnkinde,
Within whose breast remaines a bloody minde.

Yee sauage Beares in Caues and Dens that lie,
Remaine in peace if you my sorrowes heare:
And be not mooued at my miserie,
Though too extreame my passions doo appeare:
England farewell and Couentrie adue,
But Sabra, heauen aboue still prosper you.

These verses beeing no sooner finished; and ingrauen about the Barke of the Walnut tree, but with a grisly looke and wrathfull countenance he lift vp hys hand, intending to strike the Poyniard vp to the hilts in his breast: but at that same instant hee beheld *Sabra* entring the Orchard to take her wonted walkes of pleasure, whose sight hindred his purpose, and caused other bloody cogitations to enter into his minde. The Furies did incense him to a wicked deede, the which my trembling tongue faints to report: for after she had walked to the furthest side of the melancholie Orchard, he rigerously ran vnto her with hys dagger drawne, and catching her about the slender waste, thus spitefullie threatned her.

Now stubburne Dame (quoth hee) will I obtaine my long desired purpose, and reuenge by violence thy former proude denials: First will I wrappe this dagger in thy lockes of haire, and nayle it fast into the ground: then wil I rauish thee by force and violence, and triumph in the conquest of thy chastetie: which beeing done, Ile cut thy tong out of thy mouth, because thou shalt not reueale nor discrie thy bloody rauisher: Likewise with this Poyniard will I chop off both thy hands: whereby thou shalt neither write with pen thy staine of honour, nor in Sampler sowe this proffered disgrace: Therefore except thou willingly yeelde to quench my desired loue with the pleasures of thy marriage bed, I will by force and violence inflict these vowed punishments vppon thy dellicate body: be not too resolute in thy denials, for if thou beest, the gorgious Sunne shall not glyde the compasse of an houre, before I obtaine my longe desired purpose, and there upon hee stepped to the Orcharde doore, and with all expedition locked it, and put the key into hys pocket: then returned hee like the hunger starued Wolfe to ceaze vppon the sillie Lambe, or like the chafed[9] Bore when he is wounded with the hunters Launce, came running to the helples Ladie, intending her present Rape, & foule dishonour: But shee thinking all hope of ayde or succour to bee voyde, fell into a dead sound, beeing not able to mooue for the space of a quarter of an hower: But yet at last hauing recouered her dead senses to their former vitall moouing, she began in this pittifull maner to defende her assayled chastetie, from the wicked Earle that stoode ouer her with hys bloodie dagger, threatning most cruelly her finall confusion.

My Lord of *Couentrie* (said shee with weeping teares, & kneeling vppon the bare ground) is vertue banished your brest? haue you a minde more tyrranous than the Tygers of *Hercania*, that nothing may suffice to satisfie your lustfull desires, but the staine of my honour, and the conquest of my chastetie? if it bee my beautie that hath intised you, I am content to haue it conuerted to a loathsome Leprosie, whereby to make mee odious in your eyes: If it bee my rich and costly garments that makes me beautifull, and so intangles you, henceforth I will attire my body in poore & simple aray, and for euermore dwell in countrie Caues and Cottages, so that I may preserue my chastetie vnspotted: If none of these may suffice to abate your tyrranous intent, but that your lust will make me times wonder, and a pointing stocke and scorne of vertuous Ladies: then will the heauens reuenge my wronges, to whome I will vncessantlie make my petitions: the birdes in the aire after their kinde will euermore exclaime against your wickednes: the siluane beastes that abide in woodes and deserts, will breath forth clamors of your wickednes: the creeping wormes that liue within the creuises of the earth, will giue dumbe signes and tokens of your wickednes, the running Riuers they will murmure at your wickednes, the woods and trees, both hearbes and flowers, with euerie sensles thing will sound some motions of your wickednessse: Returne, returne, my Noble Lord vnto your former vertues: bannish such fonde desires out of your minde: staine not the honor of your house with such blacke scandales and disgrace, beare this in minde before you doe attempt so vile a sinne. What became of *Hellens* rauishment, but the destruction of renowned *Troy*? What of *Romaine Lucresiaes*

---

[9] chafed] chased *1596*

Rape, but the banishment of *Tarquin*? and what of *Prognies* foule deflowrement
by her sisters husband, the lustfull King of *Thrace*, but the bloody banquet of his
young Sonne *Itis*, whose tender body they serued to his table baked in a Pye? At
which speeches the irefull Earle wrapped hys handes within her lockes of haire,
which was couered with a costly Caule of gold, and in this manner presently
replied vnto her.

What tellest thou me of Poets tales (said he) of *Prognies* Rape, and *Terius*
bloody banquet: thy rauishment shall be an Induction to thy Tragedie, which if
thou yeelde not willingly, I will obtaine by force and violence: therefore prepare
thy selfe eyther to entertaine the sentence pronounced, or yeelde thy body to my
pleasure. This vnrecanting and vowed resolution of the Earle, added griefe vpon
griefe, & heaped mountaines of sorrow[10] vpon her soule: twice did the haples Lady
cast her eyes to heauen, in hope the Gods would pittie hir distresse, & twice vnto
the earth, wishing the ground might open and deuoure her, & so deliuer her from
the furie of the wicked Homecide: but at last when shee saw that neyther teares,
praiers, nor wishes could preuaile, shee gaue an outward signe of consentment
vppon some conditions, vnder colour to deuise a present meanes to preserue her
chastetie, and deliuer hir selfe from his lustfull assailements. There is no condition
saide the Earle, but I will yeeld vnto, so thou wilt graunt my desire, and make me
chiefe commaunder of thy loue.

First my Lord (quoth she) shall you suffer me to sit some certaine houres vpon
this bed of violets, and bewaile the losse of my good name, which shortly shall bee
yeelded vp to your pleasure: then shall you lie and dallie in my lap thereby to make
my affections, yet freezing cold, to flame with burning brandes of loue: that beeing
done you shall receaue your wished desires. These wordes caused the Earle to
conuert his furious wrath to smiling ioy, and so casting downe his dagger, he gaue
her a curteous kisse, which shee in his conceite graciously accepted whereby hys
mind was brought into such a vaine opinion, that he thought no Heauen but in her
presence: no comfort but in her sight: and no pleasure but in her loue: then caused
he *Sabra* to sit downe vpon a bed of violets, beset about with diuers sorts of
flowers, whose lap hee made his pillow, whereon he laide hys head, intending as
he thought to increase desire: But as women in extreamitie haue the quickest
wittes: So *Sabra* busied her selfe by all meanes possible, eyther now or neuer to
remooue the cause of her deepe distresse by practising hys death, and so quit her
selfe from her importunate sutor: one while she told him pleasant tales of loue, in
hope to bring his sences to a slumber, the better to accomplish her desires: other
whiles shee played and sported with hys haire that hung dangling below his
shoulders like to threds of silke: But at last when neyther discoursing tales, nor her
dallying pastime with his haire could bring him a sleepe, she strained forth the
Organs of her voice, and ouer his heade song this wofull Dittie.

> *Thou God of sleepe and golden dreames appeare,*
> *That bringst all things to peace and quiet rest:*

---

[10] sorrow] sorrw *1596*

Close vp the glasses of his eies so cleare,
Thereby to make my fortune euer blest:
His eies, his hart, his senses and his minde,
In peacefull sleep let them some comfort finde.

Sing sweet you prettie birdes in top of Skyes,
With warbling tunes and many a pleasant note:
Till your sweet Musicke close his watchfull eies,
That on my loue with vaine desires doth dote:
Sleepe on my deare, sleepe on my loues delight,
And let this sleepe be thy eternall night.

You gentle Bees the Muses louelie birdes,
Come aide my dolefull tunes with siluer sound:
Let your inspiring melodie recorde,
Such heauenlie musicke that may quite confounde,
Both wit and sence, and tier his eies with sleepe,
That on my lap in sweet content I keepe.

You siluer streames which murmuring musicke makes,
And filles each dale with pleasant Harmonie:
Whereat the floting fish much pleasure takes,
To heare their sweet recording melodie:
Assist my tunes his slumbring eyes to close,
That on my lap now takes a sweet repose.

Let whispering windes in euerie sensles tree,
A solemne, sad, and dolefull Musicke sing:
From hilles and dales, and from each mountaine hie,
Let some inspiring sound or eccho ring:
That he may neuer more awake againe,
Which sought my marriage bed with lust to staine.

This delightfull song rocked hys sences to such a careles and heauie slumber, that he slept as soundly vpon her lappe, as if he had been couched in the softest bed of downe, whereby she found a fit opportunitie to deliuer her vndefiled body from his lustfull desires: So taking the Poyniard in her hand, which he had cast a little aside, and gazing thereon with an irefull looke, she made this sad complaint.

Graunt you immortall powers of heauen (said she) that of these two extreames I choose the best, either must I yeeld my body to bee dishonored by his vnchast desires, or staine my hands with the trickling streames of his heart blood: If I yeeld vnto the first, I shall be then accounted for a viscious Dame in euerie place: but if I commit the last I shall be guiltie of a wilfull murder, and for the same the lawe will adiudge me to a shamefull death. What shall I feare to die and loose my vertue and renowne? No, my heart shall be as tyrranous as *Danaus* Daughters, that slewe their fiftie husbands in a night, or as *Medeas* crueltie, which scattered her brothers bloodie ioynts vpon the sea shore, therby to hinder the swift pursute of her father, when *Iason* got the golden Fleece from *Calcos* Ile: Therefore stand still you glistring Lampes of heauen, stay wandring time and let him sleepe eternally. Where art thou sad *Melpomene*, that speakst of nothing but of murthers and Tragedies? Where be those Dames that euermore delights in blood? Come, come, assist me with your cruelties, let me exceede the hate of *Progne*, for her rauishment: rage hart, and take delight in blood, banish all thoughts of pitty from thy breast, be thou as mercilesse as King *Priams* Queene, that in reuenge of fiue and twenty murthred sonnes, with her owne hands staynd the pauements of *Agamemnons* Court with purple gore: these words being no sooner ended, but with wrathfull and pale countenance, she sheathed the Poyniard vp to the hilts in the closure of his breast, whereat he started, and woulde haue got vpon his feete, but the streame of blood so violently gushed from his wound, that hee declined immediatly to the earth, and his soule was forced to giue the world a dolefull adue.

But when *Sabra* beheld the bedde of violets stainde with blood, and euery flower conuerted to a crimson colour, shee sighed grieuously, but when she saw her garments all to be sprinckled with her enemies blood, and he lay wallowing at her feete in purple gore she ran speedily vnto a flowing fountaine that stoode on the further side of the Orchard, and began to wash the blood out of her clothes, but the more shee washed, the more it increased, a signe that heauen will neuer suffer wilfull murder to be hid, for what cause soeuer it is done.

This straunge spectakle or rather wonderfull accident, so amazed the sorrowfull Lady, that shee began a newe to complaine. O that this wicked murther neuer had bin done (said shee) or that my hand had beene stroken lame, by some vnluckie Plannet, when first it did attempt the deede! whether shall I flie to shrowde me from the company of vertuous women, which will for euermore shun me as a detested murtherer? If I should goe into some forraine Countrie, there heauen will cast downe vengeance for my guilt: If I should hide my selfe in woods and solitarie wildernesses, yet would the winde discouer me, and blow this bloody crime to euery corner of the world: or if I should goe liue in Caues or darkesome Dennes, within the deepe foundation of the earth, yet will his Ghost pursue me there, and haunt mee day and night: so that in no place a murtherer can liue in rest, such discontented thoughts shall still oppresse his mind. After shee had breathed forth this comfortles lamentation to the aire, she tore her blood stayned Garment from her backe and cast it into the fountaine, where it turned the water into the colour of blood: so heyhous is murther in the sight of heauen.

Thus beeing disrobed into her Petticote, she returned to the slaughtered Earle, whome shee founde couered with mosse, which added more griefe vnto her sorrowfull soule, for she greatlie feared her murther was discried, but it fell not out as she mistrusted:[11] for it is the nature and kind of a Robbin Red-brest and other birdes, alwaies to couer the bodie of any dead man, and them it was that bred this feare in the Ladies heart: by this time the day began to shut vp his bright

---

[11] mistrusted] mustrusted *1596*

windowes, and sable night entred to take possession of the earth: yet durst not the wofull and distressed *Sabra* make her repaire homewards, lest she should bee discried without her vpper garment.

During which time there was a generall search made for the Earle by his seruauntes, for they greatly suspected some daunger had befallen him, considering that they heard him the night before so wofullie complaine in his Chamber: At last with Torch light they came to the Orchard gate, which they presently burst open: wherein no sooner entring, but they found their murthered Master, lying by a bed of violets couered with mosse, likewise searching to find out the murtherer: At last they espied *Sabra* in her naked Petticote, her handes & face besprinckled with blood, & her countenance as pale as ashes: by which signes they suspected her to be the bloody bereauer of their Lord & Masters life: therefore because she descended from a noble linnage, they brought her the same night before the King, which did then keepe hys Court in the Cittie of *Couentrie*: who immediatly vpon the Confession of the murther, gaue this seuere iudgment against her: First to be conueied to Prison, there to remaine for the tearme of twelue moneths, and at the end whereof, to be burned like a most wicked offender: yet because she was the Daughter of a King, and loyall Lady to so Noble a Knight, his Maiesty in mercie graunted her this fauour: that if she could get any Knight at Armes before the time were expired, that would be her Champion, and by Combat redeeme her from the fire, she should liue: otherwise, if her Champion were vanquished, then to suffer the former Iudgement. Thus haue you heard the true discourse of all things which hapned, till my departure from England, where I left her in Prison, and since that time, fiue monthes are fullie exspired: Therefore most renowned Champion, as you loue the life of your Ladie and wish her deliuerie make no tarriance, but with all speed post into England, for I greatly feare before you ariue vppon that blessed shore, the time will be finished, and *Sabra* suffer death for want of a Champion to defend her cause.

This doleful discourse draue saint *George* with the other Knights and Champions to such an extasie of minde, that euery one departed to their lodging Chambers with dumbe signes of sorrow, being not able to speake one word, where for that night they lamented the mishap of so vertuous a Lady: The Egyptian King her father, he abandoned the sight of all companies, and repayred to the toppe of an high Tower built of Marble stone, wherein hee barred himselfe fast with yron bolts, so that none could come within the hearing of his lamentations: then raged hee vp and downe like franticke *Oedipus*, tearing his eyes from their naturall Celles, accusing heauen of iniustice, condemning earth of iniquity, and accursing man for such an execrable crime, one while wishing his daughters byrth hower, had beene her buriall day, another while, that some vnlucky Plannet would descend the firmament, and fall vppon his miserable head: being in this extreame passion, hee neuer hoped to see his daughters countenance againe, and so about midnight, being a time when desperate men practise their owne destructions, he cast himselfe headlong from the toppe of the Tower and broake his necke, and all besprinckled the flinty pauements with his blood and braines.

No sooner was the night vanished, and bright *Phœbus* entred the Zodiacke of heauen, but his bruised body liueles and senseles, was found by his seruants lying in the Pallace yard, all to be beaten in peeces against the grounde. The wofull newes of this selfe-wild murtherer, they presently told to certaine Egyptian Knights, who tooke his scattered limbs and carryed them to saint *Georges* Chamber; where they found him arming himselfe for his departure towardes England: But at this wofull spectackle, he tooke a seconde conceited griefe, in such extreame manner, that it had almost cost him his life, but that the Egyptian Knights gaue him many comfortable speeches, and by the consent of many Dukes Earles, Lords, and Barrons, with many other of the late Kings priuy Councell, they elected him the true succeeding King of Egipt by the marriage of *Ptolomies* daughter: which Royall proffer saint *George* refused not, but took vpon him the Regiment of the whole Country, so that for that day his iourney toward England was stayed, and vppon the third day following, his Coronation was appoynted, which they solemnely perfourmed, to the high honour of all the Christian Champions: For the Egyptian Pieres caused saint *George* to be apparralled in Royall Uestures like a King, he had on a sute of flaming greene like an Emerauld, and a Mantle of scarlet very richly furd, and wrought curiously with gold, then the other sixe Champions lead him vp to the Kings Throane, and set him in a Chayre of Ebony with pummells of siluer, which stood vpon an Allablaster Elephant: then came three of the greatest Lords in Egypt and set a Crowne of gold vpon his head, then followed two Knights with a Scepter and a naked Sworde, to signefie that he was chiefe Champion of all the Realme, and Lord of all that appertained to the Crowne of Egypt: This being performed in most sumptuous and stately manner, the Trumpets with other Instruments began to sound, wherat the generall company, with ioyfull voyces, cryed all together, Long liue saint *George* true Champion for England, and King of Egypt: Then was he conducted to the Royall Pallace, where for ten dayes he remayned amongst his Lords and Knights, spending the time in great ioy and pleasure: the which beeing finished, hys Ladyes distresse constrayned him to a sodaine departure, therefore he left the guiding of his Lande to twelue Egyptian Lordes, binding them all by oath, to redeliuer it at his returne, likewise charging them to interre the body of *Ptolomie* in a sumptuous Toombe, befitting the body of so Royall a Potentate: Also appoynting the sixe Champions to rayse their Tents, and muster vp anewe their souldiers, and with all speede march into *Persia*, and there by dynt of bloody warre, reuenge his former iniuries vpon the cursed Soldan. This charge being giuen, the next morning by breake of day, hee buckled on his Armour, mounted on his swift footed Steed, and bad his friends in Egipt for a season adue, and so in companie of the Knight that brought him that vnluckie newes, hee tooke his iournie with all speed toward England: In which trauaile we leaue him for a time: Also passing ouer the speedy prouision made by the Christian Champions in *Egypt* for the inuasion of *Persia*, and returne to sorrowfull *Sabra* beeing in prison, awayting each minute to receaue the finall stroke of impartiall death: for now had the rowling Plannets brought their yeares trauailes to an end: yet *Sabra* had no intelligence of any Champion that would defend her cause: therefore shee prepared her dilicate bodie to receaue her latest breath of life: the time beeing come shee was brought to the place of execution: whether she went as willinglie, and with as much ioy, as euer shee went before time vnto her marriage, for she had made her humble submission to the world, and vnfainedly committed her soule to God. She beeing at the stake (where the king was present with many thousands, as wel of Noble personages, as of Common people to behold this wofull Tragedie) the deaths-man stripped off her Garment, which was of blacke sarcenet, & in her snow-white smocke, bound her with an Iron chaine vnto the stake, then placed they round about her tender body, both Pitch, Turpentine and Gunpowder, with other merciles things, therby to make her death the more easier, and her paine the shorter. Which beeing done the King caused the Harrold to summon in the Challenger: who at the sound of the Trumpet came trasing in vpon a Rone coloured Steede, without any kinde of marke, and trapped with rich trappinges of gold & precious stones of great price: there came foorth at the Horse mouth, two tuskes like vnto an Elephants, hys nostrelles were verie large and bigge, his heade little, his breast some what broad, well pitcht, and so hard that no sword were it neuer so sharpe, was able to enter in thereat. The Champion was called the Barron of *Chester*, a bolde and hardier Knight they thought liued not then vpon the face of the whole earth: he so aduanced himselfe vp & downe as though hee had beene able to Encounter with a hundred Knights: then the King caused the Harrold to summon in the Defendant, if there were any to defend her cause both Drums and Trumpets sounded three seuerall times vp & downe the fieldes, betwixt euerie rest was full a quarter of an houre, but yet no defendant did appeare: therefore the King commaunded the Executioner to set the stake on fire presently.

At which words *Sabra* began to grow as pale as ashes and hir Ioyntes to tremble like to Aspen-leaues, hir toung that before continewed silent began to recorde a swanlike dying tale, & in this maner vttered she the passion of hir heart. Be witnes heauen, and all you bright celestiall Angells: bee witnes sun and moone the true beholders of my fact: be witnes thou cleare firmament and all the world be witnes of my innocence: the blood I shed was for the sauegard of my honor and vnspotted Chastety: Great God of heauen, if the praiers of my vnstained heart may assaile thy mighty Maiestie, or my true innocence preuaile with thy immortall power. Commaund that eyther my Lorde may come to be my Champion, or sad beholder of my death: But if my hands were stained with blood about some wicked enterprise: then heauen shew present vengeance vppon me by fire, or els let the earth open & deuoure my bodie vp aliue. At which instance she heard the sound of a shrill and lowd horne, the which S. *George* winded: (for as then hee was neere) which caused the Execution a while to bee deferred: At last they beheld a farre off, a stately Banner wauering in the Ayre, the which the Knight carried before saint *George*: then they espied nere vnto the Banner, a most valiant Armed Knight mounted vpon a cole blacke Palfray, with a mightie great Launce set charged in his Rest, by which sodaine approach they knewe him to bee some Champion that would defende the distressed Ladyes cause.

Then the King commanded the Drums and Trumpets to sound, whereat the people gaue a generall showt, and the poore Lady halfe dead with feare, began to reuiue, and her blushing cheekes to be as beautefull, as redde Roses dipt in milke, & blood mingled with snowe: but when saint *George* approached the sight of his true and constant Ladie, whom he found chayned to a stake, incompassed with many instruments of death, his hart so relented with griefe, that he almost fell beside his horse: yet remembring wherefore hee came, he recalled his courage, and intended to try his fortune in the Combat, before he would discouer himselfe vnto his Lady: And so when the Trumpets sounded deaths Alarum, the two Knights set spurres to their horses, & made them run so fiercely, that at the first encounter, they shiuered both theyr Launces to their hands, then rushed they together so rigorously with their bodies and Helmets, that they fell downe both to the earth: But saint *George* who was the more lustier Knight, nimbly leapt vppon his feete without any hurt, but the Barron of Chester lay still with his head downewards, casting from his mouth abundance of blood, he was so mightely bruised with the fall: but when he reuiued from his traunce, he tooke his shield, drawing out a mighty Fawchion, and with a wrathfull countenance ran at saint *George*: Now prowde Knight (quoth he) I sweare by all the Saints in heauen, to reuenge the blood which thou hast shed, and therewithall he stroke so violently vpon saint *Georges* shield, that it cleaued quite a sunder: then began he to waxe angry, and tooke his sword in great wrath, and gaue the Barron of *Chester* such a stroke, that he cut away arme and shoulder, and all the flesh of his side to the bare ribs, and likewise cut his legge almost cleane a sunder, in the thickest[12] place of his thigh, and yet for all that the sword entred halfe a foote into the earth, then fell the Barron of Chester to the ground, and breathed forth this lamentable cry: Nowe frowne you fatall starres eternally, that did predominate at my byrth, for he is slaine and vanquished that neuer stoopt to any Knight before this day, and thereupon the blood stopped the passage of his speech, and his soule went flying to Elizium, whereat the whole company reioyced, and applauded saint *George* for the most fortunate[13] Knight in the world: then the King deliuered *Sabra* with his owne hands to saint *George*, who most curteously receiued her, and like a kinde Knight cast a scarlet Mantle ouer her body, the which a Lady standing by bestowed vpon him, yet he minding not to discouer himselfe, but set her vpon his portly Steede, (that presently grew prowde in carrying so rich a burthen) and with his owne hands lead him by the brydle raynes: so great was the ioy throughout the City, that the belles rung without ceasing, for three dayes together, the Citezens thorough euery place that saint *George* should passe, did hang forth at their windowes, and on their walles cloth of gold and silke, with rich Carpets, Cushions, and couerings of greene veluet lay abroad in euery window: the Cleargy in Copes of gold and silke met them with solemne Processions: The Ladyes and beautefull Damsels strowd euery streete where as hee past with Roses and most pleasant flowers, and Crownd him with a wreath of greene bayes, in signe of his triumphant victory and Conquest.

In this manner went hee vnto the Kinges Pallace, not known by any what he should be, but that he was a Knight of a strange Country, yet *Sabra* many times as they walked by the way, desired to see his face, and knowe his name, in that he had aduentured so farre for her sake, and that for her deliuery had vanquished the brauest knight in England. Yet for all her perswasions hee kept himselfe

---

[12] thickest] thichest *1596*
[13] fortunate] fortunates *1596*

vndiscouered, till a troupe of Ladies in company of *Sabra* got him into a chamber richly hung with Arras cloth, and there vnlaced his Beuer, whose countenance when she beheld, and sawe that it was her Lord and husband which had redeemed her from death, shee fell into a deade sounde for very ioy: But saint *George* sprinckled a little colde water on her face, and reuiued her presently: After this he gaue her many a kinde and louing kisse, calling her the most truest, and the most loyallest Lady that euer nature framed, that to the very death would not loose one iote of her vnspotted honour: Likewise she accounted him the truest Knight and the loyallest husband, that euer heauenly *Hymen* linckt in bands of marriage with any woman. But when the King had notice that it was saint *George*, his Countries Champion, which atchieued that Noble Conquest in vanquishing the Barron of Chester, he was rauished with such ioy, that he came running in all hast to the Chamber, and most kindly imbraced him, and after he was vnarmed, & had washed his woundes in white wine and new milke, the King conducted him with his Lady to his banquetting house where they feasted for that euening, and after he kept open Court for all commers so long as saint *George* continued there, which was for the space of one month: At the end whereof he tooke his Lady and one Page with him, and bad England adewe, and then he trauelled towards *Persia*, to the other Christian Champions, whose dangerous iourney and straunge aduentures you may reade in this Chapter following.

CHAP. XVI.

How Saint George in his iournie towardes Persia, ariued in a Countrie inhabited onely by maides, where hee atchiued many strange and wonderfull aduentures: Also of the rauishment of seauen Virgins in a wood, and howe Sabra preserued her Honour from a tirrible Gyant.

AFter saint *George* with his vertuous Ladie departed from England, and had trauailed through many Countries, taking their direct courses towards *Egipt*, and the Confines of *Persia*, where the other sixe Champions remayned with their warlike Legions: At last they ariued in the Country of the *Amazonians*, a land inhabited by none but women: In which Region saint *George* atchiued many braue and Princely aduentures, which are most wonderful to rehearse, as after shall bee declared: For trauelling vp and downe the Countrie, they found euery Towne and Cittie desolate of people, yet very sumptuosly builded: the earth like wise vntilled: the pastures vncherished, and euerie field ouergrowne with weeds: whereby he deemed that some strange accident had befallen the country, either by war, or mortalitie[1] of some grieuous plague, for they could neyther set eye of man, woman, nor childe, whereby they were forced to feede on Berries & Rootes, and in steede of braue Pallaces, they were constrained to lie in broad pastures, vpon bankes of mosse, & insteede of Curtens of silke, they had the blacke and scowling cloudes to couer them.

In this extreamety they trauelled vp and downe for thirty dayes, but at last it was theyr happy fortunes to ariue before a rich Pauillion, scituate and standing in the open fields, which seemed to be the most glorious sight that euer they beheld, for it was wrought of the richest worke in the world, all of greene and crimson satten, bordred with golde and azure, the posts that bare it vp was of Iuory, the cordes of greene silke, and on the toppe thereof there stoode an Eagle of gold, and at the two corners, two great siluer Griffons shining against the sunne, which seemed in richnes to exceede the monument of *Mausalus* being one of the worlds twelue wonders. They had not there remayned long, admiring at the beauty of the workemanship, but at the entry of the Pauillion, there appeared a mayden Queene Crowned with an imperiall Diademe, who was the most fayrest creature that euer hee sawe: on her attended twenty Amazonian Dames, baring in theyr handes siluer bowes of the Turkish fashion, and at theyr backes hung quiuers full of golden Arrowes: vppon theyr heades they wore siluer Coronets, beset with Pearles and precious stones: theyr attire comelie and gallant: theyr faces faire and gentle to behold, theyr foreheads playne and white, the tramels of theyr hayre like burnisht golde, theyr browes small and proper, somewhat drawing to a browne colour: theyr visages plaine, neither too long, nor too round, but coloured like Roses and Lillies mixt together, theyr noses long and strait, their ruddy mouthes somewhat smiling, their eyes louely, and all the rest of theyr parts and liniaments by nature framed most excellent, who had made them in beauty without compare: The Queene her

---

[1] mortalitie] immortalitie *1596*

selfe was cloathed in a gowne of greene, straight gyrt vnto her body with a lace of gold, so that somewhat her rounde and Lilly white breast might be seene, which became her wonderfull well, beside all this, shee had on a crimson Kertle, lined with violet veluet, and her wide sleeues were likewise of greene silk imbrothred with flowers of golde, and with rich Pearles: when saint *George* had sufficiently beheld the beauty of this mayden Queene, hee was almost intrapped in her loue, but that the deare affection he bare to his owne Lady preuented him, whome hee woulde not wrong for all the treasures betwixt the highest heauens, and the lowest earth: At last he alighted from his horse, and humbled himselfe vnto her Excellence and thus curteously began to question with her after this manner.

Most diuine and fayer of all fayers, Queene of sweete beauty (sayd he) let a trauelling Knight obtaine this fauor at your hands, that both himselfe and his Lady whome you behold here wearied with trauell, may take our rest within your Pauillion for this night: For wee haue wandred vp and downe this Country many a day, neither seeing man to giue vs lodging, nor finding foode to cherrish vs, which made vs woonder that so braue a Country, and so beautefied with natures ornamentes[2] as this is, should be left desolate of people, the cause whereof is straunge I knowe and full of woonder.[3]

This question beeing curteously demaunded by saint *George*, caused the Amazonian Queene as kindly to reply: Syr Knight quoth she, (for so you seeme both by your behauiour, and gallant stature) what fauour my Pauillion may afford be assured of: But the remembrance of my Countries desolation which you speake of, breedes a sea of sorrowe in my soule, and makes me sigh when I remember it, but because you are a Knight of a strange Land, I will report it though vnto my griefe: about some twelue yeares since, it was a Nigromancers chaunce to ariue within this Country, his name is *Osmond*, the cunningst Artist this day liuing vpon the earth, for he can at his call raise all the spirits out of hell: and with his charmes make heauen to raine continuall showers of bloode, my beauty at that instance tempted him to loue, and drowned his senses so in desire, that hee assayed by all perswasions that either wit or Art could deuise, to winne me to his will: but I hauing vowde myselfe to *Dianaes* chastetie, to liue in singlenes among the *Amazonian* maides, contemned his loue, dispised his person, and accounted his perswasions as ominous as the hissing of venemous snakes: for which hee wrought the destruction of this my Realme and Kingdome: for by hys Magicke Art and damned Charmes, hee raysed from the earth a mightie Tower, the morter whereof hee mingled with virgins blood: wherein are such Inchantmentes wrought, that the light of the Sunne, and the brightnes of the Skye is quenched, and the earth blasted with a tyrrible vapour, and blacke mist, that ascendeth from the Tower, whereby a generall darkenes ouerspreades our Land, the compasse of foure and twentie Leagues: so that this countrie is cleane wasted and destroyed, and my people fled out thereof. This Tower is haunted day and night with gastlie fiends: and at hys departure into *Persia*, where hee now by Inchauntment aides the Soldan in hys Warres against the Christians, hee left the guarding of the same to a mightie and

---

[2] ornamentes] ornamenes *1596*
[3] woonder.] woonder, *1596*

tyrrible Gyant: In shape the vgliest monster that euer eye beheld, or eare heard tell: For hee is thirtie foote in length: his head three times larger than the head of an Oxe: his eyes bigger than two pewter dishes, and hys teeth standing out of hys mouth more than a foote: wherewith he will breake both Iron and Steele: his armes big and long without any measure, and all his bodie as blacke as any coale, and as hard as brasse: Also of such a strength that he is able to carrie away at once, three Knights Armed, and he neuer eateth any other meate but raw flesh of mankinde: he is so light and swift that a horse cannot run from him, and oftentimes hee hath beene assayed with great Troups of Armed men, but all of them could neuer doe him any harme, neyther with sword, speare, crosbow, nor any other weapon.

Thus haue you heard most noble and curteous Knight, the true discourse of my vtter ruine, and the vengeance shewed vppon my Countrie by this wicked Nigromancer: for which I haue remayned euer since in this Pauilion amongst my maydes, where wee pray both day and night, that some vnhappie fortune, or tyrrible vengeance may fall vpon this wicked Coniurer.

Now as I am true English Knight (replied S. *George*) no sooner shall the morninges Sunne appeare but I wil take my iournie to that inchaunted Tower: in to which Ile enter in despite of the Gyant, and breake the Inchantment, or make my graue within the Monsters bowelles: which if I happely perfourme, then will I trauaile into *Persia*, and fetter vp the most wicked and damned Nigromancer, and like a blood hound lead him vp and downe the world in Chaynes.

Most dangerous is the aduenture (quoth the *Amazonian* Queene) from whence as yet did neuer Knight returne: But if thou be so resolute and Noble minded as to attempt the enterprise, then happie bee your fortune. And knowe braue Knight, that this tower lieth westward, from hence some threescore miles, and thereupon shee tooke him by the hand, and caused *Sabra* likewise to alight from her Palfray and led them both into her Pauilion: where they were feasted most royally, and for that night slept securely: But when the dayes bright windowes opened, and the Morning Sunne began to glister, in all the haste saint *George* that valiant minded Champion, arose from his sweet content, and Armed himselfe: where after hee had taken hys leaue of the Queene, and gaue her thankes for hys curteous entertainement, and also taken his leaue of *Sabra*: whome he left in companie of the Queenes maides, till hys returne with conquest, and so rode foorth till it was Noone, and then he entred into a deepe Ualley, and euer hee rode lower and lower. It was then a faire day, and the Sun shined cleare: but by that time he had ridden two miles and a halfe, he had lost both the light of the Sunne, and also the sight of heauen: for it was there as darke as night, & more dismall than the deepest dungeon.

At last he found a mighty riuer with streames as blacke as pitch, and the bankes were so high, that the water coulde scarce bee seene running vnderneath, and it was so full of Serpents, that none could enter amongst them that euer returned backe with life: Aboue his heade flewe monstrous byrds and diuers Griffons, who were able to beare away an Armed Knight horse and all, and were in as great multitudes, as though they had beene Starlings: Also there were flyes as bigge as nuts, and as blacke as pitch, which stung him and his horse so grieuously, that there issued downe such store of bloode, that it changed his horse from a sable to a crimson colour: likewise the Griffons strook at saint *George* with theyr talents so furiously, that had not hee defended himselfe with his shield, which couered his whole body, hee had beene pierced to the hart.

In this dangerous manner rode he on, till he came to the gates of the inchaunted Tower, where as the Gyant sate in his yron coate vpon a blocke, with a mace of steele in his hand, who at the first sight of saint *George*, beate his teeth so mightely together, that they rung like the strokes of an Anuile, and ran raging like a Fiende of hell, thinking to haue taken the Champion horse and all in his long teeth, that were as sharpe as steele, and to haue borne them presently into the Tower: But when saint *George* perceiued his mouth open, he tooke his sword and thrust therein so far, that it made the Gyant to roare so lowd, that the Elements seemed to thunder, and the earth to tremble, his mouth smoakt like a fiery Furnace, and his eyes rowled in his head like brands of flaming fier: the wounde was so great, and the blood issued so fast from the Gyants mouth, that his courage began to quayle, and against his will, he was forced to yeeld to the Champions mercy, and to beg for life, to which saint *George* agreed, but vppon condition, that the Gyant would discouer all the secrets of the Tower, and euer after be sworne his true seruant, and to attend on him with all dilligence: To which the Giant swore by hys own soule, neuer to leaue him in exstreamitie, & to answere him truely to all questions whatsoeuer: Then saint *George* demaunded the cause of the darkenes, and how it might be ceased, to which the Gyant answered in this manner.

There was within this Countrie about some twelue yeares since, a cunning Nigromancer that by Inchauntment built this Tower, the which you nowe behold,[4] and therein caused a tyrrible fire to spring from the earth, that cast such a smoake ouer the whole land: whereby the people that were wont to dwell therein are fled and famished for hunger: Also this Inchaunter by his Arte, made the Riuer that you haue passed, the which did neuer man before this time without death: Also within the Tower nere vnto the fire, there standes a faire and plentifull fountaine: to which if euer any Knight be able to attaine, and cast the water thereof into the fire: then shall the darkenes euer after cease, and the Inchantment end: for which cause I haue beene bound to guard and keepe this Tower from the atchiuement of any Knight.

Thus when the Giant had ended hys discourse, saint *George* commaunded him to remaine at the Gate, for hee would aduenture to end the Inchauntment, and deliuer the Countrie from so grieuous a plague: Then went hee close by the windowes of the Tower, the which were sixteene speares in length and breadth, til he came to a little wicket, through which hee must needes enter: yet was it set as thicke with pickes of steele, as the pricks of an Urchens skinne, to the intent that no Knight should approach neare vnto the dore, nor once attempt to enter the Tower: yet with great danger he opened the wicket: whereout came such abundance of smoake, that the darkenes of the countrie doubled: so that neyther Torch nor Candle woulde burne in any place: yet neuertheles saint *George* entred, and went downewardes vpon stayers, where hee could see nothing: but yet felt so many great blowes vpon his Burgonet, that he was constrayned to kneele vpon his knees, &

---

[4] behold] beheld *1596*

with his shield to defend himselfe, or els he had beene brused to peeces: At last hee came to the bottome, and there hee found a faier great vault, where he felt so tyrrible a heate, that he sweat exceedingly, and as he felt about him, hee perceaued that he approached neere the fire, and going a little further he espied out the Fountaine, whereat hee greatlie reioyced: and so he tooke his shield, and bore therein as much water as he could and cast it into the fire: In conclusion, labouring so long till the fire was cleane quenched, then began the skyes to receaue their perfect lightnes, and the golden Sunne to shine most clearelie about him, whereby hee plainely perceaued how there stoode vpon the stayers many great Images of Brasse, holding in their handes mightie Maces of steele, the which had done him much trouble at his comming downe: but then their power was ended, the fire quenched, and the Inchauntment finished.

Thus when saint *George* through hys inuincible fortitude had performed this dangerous aduenture, hee grew wearie of trauaile: what with heate and sweating, and the mightie blowes he receaued from the Brazen Images, that he returned againe to the little wicket: whereas the deformed Gyant still remayned: who when he beheld the Champion returne both safe and sound, hee fell vppon hys knee before him and said.

Sir Knight you are most welcome, and happilie returned: for you are the flower of Chiualrie, and the brauest Champion in the world. Commaund my seruice, dutie and obedience: for whilst I liue, I doe protest by the burning Banckes of *Acharon*, neuer to follow any Knight but you, and thereupon I kisse your golden spurre, which is the Noble badge of Knighthood.

This humble submission of the Gyant caused the Champion to reioyce, not for his ouerthrow, but that he had gotten so mighty a seruant: then vnlaced he his Helmet, and laie downe after hys wearie Encounter, where after hee had sufficiently rested himselfe, he tooke his iournie in companie of the Gyant to the *Amazonian* Queene: where he left hys Lady, in companie of her virgins: who like a kinde, modest, and vertuous wife, during all the time of her husbands absence, continually praied to the immortal powers of heauen, for his fortunate successe, and happy returne, otherwise resoluing her selfe, if the lowring destenies should crosse hys intent, and vnluckilie end his dayes before the aduenture were accomplished: then to spende the remnant of her life, amongst those happie virgins: But on the sodaine before the Queene and her virgins were a ware, *S. George* ariued before the Pauillion, dutifully attended on by the Giant: who bore vpon his shoulder the body of a tal Oake, by which the Queene knewe that his prowesse had redeemed her country from darkenes, and deliuered her from her sorrow, care, and trouble: so in companie of her maides very gorgeously atired, she conducted the Champion to a bower of Roses, intermingled with creeping vines, the which in his absence, they had planted for hys Ladies delight: there found he *Sabra* at her diuine prayers, like a solitarie Widdow, clad in mourning habilliments: but when shee beheld her Lord returne in saftie, she banished griefe, & in al haste ran vnto him, & in his bosome rauished her selfe with pleasure: But to speake how the *Amazonian* Queene feasted them, and in what maner shee and her Maides deuised pastimes for their contents, were too tedious to repeate: but when night gaue end to their pleasures, & sleep summoned all things to a quiet silence, the Queene brought them to a very sumptuous lodging: wherein stood a bed framed with Ebon wood ouerhung with manye pendants of gold, the Tike was stuft with Downe of Turtle-Doue, the sheetes of *Mædian* silke: thereon lay a rich quilt wrought with cotten, couered with dammaske, and stitcht with threds of gold. The Queene bestowed on saint *George* at hys going to bed, an imbrothered shirt, curiouslie wrought with many rare deuises, as the labors of *Hercules*, the triumphs of *Mars*, & the loues of many Potentates wrought in such curious manner, as though Arte her selfe had beene the contriuer. *Sabra* at her going to bed was likewise presented by the Queenes maidens, with a light Kirtle of chaungable violet, somewhat blushing on a red colour: Also they put a white Kerchiefe of silke vpon her head, some what lose and vntied: so that vnder the same her Iuorie throat might be easilie seene, and her faire golden haire flying about her necke: ouer them was cast a mantle of greene silke, which made the bed seeme more beautifull, than *Floraes* richest ornament: By them the Queene and her virgins sate makeing sweete musicke vpon their siluer tuned Lutes, till golden sleepe had closed vp their eyes: The which beeing done the Queene with her Ladies departed likewise to their naturall restes: But all this while the Giant neuer entered the Pauillion, but slept as soundly vnder the roote of a Pine tree, as saint *George* did in his imbrothered bed, for he knew not what pleasures belonged thereunto, nor neuer before that time behelde any womans face: At last the night withdrew her blacke Curtens, and gaue the morning leaue to appeare, whose fearefull light caused saint *George* to forsake hys bed, and to walke some few miles to ouerveiw the Countrie: In which iournie hee tooke such exceeding pleasure, that hee thought it the goodliest Realme that euer hee saw: for he perceiued well, how that it was full of worldlie wealth.

   At last hee climbed vp to the toppe of a high Mountaine beeing some two miles from the Queenes Pauilion: whereon he stood and beheld many stately Townes and Towers, high and mightie Castels, many large woods & meadowes, and manie pleasant Riuers, and about the Townes faire Uines, goodlie Pastures and fields: At last he behelde the Cittie of *Argenia* shining against the Sun, the place where the Queene in former time was wont to keepe her Court: which Cittie was inuironed with deepe Ditches, the wals strongly builded, & more than fiue hundred Towers made of lime and stone: also he saw many faire Churches couered with Lead, hauing toppes and spiers of gold, shining most gorgeously with weather Cockes of siluer glistring against the Sun: also he saw the Burgesses houses stande like Pallaces closed with high and strong walles, barred with chaines of Iron from house to house: whereat in his hart he praised much the Noblenes and richnes of the Cittie, and saide to himselfe that it might well be called *Argenia*, for it seemed to be of Argent, that is as much to say of siluer.

   During the time of the Champions pleasurable walke, which continued from the breake of day, to the closing of the euening, behapned a wofull Tragedie nere vnto the Queenes Pauilion, committed by the monstrous Gyant, whome S. *George* brought from the Inchaunted Tower: For that same morning when the Sun had mounted some few degrees into the firmament: Seauen of the Queenes Uirgins in *Sabraes* companie, walked into a pleasant thicket of trees adioyning to her Pauilion, not onely to take the pleasure of the mornings aire: but to heare the chirping mellodie of birdes: In which thicket or groaue vnder a Pyne tree this Giant lodged the passed night: for no sooner came these beautiful Ladies vnder the branches of the trees, but the Giant cast his eye vpon them, whose rare perfections so fired the heart of the lustfull Gyant, that hee must eyther quench his desires with the spoyle of their chasteties, or end hys dayes in some monstrous manner: Therefore he starts vp from the place where he lay, and with a wrathfull countenance ran amongst the Ladies, and catching them all eyght at once betwixt hys Armes, hee bore them to the furthest side of the groue, where hee rauished seauen of the Queenes Maidens, and afterward deuoured them aliue into his loathsome bowels: But *Sabra* beeing the eighth of that wofull number, which in her sight she beheld butchered by that bloodie wolfe: still continuing the time of their rauishments, making her supplication to the Gods, that they would in mercie defend her chastetie from the lustfull rape of so wicked a monster, and immediately vpon these wordes she saw an vglie toade come crauling before her: through which by pollicie shee saued her life, and preserued her Honour: For she tooke the toade betwixt her hands, & crushed the venome from her impoysoned bowels, wherewith shee all to be sprinckled her face: so that presently her faier beautie, was chaunged into loathsome blisters: for she then seemed more liker a creature deformed with Leprosie, than a Ladie of excellent feature. At length shee beeing the last of all, her time came that she should be deflowred, and the lustfull Gyant came to fetch her: but when hee beheld her visage so inuenomed, he loathed her sight, seeking neyther to rauish her, nor proffering to deuoure her: but discontentedly wandred away, greatly greeuing at the committed crime, and sorely repenting himselfe of so wicked a deede: not onely for the spoyle of the seauen Uirgins, but for the wronges proffered to so Noble a Knight: who not onelie graunted him libertie of life, but receaued him into his seruice: therefore he raged vp and downe the groaue, making the earth to tremble at hys exclamations: one while cursing his fortune and houre of creation: another while banning hys Sire and diuelish Dam: But when he remembred the Noble Champion saint *George*, whose angry frowne he would not see for all the world: therefore to preuent the same, he runne his heade most furiously against a knobbed Oake and brayned himselfe: where wee will leaue him now weltring in hys blood, and speake what became of *Sabra* after this bloody accident: for after she had wandred vp and downe the thicket many a wearie steppe, incensing heauen against the Giants crueltie: the Sunne began to set, and the darke night drew on, which caused her thus to complaine.

O you immortall powers of heauen, and you celestiall Planets, beeing the true guiders of the firmaments! open your bright celestiall gates, and send some fatall Plannet, or some burning thunderbolt, to rid mee from the vale of miserie, for I will neuer more returne to my beloued Lord, sith I am thus deformed, and made an vglie creature, my loathsome face will proue a corasiue to his hart, and my bodie a torment to his soule, my sight will be displeasant, my company hated, my presence loathed, and euery one will shun my sight as from a Crocadiles: therefore I will remaine within this groue, till the heauens either bring mee to my former beauty, or ende my languishing misery: yet witnesse heauen of my loyalty vnto my Lorde, and in what extreamity I haue maintained my chastety, in remembrance of my true loue here will I leaue this chaine of gold, for my beloued Lord to finde, that he may knowe, for his sake I haue indured a world of woe: At which speeches she tooke her Chayne (which was doubled twenty times about her necke) and left it lying all besmeard in the blood of those virgins whome the Gyant had rauished and slayne, and so betooke herselfe to a sad and solitary life, intending neuer to come in the sight of men, but to spend her dayes wandring in the woods: where we will likewise leaue her for a time & speake of saint *George*, who by this was returned to the Queenes Pauillion, where hee missing his Lady, and had intelligence how that shee in company of seauen other Ladies, walked in the morning into a pleasant groue, to heare the mellody of byrdes, and since that time no newes hath beene heard of them: for as then it grewe towardes night, which caused saint *George* greatly to mistrust that some mischance had befalne his Lady: then he demaunded what was become of the Giant, but answere was made that hee was neyther seene nor heard off since morning, which caused him greatly to suspect the Gyants treachery, and how that by his meanes the Ladyes were preuented of theyr purposed pleasures.

Therefore in all hast like a franticke man he ran into the thicket, filling each corner with clamours and resounding ecchoes of her name, and calling for *Sabra* through euery bramble bush: but there he could neyther heare the voyce of *Sabra*, nor the answere of any other Ladie, but the wofull eccho of his exclamations, which ratled through the leaues of trees: then began he to waxe something melancholie & passionate, wearing the time away with wofull lamentations, till bright *Cinthia* mounted on the Hemispheeres: by whose glistring beames, he saw the ground besprinckled with purple gore, & found the chaine that *Sabra* was wont to weare about her necke all besmeerde in blood: he bitterlie complained against his owne fortune, & his Ladies haples destenie, for he supposed then that the Gyant had murthered her.

O discontented sight (said he) heere lies the blood of my beloued Ladie, the truest woman that euer Knight inioyed: that bodie which for excellence deserued a Monument of gold, more richer than the Toombe of *Angelica*, I feare lyes buried in the bowels of that monstrous Gyant, whose life vnhappilie I graunted. Here is the chaine besmeered with blood, which at our first acquaintance I gaue her in a Courtlie Maske. This golden chaine I say stained with the blood of my deare Ladie, shall for euermore bee kept within my boosome, nere vnto my bleeding hart, that I may still remember her true loue, faith and constancie: but fond foole that I am, why doe I talke in vaine? It will not recompence her murthered soule, the which me thinks I heare howe it calles for reuenge in euerie corner of this groaue: It was I that left her careleslie within the daunger of the Gyant, whome I little mistrusted:[5] therefore will I meete her in the Elizian shades, and craue remission for my committed trespasse, for on this Oake I will abridge my life, as did the worthie Knight *Melmerophon*[6] for the loue of his Ladie *Sillera*: which lamentation beeing no sooner ended, but he tooke the chaine of gold and fastned one ende to the Arme of a great Oake, and the other end to hys owne necke, intending presentlie to strangle himselfe, but heauen preuented his desperate intent after a straunge

---

[5] mistrusted] mustrusted *1596*
[6] *Melmerophon*] *Melmeropolion 1608; 1616*

manner: For vnder the same tree the brayned Gyant lay not yet fully dead, who in this manner spake to saint *George*.

O stay thy hand most Noble and inuincible Knight the worlds chiefe wonder for admired Chiualrie, and let my dying soule conuert thee from so wicked a deed: Seauen virgins in this Thicket haue I rauished, and buried all their bodyes in my accursed bowelles: but before I could deflower[7] the eighth, in a straunge manner hir bright beauty was conuerted in to a loathsome leprosie, whereby I detested hir sight, and left hir chastetye vndefiled: but by hir sad complaynts I since haue vnderstood, how that she is your Ladie and Loue, and to this hower she hath hir residence with in the cercuite[8] of this thicket, and thereuppon with a dolefull grone which seemed to shake the ground he bad adue to the world: then saint *George* being glad to heare such tydings reuerted from his desperate intent, and searched vp and downe the Groue, till he found *Sabra* where shee sate, sorrowing vnder the braunches of a mulberie tree, betwixt whome was a sad and heauie greeting, and as they walked backe to the Queenes Pauillion, shee discoursed[9] to him the truth of this bloody stratagem: where shee remayned till the *Amazonian* Queene had cured her leprosie by the secret vertue of her skill: of whome after they had taken leaue, & giuen her thankes for her kinde curtesies, saint *George* with hys Ladie tooke their iournie towards *Persia*, where the Christian Armies lay incampt: At whose ariuall you shall heare strange and woonderfull thinges, the like was neuer done in any age.

---

[7] deflower] deflower, *1596*
[8] cercuite] crcuite *1596*
[9] discoursed] discoused *1596*

CHAP. XVII.

How Saint George and his Ladie lost themselues in a wildernes, where she was deliuered[1] of three goodlie boies: The Fayerie Queenes Prophecie vppon the Childrens fortunes: Of Saint Georges returne into Bohemia, where he christned his Children, and of the finding of his Fathers graue, ouer which he built a statelie Toombe.

SAint *George* hauing atchiued the aduenture of the Inchaunted Tower, and *Sabra* the Furie of the lustfull Gyant: they tooke their iournie towards *Persia*, where the Christian Champions lay incamped before the Soldans great Cittie of Graund *Belgor*, a place most straungely fortefied with spirits and other gastlie illusions by the Inchauntment of *Osmond*, whome you heard before in the last Chapter, to bee the rarest Nigromancer in the world: But as the English Champion with his Ladie trauailed[2] thetherward, they hapned into a Desart, and mightie Wildernes, ouergrowne with loftie Pines, & Ceder trees, and many huge and mightie Oakes, the spreading braunches whereof, seemed to withold the light of heauen from their vntroden passages, and the toppes for exceeding height to reach into the Elements: the Inhabitantes were Siluaines, Satiers, Faieries, and other woodie Nimphes, which by day sported vp and downe the Forrest, and by night tended the pleasure of *Proserpine* the Fayrie Queene. The musicke of siluer sounding birds, so chearefullie resounding through the woodes, and the whistling winde made such melodie amongst the leaues of trees, that it rauished their sences like the harmonie of Angels, & made them thinke they had entred the shades of gladsome Elizium:[3] one while they wondred at the beautie of the Woods, which nature had ornefied with a Sommers liuerie: another while at the greene and fragrant grasse, drawne out in round circles by the Fayries daunces: so long till they had lost themselues amongst the vnknown passages, not knowing how nor by what meanes to recouer the perfect path of their intended iournie, but were constrained to wander in the Wildernes like solitarie Pilgrims, spending the daie with wearie steps, and the night with vaine imaginations, euen as a childe when hee hath lost himselfe in a populous Cittie, runneth vp and downe not knowing how to returne to his natiue dwelling: Euen so it hapned to these two lost and disconsolate trauailers: for when they had wandred many dayes one waie, and finding no end to their toyles, they retired backeward to the place of their first setting foorth: where they were wont to heare the noyse of people resound in Countrie Uillages, and to meete trauailers posting from place to place: but now they heard nothing but blustring of windes, ratling in the woods, making the brambles to whistle, and the trees to groane, and now and then to meete a speckled beast like to the rainebow, weltring from his Den to seeke his naturall sustenance: In their trauaile by night they were wont to heare the crowing Cocke, recording glad tydings of the chearefull dayes approach, the

---

[1] *deliuered*] *deluered 1596*
[2] trauailed] *trauiled 1596*
[3] Elizium] *Elizian 1596*

naying of horses in pasture fields, and the barcking of dogs in Farmers houses: but now they were affrighted with the roring of Lyons, yelling of Caues, the crooking of Toades in rootes of rotten trees, and the rufull sound of *Prognies* rauishment, recorded[4] by the Nightingale.

In this solitarie manner wearied they the rouling time away, till thrice three times the siluer Moone had renewed her borrowed light: by which time the burthen of *Sabraes* wombe began to grow painefull, and the fruite of her bodie to waxe ripe, the houre of her deliuerie drew on, wherein she required *Lucinaes* help to make saint *George* the father of a Princely Sonne: time called for Midwiues to aide & bring her Babe into the world, and to make her a happie mother: but before the painefull houre of her deliuerie approacht, Saint *George* had prouided her a bower of Uine braunches, which he erected betwixt two pleasant Hilles: where in steede of a Princely Cabbinet, behung with Arras and rich Tapestrie, shee was constrained to suffice her selfe with a simple lodging, couered with Roses and other fragrant flowers: her bedde hee made of greene mosse and thistle Downe, beeset curiously rounde about with Oliue braunches, and the sprigges of an Orring tree, which made it seeme more beautifull than *Floraes* Pauillion, or *Dianaes* Mansion: but at the last when shee felt the paynes of her wombe grow intollerable, and the seed readie to be reaped, and how she was in a Wildernes deuoyde of womens company, that should be readie to assist her in so secret a matter, shee cast her selfe downe vppon her mossie bed, and with a blushing countenance she discouered her minde in this order to saint *George*.

My most deare and louing Lord (quoth shee) my true & onely companion at all times and seasons except at this houre, for it is the painefull houre of my deliuerie: therefore depart from out the hearing of my cryes, and commit my fortune to the pleasures of the heauens: for it is not conuenient for any mans eye to behold the secrets of a woman in such a case: stay not I say deare Lorde to see the Infant now sprawling in my wombe to be deliuered from the bed of his creation, forsake my presence for a time, and let mee like the Noble Queene of Fraunce, obtaine the fauour of some Fayrie to be my Midwife, that my Babe may be as happily borne in this Wildernes, as was her valiant Sons *Vallentine* and *Orson*: the one of them was cherisht by a King, and the other by a Beare; yet both of them grew famous in their deedes: My paine is great deare Lord, therefore depart my Cabbinet, and before bright *Phœbus* lodgeth in the West, I shall eyther be a happie mother, or a liueles body: thou a ioyfull Father, or a sorrowfull Widdower. At which wordes Saint *George* sealed agreement with a kisse and silently departed without any reply: but with a thousand sighes he bad her adue, and so tooke his way to the top of a Mountaine, being in distance from hys Ladies abyding a quarter of a mile: there kneeled hee during the time of her trauailes, with hys bare knees vpon the bowels of the earth, neuer ceasing prayer, but continually soliciting the Maiestie of God, to graunt his Lady a speedy deliuerie: at whose diuine orizons the heauens seemed to relent, and all the time of her paine, couered the worlde with a vale of darkenes: whole flights of birdes, with Troupes of vntamed beasts came flocking round about

---

[4] recorded] recoroded *1596*

the Mountain where he kneeled, and in their kindes assisted his celestiall contemplations: where I will leaue him for a time, and speake what hapned to *Sabra* in the middle of her paynes and extreamitie of her trauailes: for after saint *Georges* departure, the furie of her griefe so raged in her wombe, that it exceeded the boundes of reason, whereby hys hart was constrained to breath so many scortching sighes, that they seemed to blast the leaues of trees, and to wither the flowers which beautefied her Cabbinet: her burthened tormentes caused her star-bright eyes like fountaines to distill downe siluer drops, and all the rest of her bodie to tremble like a Castle in a tyrrible earthquake: so grieuous was her paynes, and rufull was her cryes, that shee caused the mercilesse Tygers to relent, and vntamed Lyons with other wilde Beastes, like sillie Lambes to sit and bleate: her grieuous cryes and bitter moanes, caused the Heauens as it were to bleede their vapours downe, and the earth to weepe a spring of teares: both hearbes and trees did seeme to droope, hard stonie Rockes to sweate when shee complayned.

At last her pittifull cries pearced downe to the lowest vaults of direfull *Dis*, where *Proserpine* sits Crowned amongst her Fayries, and so preuailed: that in all haste she ascended from her regiment to worke this Ladies safe deliuerie, and to make her mother of three goodlie boyes: who no sooner ariued in *Sabraes* loging, but she practised the dutie of a Midwife, eased the burden of her wombe, and safelie brought her Babes into the world: At whose first sight the heauens began to smile, and the earth to reioyce, as a signe and token that in time to come, they would proue three of the Noblest Knights in the world.

This courteous deede of *Proserpine* beeing no sooner performed: but she laide the three boyes in three most rich and sumptuous Cradles, the which she caused her Fayries to fetch inuisible from three of the richest kinges in the world, and therewithall mantles of silke, with other things therunto belonging: Likewise she caused a winged Satier to fetch from the furthiest borders of *India*, a couering of dammaske Taffetie imbrodered with gold, the most richest ornament that euer mortall eye behelde: for thereon was wrought and liuelie portraied by the curious skill of *Indian* weauers, how God created heauen and earth, the wandring courses both of Sunne and Moone, and likewise howe the golden Plannets daylie doe prodominate: Also there is no Storie in anye age remembred since the beginning of the world, but it was thereon most perfectly wrought: So excellent it was that Art herselfe could neuer deuise a cuninger. With this rich and sumptuous ornament shee couered the Ladies Childe-bed: whereby it seemed to surpasse in brauerie the gorgeous bed of *Iuno* Queene of heauen: when first she entertained imperious *Ioue*. After this *Proserpine* laid vnder euerie childes pillow a siluer Tablet, wheron was written in letters of gold, their good and happy fortunes. Under the first were these verses caractered, who at that time lay frowning in hys Cradle like the God of Warre.

> *A Souldier bold a man of wondrous might,*
> *A King likewise this royall babe shal die:*
> *Three golden Diadems in bloody fight,*
> *By this braue Prince shall conquered be:*

The Towers of fayer Jerusalem and Roome,
Shall yeeld to him in happy time to come.

Under the pillow of the second Babe was caractered these verses following: who lay in his cradle smiling like *Cupid* vpon the lappe of *Dido*, whome *Venus* transformed to the liknes of *Askanius.*

This child shall likewise liue to be a King,
Times wonder for deuice and Courtly sport:
His Tiltes and Turniments a broad shall ring,
To euery coast where noble[5] Knightes resort:
Queenes shall atend and humble at his feete:
Thus loue and bewtie shall together meete.

Lastly, vnder the pillow of the third were these verses likewise caractred, who blushed in his Cradle like *Pallas* when shee[6] stroue for the golden aple with *Venus* and the Queene of heauen.

The Muses darling for true sapience,
In Princes Court this Babe shall spend his dayes:
Kinges shall admire his learned eloquence,
And write in brazen bookes his endles praise:
By Pallas gift he shall atchiue a Crowne,
Aduance his fame and lift him to renowne.

Thus when the Fayrie Queene had ended her Prophesie vpon the Children, and had left their golden Fortunes lying in their Cradles, she vanished away, leauing the Lady reioycing at her safe deliuerie, and woondred at the gifts of *Proserpine*: which shee coniectured to bee but shadowes to dazell her eyes, and thinges of a vading substance: but when shee had laide her handes vppon the riche couering of Dammaske Taffatie which couered her mossie bed, and felt that it was the selfe same forme that it seemed: shee cast her eyes with a chearefull looke vp to the Maiestie of heauen, and not onely gaue thankes to immortall *Ioue* for her rich receaued benefits: but for his mercifull kindnes in makeing her the happie Mother of three such goodly children: but we will now returne againe to the noble Champion Saint *George*, whome we left praying vppon the mountaine top: and as you heard before, the skies were ouerspred with Sable Cloudes, as though they had beene mourning witnesses of hys Ladies torments: but before the golden Sunne had diu'de into watry *Thetis* lap, the element[7] began to cleare, & to withdraw her former mouming Mantles: by which he supposed that heauen had pittied his Ladies paines, & granted her a safe deliuerie: therefore in all hast he retired back to the

---

[5] *noble*] om. *1596*
[6] shee] hee *1596*
[7] element] elemen *1596*

Siluaine Cabbinet, the which he found most strangely deckt with sumptuous habilliments, hys Lady lying in her Child-bed as glorious, as if shee had beene the greatest Empresse in the world, and three Princely boyes sweetlie sleeping in their seuerall Cradles: At whose first sight hys hart was so rauished with ioy, that for a time it with-held the passage of his tongue: but at last when hee found the siluer Tablets lying vnder the pillows, and had read the happie fortunes of his Children, he ran vnto his Ladie, imbraced her most louinglie, and kindely demaunded the true discourse of that strange accident, and by whose meanes the bower was beautefied so gorgeouslie, and the propounder of his Childrens Prophesie: who with a countenance blushing like the purple Morning, replied in this manner.

My most deare and welbeloued Lord, the paynes I haue indured to make you the happie Father of three louelie boyes; hath beene more tyrrible than the stroake of death: but yet my deliuerie more ioyfull than the pleasures of Elizium:[8] the windes carried my groanes to euerie corner of this Wildernes, whereby both trees and hearbes assisted my complaints, beasts, birdes, and feathered foules, with euerie sensles thinge that nature framed on this earth, seemed to agrauate my mones: but in the middle of my torments, when my soule was readie to forsake this worldlie habitation: there appeared to me a Queene Crowned with a golden Diadem, in state and gesture, like imperious *Iuno*, and in beautie to diuine *Diana*: her garments for brauerie seemed to staine the Raine-bow[9] in her brightest hue, and for diuersitie in colours, to surpasse the Flowers in the fieldes: On her attended many beautifull Nimphes, some clad in garments in colour like the marble *Ocean*, some in attire as gallant as the purple Rose, and some more glorious than the azurde firmaments: her wisedome might compare with *Apolloes*, her iudgement with *Pallas*, and her skill with *Lucinaes*: for no sooner entred she my presence but my trauailes ceased, and my wombe deliuered vp her grieuous burthen: my Babes beeing brought to light by the vertue of her skill, she prepared these rich and sumptuous Cradles, the which were brought inuisible to my Cabbinet: Likewise these Mantles[10] & this imbrothered Couerled she franckly bestowed vpon me, and so immediatlie vanished away.

At which wordes saint *George* gaue her so many kinde imbraces, and kissed her so louingly, as though it had bin the first day of their Nuptials: At last her hunger increased, and her desires thirsted so much after foode, that except shee receaued some comfortable sustenance, her life were in danger. This extreame desire of *Sabra*, caused S. *George* to buckle on his Armour, & to vnsheath his trustie sword, ready to gorge the intrails of some Deare: who swore by the honor of true Knighthood, neuer to rest in peace, till he had purchased his hearts content. My Loue (quoth he) I will aduenture for thy sake, more daungers than *Iason* did for *Medeas* loue: Ile search the thickest Groues, and chase the nimble Doe to death: the flying Foule Ile follow vp & downe from tree to tree, till ouer wearied they doe fall and die: For loue of thee and these my tender Babes, whome I esteeme more dearer than the Conquest of rich *Babilon*: I will aduenture more daungers than did

---

[8] Elizium] Elizian *1596*
[9] Raine-bow] Raine-baw *1596*
[10] Mantles] Mantled *1596*

Hercules for the loue of *Dianaria*, and more extreames than *Turnus* did in hys blody battels, & thereupon with hys Fauchion readie charged, he traced the woods, leauing no thornie brake nor mossie Caue vnsearcht, till he had found a heard of fallow Deare: from which number hee singled out the fattest to make hys Lady a bountifull banquet: but in the time of his absence there hapned to *Sabra* a straunge and wonderfull accident: for there came weltring into her Cabbinet three most wilde and monstrous beastes, a Lyon, a Tyger, and a shee Wolfe, which tooke the Babes out of their cradles, and bore them to their secret Caues.

At which sight, *Sabra* like one distraught of sence, started from her bed, and to her weake power offered to follow the Beastes: but all in vaine: for before shee coulde get without her Cabbinet, they were past sight, and the Childrens cryes without her hearing: then like a discontented woman she turned backe, beating her breasts, rending her haire, and raging vp and downe her Cabbinet, vsing all the rigour she could deuise against her selfe, and had not Saint *George* returned the sooner, she had most violently committed her owne slaughter: but at his returne when he beheld her face stayned with teares, her head disrobde of ornaments, and her Iuorie breastes all to bee rent and torne, he cast downe his venison, and in all haste asked the cause of her sorrow.

O (said she) this is the wofullest day that euer hapt to me: for in the time of your vnhappie hunting a Lyones, a Tygresse, and a Wolfe came into my Cabbinet and tooke my Children from their Cradles, what is become of them I know not: but greatly I feare by this time, they are intoombed within their hungry bowels.

O simple Monuments (quoth he) for such sweete Babes! Well *Sabra*, if the monsters haue bereaued mee of my children: this bloody sword that diu'de into the intrailes of fallow Deare, shall riue my wofull heart in twaine. Accursed be this fatall day: the Planets that predominate, & Sunne that shines thereon: Heauen blot it from the yere, and let it neuer more be numbred, but accounted for a dismall day through all the world: let all the trees bee blasted in these accursed woods: let hearbes and grasse consume a way and die, and all thinges perish in this Wildernes: but why breath I out these curses in vaine, when as me thinks I heare my Children in vntamed Lyons dens crying for help and succour: I come sweet Babes I come, eyther to redeeme you from the Tygers wrathfull Iawes, or make my graue within their bowels: then tooke hee vp hys sword besmeered all with blood, and like a man bereaude of wit and sence raged vp and downe the Wildernes, searching euerie corner for hys Children: but hys Lady remayned still in her Cabbinet lamenting for their losse, washing their Cradles with her Pearled teares that trickled downe her stayned cheekes like siluer drops.

Many waies wandred saint *George*: sometimes in vallies where Wolfes and Tygers lurke: sometimes on mountaine toppes where Lyons whelpes doo sporte and play, and many times in dismall thickets where Snakes and Serpents liue.

Thus wandred S. *George* vp & downe the Wildernes for the space of two dayes, hearing no newes of hys vnchristened Children: At last he approached the sight of a pleasant Riuer, which smoothlie glided downe betwixt two Mountaines: into whose streames he purposed to cast himselfe, and so by a desperate death giue end to hys sorrowes: But as hee was committing his bodie to the mercie of the waters, and his soule to the pleasure of the heauens, hee heard a farre off the rufull scrike as he thought of a comfortles Babe: which sodaine noyse caused him to refraine hys desperate purpose, and with more discreation tender his owne safetie: Then casting his eye aside, it was his happie destenie to spie the three inhumane beastes lying at the foote of the hill, tumbling themselues against the warme Sunne, and his three prettie babes sucking from their wombes their most vnkindly milke: which spectackle so incouraged the Champion, that without further aduisement, with his single sword he assayled at one time the three Monsters, but so furiously they pursued him, that he little preuailed, and being almost breathlesse, was forced to leape into an Oringe tree, else had hee beene buried in theyr mercilesse bowels: but when the three wilde beasts perceiued him aboue theyr reaches, and that by no meanes they could come neere him, with theyr wrathfull iawes they so rent and tore the roote of the tree, that if by pollicie hee had not preuented them, the tree had beene puld in pieces, for at that time it was so full of ripe Oringes, and so ouerloden, that the branches seemed to bend, and the boughes to breake: of which frute he cast such abundance downe to the beastes, whereby they restrained theyr furies, and fedde so fast thereon, that in short time they grew drunke, and quite ouercome with a dead and heauy sleepe, this good and happy fortune caused *S. George* nimbly to leape from the tree, and with his keene edged sword, deliuered theyr monstrous heades from theyr bodies, the which being done he went to his children, lying comfortlesse vppon a mossy banke, who so pleasantly smiled in his face, that they made him greatly to reioyce, and to receiue as great pleasure in theyr sights, as though hee had beene honoured with the Conquests of *Cæsar*, or the Royalty of *Alexander*, therefore after he had giuen them his blessing, he tooke them vp in his Armes, and spake these wordes following.

Come, come my pretty Babes, your safe deliueries from these inhumane Monsters, will adde long life vnto your mother, and hath preserude your father from a desperate death: from henceforth let heauen be your guides, and send you as happy fortunes as *Remus* and *Romulus*, the first founders of imperious *Rome*, which in theyr infancies were nurced with the milke of a rauenous Wolfe: and as prosperous in your aduentures, as was that *Persian* Potentate, which fed vppon the milke of a Bitch: At the ende of which speeches he approached the Cabbinet, where he left his Lady mourning for the losse of her children: but at his returne, he found her almost without sence or moouing, being not able to giue him a ioyfull welcome, whereat hee fell into this extreame passion of sorrow.

O fortune, fortune (quoth hee) how many griefes heapest thou vppon my heade? wilt thou needes inioyne me to an endles sorrow? See, *Sabra* see, I haue redeemed our sonnes and freed them from the Tygers bloody iaws, whose wrathfull countenance did threaten death: Which comfortable speeches caused her presently to reuiue, and to take the silly Infants in her Armes, laying them sweetly vpon her yuorie bosome, at which they seemed to smile as pleasantly, as *Cupid* vpon the lappe of *Dido*, when *Aeneas* sported in the Court of Carthage, the kinde imbraces, louing speeches, and ioyfull conference that past betwixt the Champion and his Lady, were now too long to be discoursed: But to be short, they remayned in the wildernesse without further disturbance either of wilde beasts or other accident, till *Sabra* had recouered her Child-bed sicknes: and then beeing conducted by a happie starre, they returned backe the readie way to Christendome: where after some few dayes trauaile they ariued in the *Bohemian* Court, where the King of that Countrie, with two other bordering Princes, most Royally Christned his Children: The eldest they named *Guy*: the second *Alexander*: and the third *Dauid*: the which being performed, and the Triumphes ended: which in most sumpteous manner continued, for the space of one month: then the Bohemian King for the great loue hee bare vnto *S. George*, prouided most honourably for his childrens bringing vp: First, he appoynted three seuerall Embassadours, with all things necessary for so Princely a charge, to conduct the three Infants to three seuerall Countries: the first and eldest, whose fortune was to be a souldier, he sent to the imperiall Citty of *Rome*, (being then the wonder of the world for Martiall discipline) there by the Emperour to bee trayned vp. The seconde, whose fortune was to bee a Courtly Prince, hee sent to the rich and plentifull Country of England, being the pride of Christendome for all delightfull pleasures: The third and last, whose fortune was to prooue a Scholler, he sent into *Germany*, to the Uniuersity of *Wittenberge*, beeing thought at that time to bee the excellenst place of learning, that remayned throughout the whole world.

Thus were saint *Georges* Children prouided for by the Bohemian King: For when the Embassadours were in a readinesse, the ships for theyr passage furnished, and their attendance appoynted, saint *George* in the company of his Lady, the King of Bohemia with his Queene, and a trayne of Lords, gentlemen, and Ladyes, conducted them to shipbord, where the winde serued them so prosperously, that in short time they bid adew to the shore, and sayled chearefully away: But as saint *George* returned backe to the Bohemian Court, it was his chaunce to come by an olde ruinated Monastery, vnder whose walles in former time his Father was buried, the which he knewe by certaine verses that was carued in stone ouer his graue by the Commons of the Country (as you may reade before in the beginning of this History.) Ouer the same, he requested of the King, that hee might erect a stately Monument, that the remembrance of his name might liue for euer, and not be buried in the graue of obscurity.

To which reasonable demaund, the King most willingly consented, and in all hast gaue speciall commandement, that the cunningest Architectors that remayned within his Dominion, should forthwith be sent for, and withall gaue a tun of gold forth of his owne treasury towards the performance thereof.

The sodaine report of this memorable deede, being bruted abroade, caused workemen to come from euery place of their owne accord with such willingnes, that they in short time finished it. The foundation of the Toombe, was of the purest Marble, whereon was ingrauen the frame of the earth, and how the watry Ocean was deuided: with woods groues, hilles and dales, so liuely portrayed, that it was a wonder to behold: the props and Pinacles of Allablaster, beset with knobs of Iasper stone, the sides and Pillers of the clearest Iette, vpon the topp stoode foure golden Lions, holding vp as it were an Element, therein was curiously contriued the golden Sunne and Moone, & how the heauens haue vsuall courses, with many other excellent thinges wrought both in gold and siluer, which for this time I omit, because I am forced at large to discouer the Princely proceedings of saint *George*, who after the Monument was finished, he with his Lady most humbly tooke their leaue of the King, thanking him for his loue, kindnes, and curtesie, and so departed towards *Egypt* and *Persia*, of whose aduentures you shall heare more in this Chapter following.

How S. George with his Lady ariued in Egypt: of their royall entertainements to the Citie of Ground Cayer: And also how Sabra was crowned Queene of Egypt.

MAny strange accidents and dangerous aduentures, S. *George* with his Lady passed before they ariued within the territories of Egypt, that I want memory to relate them, and Arte to describe them: But at last when fortune smiled, which before had long time crossed their intents with her inconstant chances, and had cast them happily vpon the Egyptian shore, being the nurse and mother of *Sabraes* first creation. The twelue Peeres with whome S. *George* beforetime had committed the guiding of the Land, and keeping of his Crowne, as you heard before discoursed, now met him and his Lady at the Sea side,[2] most richly mounted vpon their costly trapped Steeds, and willingly surrendred vp his Scepter, Crowne and Regiment: and after, in companie of many Princely Estates, both of Dukes, Earles, Lords, Knights, and royall Gentlemen, they attended them to the Citie of graund Cayer, beeing then vnder the subiection of the Egyptian Monarchy, and the greatest Cittie in the world: for it was in breadth and compasse full three score miles, and had by iust account within the walles twelue thousand Churches, besides Abbies, Priories, and houses of Religion: but when S. *George* with his stately attendants entred the gates, they were presently entertayned with such a ioyfull sound of Belles, Trumpets, and Drummes, that it seemed like the inspiring melodie of heauenly Angels, and to exceed the Royaltie of *Cæsar* in Rome, when hee returned from the worlds conquest. The streetes were beautified with stately Pageants, contriued by schollers of ingenious capacitie, the pauements strowed with all maner of odoriferous flowres, and the walles hung with Indian Couerlets and curious Tapestrie.

Thus passed they the streetes in great solemnitie, wondring at the curiositie of the Pageants, and listning to their learned Orations, till they entred the gates of the Palace; where, in the first entry of the Court was contriued ouer their heads, a golden pendant firmament, as it were supported by a hundred Angels: from thence it seemed to rayne *Nectar* and *Ambrosia*: Likewise there descended, as it were from the clouds, *Ceres*, the goddesse of plentie, sitting vpon a throne of gold, beautified with all maner of springing things, as of Corne, Oliues, Grapes, Hearbs, Flowers, and Trees: who, at the comming by of S. *George* and his Ladie, presented them with two garlands of wheate, bound vp most curiously in bands of siluer, to signifie that they were happily returned to a plentifull countrey, both of wealth and treasure. But at *Ceres* ascension vp into the firmament, there was seene most strange and pleasant fireworkes, shooting from place to place, as though the fierie Planets had descended heauen, and had generally consented to make them delightfull pastimes: But as Saint *George* with his Lady crowned with Garlands of

---

[1] *The 1596 edition is defective, lacking everything after the first page of Chapter XVIII. The whole of Chapters XVIII and XIX have been supplied from the 1608 edition.*
[2] side] sids *1608*

Wheat, passed through the second Court, they beheld a Pageant most strangely contriued: wherein stoode *Mars* the angrie God of warre, inuironed with a Campe of armed Souldiers, as if they were with their weapons readie charged to assault some strong Hold, or inuincible Cittie: their siluer Trumpets seemed to sound cheerefully, their thundring Drums couragiously, their silken streamers to flourish valiantly, and themselues to march triumphantly. All which seemed to bee of more content to Saint *George*, then all the delightfull pleasures before rehearsed: for there was nothing in all the world that more reioyced his heart, then to heare the pleasant sound of warres, and to see Souldiers brandish forth their steeled weapons. After hee had sufficiently delighted himselfe in these Martiall sportes, and was ready to depart, the god of warre descended his throne, and presented him with the richest Armour that euer eye beheld, and the brauest sword that euer Knight handled: for they had beene kept within the Cittie of Graund Cayer for the space of fiue hundred yeeres, and held for the richest monuments in the Countrie. Also he presented *Sabra* with a myrrour of such an inestimable price, that it was valued at a Kings Dominion: for it was made by Magicke Art: the vertues and qualities thereof were so pretious, that it is almost incredible to report: for therein one might beholde the secret misteries of all the liberall Sciences, and by arte discouer what was practised in other Princes Courts: if any hill or mountaine within a thousand miles of the place where it remained, were inriched with a mine of gold, it would describe the place and countrey, and how deepe it lay closed in the earth: by it one might truly calculate vpon the birth of children, succession of Princes, and continuance of common-weales, with many other excellent gifts of vertues, which for this time I omit. Then in great state passed S. *George* to the third Court, which was as richly beautified with as gallant sights as the other twane: for there was most liuely portraied ye maner of Elizium, how *Ioue & Iuno* sate inuested on their royall thrones, and likewise how all the gods & goddesses tooke their places by degrees in Parliament: the sight was pleasant, & the deuice most excellent, their musicke admired, and their songs most heauenly.

Thus passed S. *George* with his Lady through the three Courts, till they came to the Pallace: wherein was prouided against their comming, a statelier banquet then had the Macedonian Monarch, at his returne to Babylon, when he had conquered the middle earth: the curious cates and well appoynted dishes were so many, that I want Art or eloquence to describe them: but to be short, it was the sumptuoust banquet that euer they beheld, since their departure from the English Court, and so artificially serued, as though that all the Kings of the world had beene present. Many daies continued this sumptuous cheare, and concluded with such princely triumphes, as Arte her selfe wants memorie to describe.

The Coronation of Sabra, which was royally performed within three moneths following, requires a golden pen to write it, and a tongue washt in the conseruatiues of ye Muses hony to declare it. Egypt was honoured with triumphs, and Graund Cayer with tilts and turnaments. Through euery towne was proclaimed a solemne and feastiuall day, in ye remembrance of their new crowned Queene: no tradesman nor Artificer was suffred to worke vpon that day, but were charged vpon paine of death to hold it for a day of tryumphs, a day of ioy, & a day of pleasure: in which royalties, S. *George* was a principall performer, till thirst of honour summoned him to Armes: the remembrance of the Christian Champions in Persia, caused him to breuiat the pastimes, & to buckle on his steeled Corslet, which had not glistered in the fields of *Mars* in foure and twenty months: of whose noble deeds, and aduenturous proceedings, I will at large discourse, and leaue all other pastimes, to the new inuested Queene and her Ladies.

CHAP. XIX.

The bloudie battell betwixt the Christians and the persians, and how the Nigromancer Osmond raysed vp by Magicke Arte, an Armie of spirits to fight against[1] the Christians: How the sixe Champions were inchaunted, and recouered by Saint George: The miserie and death of the Coniurer: and how the Souldan brained him selfe against a Marble piller.

NOw must we returne to the Christian Champions, and speake of their battels in Persia, and what happened to them in S. *Georges* absence: for if you remember before, being in Egypt, when he had newes of his Ladies condemnation in England, for the murther of the Earle of Couentrie, he caused them to march into Persia, and incouraged them to reuenge his wrongfull imprisonment vpon the Souldan and his Prouinces: into which Countrey after they had marched some fiftie miles, burning and spoyling his Territoryes, they were intercepted by the Souldanes power which was about the number of three hundred thousand fighting men: but the mustrer-rolles of the Christians were likewise numbred, and they surmounted not to aboue one hundred thousand able men: at which time, betwixt the Christians and Pagans happened a long and dangerous battell, the like in any age was seldome fought: for it continued without ceasing, for the space of fiue dayes, to the great effusion of bloud on both parties.

But at last the Pagans had the worst: for when they beheld their fields bestrowed with mangled bodies, and that the riuers for twentie miles compasse did flow with Crimson bloud, their hearts began to faile, and incontinently fled like sheepe before the wolfe. Then the valiant Christians thirsting after reueng, speedily pursued them, sparing neither young nor old, till the waies were strowed with liueles bodies, like heapes of scattered sand: In which pursuite and honourable Conquest, they burned two hundred Forts and townes, battering their Towers of stone as leuell with the ground, as haruest reapers doe fields of ripened corne: But the Souldan himselfe, with many of his best approoued souldiers escaped aliue, & fortified the Cittie of Graund Belgor, being the strongest Towne of warre in all the Kingdome of Persia: before whose walles wee will leaue the Christian Champions planting their puissant forces, and speake of the damnable practises of *Osmond* within the towne, where he accomplisht many admirable accidents by Magicke Art: for when the Christian Armie had long time giuen assault to the walles, sending their fiery bullets to their loftie battlements like storms of winters haile, whereby the Persian souldiers were not able any longer to resist, they began to yeeld & commit their liues to the mercies of the Christian Champions: but when ye Souldan perceiued his souldiers cowardice, and how they would willingly resigne his happie gouernement to forraine rule, hee incouraged them still to resist the Christians desperate encounters, and within thirtie dayes, if they had not the honour of the war, then willingly to condiscend to their Countries conquest: which princely resolution incouraged the souldiers to resist, intending neuer to yeeld vp their Cittie, till death

---

[1] *against] agrinst 1608*

had made triumph in their bodies. Then departed he into a secret Tower, where he found *Osmond* sitting in his Chaire, studying by Magicke, how long Persia should remaine vnconquered: who at his entrance droue him from his charmes with these speeches:

Thou wondrous man of Art (sayd the Souldan) whom for Nigromancie the world hath made famous. Now is the time to expresse the loyaltie and loue thou bearest thy Soueraigne: Now is the time thy Charming Spels must worke for Persiaes good: thou seest my fortunes are deprest, my souldiers dead, my Captaines slaughtered, my Cities burned, my fields of Corne consumed, and my Countrey almost conquered: I that was wont to couer the Seas with Fleetes of ships, now stand amazed to heare the Christians Drums, that sound foorth dolefull Funerals for my souldiers: I that was wont with armed Legions to drinke vp riuers as wee marched, and made the earth to groane with bearing the number of our multitudes: I that was wont to make whole kingdomes tremble at my frownes, and force imperious Potentates to humble at my feete: I that haue made the streetes of many a Cittie run with bloud, and stoode reioycing when I saw their buildings burne: I that haue made the mothers wombs the Infants toombes, and caused Cradles for to swimme in streames of bloud, may nowe behold my Countries ruine, my kingdomes fall, & mine owne fatall ouerthrow: Awake, great *Osmond*, from thy dreaming traunce, awake, I say, and raise a troupe of blacke infernall fiendes to fight against the damned Christians, that like to swarmes of Bees doe flocke about our wals: preuent, I say my lands inuasion, and as I am great Monarch of Asia, Ile make thee King ouer twentie Prouinces, & Sole Commaunder of the Ocean: rayse vp, I say, thy charmed spirits: leaue burning Acharon emptie for a time, to ayd vs in this bloudie battell.

These words being no sooner ended, but there ratled such a peale of Cannons against the Cittie[2] wals, that they made the verie earth to shake: whereat the Nigromancer started from his Chaire, and in this maner incouraged the Souldan:

It is not Europe (quoth hee) nor all their pettie bands of armed Knights, nor all the Princes in the world, that shall abate your princely dignitie: Am not I the great Magician of this age, that can both lose and bind the fiends, and call the blacke-faste Furies from low *Cossitus*? Am not I that skilfull Artist, which framed the charmed Tower amongst the Amazonian Dames, which all the Witches in the world could neuer spoyle? Therefore let Learning, Arte, and all the secrets of the deepes, assist mee in this enterprize, and then let frowning Europe doe her worst: my charmes shall cause the heauens to rayne such ratling showers of stones vpon their heads, whereby the earth shall be ouerloaden with their dead bodies, and hell ouerfilled with their hatefull soules: sencelesse trees shall rise in humane shapes, and fight for Persia. If wise *Medea* were euer famous for Arts, that did the like for safegard of her fathers state: then why should not *Osmond* practise wonders for his Soueraignes happines? Ile raise a troupe of spirits from the lowest earth, more blacke then dismall night, the which in vgly shapes shall haunt them vp and downe, and when they sleepe within their rich Pauillions, legions of fierie spirits will I

---

[2] Cittie] Cttie *1608*

vprayse from hell, that like to Dragons spitting flames of fire, shall blast and burne
the damned Christians in their Tents of warre: The fields of Graund *Belgor* shall be
ouerspred with venemous Snakes, Adders, Serpents, and impoysoned Toades, the
which vnseene shall lurke in Mossie ground, and sting the Corronets of warlike
horses: downe from the Chrystall firmament, I will coniure a troupe of ayrie spirits
to descend, that like to virgins clad in princely ornaments, shall linke these
Christian Champions in the chaines of loue: their eyes, which shall be like the
twinkling Lamps of heauen, shall dazell so their warlike thoughts, and their louely
countenance more bright then Angels, shall leade them captiues to a Tent of loue,
the which shall be artificially erected vp by my Magicke Spels: their warlike
weapons that were wont to sweate in Pagans bloud, shall in my charmed Tent bee
hung vpon the bowers of peace: their glistring Armours that were wont to shine
within the fields of Affrica, shall henceforth be euermore stayned with rust, and
themselues surnamed for Martiall discipline, the wondrous Champions of the
world, shall surfet with delightfull loues, and sleepe vpon the laps of ayrie spirits,
that shall descend the Elements in virgins shapes, terrour and despaire shall
mightily oppresse their mercilesse Souldiers, that they shall yeeld the honorable
conquest to your excellencie: such strange and wondrous accidents by Art shall bee
accomplished, that heauen shall frowne at my Inchauntments and the earth tremble
to heare my Coniurations. Therefore most mightie Persian, number vp thy scattered
bands, and to morrow in the morning set open thy gates, & march thitherward with
thy armed souldiers: leaue not a man within the Citie, but let euery one that is able
to carrie Armes, fight in the honour of Persia, and before the closing of the night,
Ile make thee Conquerour, and yeelde vp the brauing Christians as prysoners to thy
mightinesse.

   If this proue true, renowmed *Osmond*, as thou hast promised (sayd the Souldan)
earth shall not harbour that too deare for thee: for thou shalt haue my selfe, my
kingdomes, Crownes and Scepters at commaund: the wealthie Riuer *Ganges*, shall
pay thee yearely tribute with her treasure: *Pactulus* shall yeelde his ritches to thy
pleasure, the place where *Midas* washt his golden wish away. All things that nature
framed precious, shalt thou be Lord and Sole commaunder of, if thou preuent the
inuasion of my Countrey: and thereupon he departed the Chamber, and left the
Nigromancer in his studie: and as hee gaue commaundement his Captaines made in
readinesse their souldiers, and furnished their warlike horses, and by the Sunnes
vprising, marched into the fields of *Belgor*: where vpon the Northside of the
enemie they pitched their Campe. On the other side, when the warlike Christians
had intelligence by their Courts of gard, howe the Pagans were entred the fieldes,
readie to giue them battell, sudden Alarums sounded in their eares, rumors of
conquest encouraged so their Souldiers, that presently they were in readinesse to
entertayne the Persians to a bloudy banquet. Both armies were in sight, with bloud
red colours wauering in the ayre: the Christian Champions richly mounted on their
warlike coursers, placed themselues in the forefront of the battell like couragious
Captaines, fearing neyther death, nor the vnconstant chance of fortune. But the
Souldan with his petty Princes like cowards, were inuiron'd and compast with a
ring of armed Knights, where in stead of nimble Steedes, they sate in iron
charriots. Diuers heroicall and many princely incouragements past betweene the

two Armies, before they entred battell: but when the Drums began to sound alarum, and the siluer Trumpets gaue dreadfull ecchoes of death: when the Crosse of Christendome began to flourish, and the Armes of *Mahomet* to aduance; euen then began so terrible and bloudie a battell, that the like was neuer found in any age: for before the Sunne had mounted to the top of heauen, the Pagans receiued so greate a massaker, and fell so fast before the Christian Champions, that they were forst to wade vp to the knees in bloud, and their souldiers to fight vpon heaps of slaughtered men: the fields were conuerted from a greene colour to a purple hewe, the dales were steept in crimson gore, and the hils and mountaines hung with dead mens ratling bones.

But let vs not forget the wicked Nigromancer *Osmond*, that during the time of that dangerous encounter kneeled in a low valley neere vnto the campes, with his blacke haire hanging downe vnto his shoulders like a wreathe of snakes, and with his siluer wand circling the earth; where when hee heard the sound of Drums thundring in the ayre, and the brazen Trumpets giuing dreadfull sounds of warre, hee entred into these fatall and damned speaches:

Now is the battell (quoth he) furiously begunne, for me thinks I heare the Souldan cry for helpe: nowe is the time my charming spels must worke for Persiaes victorie, and Europes fatall ouerthrow: which being sayd, thrice did he kisse the earth, thrice behold the elements, and thrice besprinckled the circle with his owne bloud, the which with a siluer razor he let from his left arme, and after began againe to speake in this maner:

Stand still, you wandring lamps of heauen, mooue not, sweete starres, but linger on, till *Osmonds* Charmes bee brought to full effect. O thou great *Dæmon*, prince of damned ghosts, thou cheife commaunder of those fearefull shapes, that nightly glide by misbeleeuing trauellers, euen thou that holdest a snakie scepter in thy hand, sitting vpon a throne of burning steele, euen thee that bindest the furies vp in chaines, euen thee that tossest burning firebrands abroad, euen thee whose eyes are like two blazing and vnlucky Commets, euen thee I charge to let thy furies loose, open thy brazen gates and leaue thy boyling cauldrons empty: send vp such Legions of infernall fiends, that may in number counteruayle the blades of grasse that beautifie these bloudy fieldes of Belgor.

These fatall speeches being no sooner finished, but there appeared such a multitude of spirits, both from the earth, water, ayre, and fire, that it is almost incredible to report, the which hee caused to runne into the Christian Armie: whose burning Fauchions not onely annoyed the souldiers with feare and terror, but also fiered their horses manes, burned their trappings, consumed their banners, scorched trees and hearbes, and dimmed the elements with such an extreme darkenesse, as though the earth had beene couered with eternall night: he caused his spirits likewise to rayse such a terrible tempest, that it tore vp mighty Oakes by the rootes, remoued hilles and mountaines, and blew men into the ayre horse and all: yet neyther his Magicke Artes, nor all the Furies of his wicked spirits could any whit daunt the most noble and magnanimious mindes of the six Champions of Christendome: but like vnconquered Lyons they purchast honour where they went, colouring their swords in Pagans bloud, making the earth true witnes of their victorious and heroicall proceedings, whome they had attyred in a bloud red liuery:

and though Saint *George* (the cheife Champion of Christendome for Martiall discipline, and princely atcheiuements) were absent in that terrible battell: yet merited they as much honor & renowne, as though he had beene there present: for the accursed Pagans fell before their warlike weapons, as thicke as leaues doe fall from the trees, when the blustring stormes of winter enter on the earth. But when the wicked Nigromancer *Osmond* perceiued, that his Magicke spels tooke small effect, and how in despite of his Inchauntments the Christians got the better of the day, he accursed his Art, and banned the houre and time wherein hee first attempted so euill and wicked an enterprise, thinking them to be preserued by Angels or else by some celestiall meanes: but yet not purposing to leaue off at the first repulse, he attempted another way by Nigromancie to ouerthrowe the Christians.

First he erected vp by Magicke Art a stately Tent, outwardly in show like to the compasse of the earth: but furnished inwardly with all the delightfull pleasures that eyther Art or reason could inuent, onely framed to inchaunt the Christian Champions with intising delights, whome he purposed to keepe as prisoners therein: then fell hee againe to his coniuration, and bound a hundred spirits by due obedience to transforme themselues into the likenes of beautifull virgins, which in a moment they accomplished, and they were framed in forme and beautie like to the darlings of *Venus*, in comelinesse comparable with *Thetis* dauncing on the siluer sands, & in all proportions like *Daphne*, whose beautie caused *Apollo* to descend the heauens: their limmes were like the loftie Cedars: their cheekes to Roses dipt in milke, and their eyes more bright then the starres of heauen: also they seemed to carrie in their hands siluer bowes, and on their backes hung quiuers of golden Arrowes: Likewise vpon their brests they had pictured ye God of loue, dauncing vpon *Mars* his knee.

Thus in the shape of beautious Damsels, caused he these spirits to enter the Christian Armie, and with the golden baite of their intising smiles, to tangle the Champions in the snares of loue, & with their smiling beauties lead them from their souldiers, and to bring them prisoners into his inchaunted tent. Which commaundement being no sooner giuen, but these virgins, or rather infernall furies, more swift then the windes, glided into the Christians Armie; where their glistering beauties so dazeled the eyes of the sixe Christian Champions, and their sober countenances so intrapped their hearts with desire, that their princely valours were abated, and they stood gazing at their excellent proportions, as though *Medusaes* shaddowes had beene pictured vpon their faces, to whome the intising Ladyes spake in this maner.

Come, Princely Gallants, come, away with Armes, forget the soundes of bloudy warre, and hang your angry weapons on the bowre of peace: *Venus* you see hath sent her messengers from *Paphos*, to lead you to the paradise of loue: there heauen will raine downe *Nectar* and *Ambrosia* sweete for you to feede vpon; and there the melody of Angels will make you musicke: there shall you fight vpon beds of silke, and encounter with inticing kisses. These golden promises so rauished the Champions, that they were inchaunted with their loues, and vowed to take their last farewell of Knighthood and magnanimious Chiualry.

Thus were they led from their warlike companies to the Nigromancers inchaunted tent, leauing their souldiers without guiders in danger of confusion. But the Queene of chaunce so smiled vpon the Christians, that at the same time S. *George* ariued in Persia with a fresh supply of Egyptian Knights: of whose noble atcheiuements I purpose now to speake off: For no sooner had he entred the battell & placed his squadrons, but he had intelligence of the Champions misaduentures, and how they lay inchaunted in a Magicke tent, sleeping in pleasure vpon the laps of infernall furies, the which *Osmond* had transformed, by his charmes, to the likenes of beautifull Damsels: which vnexpected newes constrained S. *George* to breathe from his sorrowful heart this wofull lamentation.

Unconstant fortune (quoth he) why doest thou entertaine me with such bitter newes? are my fellowe Champions come from Christendome to win immortall honour with their swords, and lie they now bewitcht with beauty? Come they from Europe to fight in cotes of steele, and will they lye distraught in tents of loue? Came they to Asia to purchase Kingdomes, and by bloudy war to ruinate countreys, & will they yeeld their victories to so foule disgrace? O shame and great dishonour to Christendome! O spot to Knighthood and true Chiualrie! this newes is far more bitter to my soule, then was the poysoned dregs y^t *Antipater* gaue to *Alexander* in his drunkennes, and a deadlier paine vnto my heart, then was ye iuyce that *Hanniball* suckt from his fatall ring. Come, Champions, come you followers of those cowardly Champions, vnsheath your warlike weapons, and follow him whose soule hath vowed eyther to redeeme them from the Nigromancers charmes, or dye with honour in the enterprize. If euer mortall creatures warred with damned furies, & made a passage to inchaunted dales, where deuils daunce, & warlike shaddowes in the night: then souldiers, let vs march vnto that blacke pauilion, and chaine the cursed charmer to some blasted Oake, that hath so highly dishonoured Christendome.

These resolute speaches being no sooner finished, but the whole armie, before daunted with feare, grewe so couragious, y^t they protested to follow him through more dangers, then did the Grecian Knights with noble Iason in the Ile of Calcos. Now began the battell againe to renew, & the drums to sound fatall knels for the Pagan souldiers, whose soules the Christian swords by numbers sent to burning Acharon: but S. *George*, that in valour exceeded the rest, as much as the golden Sun surpasseth the smallest starres in brightnes, with his sword made lanes of slaughtered men, and with his angry Arme made passage through the thickest of their troups, as though that death had beene commaunder of the battell: he caused Crownes and' Scepters to swim in bloud, and headlesse Steedes with ioyntlesse men to fall as fast before his sword, as drops of raine before a thunder, & euer in the greatest danger, he incouraged his Souldiers in this maner: Now for the fame of Christendome, fight, Captaines, bee nowe triumphant conquerours, or Christian Martyrs.

These words so incouraged the souldiers hearts with inuincible valour, that they neyther feared the Nigromancers charmes, nor all his flaming dragons, nor fiery drakes, that filled the ayre with burning lights, nor daunted at the strange encounters of hellish Legions, that like to armed men with burning Fauchions haunted them: so fortunate were their proceedings, that they followed the inuincible Champion to the inchaunted tent, where as the other Champions lay surfetting in loue, whilest thousands of their freinds fought in fearefull cotes of steele, and merited renowme by their noble atchieuements: for no sooner ariued S. *George* with his warlike followers before the Pauilion, but he heard as it were, the melodie of the Muses: likewise his eares were almost rauished with the sugred songs of the inchaunted virgins, which like the musicke of *Orpheus* harpe, caused both stones and trees to daunce, and made elements to shew more brighter then the mornings beautie with drops of hony trickling downe their christall cheekes: the Doues did kisse when they beganne to sing: the running waters daunced, and euery senceles thing did seeme to breathe out sighes for loue: so pleasurable and heauenly were the sights in the Tent, and so delightfull in his eyes, that he had beene inchaunted with their charmes, if hee had not continually borne the honour of Knighthood in his thoughts, and that the dishonour would redound to Christendomes reproache: therefore with his sword he let driue at the Tent, and cut it into a thousand peeces; the which being done, he apparantly beheld where the Nigromancer sate vpon a blocke of steele, feeding his spirits with drops of bloud: whom when the Champion beheld, he caused his souldiers to lay hold vpon him, and after chayned him fast to the roote of an olde blasted Oake: from whence, neyther his artes, nor help of all his charmes, nor all the legions of his deuils could euer after lose him: where we wil leaue him to his lamentations, filling the ayre with ecchoes of cries, and speake how S. *George* redeemed[3] the Champions from their inchauntments.

First, when he beheld them disrobed of their warlike attire, their furniture hung vp, and themselues securely sleeping vpon the laps of Ladyes, he fell into these discontented speeches:

O heauens (sayd he) how my soule abhorres this spectacle! Champions of Christendome, arise, braue knights, stand vp, I say, and looke about like men: are you the chosen Captaines of your countries, and will you burie all your honours vp in Ladies laps? for shame arise, I say, they haue the teares of Crocodiles, the songs of Syrens to inchaunt: to Armes, braue Knights, let honour be your loues: blush to behold your freinds in Armes, and blush to see your natiue countrymen steeping the fieldes of Belgor with their blouds. Champions, arise, S. *George* calles, the victorie will tarry till you come: arise, and teare this womannish attire, and surfet not in silken robes: put on your steely Corslets, your glistering Burgonets, and vnsheath your conquering weapons, that Belgors fields may bee conuerted into a purple Ocean.

These Heroicall speaches beeing no sooner finished, but the Champions like men amazed, rose from their Ladyes bosomes, and being ashamed of their follies, they submissiuely craued pardon, and vowed by protestations, neuer to sleepe in beds of downe, nor neuer vnbuckle their shields from their wearie armes, till they had wonne their credits in the fields again: nor neuer more would be counted his deserued followers, till their triumphs were inrouled amongst the deedes of Martiall Knights. So arming themselues with their approued Corslets, and taking to

---

[3] redeemed] redeeme *1608*

them their trustie swords, they accompanied S. *George* to the thickest of their enemies, and left the Nigromancer chayned to the tree, which at their departure breathed foorth these bitter curses:

Let helles horror, and tormenting paines (quoth hee) be their eternall punishments: let flaming fire descend the elements, and consume them in their warlike triumphes, and let their wayes be strowed with venimous Porthers, that all their legges may ranckle to their knees, before they march to cursed Christendome. But why exclaime I thus in vaine, when heauen it selfe preserues their happinesse? Now all my Magick charmes are ended, and all my spirits forsake me in my needes, and here am I fast chained vp to starue and die. Haue I had power to rend the vales of earth, and shake the mightie mountaines with my charmes? Haue I had power to rayse vp dead mens soules from kingly toombes, and can I not vnchaine my selfe from this accursed tree? O no, for I am fettred vp by the immortall power of the Christians God; against whom, because I did rebell, I am nowe condemned to euerlasting fire. Come all you Nigromancers in the world, come all you Sorcerers and Charmers, come all you Schollers from the learned Uniuersities, come all you Witches, Beldames, and Fortune-tellers, and all that practise deuillish artes, come take example by the story of my fall.

This being sayd, he violently with his owne hands tore his eyes from his head, as a sufficient reuenge, because by the directions of their sights, he was first traind in that damned Arte: then betwixt his teeth hee bit in two his lothesome tongue, because it murmured forth so many fatall charmes: then into his thirstie bowels hee deuoured his hands, because they had so often held the siluer wand, wherewith hee had made his charmed circles, and for euery letter, marke, and character, that belonged to his Coniurations hee inflicted a seuerall torment vpon himselfe: and at last, with sightles eyes, speachles tongue, handlesse armes, and dismembred body, he was forced to giue vp his condemned ghost: where, after his ayre of life was vanished from his earthy trunck, the heauens seemed to smile and triumph at his sudden fall, and hell began to rore at the conquest of his death: the ground whereon he died, was euer after that time vnfortunate, and to this present time, it is called in that country, a vale of walking spirits.

Thus haue you heard the damned life and miserable fall of this accursed Nigromancer *Osmond*, whome wee will nowe leaue to the punishments due to such a wicked offender, and speake of the seuen noble and magnanimious Christian Champions.

After S. *George* had ended their Inchauntments, they neuer sheathed vp their swords, nor vnlocked their Armour, till the subuersion of Persia was accomplished, and the Souldan with his pettie Kings taken prysoner. Seuen dayes the battle continued without ceasing: they slew two hundred thousand Souldiers, besides a number that fled away and drowned themselues: some cast themselues headlong downe from the top of high trees, some made murther of themselues, and some yeelded to the mercies of the Christians: But the Soldan with his Princes riding in their Iron chariots, endured the Christians encounters, till the whole armie were discomfited, and then by force and violence they were compelled to yeelde. The Soldan hapned into the hands of S. *George*, and sixe of his Uiceroyes to the other sixe Champions, where after they had sworne aleageance to the Christian Knights, and had promised to forsake their *Mahomet*, they were not onely set at libertie, but vsed most honourably: but the Souldan himselfe hauing a heart fraught with despight and tyrannie, condemned the Champions courtesies, and vtterly disdained their Christian gouernments, protesting that the heauens shoulde first lose their wonted brightnes, and the Seas forsake their swelling Tides, before his heart shoulde yeelde to their intended desires: whereupon Saint *George* beeing resolued to reuenge his former iniuries, commaunded that the Souldan should bee disrobed from all Princely attire, and in base apparell sent to pryson, euen to the same Dungeon where he himselfe had indured so long imprysonment, as you heard in the beginning of the Historie: which strickt commaundement was presently performed: In which Dungeon the Souldan had not long continued, sufficing his hungrie stomacke with the bread of mustie branne, and stanching his thirst with Channel water, but he began to grow desperate and weary of his life, and at last fell into this wofull lamentation:

O heauens (quoth he) now haue you throwne a deserued plague vpon my head, and all those guiltlesse soules that in former times my tyrannies haue murthered, may now be fully satisfied: For I that was wont to haue my table beautified with Kings, am now constrained to feede alone in a Dungeon: wherefore sorrow is my foode, & despaire my seruitor: I that haue famished thousands vp in wals of stone, am now constrayned to feede vpon mine owne flesh, or else to starue and dye: yet shall these cruell Christians know, that as I liu'd in tyranny, so will I die: for I will make a murther of my selfe, that after this life, my angry ghost may fill their sleepes with gastly visions.

This being said, hee desperately ranne his head against a Marble piller, standing in the middle of the Dungeon, and dasht his braines from out his hatefull head: the newes of whose death, when it was bruted to the Champions eares, they proffered no violence to his liueles body, but intoombed him in a sumptuous Sepulchre, and after that, S. *George* tooke vpon him the gouernment of Persia, and there established good and Christian lawes: also hee gaue to the other sixe Champions, sixe seuerall kingdomes belonging to the Crowne of Persia, & surnamed them his Uiceroyes or pettie Kings. This being done, hee tooke truce with all the world, and triumphantly marched towards Christendome, with the Conquest of three imperiall Diadems, that is to say, of Egypt, Persia, and Moroco: In which iournie he erected many stately Monuments, in remembraunce of his victories and heroicall atcheiuements, and through euery Countrey that they marched, there flocked to them an innumerable company of Pagans, that desired to follow him into Christendome, and to bee christened in their faith, protesting euer to forsake their gods, whose worshippers were none but tyrants, and such as delighted in nothing but shedding of bloud. To whose requests, S. *George* presently condescended: not onely in graunting them their desires, but also in honouring them with the fauour of his princely countenance. This courtesie of the English Champion merited such a glistering glorie through the world, that as far as euer the swelling Ocean flowes, and as far as euer the golden globes of heauen extend their lights, S. *Georges* honour was bruted: and not onely his matchles aduentures caractred in brazen tables, but his martiall exployts painted in euery temple: so that the heathen Poets contriued Histories of his deeds, and cannonized his name amongst ye worthies of the world.

In this Princely maner marched S. *George* with his warlike troups through the territories of Affrica and Asia, in greater royalty, then did *Darius* with his Persian souldiers towards the campe of time-wondring *Alexander*. But when the Christian Champions approched the sight of the watry world, and began to goe aboord their shippes, the earth seemed to mourne at their farewels, and the seas to reioyce at their presence, the waues couched as smooth as Chrystall yce, and the windes blewe such gentle gale, as though the sea-gods had beene the directors of their fleete: the Dolphins daunced about the waters, and the louely Mare-maides, in multitudes lay dallying amidst the streames, making them delightfull pastime: the skies seemed to smile, and the Sunne to shew such a glistering brightnes vpon the chrystall waters, that the seas seemed to be of siluer.

Thus in great pleasure they passed the time away, committing their fortunes to the mercy of the windes and the waters; who did so fauourably serue them, that in short time they ariued vpon the bankes of Christendome: where being no sooner come on shore, and past the dangers of the Seas, but Saint *George* in the presence of thousands of his followers, kneeled downe on the ground, and gaue God prayse for his happy ariuall, by these words following:

O thou omnipotent God of new Jerusalem, we not onely giue thee condigne prayse, for our late atcheiued victories against thy enemies, who by their wickednesse seeke dayly to pull thee from thy celestiall throne, but also do render thee hearty thankes, that hast deliuered vs safely from the furies of the raging Seas, that otherwise might haue drenched vs in her deuouring gulfe, as thou diddest *Pharao* with his golden Chariots, and his inuincible Legions: therefore, great King of Iuda, vnder whose name wee haue taken many things in hand, and haue atcheiued so many victories, grant that these true oblations from our tender hearts may be acceptable in thy sight, which be no fained ceremonies: but the inward deuotions of our soules: and there withall letting fall a showre of teares from their eyes, and discharging a volley of sighes from their brests, as a signification of the integritie of their soules, he held his peace: then gaue he commaundement that the Armie should bee discharged, and euery one rewarded according to his desert, which within seuen dayes was performed, to the great honour of Christendome.

After this S. *George* earnestly requested the other sixe Champions, that they would honour him with their presence home to his Countrie of England, and there receiue the comfort of ioyfull ease, after the bloudy encounters of so many dangerous battels. This motion of S. *George* not onely obtained their consents, but added a forwardnesse to their willing minds: So incontinently they set forward towards England, vpon whose Chalkie cliffes they in a short time ariued, and after this tooke their iournie towards the Cittie of London, where their entertainments were so honourably performed, as I want the eloquence of *Cicero*, and the Rethoricke of *Caliope* to describe it.

Thus, gentle Reader, hast thou heard the first part of the honourable liues, and princely atcheiuements of these worthie Champions, which if with a kind curtesie thou accept of, my wearie Muse shall take in hand the second part: wherein is described the fortunes of Saint *Georges* children: the loues of many gallant Ladyes:

the Combats and Turnaments of noble Knights: the Tragedies of mighty Potentates: and finally, the honourable deaths of these renowned Champions. Thus fare you well, from my house at London, the two and twentie day of Nouember.

1608

FINIS.

R. I.

The second Part of

the famous History of the sea-
uen Champions of Christen-
dome.

Likewise shewing the Princely prowesse of
Saint Georges three Sonnes, the liuely
Sparke of Nobilitie.

With many other memoriall atchiuements
worthy the golden spurres of
Knighthood.

LONDON,
Printed for Cuthbert Burbie, and are to
be solde at his shop, vnder the
Royall Exchange
1597.

TO THE RIGHT HONORABLE

THE LORDE WILIAM HOWARD,
Richard Iohnson wisheth encrease
of all prosperity.

As it hath, Right Honorable, of late pleased your most noble brother in kindenes to accept of this history, and to grace it with a fauourable countenaunce. So am I nowe embouldened to dedicate this second part vnto your honour, which here I humbly offer to your Lordships handes, not because I thinke it a gift worthy the receauer: but rather that it should be, as it were a witnes of the loue and duety which I beare to your Right Noble House.

And when it shall please you to bestowe the reading of these my rude Discourses, my humble request is, that you would thinke I[1] wish your Honor as many happy dayes, as there be letters contayned in this Historie.

Thus praying for your Honors chiefe happynes, I end.

Your Honors in all dutifull loue
to his poore power. R. I.

To the Gentle Reader.

I Haue finished the seconde part of the seuen Champions of Christendome, onely for thy delight, being thertoo incouraged by thy greate curtesie in the kinde acceptation of my first part. I haue no eloquent phrases to inuite thy willingnes to read, onely a little barren inuention, wherof I haue no cause to boast, so excellently the wits of many in these daies in that kinde exceed. Onely thy curtesie must be my Buckler, against the carping malice of mocking iesters, that being worst able to doe well, scoffe commonly at that they cannot mend, censuring all thinges, doing nothing, but (monkey like) make apish iests at any thinge they see in Print: and nothing pleaseth them, except it sauor of a scoffing or inuectiue spirite. Well, what those say of me I doe not care, thy delight onely is my desire: And accept it and I am satisfied, reiect it and this shall bee my

---

[1] I] 1 I *1597*

penaunce neuer againe to come in Print. But hauing better hope, I boldly leade thee to this maine from this doubtfull floude of suspition where I rest. Walke on in the historie, as in an ouergrown & ill husbanded garden: if among all the weedes thou finde one pleasing flower I haue my wish.

Thine *Richard Iohnson,*

The second part of the most honoura-
ble Historie of the seauen Champions of
Christendome.

How Sa. Georges three sonnes were entertained into the famous Cittie of London, and after how their Mother was slaine in a wood with the prickes of a thornie brake, her blessing she gaue her sonnes, S. Georges lamentation ouer her bleeding bodie: and likewise of the Iourney the seuen Champions intended to Ierusalem to visit the Sepulcher of Christ.

AFter Saint *George* with the other six Champions of Christendom (by their inuincible conquests) had brought into subiection al the Easterne Parts, and by dint of bloodie warres yoaked the stubborne Infidels euen to the furthest boundes of *India*, where the golden Sunne beginneth to arise, as you heard discoursed in the former Part of this Historie, they returned with the conquest of Imperiall Diadems, regall crownes and kingly scepters to the rich and plentifull Country of *England*: where in the famous Citie of *London* they manie a day soiourned, a place not onely beautefied with sumptuous buildings, but grac'd with a number of valiant Knights and gallant Gentlemen of courtly behauiour, and therewithal adornd with troopes of Ladies, of diuine and celestiall beauties, that trip it vp and downe the streetes like to the *Grecian* Queenes, when as they tyed the *Phrigian* Warriers in the silken snares of loue: whereby it seemed rather a paradice for heauenlye Angels, than a place for earthly inhabiters.

Here the Christian Champions laide their Armes aside, here hung they vp their weapons on the bowers of peace, here their glistering corslets rusted in their Armories, here was not heard the warlike sound of drums nor siluer trumpets, heere stood no Centinells nor Courts of guard, nor barbed steedes prepared to the battaile, but all things tended to a lasting peace.[1] They that had wont in steeled coates to sleep in champion fields, lay dallying now in beds of silke: they that had wont with wearie armes to weeld the warlike fawchions, sate now embracing louely Ladies on their knees: and they whose eares had wont to heare the rufull cryes of slaughtered souldiers, were now orecloyd with musickes pleasant harmonie.

In this delicious manner liued these Champions in the Cittie of *London*, burying the remembrance of all theyr former Aduentures in the lakes of obliuion, and spending their times in honorable Tiltes and courtly Turnaments: wher S. *George* performed manie atchiuements in honor of his beloued Ladie, & the other Knights in honor of their Mistresses.

But at last Saint *Georges* three Sonnes, *Guy*, *Alexander* and *Dauid*, being all three borne at one birth, as you heard before in the wildernesse, and sent into three

---

[1] peace.] peace, *1597*

seuerall Kingdomes by their carefull Father to be trained vp: the one into *Rome* to the warlike *Romanes*, another vnto *Wittenberg* to the learned *Germanes*, the third into *Brittaine* to the valiant *English*. But now being growne to some ripenes of age and agilitie of strength, they desired much to visit their parents, whom they had not seene from their infancies lying in their cradles: and to craue at hys hands the honor of true Knighthood, and to weare the golden Spurre of Christendome.

This earnest & princely request so highly pleased theyr Tutors, that they furnished them with a stately traine of Knights, and sent them honourably into *England* where they arriued all three at one time in the famous Cittie of *London*, where their entertainments were most princely, and their welcomes so honorable, that I want arte to describe and memorie to expresse.

I omit what sumptuous Pageants and delightfull Showes the Cittizens prouided, and how the streetes of *London* were beautefied with tapestrie, the solemne bels that rung them ioyfull welcomes, and the siluer strained instruments that gaue them pleasant entertainment. Also I passe ouer their fathers ioy, who prized their sightes more precious in his eyes, than if hee had been made sole Monarch of the golden mynes of rich *America*: or that euerie haire that grew vppon his head had been equalled with a kingdome, & he to giue as manie golden diademes in his Armes. Also the Mothers welcomes to her Sons, who gaue them more kisses than shee breathed foorth groanes at their deliueries from her painful womb in the wildernesse.

The other Champions curtesies were not the least nor of the smallest in account to these three yong Gentlemen: but to be short, Saint *George* (whose loue was deare vnto his Children) in his owne person conducted them vnto their lodgings, whereas they spent that day and the night following in royall banquetting amongest theyr Princely Frends.[2]

But no sooner appeared the Mornings Sunne vppon the Mountaine tops, and the cleare countenaunce of the Elements made motion of some insuing pastime, but S. *George* commaunded a solempne Hunting for the welcome of his Sonnes.

Then began his knights to arme themselues in troops, and to mount vpon their nimble *Iennets*, and some with well armd Boare speares in their handes, prepared for the game on foote: but S. *George* with his Sonnes clad in green vestments like *Adonis*, with siluer hornes hanging at their backes in scarffes of coloured silke, were stil the formost in this Exercise. Likewise *Sabra* (intending to see her Sonnes valours displaied in the field, whether they were in courage like their Father or no) caused a gentle Palfray to be prouided, whereon she mounted her Princely Person to be a witnes of these Siluane sportes: she was armd with a curious brest-plate wrought like to the scales of a Dolphin, and in her hand she bare a siluer bow of the Turkish fashion, like an Amazonian Queen, or *Diana* hunting in the groues of *Arcadie*.

Thus in this gallant manner rode forth these Hunters to their Princely pastimes, where after they had ridden some six miles from the Cittie of *London*, fell from Sa. *Georges* nose three drops of purple blood, whereat hee sodainly started, and

---

[2] Frends] Frend *1597*

therewithall he heard the croaking of a Flight of night Rauens, that houered by the Forrest side, all which he iudged to be dismall signes of some insuing stratagem: but hauing a princely mind he nothing discouraged thereat, nor little mistrusted the wofull accident that after happened, but with a noble resolution entered the Forrest, accounting such foretelling tokens for olde wiues ceremonies. Wherein they had not passed the compasse of halfe a mile, but they started a wilde & swift Stag, at whom they vncoupled their Hounds, and gaue bridle to their horses, and followed the game more swifter, than Pirates that pursue the Merchants vppon the seas. But now behold how frowning Fortune chaunged their pleasant pastimes to a sad and bloodie tragedie: for *Sabra* proffering to keepe pace with them, delighting to behold the valiant incounters of her yong sonnes, and being careles of her selfe thorough the ouer swiftnes of her Steede, shee slipped beside her saddle, and so fell directly vpon a thornie brake of brambles, the prickes whereof more sharpe than spikes of steele entered to euerie part of her delicate bodie: some pierced the louely closets of her starre bright eyes, whereby (instead of christall pearled teares) there issued drops of purest blood: her face before that blushed like the mornings radiant countenance, was now exchanged into a crimson red: her milk white hands that lately strained the yuorie Lute, did seeme to weare a bloodie scarlet gloue: and her tender paps that had so often fed her Sonnes with the milke of nature, were all berent and torne with these accursed brambles: from whose deep wounds there issued such a streame of purple gore, that it conuerted the grasse from a liuely green to a crimson hieu, and the abundance of blood that trickled from her breast, began to inforce her soule to giue the world a wofull farewell. Yet notwithstanding, when her beloued Lord, her sorrowfull Sonnes, and all the rest of the wofull Champions, had washed her wounded bodie with a Spring of teares, and when she perceiued that she must of force commit her life to the furie of imperious death, shee breathed foorth this dying Exhortation.

Deare Lord (said she) in this vnhappie Hunting must you loose the truest Wife that euer lay by Princes side: yet mourne you not, nor greeue you my Sonnes, nor you braue Christian Knights, but let your warlike drummes conuay me royally vnto my Toombe, that all the world maye write in brazen Bookes, how I haue followed my Lord (the Pride of Christendome) thorough many a bloodie field, and for his sake haue left my Parents, Frends, and Countrey, and haue trauelled with him through manie a daungerous Kingdome: but now the cruell Fates haue wrought their latest spites, and finished my life, because I am not able to performe what loue he hath deserued of me. And now to you my Sonnes, this blessing do I leaue behinde: euen by the paines that fortie weekes I once indured for your sakes, when as you lay enclosed in my wombe, and by my trauels in the wildernes, whereas my grones vpon your birth day did (in my thinking) cause both trees and stones to drop downe teares, when as the mercilesse Tygers & tamelesse Lyons did stand like gentle Lambes, and mournd to heare my lamentations: and by a Mothers loue that euer since I haue borne you, imitate & follow your Father in all his honorable attempts, harme not the silly Infant, nor the helplesse Widdow, defend the honour of distressed Ladies, and giue freely vnto wounded Souldiers: seeke not to stain the vnspotted virgins with your lusts, and aduenture euermore to redeeme true Knights from captiuitie: liue euer professed enemies to paganisme, and spend your liues in the quarrel and defence of Christ, that Babes (as yet vnborne) in time to come may speake of you, and record you in the Bookes of fame to be true christian Champions. This is my blessing, and this is the Testament I leaue behinde: for now I feele the chilnesse of pale death closing the closets of my eyes. Farewell vaine world, deere Lord farewell, sweet Sonnes, you famous fellowes of my *George*, and all true Christian Knights, adieu.

These words were no sooner ended, but with a heauie sigh she yeelded vp the ghost: whereat Saint *George* (being impatient in his sorrowes) fell vpon her liuelesse bodie, rending his haire, and tearing his Hunters attyre from his backe into a thousand peeces: and at last when his griefes somewhat diminished, he fell into these bitter lamentations.

Gone is the Starre (said he) that lightned all ye Northerne world, withered is the Rose that beautefied our Christian fields, dead is the Dame that for her beautie stained all Christian women: for whom Ile fill the aire with euerlasting moanes. This day hencefoorth be fatall to all times, and counted for a dismall day of death. Let neuer the Sunne shew foorth his beames thereon a gaine, but clowdes as blacke as pitch couer the earth with fearfull darknes. Let euerie Tree in this accursed Forrest, hencefoorth be blasted with vnkindly windes: let brambles, hearbs and flowers consume and wyther, let grasse and blooming buds perish and decay, and all things neere the place where shee was slaine, bee turned to a dismall, blacke and sable colour, that the Earth it selfe in mourning garments may lament her losse. Let neuer Birde sing cherefully in top of trees, but like the mournfull musicke of the Nightingale, fil all the aire with fatall tunes: let bubling riuers murmure for her losse, & siluer Swans that swim thereon sing dolefull melodie: let all the dales belonging to these fatal woods be couered with greene bellyed serpents, croaking toades, hissing snakes, and sight-killing cockatrices: in blasted trees let fearfull Rauens shrike, let howlets crye, and crickets sing, that after this it may be called a place of dead mens wandring ghosts. But fond wretch, why doo I thus lament in vaine, and bathe her bleeding bodie with my teares, when greefe by no meanes will recall her life? Yet this shall satisfie her soule, for I will goe a Pilgrimage vnto *Ierusalem*, & offer vp my teares to Iesus Christ vpon his blessed Sepulcher, by which my stained soule may be washt from this bloody guilt, which was the causer of this sorrowfull dayes mishappe.

These sorrowfull words were no sooner ended, but hee tooke her bleeding limmes betweene his fainting armes, and gaue a hundred kisses vpon her dying coloured lips, retayning yet ye colour of Alablaster new washt in purple blood, and in this extasie awhile lying, gaue waye to others to vnfold their woes.

But his Sonnes whose sorrowes wer as great as his, protested neuer to neglect one day, but duly weepe a sea of teares vpon their Mothers graue, till from the Earth did spring some mournfull flower, to beare remembrance of her death, as did the Uiolet that sprung from chast *Adonis* blood, when *Venus* wept to see him slaine. Likewise the other sixe Champions (that all the time of their lamentations stood like men drownd in the depth of sorrow) began now a little to recouer themselues: and after protested by the honour of true Knighthood, and by the Spur and golden Garter of S. *Georges* leg, to accompanie him vnto the holy Land, bare footed without either hose or shoo, onely clad in russet gaberdines, like the vsuall

Pilgrimes of the world, and neuer to returne till they haue payd their vowes vpon that blessed Sepulcher.

Thus in this sorrowful manner wearied they the time away, filling the woods with Echoes of their lamentations and recording their dolors to the whistling windes: but at last, when blacke Night began to approach, and with her sable mantles to ouer-spred the christall firmament, they retyred (with her dead bodie) backe to the Citie of *London*, where the report of this tragicall accident, drowned their friends in a sea of sorrow: for the newes of her timelesse death was no sooner bruted abroad, but the same caused both olde and young to lament the losse of so sweete a Ladie. The siluer headed age that had wont in scarlet gownes to meete in Councell, sat now at home in discontented griefes: the gallant youths and comely virgins that had wont to beautefie the streetes with costlye garments, went drouping vp and downe in blacke and mournfull vestures: and those remorcelesse hearts that sildome were opprest with sorrow, now constrained their eyes like fountaines to distill a floud of brinish and pearly teares.

This generall griefe of the Citizens continued for the space of thirtie dayes, at the ende whereof Saint *George* with his Sonnes and the other Champions interred her bodie verie honourably, and erected ouer the same a rich and costly Monument (in sumptuous state like the toomb of *Mausolus*, which was called one of the Wonders of the World: or like to the Pyramides of *Greece*, which is a staine to all Architectures): for thereon was portrayed the Queene of Chastitie with her Maydens, bathing themselues in a christall Fountaine, as a witnesse of her wondrous Chastitie, against the lustfull assailements of manie a Knight. Thereon was also most liuely pictured a Turtle-doue sitting vpon a tree of gold, in signe of the true loue that she bore to her betrothed husband. Also a siluer coloured Swan swimming vpon a Christall riuer, as a token of her beautie: for as the Swan excelleth al other fowles in whitenes, so she for beautie excelled all Ladies in the world.

I leaue to speake of the curious workmanship of the pinacles that were framed all of the purest ieat, the pummels of siluer and Iasper stones. Also I omit the Pendants of gold, the Scutchions of Princes, & the Armes of Countreyes that beautefied her Toombe: the discourse whereof requires an Oratours eloquence, or a penne of golde dipt in the dew of *Hellicon* or *Pernassus* Hill, whereas the Muses doo inhabit. Her Statue or Picture was carued cunningly in alablaster, and layd as[3] it were vppon a pillow of greene silke, like vnto *Pigmalions* yuorie Image, and directly ouer the same hung a siluer Tablet, whereon in letters of golde was this Epitaph written.

> *Here lies the wonder of this worldly age*
> *For beautie, wit, and princely maiestie,*
> *Whom spitefull death in his imperious rage*
> *Procurde to fall through ruthlesse crueltie:*

---

[3] as] (as *1597*

In leauie sports within a fragrant wood,
Vpon a thornie brake she spilt her blood.

Let Virgins pure and Princes of great might,
With siluer perled teares imbalme this tomb,
Accuse the fatall sisters of despight,
For blasting thus the pride of natures bloom:

For here she sleeps within this earthly graue,
whose worth deserues a golden tomb to haue

Seauen yeares she kept her sweet Virginitie,
In absence of her true betrothed Knight,
When thousands did perceiue her chastitie,
Whilst he remaind in prison daye and night:
But yet we see that things of purest prize,
Forsakes the earth to dwell aboue the skies.

Maidens come mourne with dolefull melody
And make this monument your setled bower
Here shed your brackish teares eternally,
Lament both yere, month, week, day, hower:
For here she rests whose like can nere be found
Her beauties pride lyes buried in the ground.

Her wounded hart that yet doth freshly bleed,
Hath causd seuen knights a iourny for to take
To faire Ierusalem in Pilgrimes weed,
The furie of her angrie ghost to slake:
Because their siluane sports was chiefest guilt,
And onely cause her blood was timeles spilt.

Thus after the Toomb was erected, and the Epitaph ingrauen in a siluer Tablet, and al things performed according to Saint *Georges* direction, he left his Sonnes in the Cittie of *London* vnder the gouernment of the English King: and in companie of the other sixe Champions, he tooke his iourney towards *Ierusalem*.

They were attired after the manner of Pilgrimes, in russet gaberdines downe to their foote, in their hands they bore staues of Ebon wood tipt at the endes with siluer, the pikes whereof were of the strongest *Lydian* steele, of such a sharpnes that they were able to pierce a target of Tortoys shell: vppon their breasts hung Crosses of crimson silke, to signifie that they were Christian Pilgrimes, trauelling to the Sepulcher of Christ.

In this manner set they forward from *England* in the Spring time of the yeare, when *Flora* had beautefied the earth with Natures tapestrie, and made their passages as pleasant as the Gardens of *Hesperides*, adorned with all kinde of odoriferous flowers. When as they crossed the seas, the siluer waues seemed to lye as smoothe as christal yce, and the Dolphins to daunce aboue the waters, as a signe of a prosperous iourney. In trauelling by land, the wayes seemed so short and easie, and the chirping melody of birdes made them such musique as they passed, that in a short season they arriued beyond the borders of Christendome, and had entred the confines of *Africa*.

There were they forced insted of downie beds nightly to rest their wearie limmes vpon heapes of sun burnt mosse: and in sted of silken curtens and curious canopies, they had the clowdes of heauen to couer them. Now their naked legs and bare feet, that had wont to stride the stately steedes, and to trample in fields of Pagans blood, were forced to clyme the craggie mountaines, and to endure the torments of pricking briers, as they trauayled thorough the desert places and comfortlesse solitarie wildernesses.

Manie were the dangers that hapned to them in theyr Iourney, before they arriued in *Iudea*, and most princely their atchieuements, and honourable their aduentures: which for this time I passe ouer, leauing the Champions for a time in their trauell towards the holy Sepulcher of Christ, and speake what happened to Sa. *Georges* three Sonnes in visiting their Mothers Tombe in the Cittie of *London*.

CHAP. II.

Of the strange giftes that S. Georges *sonnes offered at their Mothers Toombe, and what hapned thereupon: how her Ghost appeared to them, and counselled them to the pursute of their Father: also, how the Ki. of* England *installed them with the honor of knighthood, and furnished them with abiliments of warre.*

THe swift foote steedes of *Titans* fierie Carre had almost finished a yere, since *Sabraes* Funerall was solemnized: in which time Saint *Georges* three Sonnes had visited their Mothers Tomb oftner than there were dayes in the yeare, and had shed as manie teares thereon in remembraunce of her loue, as there were starres in the glistering veyle of Heauen: but at last these three yong Princes fell at a ciuill discord and deadly strife, which of them should beare the truest loue vnto their Mothers dead bodie, and which of them should be held in greatest esteeme. For before manie dayes were expired, they concluded to offer vp three seuerall deuotions at her Tombe: and he that deuised a gift of the rarest prize and of the straungest qualitie, should bee held in the greatest honour, and accompted the noblest of them all. This determination was speedily perfourmed, and in so short a time accomplished, that it is wonderfull to discourse.

The first thinking to exceed his brothers in the strangenes of his Gift, made repaire vnto a cunning Inchauntresse, which had her abiding in a secret caue adioyning to the Cittie, whom he procured (through manie rich giftes and large promises) by arte to deuise a meane to get the honor from his Bretheren, & to haue a gift of that strange nature, that all the world might wonder at the report thereof.

The Inchauntresse (being won with his promises) by her artes and magicke spells, deuised a Garland contayning all the diuersitie of flowers that euer grew in earthly Gardens: and though it were in the dead time of winter, when as the siluer ysicles had disroabd both hearb and flower of their beauties, and the Northerne snow lay freezing on the mountaine tops, yet was this Garland contriued after the fashion of a rich Imperial Crowne, with as manie seuerall Flowers as euer *Flora* placed vppon the downes of rich *Arcadia*: in diuersitie of colours lyke the glistering Raine-bow, when as it shineth in her greatest pride: and casting such an odoriferous sent and sweete sauour, as though the Heauens had rained downe showers of Campheere, Bisse, or Amber-greece.

This rare and exceeding Garland was no sooner framed by Inchauntment, and deliuered into his hands, but he left the Inchauntresse sitting in her Ebon chaire vpon a blocke of steele (practising her fatall artes), with her hair hanging about her sholders, like wreaths of snakes or inuenomed serpents: and so retourned to his Mothers tombe, where he hung it vppon a pillar of siluer that was placed in the middle of the Monument.

The second Brother like wise repaired to the Tombe, and brought in his hand an yuorie Lute, wheron he plaid such inspiring melodie, that it seemed like the harmony of Angels, or the celestiall musique of *Apollo* when hee descended heauen for the loue of *Daphne*, whom hee turned into a Baytree. The musicke being finished, he tied hys Lute in a damaske scarffe, and with great humilitie hee hung it at the west ende of the Tombe vppon a knobbe of Iasper stone.

Lastly, the third Brother likewise repaired with no outward deuotion or worldly gift: but clad in a vesture of white silke, bearing in his hand an instrument of death, like an innocent Lambe going to sacrifice: or one readie to be offered for the loue of his mothers soule.

This strange manner of repaire, caused his other brothers to stand attentiuely, and with vigilant eyes to behold the conclusion.

First, after he had (submissiuely and with great humilitie) let fall a shower of siluer teares from the cesternes of his eyes, in remembrance of his Mothers timeles tragedie, he prickt his naked breast with a siluer bodkin, the which he brought in his hand, from which there trickeled downe some thirtie drops of blood, which he after offered vp to his Mothers Tombe in a siluer bason, as an euident signe that there can be nothing more dearer, nor of more precious price, than to offer vp his owne blood for her loue. This ceremonious gift caused his two other Brothers to swell in hatred like two chafed Lions, and with furie to run vpon him, intending to catch him by the haire of the head, and to drag him round about their Mothers Tomb, till his braines were dasht against the marble pauement, and his blood sprinkled vppon her graue: but this wicked enterprize so mooued the Maiestie of heauen, that ere they could accomplish their intents, or staine their hands in his blood, they heard (as it were) ye noyse of dead mens bones ratling in the ground. And thereupon (looking fearfully about) the Toombe seemed of it selfe to open, and thereout to appeare a most terrible and ghastly shape, pale, like vnto ashes, in countenance resembling theyr Mother with her breast besmeard in blood, and her bodie wounded with a hundred scarres: and so with a dismall & rufull looke she spake vnto her desperate Sonnes in thys manner.

Oh you degenerate from Natures kinde, why doo you seeke to make a murther of your selues? can you indure to see my bodie rent in twaine, my heart split in sunder, and my wombe dismembred? Abate this furie, staine not your hands with your owne bloods, nor make my Tombe a spectacle of more death. Unite your selues in concord, that my discontented soule may sleepe in peace, and neuer more be troubled with your vnbridled humours. Make hast I say, and arme your selues in steeled corslets, and follow your valiant Father to *Ierusalem*, for he is there in danger and distresse of life. Away I say, or els my angry ghost shall neuer leaue this world, but haunt you vp and downe with gastly visions.

This being said, she vanished from their sight, lyke to the brittle[1] ayre, whereat for a time they stood amazed and almost distraught of their wits, thorough the terrour of her words: but at last recouering their former senses they all vowed by the eternall Maiestie of Heauen, neuer to proffer the like iniurie againe, but to liue in brotherly concord and vnitie till the dissolution of their earthly bodyes. So in all hast they went vnto the King, and certefied him of all things that had happened: and falling vpon theyr knees before his Maiestie, requested at his hands the honour

---

[1] brittle] brittlo *1597*

of Knighthood, and leaue to depart in the pursute of their Father and the other Champions, that were fallen in great distresse.

The King purposing to accomplish their desires, and to fulfill their requests, presently condiscended, and not onely gaue them the honour of Knighthood, but furnished them with rich abiliments of warre, answerable to their magnanimious mindes. First he frankly bestowed vppon them three stately Palphryes, bred vpon the bright mountaines of *Sardinia*: in collour like to an Irone gray, bewtifyed with siluer hayres, and in pace more swifter then the Spanish Ginets, which be a kinde of horse ingendred by the winds vpon the Alpes, that be certaine craged mountaines that deuide the Kingdomes of *Italy* and *Spaine*: in bouldnes and courage, they were like to *Beucephalus* the horse of *Macedonian Alexander*, or to *Cæsars* steedes that neuer daunted in the field, for they were trapped with rich trappings of golde after the *Moroco* fashion with Saddels framed like vnto Irone chaires with backs of Steele, and their foreheads were beautified with spangled plumbes of purple feathers, whereon hung many golden pendants: the king like wise bestowed vpon them three costly swoords wrought of purest Lidian steele, with Launces bound about with plates of brasse, at the toppes thereof hung silken Streamers beautified with the English Crosse, being the crimson badge of Knight-hood, and honor of aduenterous champions: Thus in this Royall manner rode these three young Knights from the City of *London* in companie of the King with a traine of Knights and gallant Gentlemen which conducted them vnto the Sea side, where they left them vnto their future fortunes and returned backe to the English Court.

Now is Saint *Georges* sonnes floting on the Seas, making their first aduentures in the world, that after ages might aplaude their atchiuement, and inrole theyr fames in the records of honor, heauen prosper them succesfully, and gentle fortune smile vpon their trauailes, for three brauer knights did neuer crosse the seas, nor make their aduentures into straunge Countries.

CHAP. III.

How Saint Georges *sonnes after they were knighted by the English King, trauailed towards* Barbarie, *and how they redeemed the Dukes Daughter of* Normandie *from rauishment, that was assayled in a wood by three tawnie Negroes: and also of the tragicall tale of the Virgins strange miserie, with other accidents[1] that happened.*

MAny daies had not these three magnanimous knights indured ye dangers of the swelling waues, but with a prosperous and succesfull winde, they arriued vpon the territories of *France*: where beeing no sooner safely set on shoare, but they bountifully rewarded theyr Marriners, & betooke themselues to their intended trauells.

Now began their costly trapped Steeds to pace it like the scudding Windes, and with their warlike hooues to thunder on the beaten passages: now began true honour to florish in their princely brests, and the renowne of their Fathers atchieuements to incourage their desires. Although but tender youth sate budding on their cheekes, yet portly manhood triumpht in their harts; and althogh their childish armes as yet neuer tried the painfull aduentures of Knighthood, yet bore they high and princely cogitations in as great esteeme, as when their Father slewe the burning Dragon in *Aegypt*, for preseruation of their mothers life.

Thus trauelled they to the further Parts of the Kingdome of *France* (guided onely by the direction of fortune) without anie aduenture worth the noting, till at last ryding through a mightie Forrest standing on the Borders of *Lusitania*, they heard (a farre off as it were) the rufull cryes of a distressed woman: which in this manner filled the ayre with the Eccho of her moanes.

Oh heauens (sayd shee) bee kinde and pittifull vnto a Maiden in distresse, and send some happy passengers that may deliuer me from these inhumane monsters.

This wofull and vnexpected noyse, caused the Knights to alight from their horses, and to see the euent of this accident. So after they had tied their Steeds to the bodie of a Pine tree by the reynes of their bridles, they walked on foote into the thickest of the Forrest with their weapons drawne, readie to withstand anie assailment whatsoeuer: & as they drew neerer to the distressed Uirgin, they heard her breathe foorth this pittie moouing lamentation the second time.

Come, come, some curteous Knight, or els I must forgoe that precious Iewell, which all the world can neuer againe recouer.

These words caused them to make the more speed, and to run the neerest way for the Maidens succour. At last, they approached her presence, where they found her tyed by the locks of her owne haire to the trunke of an orenge tree, and three cruel and inhumane *Negroes* standing readie to despoyle her of her chastitie, and with their lusts to blast the blooming bud of her sweete and vnspotted Uirginitie.

But when Saint *Georges* Sonnes beheld her louelye countenance besmeared in dust, that before was as beautifull roses in milk, and her christall eyes the perfect

---

[1] *accidents*] acdents *1597*

patterns of the Lampes of heauen, inbrewd in floods of teares, at one instance they ran vpon the *Negroes*, and sheathed their angry weapons in their loathsome bowels, the leachers being slaine, their bloods sprinckled about the Forrest, and their bodies cast out as a pray for rauenous beastes to feede vpon: they vnbound the Mayden and like curteous Knightes demaunded the cause of her captiuity, and by what meanes she came into that solitarie Forrest? Most Noble Knights quoth shee, and true renounded men at armes, to tell the cause of my passed miseries were a pricke vnto my soule, and the discourse thereof will burst my heart with griefe but considering your Nobilities the which I perceiue by your Princely behauiours, and your kinde curtesies extended towards me, being a Uirgin in distresse, vnder the hands of these lustfull Negroes, whom you haue iustly murdred, shall imbolden me, though vnto my hearts great griefe, to discourse the first cause of my miserable fortune.

My Father (quoth shee) whilst gentle fortune smilde vpon him, was a Duke and sole commaunder of the state of *Normandy*, a countrie now scituated in the kingdom of *Fraunce*, whose lands & reuenewes in his prosperitie was so great that hee continually kept as stately a traine, both of Knights and gallant gentlemen as any Prince in *Europe*, whereat the King of *France* greatly enuied, and by bloody warres deposed my Father from his princely dignitie, who for sauegard of his life in company of mee hys onely heire and daughter, betooke vs to these solletarie woods, where euer since we haue secretly remained in a poore cell or hermitage yᵉ which by our industrious paines hath been builded with plants of Uines and oaken bows, and couered ouer head with cloddes of earth, and turffes of grasse, seauen yeares we haue continued in great extreamitie sustaining our hungers with the fruites of trees, and quenching our thirstes with the dewe of heauen, that falleth nightly vpon fragrant flowers: heere in steede of Princely attyre, imbrothered garments and damaske vestures, we haue beene constrained to cladde our selues in flowers, the which we haue cunningly wouen vp together.

Heere insteade of musicke, that had wont each morning to delight our eares, we haue the whistling windes resounding in the woods: our clockes to tell the minutes of the wandring nights, are snakes and toades that sleep in rootes of rotten trees, our cannopeies to couer vs, are not wrought of *Median* silke, the which the Indian Uirgins weaue vppon their siluer loombes, but the sable cloudes of heauen, when as the cheerefull day hath clos'd her christall windows vp.

Thus in this manner continued wee in this soletary wildernes, making both birds and beastes our chiefe companions, till these mercilesse Moores (whose hateful brests you haue made like watry fountaines to water the parched earth with streames of blood:) who came into our cell, or simple cabinet, thinking to haue found some store of treasure. But casting their gazing eyes vpon my beutie, they were presently inchaunted with a lustfull desire, onely to crop the sweete bud of my virginitie. Then with a furious and dismall countenaunce, more blacke than[2] the sable garments of sad *Melpomine*, when wyth her strawberie quill she writes of bloodie tragedies: or with a heart more crueller, than was *Neroes* the tyrannous

---

[2] than] than than *1597*

Romane Emperour when he beheld the entrailes of his naturall Mother layde open by his inhumane and mercilesse commaundement: or when he stood vpon the highest toppe of a mightie mountayne to see that famous and Imperiall Cittie of *Roome* set on fire by the remorselesse handes of his vnrelenting Ministers, that added vnhallowed flames to his vnholie furie.

These mercilesse and wicked minded *Negroes* with violent handes tooke my aged Father, and most cruellye bound him to the blasted bodie of a wythered oake, standing before the entrie of his Cell: where, neither the reuerent honor of his siluer haires, that glistered like the frozen ysicles vpon the Northerne Mountaines, nor the strayned sighes of his breast, wherein the pledge of wisedome was inthronized, nor all my teares or exclamations could anie whit abate their cruelties, but like grim dogs of *Barbarie*, they left my Father fast bound vnto the tree, and like egregious vipers tooke me by the tramells of my golden haire, and dragd me like a silly Lambe vnto this slaughtering place, intending to satisfie their lustes with the flower of my chastitie.

Here I made my humble supplication to the Maiestye of Heauen, to bee reuenged vppon their cruelties: I reported to them the rewards of bloodie rauishments by the example of *Tereus* that lustfull King of *Thrace*, and hys furious Wife, that in reuenge of her Sisters rauishment caused her Husband to eate the flesh of his owne Sonne. Likewise (to preserue my vndefiled honor) I told them, that for the Rape of *Lucrece* the Romane Matron, *Tarquinius* and his name was for euer banished out of *Rome*: with manie other examples, like the Nightingale, whose doleful tunes as yet recordeth nothing but rape and murther. Yet neither the frownes of heauen, nor the terrible threates of hell, could mollifie their bloodie mindes: but they protested to perseuer in that wickednes, & vowd that if all the leaues of the Trees that grew within the Wood were turned into Indian Pearle, & made as wealthie as the golden Streames of *Pactolus*,[3] where *Mydas* washt his golden Wish away: yet shuld they not redeeme my chastitie from the staine of their insatiable and lustfull desires.

This being said, they bound mee with the tramells of myne owne haire to this Orenge tree, and at the very instant they proffered to defile my vnspotted bodie, but by the mercifull working of God, you happily approached, & not only redeemed me from their tyrannous desires, but quit the world from three of the wickedest creatures that euer nature framed. For which (most noble and inuincible Knights) if euer Uirgins prayers may obtaine fauor at the Maiestie of Heauen, humbly will I make my supplications, that you may proue as valiant champions, as euer put on helmet: and that your fames may ring to euerie Princes eare, as far as bright *Hiperion* showes hys golden face.

This tragicall tale was no sooner ended, but the three Knights (whose remorcefull hearts sobbed with sighes) imbraced the sorrowfull Maiden betwixt their armes, & earnestlye requested her to conduct them vnto the place, whereas she left her father bound vnto the withered oke. To which shee willingly consented, and thanked them highly for their kindnes: but before they approched to the olde

---

[3] *Pactolus*] *pactolus* 1597

mans presence, what for the griefe of his banishment and the violent vsage of his Daughter, he was forced to yeeld vp his miserable life to the mercies of vnauoydable death.

When Saint *Georges* valiant Sonnes (in companie of this sorrowfull Maiden) came to the tree, and (contrarie to their expectations) found her Father cold and stiffe, both deuoyd of sense and feeling, also finding his hands & face couered with greene mosse, which they supposed to be done by the Roben red-breast and other little birds, who naturally couer the bare parts of anie bodie which they finde dead in the field, they fell into a new confused extremitie of greefe.

But especially his Daughter seeming to haue lost all ioy and comfort in this World, made both heauen & earth to resound with her exceeding lamentations, and mourned without comfort like weeping *Niobe*, that was turned into a rocke of stone, her griefe so abounded for the losse of her children: but when the three young Knights perceiued the comfortles sorrow of the Uirgin, and how she had vowd neuer to depart from those solitary groues, but to spend the remnant of her daies in company of his deadly body, they curteously assisted her to burie him vnder a ches-nut tree, where they left her continually bathing his senceles graue with her teares and returned backe to their horses, where they left them at the entry of the Forrest tied vnto a lofty pine, & so departed on their Iorney.

There we will leaue them for a time, and speak of the seauen Champions of Christendome, that were gone on Pilgrimage to the Cittie of *Ierusalem*, and what strange aduentures happened to them in their trauels.

CHAP. IIII.

Of the Aduenture of the Golden Fountaine in Damasco: how sixe of the Christian Champions were taken prisoners by a mightie Giant, and after how they were deliuered by Saint George: and also how he redeemed fourteene Iewes out of prison: with diuers other strange accidents that happened.

LEt vs now speake of the fauourable clemencie that smiling Fortune shewd to ye Christian Champions in their trauells to *Ierusalem*. For after they were departed from *England*, and had iourneied in their Pilgrimes attire thorough manie strange Countreys, at last they arriued vpon the Confines of *Damasco*, which is a Countrey not onely beautefied with sumptuous and costly buildings framed by the curious Architecturie of mans deuice, but also furnished with all the precious gifts that Nature in her greatest liberalitie could bestow.

In this fruitefull Dominion long time the Christian Champions rested their wearie steps, and made theyr abode in the house of a rich and curteous Iew, a man that spent his wealth chiefly for the succour and comfort of trauellers, and wandring Pilgrims, his house was not curiously erected vp of carued timber work, but framed with quarries of blewstones, and supported by many stately pillors of the purest marble: The gates and entrie of his house were continually kept open in signe of his bountifull minde, ouer the portall thereof hung a brazen table, whereon was most curiously ingrauen the picture of *Ceres* the Goddesse of plenty deckt with garlands of wheate, wreathes of Oliues, bunches of Uines, and with all manner of fruitfull things, the chamber wherein these Champions tooke their nightly reposes and golden sleepes, was garnished with as many windows of Christall glasse, as there were daies in the yeere, and the wals painted with as many stories as there were yeeres since the world began: it was likewise built foursquare, after the manner of piramides in Greece, at the east ende whereof was moste liuely portraied, bright *Phœbus* rising from *Auroras* golden bed, whose glistering countenance at his departure, distaind the ellements with a purple colour. At the west side *s*was likewise portraied how *Thetis* trippes vpon the siluer sands when as *Hiperions*[1] carre driues to the watrie Ocean, and takes his nights repose vpon his louers bosome: on the North side was painted mountaines of snow whose tops did seeme to reach to heauen, & mightie woods ouer hung with siluer Isickles, which is the nature of the Northerne Climate.

Lastly vpon the west side of the chamber satte the God of the seas riding vpon a Dolphins backe, with an hundred Mermaides following him, with their golden tramels floting vpon the siluer waues, there the Tritons seemed to daunce aboue the Christal streams with a number of other siluer scaled fishes that made the sea delightfull in pleasure.

Ouer the roofe of the Chamber was most perfectly portraied the foure ages of the World, which seemed to ouerspred the rest of the curious workes.

---

[1] *Hiperions*] *Hiperious 1597*

First the golden age was pendant ouer the East: the second being the siluer a mettle some what bazer than the first, seemed to ouerspred the freezing North. The thirde, which was the brazen age, beautifyed the westerne parts: The fourth and last being of Irone, being the basest of them all, seemed to bee pendant ouer the Southerne clymate.

Thus in this curious Chamber rested these wearie Champions a long season, where their food was not delicious but wholsome, and their seruices were not curious, but comely: answerable to the braue mindes of such Heroycal Champions: the curteous Iew their friendly hoast whome nature had honored with seuen comely Sonnes dayly kept them company, and not only shewed them the curiositie of this habitation, but also discribed the pleasant scituation of his Countrie, how the townes & Cities were ornefied with all manner of delights, that they seemed like the immortall Pallaces of heauen, where celestiall Angelles doe record their Hermonies, and the fieldes and flowring medowes so beautified with natures gladsome ornaments, that they seemed for pleasure to exceede the paradice of *Elizium*,[2] where crowned soules doe liue in endles glory.

The dayes were spent away in such manner discourses to the exceeding pleasure of the Christian Knights, and euermore when darke night approched, and the wonted time of sleepe sommoned them to their silent and quiet restes, the Iewes children beeing seuen of the brauest and comlyest boyes that euer dame nature framed, tyred the Christian Champions eares wyth suche sweete inspiring Melodies which they strayned from theyr Iuory Lutes, that not *Arion* (when all the Arte of musique consented with his tune, voyce, and hand, when hee won mercy of the Dolphin, being forsaken of men) was comparable thereto. Whereby the Christian Champions were inchaunted with such delights, that theyr golden sleepes seemed to be as pleasant as the sweete ioyes of Paradice.

But vpon a time, after the curteous Iew had intelligence how they were Christian Knights, and those admired martiall Champions, whom fame had canonized to be the Wonders of the world for martiall discipline and Knightly aduentures: finding a fit opportunitie as hee walked in their companies vpon an euening vnder an arbour of vine branches, he reuealed to them the secretes of his soule, and the cause of his so sad and solitarie dwelling. So standing bareheaded in the middle of the Champions, with his white haires hanging downe to his shoulders in colour like to the siluer Swanne, and more softer than the downe of thistles, or *Median* silke vntwisted, he began with a sober countenance and gallant demeanour to speake as followeth vnto them, that setled them attentiuely to heare.

I am sure (quoth he) you inuincible Knights, that yee meruaile at my solitarie course of liuing, and that you greatly muse wherefore I exempt my selfe from the companie of all worldlings, except my seuen Sonnes, whose sights be my chiefest comfort, and the onely prolongers of my life. Therefore prepare your eares to entertaine the strangest Discourse that euer tung pronounced, or ouer-wearied aged man in the height of his extremitye delyuered.

---

[2] *Elizium*] *Elizum 1597*

I was in my former yeres (whilst Fortune smilde vppon my happines) the principal Commaunder and chiefe Owner of a certaine Fountaine, of such a wonderfull & precious vertue, that it was valued to be worth the Kingdome of *Iudea*: the water thereof was so strange in operation, that in foure and twentie howers it wold conuert anie mettall, as of brasse, copper, yron, lead or tinne, into rich refined golde: the stonie flint it would turne into pure siluer, and anie kinde of earth into excellent mettal. By the vertue thereof I haue made the leaues of Trees more richer than Indian Pearle, and the blades of grasse of more value than the Iewels that be found in the countrey of *America*.

The richnesse thereof was no sooner bruted through the world, but it caused many forraine Knights to trie the aduenture, and by force of armes to bereaue me of the honor of this Fountaine. But at that time Nature graced me with one and twentie Sonnes, whereof seuen be yet liuing, and the onely comfort of myne age: but the other fourteene (whom frowning Fortune hath bereaued me of) manie a day by their valiant prowesse and matchles fortitudes defended the Fountaine from manie furious assaylers: for there was no Knight in all the world that was found so hardie nor of such inuincible courage, that if they once attempted to incounter with anie of my valiaunt Sonnes, but they were either taken prisoners, or slaine in the combat.

The fame of their valors, and the riches of the Fountaine rung through manie strange Countreyes, and lastly came to the eares of a furious Giant, dwelling vppon the Borders of *Arabia*: who at the report thereof came armed in his steely coate with a mightie bat of yron on his necke, like to the furious *Hercules* that burst the brazen gates of *Cerberus* in twaine, and in state and bignes like the Sonne of *Ioue* that bore the mightie mountaine *Atlas* vpon his shoulders: he was the conquerour of my sonnes, and the first causer of my sodaine downfall. But when I had intelligence of the ouerthrow of fourteen of my sons, and that he had made conquest of the wealthie fountaine, I with the rest of my Children, thinking all hope of recouerie to be past, betooke our selues to this solitarie course of life, where euer since in this mansion or hermitage we haue made our abode and residence, spending our wealth to the releefe of trauelling Knightes and wandering Pilgrimes, hoping once againe that smiling Fortune would aduance vs to some better happe: and to bee plaine right worthy Champions my hope was neuer at the height of full perfection till this present time, wherein your excellent presences almost assure me that the hideous monster shalbe conquered, my fountaine restored, my Sonnes[3] deaths (for dead sure they are) reuenged.

The Champions with great admiration gaue eare to the strange discourse of this reuerent Iew, and intended in requitall of his extraordinarie kindnesse to vndertake this aduenture. And the more to encourage the other, Saint *George* began in this manner to deliuer his mind, speaking both to the Iew their hoast, and his valiant fellow Champions.

I haue not without great wonder (most reuerent and curteous olde man) heard the strange discourse of thy admirable fountaine, and doe not a little lament that

---

[3] Sonnes] Sounes *1597*

one of so kinde & liberall a disposition should be dispossessed of so exceeding riches, for that wealth to a liberal nature is alone conuenient: neither am I lesse sorry, that so inhumane a monster and knowen enemie to all curtesie and kinde should haue the fruition of so exceeding great Treasure: for to the wicked, wealth is the cause of their more wickednes.[4] But that which most grieueth me, is: that hauing so many valiant Knights to thy Sonnes, they all were so vnfortunate to fall into the handes of that relentlesse Monster. But be comforted kinde olde man, for I haue hope by the power of heauen we were directed hither to punish that hateful Giant, reuenge the iniuries offered to thine age, satisfie with his death the death of thy children if they be dead, and restore to thy bounteous possession that admirable rich fountaine.

And nowe to you my valiant Companions I speake, that with mee through many dangers haue aduentured: let vs couragiously attempt this rare aduenture, wherein such honor to our names, such happines to our frends, such glory to God consistes, in recouering right to the wronged, and punishing rightfully the wrongers of the righteous. And that there be no contention among vs who shall begin this aduenture, for that I knowe all of you thirstie after honor, let lots bee made, and to whome soeuer the cheefe lot falleth let him be formost in assailing the Giant, and God and all good fortune be our guides.

The exceeding ioy which the old Iew conceiued, at the speeches of Saint *George*, had neere hande bereft him of the vse of sense, so aboue measure was he ouerioyed. But at length recouering vse of speech, he thus thankfully brake foorth.

How infinitely I finde my selfe bounde vnto you, you famous and vndoubted Christian Champions, all my ablenes is not able to expresse: onely thankfulnes from the exchequer of a true heart shall to you bee rendred.

The Champions without more words disrobing themselues from their Pilgrims attyre, euerie one selected foorth an armor fitting to their portely bodyes, and in steed of their Ebone staues tipt with siluer, they welded in their handes the steeled blades, and their feete that had wont to indure a paineful pilgrimage vpon the bare ground, were now redy prest to mount the golden stirrop, but as I said, they purposed not generally to assaile the Giant, but singly euerie one to trie his owne fortune thereby to obtaine the greater honor, and their deeds to merrit the higher fame, therfore the lots being cast amongst themselues which of them should beginne the aduenture. The lot fell first to Saint *Denis* the Noble Champion of *France*, who greatly reioyced at his fortune, and so departed for that night to get things in readines, but the next morning no sooner had the golden Sunne displaide his bewty in the East, but Saint *Denis* arose from his sluggish bed, and attyred himselfe in costly armor, and mounted vpon a steede of Irone gray with a spangled Plumbe of purple feathers on his burgonet, spangled with starres of golde, resembling the azure firmament beautifyed with starres.

After he had taken leaue of the other Champions, and had demaunded of the Iew where the Giant had his residence, he departed forward on his iourney: and before the Sunne had mounted to the top of heauen, he approached to the Giants

---

[4] wickednes.] wickednes *1597*

presence, which as then sate vppon a block of steele directly before the golden Fountaine, satisfying his hunger with raw flesh, and quenching his thirst wyth the iuyce of ripe grapes.

The first sight of his vgly and deformed proportion almost daunted the valor of the French Champion, so as he stood in a maze, whether it were better to trie the aduenture, or to returne with dishonor backe to his other fellow Knights. But hauing a heart furnished with true magnanimitie, he chose rather to dye in the incounter, than to returne with infamie: so committing his trust to the vnconstant Queene of chaunce, he spurred foorth his horse, and assayled the Giant so furiously, that the strokes of his sword sounded lyke weightie blowes hammered vpon an anuyle.

But so smally regarded the Giant the puissant force of this single Knight, that he wold scarce rise from the place where he sate: but yet remembring a vision that a little before appeared vnto him in his sleepe, which reueald vnto him, how that a Knight should come from the Northerne clymates of the earth, which should alone ende the aduenture of the Fountaine, and vanquish him by fortitude: therefore not minding to be taken at aduantage, he sodainly started vp, and with a grim and furious countenaunce he ran vpon Saint *Denis*, and tooke him horse, armour, furniture and all vnder his left arme, as lightly as a strong man would take a sucking infant from his cradle, and bore him to a hollow rocke of stone, bound about with barres of yron, standing neere vnto the Fountayne, in a valley betwixt two mightie mountaines. In which prison he closed the French Champion, amongst fourteen other Knights, that were al Sonnes to the curteous Iew as you heard before discoursed, and being proud of this attempt he returned backe to his blocke of steele, where we wil leaue him sitting, glorying in his own conceite, and speake of the other champions remaining in the Iewes house, expecting the French knightes fortunate returne: but when the sable Curtaines of darknes were drawne before the christall windowes of the day, and night had taken possession of the elements, and no newes was heard of the Champions successe, they iudged presently that eyther hee was slaine in the aduenture, or discomfited and taken prisoner.

Therefore they cast lots againe which of them, the next morning should trye his fortune, and reuenge the French knights quarrel, but the lot fel to Saint *Iames* the Noble champion of Spaine, whereat his Princelie heart more reioyced, then if he had beene made King of the Westerne World.

So vpon the next morning by the breake of day, he attyred himselfe in rich and costly armor like the other Champion, and mounted vppon a Spanish Ginnet, in pace more swifter then the winde, and in portly state like to *Beucephalus* the proud steede of *Macedonian Alexander*: his caparison was in color like to the waues of the Sea, his Burgonet was beautified with a spangled plumbe of sable feathers: and vpon his brest hee bore the armes of Spaine.

Thus in this gallant manner departed he from the Iewes habitation, leauing the other Champions at their deuine contemplations for his happie successe, but his fortune chanced contrarie to his wishes, for at the Giants first encounter he was likewise born to the rock of stone, to accompany Saint *Denis*.

This Giant was the strongest and hardiest knight at armes that euer set foote vpon the confines of *Damasko*, his strength was so inuincible, that at one time hee durst encounter with a hundred knights: but now returne we againe to the other champions, whome when night approached, and likewise missing the company of Saynt *Iames* they cast lots the third time, and it fel to the Noble champion of Italy Saint *Anthony*, whome on the next morning attyred himselfe in costly habiliments of war, and mounted vpon a Barbarian Palfrie as richly as did the valiant *Iason* when he aduentured into the Ile of *Colcas*, for the golden fleece: and for *Medeas* loue, his Helmet glistered like an Isie mountaine, deckt with a plumbe of ginger coloured feathers, and beautified with many siluer pendants. But his shining glory was soone blemished with a cloude of mischance, although hee was as valiant a knight as euer brandisht weapon in the fields of Mars, yet hee founde a disabilitie in his fortitude, to withstand the furious blowes of the Giant, that hee was forced to yeeld himselfe prisoner like the former Champions.

The next lot that was cast, chanced to Saint *Andrew* of Scotland, a Knight as highly honoured for martiall discipline as any of the rest, his steede was of the breede of the Flemish Mares, clad with a caparison after the maner of the Grecians, his Armor varnished with greene oyles, like the color of the Somer fields, vpon his brest he bore a crosse of purple silke, and on his burgonet a plumb of greene feathers: but yet fortune so frowned vpon his enterprize, that he nothing preuayled, but committed his life to the mercy of the Giant, who likewise imprisoned him with the other Knights.

The fift lot fell to Saint *Pattricke* of Ireland, as braue a knight as euer nature created, and as aduenterous in his atchiuements: If euer *Hector* vpon the Phrigian steede Praunst it vp and downe the streetes of *Troy*, and made that age admire his fortitude: this Irish knight might counter-uaile his valor.

For no sooner had the siluer Moone forsooke the Azure Firmament, and had committed her charge to the golden burnisht Sunne: But Saint *Pattricke* approached the sight of the Giant, mounted vppon his Irish hobby, cladde in a corselet of prooffe, beautified with siluer nayles: his plumbe of feathers, was of the color of Uirgins hayre, his horse couered with a vale of Orenge tawny silke, and his saddle bound about with plates of Steele, like to an Iron chayre.

The sight of this valliant Champion so daunted the courage of the Giant, that hee thought him to bee the knight that the vission had reuealed, by whome the aduenture shoulde bee accomplished: therefore with no cowardly fortitude hee assayled the Irish knight, who with as Princely valor indured the incounter: but the vnkinde destinies not intending to giue him the honor of the victory, compelled[5] the Champion to yeeld to the Giants forces, and like a Captiue to accompany the other imprisoned Champions.

The next lot fell to Saint *Dauid* of Wales, who nothing discouraged at the discomfiture of the other Christian knightes, but at the mornings Suns vpryse into the azure firmament, glistered in his siluer Armor before the fountaine, with a golden Griffon shyning on his brest, where he endured long & daungerous combate with the Giant, making the skyes to resound with echoes of their stroakes, but at last when the Giant perceaued that Saint *Dauid* beganne to growe almost

---

[5] compelled] ecompelled *1597*

breathlesse, in defending the huge and mightie blowes of his steeled batte, and chiefely through the long incounter, the Giant renewed his strength, and so redoubled his stroakes that Saint *Dauid* was constrayned[6] lyke the other Christian Champions to yeeld to the Gyants mercies.

But now the inuinsible and heroyecall Champyon of England Saint *George*, hee that is fames true knight, the mappe of Honour, and the worlds wonder, remayning in the Iewes pauilion, and pondring in hys minde of the bad successe of the sixe Champions, and that it was his turne to try his fortune the next morning in the aduenture: he fell vpon his knees and made this humble supplycation to the Maiesty of God. O thou creator of this worldly Globe (quoth he,) O thou that hast fought for thy christian Knights in fields of purple bloud, and made the enemies of heauen to swim in streames of Crimson gore, O thou that hast giuen mee still the victory, graunt that I may confounde this bloudy and vnhumaine monster, that hath discomfited sixe of the brauest knights that euer nature framed, euen as thou wast my ayde when I slewe the burning Dragon in Egipt: and when I conquered the terrible Giant that kept the inchaunted Castle amongst the *Amazonians*, euen so let me accomplish this daungerous aduenture, that all christians and christian Knights may applaude thy name, and in thy defence and iust quarrell, may stil be honored with the golden pledge of knighthood.

In this manner spent hee away the night in making his deuine orations to heauen, for the happy successe of the next daies enterprize, whereon he vowed by the honor of his golden Garter, either to returne a worthy conquerer, or to dye a faithfull Martir. And when the day began to beautifie the Easterne Elements with a purple color, he repayred to the Iewes armory, and clad himselfe in a blacke Corselet, and mounted vpon a pitchy coloured steede, adorned with a bloud-red caparison, in signe of a bloudy and tragicall aduenture, his plume of feathers was like a flame of fire quencht in blood as a token of speedy reuenge, hee arm'd himselfe not with a sturdy Launce, bounde about with plates of brasse, but tooke a Iauelin made of steele, the one end far more sharper then the pointe of a needle, the other end a ball of Iron in fashion of a mace or[7] club.

Being thus armd according to his wished desires, hee tooke leaue of the Iew and his seauen Sonnes, who sate attyred in blacke and mournfull ornaments, praying for his happie and fortunate successe: and so departed speedily to the golden Fountaine, where hee found the Giaunt sleeping carelesly vpon his blocke of steele, dreading no insuing dangers.

But when the valiant Champion Saint *George* was alighted from his horse, and had sufficiently beheld the deformed proportion of the Giant: how the hair of his head stood staring vpright like to the bristles of a wilde Boare, his eyes gazing open like two blazing Comets, his teeth long and sharpe like to spikes of steele, the nayles of hys hands like the tallants of an Eagle, yet ouer them was drawen a paire of yron gloues: and euerie other limme huge and strongly proportioned like to the bodie of some mightie Oake, the worthie Champion awakened him in this order.

---

[6] constrayned] constrayed *1597*
[7] or] of or *1597*

Arise (sayd he) thou vnreasonable deformed Monster, and either make deliuerie of the captiue Knights, whom thou wrongfully detainest, or prepare thy vgly selfe to abide the vttermost force of my warlike arme and death-prepared weapon.

At which words the furious Giant started vp, as one sodainly amazed or affrighted from his sleepe: and without making anie reply at all, taking his yron Mace fast in both his hands, he did with great terror let driue at the most worthie English Champion, who with exceeding cunning nimblenes defended himselfe from certaine danger by speedie auoyding the blowes violence, and withall returned on his aduersarie a mightie thrust with the pointed or sharpe ende of his Iauelin, which rebounded from the Giants bodie, as if it had been runne against an Adamantine piller.

The which the inuincible Saint *George* perceiuing, he turned the heauie round ball ende of his massie iaueline, and so mightely assayled the Giant, redoubling his heauie blowes with such couragious fortitude, that at last he beate his braines out of his deformed head: whereby the Giant was constrained to yeeld vp his ghost, and to giue such a hideous roare, as though the whole frame of the Earth had been shaken with the violence of some storme of thunder.

This beeing done, Saint *George* cast his loathsome carkasse as a pray for the fowles and rauenous beastes to seaze vppon: and after verie diligently searched vp and downe, till he found the Rocke wherein all the Knightes and Champions were imprisoned: the which wyth hys steely Iauelin he burst in sunder, and deliuered them presently from their seruitudes, and after returned most triumphantly backe to the Iewes Pauilion, in as great maiestie and roialtie as *Vaspasian* with his Romane Nobles and Peeres returned into the confines of flourishing *Italy*, from the admired and glorious conquest of *Ierusalem* and *Iudea*.

But when the reuerend olde Iew sawe the English champion returned with victorie, together with his other sixe fellow champions, and likewise beheld hys fourteene Sonnes safely deliuered, his ioy so mightely exceeded the bounds of reason, that he sodainly swonded, and lay for a time in a dead traunce, with the exceedingnes of plesure he conceiued.

But hauing a little recouered his decayed senses, hee gladly conducted them into their seuerall Lodgings, and there they were presently vnarmed, and their woundes washed in white wine and new milke, and after banqueted them in the best manner hee could deuise. At which Banquet there wanted not all the excellencie of musique that the Iewes seauen yonger Sonnes could deuise, extolling in their sweete Sonnets the excellent fortitude of the English champion, that had not onely deliuered their captiued Bretheren, but restored by that vgly Giants deserued death their aged Father to the repossession of his golden Fountaine.

Thus after Saint *George* with the other sixe Champions had soiourned there for the space of thirtie dayes, hauing placed the Iew with his Sonnes in their former desired dignities, that is in the gouernment of the Golden Fountaine, they cloathed themselues againe in theyr Pilgrimes attyre, and so departed forward on theyr intended Iourney to visite the holy Sepulcher of our Sauiour Christ.

Of whose noble Aduentures you shall heare more in the Chapter following.

Of the Champions returne from Ierusalem from the Sepulcher of Christ, and after how they were almost famished in a wood: and[1] how saint George obtained them food by his valour in a Giaunts House with other things that happened.

THe Champions after this neuer rested trauelling till they arriued at the holy Hill of Mount *Sion*, and had visited the blessed Sepulcher of Christ, the which they found most richly built of ye purest marble, garnished curiously by cunning Architecturie, with manie carbuncles of Iasper, and pillors of ieate. The Temple wherein it was erected, stood seauen degrees of staires within the ground, the gates whereof were of burnisht golde, and the portalles of refined siluer, cut as it dyd seeme out of a most excellent nature beautefied Alablaster Rocke.

By it continually burned a sweet smelling Taper, alwayes maintained by twelue of the Noblest Uirgines dwelling in all *Iudea*, attending still vppon that blessed Sepulcher, clad in silken ornaments in colour like the Lillyes in the flourishing pride of Summer: the which costly attire, they continually weare, as an euident signe of their vnspotted virginities: many daies offred vp these worthy Champions these ceremonious deuotions, to the sacred Tombe of Christ, washing the marble pauement with their vnfained teares, and witnessing their true and heartie zeales, with their continual vollyes of discharged sighes.

But at last vppon an Euening, when *Titans* golden beames began to descend the Westerne Elements, as those Princely minded Champions in companie of those twelue admyred Maidens, kneeled before the Sepulcher offering vp their Euening Orizons, an vnseene voyce (to the amazement of them all) from a hollow vault in the Temple vttered these words.

You magnanimous Knights of Christendome, whose true nobilities hath circled the earth vpon the wings of fame, whose bare feete for the loue of our sweet Sauiour, hath set more wearie steps vpon the parched earth, then there be stars within the golden Cannopy of heauen: returne, returne into the bloodie fields of warre, and spend not the honour of your times in this ceremonious maner: for great things by you must bee accomplished, such as in time to come shall fill large Chronicles, and cause babes as yet vnborne to speak of your honorable atchiuements.

And you chast Maidens that spend your liues in seruice of your God, euen by the plighted promise you haue made to true Uirginitie, I charge you to furnish foorth these warlike Champions with such approoued furniture as hath beene offered to this blessed Sepulcher, by those trauelling Knights, which haue fought vnder the Banner of Christ. This is the pleasure of the Heauens great Guider, and this for the redresse of wronged Innocents in earth must be with all immediate dispatch foorthwith accomplished.

This vnexpected voyce had no sooner ended, but the Temple (in their conceites) seemed full strangely to resound like the melodie of celestial Angels or the holy

---

[1] *and] and and 1597*

harmony of the heauenly Rubens,[2] as a signe that the Gods were pleased at their proceedings: then the twelue Uirgins arose from their diuine contemplations and conducted the seauen Champions to the farther side of mount *Syon*, and there bestowed franklie vppon them, seauen of the brauest Steedes that euer they beheld, with Martiall furniture answerable therunto, befitting knights of such esteeme: then the christian Champions beeing proude of their good fortunes, attyred them selues in rich and sumptious corselets, and after mounted vppon their warlike coursers, kindly bidding the Ladies adiew: they betooke them to the worlds wide iourney. This trauell began at that time of the yeare, when the Sommers queene began to spread her beauteous mantles amongst the greene and fresh boughes of the hye and mightie Cedars, when as all kinde of small birds flewe round about, recreating themselues in the beautie of the day, and with their well tuned notes, making a sweete and heauenlye melodye: at that time I say, these mightie and well esteemed knights the seauen Champions of Christendome, tooke the way from Ierusalem, which they thought to be most vsed: in which they had not many daies trauelled through the deserts and ouer many a mountaine top, but they were meruailously troubled for lacke of their accustomed and dayly victuale, and could not hide nor dissemble their great hunger, so that the warre which they sustayned with hunger, was farre greater then the battels that they had fought against the enemies of Christ, as you heard discoursed in the first part of this Historye.

So vpon a Sommers euening, when they had spent the day in great extreamitie, and night grewe on, being in a thicket of mightye trees, where as the siluer Moone with her bright beames glistred most cleerly, yet to them it seemed to bee as darke as pitch, for they were very sore troubled for lacke of that which shoulde sustaine them: and their faces did showe and declare the perplexities of their stomackes.

So they sate them downe vppon the greene and freshe hearbes, very pensiue of their extreame necessitie, procuring to take their rests that night: but all was in vayne, for that their corporall necessities would not consent thervnto: but without sleeping they walked vp and downe for that night, till the next day in the morning that they turned to their accustomed trauell and iourney, thinking to finde some food for the cherishing of their stomackes, and had their eyes alwayes gazing about, to espye some Uillage or house, wherein they might satisfye their hunger and take their restes.

Thus in this helplesse manner spent they away the next day, till the closing in of the euenings light, by which time they grewe so faint, that they fell to the ground with feeblenesse: Oh what a sorrowe was it to Saint *George*, not only for him selfe, but to see the rest of the Champions in such a miserable case, beeing not able to helpe themselues, and so parting a little from them, he lamented in this manner following.

Thou God of *Iudea*: in whose handes both life and death remaines, and at whose frownes the lowe foundation of the fastened worlde[3] tremble and quake: the outragious Seas swell and rise aboue theyr boundes, the woods and wildernes rore

---

[2] heauenly Rubens] Cherubins *1616*
[3] worlde] will *1597*

with tempestious gustes,[4] and the fruitfull earth growe barren. Oh pitty mee thou most gratious God: thou mightiest amongst the powers of heauen: thou that hast giuen me so many victories: thou that hast made me conqueror of Kinges and kingdomes: and thou by whose inuinsible power I haue tamed the black-faste furyes of darke *Cositus* that maskte abroad the worlde in humaine shapes: looke downe I say from thy Imperiall seate, euen by my Pilgrimage vnto thy Sacred shrine: showe mee some fauor,[5] and doe not consent that I and my companie perish for hunger & want of victualls: make no delay to remedie our great necessitie: let vs not be meat for birds houering in the aire, nor our bodies cast as a pray for rauenous beasts ranging in these woods: but rather if we must needes perish, let vs dy by the hands of the strongest warriers in the vniuersal world, and not basely to loose our liues with cowardlye hunger.

These and such like reasons vttered this valiaunt Champion of *England*, till such time as the day appeared and the sable curtaines of coale blacke night were withdrawen. Then returned he to the rest of his Companie, where he found them verie weake and feeble: but he encouraged them in the best manner he could deuise to take their horses, and to trie the chaunce of their vtmost vnkinde fortune.

Although Saint *George* as they trauelled was readie to dye by the way, and in great confusion of minde: yet rode he first to one then to another, comforting[6] them, and making them ride apace: which they might verie well doo, for that their horses were not so vnprouided as theyr Masters, by reason of the goodly grasse that grew in those Woods, wherewith at pleasure they filled themselues euerie night.

The golden Sunne had almost mounted to the top of heauen, and the glorious prime of the daye began to approch, when they came into a great field verie plaine, and in the middest of it was a little Mountaine, out of the which there appeared a great smoake which gaue them to vnderstand that there should be some habitation in that place.

Then the Princely minded Saint *George* said to the other Champions: Take comfort with your selues, and by little and little come forward with an easie pace: for I will ride before to see who shall be our hoast this ensuing night. And of this braue Knights and Companions, be[7] all assured, whether hee be pleasde or no, yet shall hee giue vs lodging and entertayne vs like to trauelling Knights, and therewithall he set spurres to his horse, and swiftly scowred away like to a ship with swelling sailes vpon the marble coloured Ocean: his hast was so speedy that in a short time he approached the mountaine, where at the furie & rushing of his horse in running, there arose from the ground a mightie and terrible Giant, of so great height, that he seemed to bee a bigge growne tree, and for hugenes like to a rocke of stone: but when he cast his staring eyes vpon the English knight: which seemed like two brazen plates or two torches euer flaming, he layde hand vpon a mightie club of Iron which lay by him, and came with great lightnesse to meete

---

[4] gustes] guses *1597*
[5] fauor] fouor *1597*
[6] comforting] camforting *1597*
[7] be] bee be *1597*

Saint *George*, but when he approached his presence, he thought him to bee a Knight but of small vallor and fortitude, he threw away his Iron bat, and came towards the champion, intending with his fistes and buffets to beat out his braines, but the courage of the English champion so exceeded, that he forgot the extremity of hunger, for like a couragious knight he raised himselfe in his stirrops, otherwise hee coulde not reach his head, and gaue him such a blowe vpon the forehead with his keene edged fauchion, that he cut his head halfe in sunder, and his braines in great aboundance ran downe his deformed bodie: so that amazed hee fell to the ground and presently dyed. His fall seemed to make the ground to shake, as though a stony tower had beene ouerturnd, for as he lay vpon the earth, he seemed to be a great oake blowne vp by the rootes with a tempestious whirlwinde.

At that instant the rest of the champions came to that place, with as much ioy at that present, as before they were sad and sorrowfull.

But when Saint *Denis* with the other knights, did see the greatnes of the Giant, and the deformity of his body, they aduanced his valor beyond immagination, and deemed him the fortunatest Champion that euer nature framed, holding that aduenture in as high honour, as the *Grecians* held *Iasons* prize when he turned from *Colchos* with *Medeas* golden Fleece: and with as great daunger accomplished as the twelue fearfull labours of *Hercules*: but after some fewe speaches passed, Saint *George* desired the rest of the Champions to goe and see what store of victuals the Giant had prepared for them.

Upon this they concluded, and so generally entred the Giants house, which was in the maner of a great Barne cut out of the hard stone, and wrought out of the Rocke: therein they found a mightie copper Chauldron standing vppon a treauet of steele, the feet and supporters thereof, were as bigge as great Iron pillers: vnder the same burned such a huge flaming fire, that it sparkeled like the fierye Furnace in burning *Acharon*.[8]

Within the Chaldron were boyling the fleshe of two fatte Bullockes, prepared onely for the Giants dinner: the sight of this ensuing banquet gaue them such comfort, that eueryone fell to worke, hoping for their trauel to eat parte of the meate: one turned the beefe in the Chaldron, another increased the fire, and some pulled out the coales, so that there was not anye idle in hope of the benefite to come.

The hunger they had, and their desire to eate, caused them to fall to their meate before it was halfe readye as though that it had beene ouer-sodden; but the two knights of Wales and Ireland, not intending to dine without bread and drinke, searched in a secret hollow caue, wheras they found two great loaues of bread, as bigge in compasse as the circle of a well, and two great Flagons full of the best Beere that euer they tasted, the which with great ioye and pleasure, they brought from the caue, to the great and exceeding contentment of the other Champions.

In stead of a knife to cut their victuals, Saint *George* vsed his Curtalaxe which lately had beene stayned with the hatefull Giants detested blood, and that had beene imbrewed with his loathsome braynes.

---

[8] *Acharon.] Acharon: 1597*

Thus and after this manner qualified they the pinching paines and torments of hunger, whereof they tooke as ioyfull a repast as if they had banqueted in the richest Kings Pallace in the world.

So giuing thankes to heauen for their good and happy fortunes, Saint *George* requested the Champions[9] to take horsse, and mounted himselfe vpon his palfrey, and so trauelled from thence thorowe a narrowe path, which seemed to be vsed by the Giant: and so with great diligence they trauelled all the rest of that day, till night had closed in the beautye of the heauens: at which time they had got to the top of a high mountaine, from whence a little before night they did discouer meruaylous and great[10] playnes, the which were inhabited with fayre Cities and townes, at which sight these Christian Champions receiued great contentment and ioy, and so without any staying, they made hast onwards on their iorney till such time as they came to a lowe valley lying betwixt two running riuers: where in the midst of the way they found an Image of fine Cristall, the picture & liuely forme of a beautiful Uirgin, which seemed to be wrought by the hands of some moste excellent worke-man, all to be spotted with blood.

And it appeared by the woundes that were cunningly formed in the same picture, that it was the image of some Lady that had suffred torments, aswell with terrible cuttings of yrons, as with cruel whippings: the Ladies legs and armes did seeme as though they had beene martyred and wrunge with cordes: and about the necke, as though shee had beene forceablye strangled with a napkin or towell: the cristall Picture laye vppon a rich adorned bed of blacke cloathes vnder an arbor of purple Roses: by the curious faire formed Image, sate a goodly aged man in a chaire of cipresse wood, his attire was after the manner of the *Arcadian* sheap-heards not curious but comely, yet of a blacke and sable colour, as a sure signe of some deadly discontent, his hayre hung downe belowe his shoulders, like vntwisted silke, in whitenes like downe of thistles, his beard ouer growne dangling downe, as it were frozen Isickles vpon a hauthorne tree, his face wrinkled and ouerworn with age and his eyes almost blind in bewraying the greefes and sorrows of his heart.

Which strange and woful spectacle, when the christian champions vigilantly behelde, they coulde not by any manner of meanes refraine from shedding some sorrowfull teares, in seeing before them that a woman of suche excellent beautie should be opprest with cruelty. But the pittifull English Knight had the greatest compassion, when he behelde the counterfeit of this tormented creature, who taking truce with his sorrowfull heart, he curteously desired the olde Father, sitting by this spectacle, the cause of his sorrow, and the true discourse of that maidens passed fortunes: for whose sake hee seemed to spend his daies in that solitary order, to whome the olde man with a number of sighes thus kindly replyed, braue knightes, for so you seeme by your curtesies and behauiours, to tell the storie of my bitter woes, and the causer of my endles sorrows, will constraine a spring of teares to trickle from the Conduits of my aged eyes, and make the mansion of my heart to riue in twaine, in remembring of my vndeserued miseries: as many drops

---

[9] Champions] Chompiens *1597*
[10] and great] great and *1597*

of bloud hath fallen from my heart as there be siluer haires vpon my head, and as many sighes haue I strained from my brest as there be minutes in a yeere, for thrice seuen hundred times the mornings dew hath wet my siluer hayres, and thrise seuen hundred times the winters frosts hath nipt the mountaine tops since first I made these ruful lamentations, during all which time I haue set before this christall Image, howerly praying that some curteous Knight would be so kinde, as to ayde me in my vowed reuenge, and now fortune I see hath smild vpon me, in sending you hether to work a iust reuenge for the inhumane murther of my daughter, whose perfect Image lyeth here carued in fine Christall, as the continuall obiecte of my griefe: and because you shall vnderstand the true discourse of her timeles Tragidie, I haue writte that downe in a paper booke with mine owne blood, the which my faintfull tongue is not able to reueale, and thereupon hee pulled from his bossome a golden couered booke with siluer claspes, and requested Saint *George* to read it to the rest of the kinghts, to which he willingly condescended, so sitting downe amongst the other Champions vpon the greene springing grasse, hee opened the bloudy written booke and read ouer the contents, which contained these sorrowful wordes following.

CHAP. VI.

What hapned to the Champions, after they had found an Image of fine Cristall, in the forme of a murthered Mayden: where Saint George had a golden Booke giuen him, wherein was written in blood, the true Tragedies of two Sisters: and likewise how the Champions intended a speedy reuenge vpon the Knight of the blacke Castle, for the deaths of the two Ladies.

IN former times whilste Fortune smilde vpon me, I was a welthye Sheepheard, dwelling in this vnhappye Countrye, not onely held in great estimation for my welth, but also for two faire Daughters which nature had made[1] most excellent in beautie: in whome I tooke such exceeding ioy & delight, that I accounted them my chiefest happinesse: but yet in the end, that which I thought should most content me, was the occasion of this my endles sorrowes.

My two Daughters (as I said before) were endued with wonderfull beauty, and accompanyed with no lesse honestie: the fame of whose virtues was so blazed into many partes of the worlde: by reason whereof, there repayred to my Sheepheards Cottage, diuers strange and worthye Knights, with greate desire to marrie with my Daughters. But aboue them all, there was one named *Leoger*, the knight of the blacke Castle (wherein he now remayneth) beeing in distance from this place some two hundreth leagues, in an Island incompassed with the sea.

This *Leoger* I say, being so entrapped with the beautye of my Daughters, that he desired me to giue him one of them in mariage: but I little mistrusting his treason and crueltie that after followed, but rather considering the greate honor that might redounde thereof, for that he was a woorthy knight and of much fortitude: I quickly fulfilled his desire, and graunted to him my eldest Daughter in mariage: where after that *Himens*[2] holy rites were solemnized, in great pomp and state she was conducted in company of her new wedded Lord, to the blacke Castle, more liker a Princesse in estate then a sheepheards daughter of such degree:

But yet still I retained in my company the youngest, beeing of farre more beautie then her elder Sister: of which, this trayterous and vnnaturall knight was informed and her surpassing beauty so extolled, that in a small time he forgot his new maried wife, and sweet companion, and wholly surrendred himselfe to her loue, without consideration that he had maried her other sister.[3] So this disordinate and lustful loue, kindled and increased in him euery day more and more, and hee was so troubled with this new desire, that he dayly deuised with himselfe by what meanes he might obtaine her, and keepe her in dispite of all the World: in the end he vsed this policie and deceipt to get her home into his Castle, for when the time grewe on that my eldest daughter his wife should bee deliuered, hee came in great pompe with a stately traine of followers to my cottage, and certified me that his wife was deliuered of a goodly boy, and thereupon requestest me with very faire

---

[1] made] mad *1597*
[2] *Himens*] *Himeus 1597*
[3] sister.] sister *1597*

and louing wordes, that I woulde let my daughter goe vnto her sister, to giue her that contentment which she desired, for shee did loue her more deerer then her owne soule: Thus his craftie and subtil perswations so much preuailed, that I coulde not frame any excuse to the contrarie, but muste needes consent to his demaund, so straight way when hee had in his power, that which his soule so much desired, hee presently departed, giuing me to vnderstand that hee would carry her to hys wife, for whose sight she had so much desired, and at whose comming she would receiue great ioy and contentment, her sodaine departure bred such sorrow in my heart (being the onely comfort and stay of my declyned age) that the fountaines of my eyes rained downe a shewer of Salt teares vpon my aged brest, so deare is the loue of a father vnto his child: but to be short, when this lustfull minded catiffe with his pompious traine came in sight of his Castle, he commaunded his companie to ride forwards that with my daughter hee might secretly conferre of serious matters, and so staide lingring behinde, till hee sawe his company almost out of sight and they two alone together, he found oportunitie to accomplish his lustful desires, and so rode into a little groue, which was hard at hande, close by a riuers side, where without any more tarying he caried her into the thickest part thereof, where he thought it most conuenient to performe so wicked a deede.

When he behelde the branches of the thicke trees to withholde the light of heauen from them, and that it seemed a place ouerspred with the sable mantles of night, he alighted from his horse, and willed my welbeloued daughter that shee should likewise alight: shee in whose heart raigned no kinde of suspition, presently alighted, and sate her downe by the riuers side, and washed her faire white handes in the streames, and refreshed her mouth with the christall waters.

Then this dessembling Traitor coulde no longer refraine, but with a countenance like the lustfull King of *Thrace* when hee intended the rauishment of *Progne*, or like *Tarquinius* of *Roame* when he defloured *Lucrecia*, he let her vnderstand by some outward shewes, and darke sentences the kindled fire of loue that burned in his hart: and in the end he did wholy declare his deuilish pretence and determined purpose.

So my louing daughter being troubled in minde with his lustfull assaylements beganne in manner to reprehend him, will you (said she)[4] defile my sisters bedde, and staine the honor of your house with lust: will you bereaue me of that precious Iewell, the which I holde more deerer then my life, and blot my true Uirginitie with your false desires: brought you me from the comfortable sight of my Father, to bee a ioy vnto my Sister, and will you florish in the spoile of my true chastitie? looke, looke, imoderate Knight, (I will not call thee brother) looke I say how the heauens doe blush at thy attempts, and see how chaste *Diana* sits vpon the winged firmaments, and threatens vengeance for her Uirgins sake: washe from thy heart these lustfull thoughts with shewers of thy repentant teares and seeke not thus to wrong thy mariage bed, the which thou oughst not to violate for all the kingdomes in the World.

---

[4] she)] she *1597*

Then this accursed Knight, seeing the chaste and vertuous maiden, to stand so boldely in the defence of her Uirginitie, with his rigorus hand hee tooke fast holde by her necke, and with a wrathfull countenance hee deliuered these words: do not think stubborn damsel to preserue thy honor from the staine of my desires, for I sweare by the christall Towers of Heauen, either to accomplish my intent, or put thee vnto the cruellest death that euer was deuised for anye damsell or maide: at which wordes, the most sorrowfull and disstressed Uirgin, with a shewer of Pearled teares, trickling downe her seemely blushing cheekes, replyed in this order. Thinke not false Traytor (quoth she) that feare of death shall cause me to yeeld to thy filthy desires: no, no, I will accompt that stroak ten times happy, and more welcome to my soule, then the ioyes of wedlocke: then might I walke in the *Elizian* fields amongst those dames that dyed true virgins, and liue to behold the budde of my maydens glory, withered with the nypping frostes of thy vnnaturall desires.

These wordes being well vnderstoode by the lustfull knight, who with a countenance more furious then the sauage Lyons in the Deserts of *Libia*, tooke her by the slender waste, and rigorously dasht her body against the ground, and therewithall spake these words. Understand said he, and be well perswaded, thou vnrelenting damsell, that either liuing or dead, I will performe my will and pretended purpose: for in my hart there burnes a fire that all the water in the Seas can neuer quench, nor all the drisling clouds of heauen, if they should drop eternal shewers of raine: but it is the water of thy sweet Uirginity that must quench my furious burning loue: and thereupon in a madnes he cut off a great part of the traine of her gowne, and bound it very fast to the hayre of her head, which glistered like to golden wyers, and drag'd her vp and downe the groue till the greene grasse turned to a purple color, with the bloud that issued from her body: by which crueltie he thought to inforce her to hys pleasure, but she respecting not his wicked crueltie, and the more he procured to torment her, the more earnestly she defended her honor.

When this cruell and inhumaine monster, saw that neither his flattering speeches, nor his cruell threates were of sufficiencie to preuaile, hee beganne to forget all faith and loyaltie he ought vnto the honor of Knighthood, and the respect he should beare vnto women kinde, but blasphemed against heauen, and tearing her cloathes al to peeces, hee stripped her starke naked, and with the raynes[5] of the bridle of his horse, he cruelly whipped and scurged her white and tender backe, that it was full of blewe spottes, and horrible circles of blacke and settled bloud, with such extreame crueltie that it was a very greeuous and sorrowfull sight to behold. And yet this did profite him nothing at all, for she continued in her former resolution.

He seeing that she still perseuerd in the defence of her honor, he straight waies like a bloudy monster, heaped crueltie vpon crueltie: then he tooke and bound her wel proportioned legs and christeline armes, greeuously vnto a withered tree (saying). Oh cruel and more cruell, then any woman in all the world hath euer beene: why dost thou suffer thy selfe to bee thus tormented, and not giue consent to

---

[5] raynes] haynes *1597*

procure my ease? Dost thou thinke it better to indure this marterdome, then to liue a moste louing, sweete and contented life: and therewithall his anger so increased that he stood staring on her face with his accursed eyes, fixed in such sort that he could not withdraw them backe.

The which being perceiued by this distressed Uirgin, as one farre more desirous of death then of life, with a furious voyce she saide: Oh thou traiter, thou wicked monster, thou vtter enemy to all humanitie, thou shamelesse creature more cruell then the Lyons in the desertes of *Hercania*: thou staine of Knighthood and the bloudiest wretch that euer nature framed in the worlde, wherein dost thou contemplate thus thyself? thou fleshly butcher, thou vnmercifull Tyger, thou letcherous hogge, and dishonorer of thy progenie: make an end (I say) of these my torments, for it is now too late to repent thee, gore my vnspotted brest with thy bloudy weapon, and send my soule into the bossome of *Diana*, whome I behold sitting in the celestiall pallace of heauen, accompanied with numberles troops of vestal Uirgins, ready to entertaine my bleeding goast into her glorious Mansion.

This vnpitifull knight seeing the stedfastnesse that she had in the defence of her honor, with a cruell and infernall heart he tooke a silken scarfe which the Damsell had girded at her waste, and with a brutall anger doubled it about her necke, and pinched it so straight that her soule departed from her teresticall body.

O you valiant Knights that by your Prowes comes to the reading of this dismal Tragidy, and comes to the hearing of these bloudy lines, contained in this golden booke: consider the great constancie and chastitie of this vnfortunate maiden, and let the griefe thereof mooue you to take vengeance of this crueltie shewed without any desert.

So when this infernall minded Knight sawe that shee was dead, he tooke his horse and rode after his company, and in a short time he ouer tooke them, and looked with so furious and Irefull a countenance, that there was none durst be so hardy to aske him where my daughter was, but one of his Squiers that bore me great affection for the kindnes and curtesie I ostended to him at his Ladyes and my daughters nuptials, hauing a suspition by the great alteration that appeared in his Master: and being very desirous to know what was become of the damsell for that he came alone without bringing the Damsell with him, neyther could he haue any sight of her: he then presently withdrew[6] himselfe backe, and followed the footings of the horse, hee ceased not vntill hee came to the place where this crueltie was wrought, whereas he found the maiden dead, at the vewe whereof he remained almost beside himselfe, in such sorte that hee had almost fallen to the ground: The sorrowfull Squire remained a good while before he could speake, but at last when he came againe to himselfe, he began with a dolorous complaint, crying out against the gods and fortune, because they had suffered so great a crueltie to be committed vpon this damsell.

---

[6] withdrew] withdraw *1597*

And making this sorrowfull lamentation, he vnloosed her from the tree, and layd her naked body vppon part of her apparell, the which hee found lying by, all besmear'd in blood, and afterwarde complained in this pitifull sort.

O cruell Knight (quoth he) what an infernall hart remained in thy brest, or what hellish furie did beare thee company that thy hands hath committed this inhumane sacrifice? was it not sufficient that this her surmounting[7] beauty might haue moued thee to pitty, when it is of power to moue the bloody Cannibal[8] to remorse, and constraine the sauage monsters to relent? so with these and other like sorrowfull words that the wofull Squire spake vnto the dead corpes, he cut downe branches from the trees, and gathered grasse from the ground for to couer the body, and left it lying so, that it seemed to be a mountaine of greene grasse, or a thicket of springing trees, and then determined with himselfe in the best manner that he could, to dissemble the knowledge of the bloudy facte, hee tooke his horse and went the way towards the Castle, in which hee rode so fast that he ouertooke the Knight and his companie at the entring of the gates, whereas the lustfull tyrant alighted, and without speaking to any person, he entred into his closset, by reason wherof, this kinde and curteous Squire had time to declare all things hee had seene to the new maried Lady, and the dolorous end of the constant Damsell her Sister. This soddaine and vnlooked for sorrowe mixed with anger and wrath, was such in the Lady that shee caused the Squire not to depart from the Castle, vntill such time as more occasion serued, and to keepe all thinges in secret that he had seene, and she her selfe remayned, making meruailous and great lamentations to her selfe all in secret, for that she would not be perceiued, yet with a soft voyce she said.

Oh vnfortunate Lady, borne in a sorrowfull howre, when some blazing and vnluckie Comette raigned: oh vnhappie Destenies, that made me wife vnto so cruell a knight, whose foule mis-deedes hath made the verye Elements to blush, but yet I know that Fortune will not be so far vnkinde, but that she will procure to take a strange reuenge vpon his purple-stayned soule: oh you immortall Gods, reuenge me on this wicked Homicide: if not, I do sweare that I will with mine owne hands put in practise such an enterprize, and so staine my vnspotted heart with wilful murther, that all the Gods aboue and all the bright celestiall powers of heauen, shall looke from their immortall Palace and tremble at the terror of my hate.

This being said, she tooke in her hand a Dagger of the knights, and in her armes her younge sonne, being but of the age of fortie dayes (saying) now do I wish so much euill vnto the worlde, that I will not leaue the sonne of so wicked a father aliue, but I will wash my hands in their accurssed bloodes, if they were in number to King *Priams* children: and so in this irefull order entred she the chamber where the knight her husband was, and finding him tumbling vpon his bed from the one side to the other, with out taking any rest, but in his furye renting and tearing the silken Ornaments, with a sorrowfull weeping and terrible voyce she called him Traitor: and like a fierce Tigresse, with the Dagger that she brought in her hand, before his face she cut the throat of the innocent Babe, and threwe it to him on the bed, and therewithal said: take there (thou cruel Traitor) the fruite that thy wicked

---

[7] surmounting] surmounted *1597*
[8] Cannibal] Camibal *1597*

seed created in my bodye, and then threwe she the Dagger after him in hope to haue killed him: but Fortune would not that it shoulde take effecte, for it strooke against the testerne of the bed, and rebounded backe vnto her handes, which when the Lady sawe that it nothing preuayled, she returned vppon her selfe her outragious furie: so taking the bloodye Dagger she thrust it to her heart, in such sorte, that it parted it in two peeces, and so she fell downe dead betwixt his armes, that was the occasion of all this bloody crueltie.

The great sorrowe that this false and vnhappy knight receiued was so strange, that he knewe not what counsell to take: but thinking vppon a seuere vengeance that might succeede these cruell actes, he straight wayes procured that the body of the Lady, should be secretly[9] buryed, which beeing doone by him selfe in the saddest time of the night, in a solitarie garden vnder his castle wall, where he heard a hollowe voyce breath from the deepest vawltes of the earth, these manner of speaches following.

That for the bloody facte which he so lately had committed, his lyfe drewe neere to a shamefull end: and that his Castle with all his treasure therein, should be destroyed or fall into the handes of him whose Daughters he had so cruelly murthered.

After this, he determined to vse a secret policie: which was, to set watch and warde in euery passage neere vnto his Castle, and to arrest all such trauellers, as by aduenture landed vpon that Island, not suffering them to passe vntill such time as they had promised him by oath to ayde and assist him euen vnto death, against all his enemies:

In the meane time, the aforenamed Squire which had seene and heard all the tragicall dealings that hath beene heere declared, in the best wise he could, returned againe vnto my cottage & tolde me all that you haue heard, which was vnto me very sorowful and heauy newes: iudge here then gentle knights and ye beholders of this woful tragedy, what sorow I vnfortunate wretch sustained, and what angwish I receiued: for at the hearing therof, I fell into a senceles[10] sounde, and being come againe vnto my selfe, I all to besmear'd my milk white hayre in dust, that before were as cleare as the tryed siluer, and with my teares being the true signs[11] of sorrow, I bathed the bosome of my mother earth, and sighes pressed with such aboundance from my tormented heart, that they staide the passage of my speach, and my tongue could not reueale the griefe that my wofull thoughts conceiued.

In this dumbe silence and sorrow of minde I remained three daies and three nightes, numbring my silent passions with the minutes of the day, and my mightie griefes, with the starres of heauen, when frostie bearded winter hath cladde the elements with twinkling Diamonds:[12] but at last, when my amazed griefes were something abated, my eyes (almost blind with weeping) required some sleepe thereby to mitigate the sorrows of my heart: I made my repayre into a pleasant meddow adioyning neere vnto my cottage, where amongst the green springing

---

[9] secretly] secrtely *1597*
[10] senceles] *thus catchword*; les *1597*
[11] signs] sings *1597*
[12] Diamonds] Diamons *1597*

downes I purposed to take some rest, and to locke vp the closets of my tearfull eyes
with golden slumbers, thinking it to be the greatest content my sobbing heart
required: But before I could settle my sences to a quiet sleepe, I was constrained to
breath this wofull lamentation from my oppressed soule: O vnhappie chaunce
(quoth I) O cruell fortune: why didst thou not make me passe this bitter and
sorrowful life in my childhood, or why did not the heauens permitte and suffer me
to be strangled in my mothers wombe, or to haue perished in my cradle, or at my
nursses pap? then had my heart neuer felt this sorrowe, my eares neuer heard the
murther of my children, nor mine eyes neuer to haue wept so many helplesse
teares.

O you mountaines, you vntamed beastes: O you deepe Seas, you lustfull
heauens, and you powers of reuengefull hell: come all I say and willinglie assist
mee in this mortall Tragidie, that these my aged handes which neuer yet practist
any hainous crime, may now be stainde in his accursed bloud, that hath bereau'd
me of the prop and stay of declined age, my daughters (I mean) whose bleeding
goastes will neuer bee appeased, nor neuer sleep in quiet vpon the ioyful bankes of
Elizian fields, but wander vp and downe the worlde, filling each corner of the earth
with fearefull clamors of murder and reuenge, nor neuer shall the furies of my
angry soule bee pacified, vntill my eyes beholde a streame of purple gore run
trickling from the detestable brest of that accursed rauisher, and that the bloud may
issue from his guiltie heart like a fountaine with a hundred springes, whereby the
pauements of his Castle may be sprinckled with the same, and the wals of his
Turrettes colored with a crimson hew, like to the streetes of *Troy*, when as her
chanels ran with bloud: at the end of this sorrowfull lamentation, what for griefe,
and what for want of natural rest, my eyes closed together and my sences fell into a
heauy sleepe.

But as I say: slumbring in the greene meadowes, I dreamed that there was a
great and fierce wilde man, which stood before me with a sharp faushion in his
hand, making as though he would kill me, wherat me thought I was so frighted,
that I gaue (in my troublesome dreams) many terrible shreekes, calling for succour
to the emptie ayre. Then me thought there appeared before my face a company of
curteous Knightes, which saide vnto mee, feare not old man, for we be come from
the soules of thy daughters to aide and succour thee, but yet for all this, the wilde
man vanished not away, but stroke with his faushion vppon my brest, whereat it
seemed to open, and howe that the wilde centaure put his hande into the wounde
and pulled out my heart, so straight at the same instant mee thought that one of the
Knightes lykewise layde hold vpon my hart, and stroue together with much
contention who should pull it from the others handes, but in the end each of them
remained with a peece in his hand, and my heart parted in two.

Then the peece which remained in the wilde mans power turned into a hard
stone, and the peece which remained in the power of the Knight, conuerted into
redde bloud, and so they vanished away.

Then straight after this there appeared before my eyes the Image of my
murthered daughter in the selfe same manner and forme as you behold her heere
portrayed who with a naked bodie all besmear'd in bloud, reported vnto mee the
true discourse of her vnhappie fortunes, and tolde me in what place, and where her

body lay in the woods dishonored for want of buriall: Also desiring me not of my selfe to attempt the reuengement, for it was impossible, but to intombe her corpes by her mother and cause the picture of her body to bee moste liuely portraied and wrought of fine christall in the same manner that I found it in the woods, and after errect it neere vnto a common passage, where aduenterous Knights do vsually trauaile. Also assuring mee that thether shoulde come certaine christian Champions that should reuenge my iniuries and inhumane murther.

Which words being finished, me thought she vanished away, with a greeuous and heauie grone, leauing behinde her certaine droppes of bloud sprinkled vpon the grasse: Whereat with great perplexitie and more sorrow I awaked out of my dreame, bearing it in my greeuous minde, not reuealing it, not so much as to the brittle ayre, but with all expedition performing her bleeding soules request.

Where euer since most curteous and noble Knights, I haue heere lamented her vntimely death and my vnhappie fortune, spending the time in writing her doleful Tragidy in bloud red lines, the which I knowe to your great griefe, you haue read in this book of gold.

Therfore most curteous Knights if euer honor incouraged you to fight in Noble aduentures, I now most earnestly intreate you with your magnanimious fortitudes to assist me to take reuengement, for the greate crueltie that hath beene vsed against my vnfortunate daughter. At the reading of this sorrowfull historie, Saint *George* with the other Champions did shed many teares, wherewith there did increase in them a further desire of reuengement, and being moued with great compassion, they protested by their promisses made to the honor of Knighthood, to perseuer speedily on their vowed reuenge and determined purpose: also calling heauen to be witnesse to their plighted oathes, protesting that sooner shoulde the liues of all the famous Romaines bee raised from death from the time of *Romulus* to *Cæser*, and all the rest vnto this time, then to be perswaded to returne from their promisses, and neuer to trauell backe into Christendome till they had performed their vowes, and thus burning with desire, to see the end of this sorrowfull aduenture: Saint *George* clapped vp the bloudy written booke, and gaue it againe to the Shepheard, and so they proceeded forwards towards the Iland where the Knight of the black Castle had his residence, guided onely by the direction of the old man, whose aged limbes seemed so lusty in traueling that it prognosticated a luckie euent: In which iorney wee will leaue the Champions for a time, with the wonderfull prouision that the Knight of the blacke Castle made in his defence, the successe whereof will be the strangest that euer was reported, and returne and speake of Saint *Georges* three Sonnes in the persute of their Father where we left them (as you heard before) traueling from the Confines of Barbarie where they redeemed the *Normaine* Lady from the Tawny Moores.

CHAP. VII.[1]

A wonderfull and strange aduenture that hapned to Saint George his Sonnes, in the persute of their Father, by finding certaine droppes of bloud, with Virgins hayre scattered in the fieldes, and how they were certified of the iniurious dealing of the Knight of the blacke Castle against the Queene of Armenia.

MAny and dangerous were the aduentures of the three valiant Princes in the persute of their father Saint *George*, and many were the Countries, Ilands, and Princes Courts, that they searched to obtaine a wished sight of his martiall countenance, but all to small purpose, for fortune neither cast them happilie vpon that coast, where he with his famous Champions had their residence, nor luckily sounded in their eares the places of their arriuals.

In which persute I omit and passe ouer many Noble aduentures that these three Princes atchiued, as well vpon the raging ocians as vpon the firme Land, and wholie discourse vppon an accident that hapned to them in an Iland bordering vpon the confines of *Armenia*, neere vnto the Iland where the Knight of the blacke Castle remained as you heard in the last Chapter, vpon which coast after they were arriued, they trauelled in a broad and straight path vntill such time as they came to a verie faire and delectable forrest, where as sundry chirping birdes had gathered themselues together, to refreshe and shrowd themselues from the parching heat of the golden Sunne: filling the ayre with the pleasures of their siluer tuned notes.

In this Forrest they trauelled almost two howers, and then they went vp to a small mountaine which was at hand, from the which they discouered very faire and wel towered townes with Princely pallaces very sumptuous to behold: likewise they discouered from the Hill a fayre fountaine wrought all of marble like vnto a Piller, out of which did proceede foure spoutes running with water, which fell into a great Cesterne, and comming to it they washed their handes and refreshed their faces, and so departed.

After they looked round about them on euery side, and toward their right handes they espied amongst a company of greene trees, a small Tent of blacke cloth, towards which these yong Princes directed their courses with an easie pace, but when they had entred the Tent, and sawe no bodie therin, they remained silent a while, harkning if they could heare any sturing, but they could neither see nor heare any thing, but onely they found the print of certain little feete vpon the same, which caused them more earnestly to desire to know whose foote steps they were, for that they seemed to be of some Ladies or Damsels: so finding the trace they followed them, and the more the knights followed, the more the Ladies seemed to hast: so long they persued after the trace, that at the end they approached a little mountain wheras they found scattered about, certaine lockes of yellow haire, which seemed to be thrids of golde, and stooping to gather them vp, they perceiued that some of them were wet with spots of blood, whereby they wel vnderstood, that in great anger they were pulled from some Ladies head: likwise they saw in diuers places how the earth was spotted with droppes of crimson blood: then with a more desire then they had before, they went vp to the top of that litle mountaine, and hauing lost the footesteps, they recouered it againe by gathering vp the hayre, where they had not traueled far vp the mountaine, but towards the waters side they heard a greeuous complaint, which seemed to be the voice of a woman in great distresse, and the woordes which the knights did vnderstand were these: O loue, now shalt thou no more reioyce nor haue any longer dominion ouer me, for death I see is ready to cut my thrid of life and finish these my sorowful lamentations how often haue I askt reuengement at the powers of heauen against that wicked wretch that hath bene the causer of my banishment, but yet they will not hear my request: how ofte haue I made my sad complaints to hell? yet hath the fatall furies stopt their eares against my woful cryes. And with this she held her peace, giuing a sorowful sighe: which being done, the three christian knights turned their eyes to the place from whence they heard this complaint, and discouered amongst certaine greene trees a Lady who was endued with singuler beautie, being so excellent that it almost depriued them of their harts & captiuated their sences in the snares of loue, which libertie as yet they neuer lost: she had her haire about her eares, which hung defusedly downe her comely sholders, through the violence she vsed against her selfe, and leaning her cheeke vpon her delicate white hand that was allto bespotted with blood, which was constraind by the scratching of her nailes vpon her Rosie colored face: by her stood another damsel which they coniectured to be her daughter for she was clad in virgin colored silk mor whiter then the Lillyes of the fields: and as pleasante to beholde as the glistring Moone in a cleare winters freezing night: yet for all this delectable sight, the three princely[2] knights wold not discouer themselues but stood closely behinde the three pine trees which grew neere vnto the mountaine to heare the euent of this accident, but as they stoode cloaked in silence, they heard her thus to confer with her beautiful daughter. Oh my *Rosana* (quoth she) the vnhappie figure of him, that without pitty hath wounded my heart and left me comfortles with the greatest cruelty that euer knight or gentleman left Lady: how hath it been possible that I haue had the force to bring vp the child of such a father which hath bereaud me of my libertie? O you soueraigne gods of heauen, grant y^t I may establish in my minde the remembrance of the loue of thy adulterous father: oh girle borne to a further griefe, heere doe I desire the guider of thy fortunes, that thy glistring beautie may haue such force and power, whereby the shining beames thereof may take reuengement of the dishonor of thy mother: giue eare deare childe I say vnto thy dying mother, thou that art born in the dishonor of thy generation, by the losse of my virginity, heere doe I charge thee vpon my blessing, euen at my houre of death, & swear thee by the omnipotent God of heauen, neuer to suffer thy beauty to be enioyd by any one, vntill thy disloyal fathers head bee offered vp in a sacrifice vnto my graue, thereby somewhat to appease the furie of my discontented soule, and recouer part of my former glorie.

---

[2] princely] princly *1597*

These and such like words spake this afflicted queene, to the wonderfull amazement of the three yong Knightes, which as yet intended not to discouer themselues, but to marke the euent, for they coniectured that her woful complaintes were the induction of some strange accedent: Thus as they stoode obscurely behinde the trees, they sawe the young and beautifull Damsell giue vnto her dying mother, paper, penne and Inke, the which shee pulled from her Iuorie bosome, wherewith the greeued queene subscribed certain sorrowful lines vnto him y^t was the causer of her banishment: and making an end of her writing, they heard her (with a dying breath) speake vnto her daughter these sorrowfull words following. Come daughter (quoth shee) beholde thy Mother at her latest gaspe, and imprint my dying request in thy heart as a table of brasse, that it neuer may be forgotten, time will not giue me longer respit, that with wordes I might shewe vnto thee my deepe affections, for that I feele my death approaching and the fatall sisters ready to cut my thrid of life a sunder betweene the edges of their shieres, insomuch that I moste miserable creature do feele my soule trembling in my flesh, and my heart quiuering at this my last and fatal houre, but one thing (my sweet and tender child) doe I desire of thee before I dye: which is, that thou wouldest procure that this letter may bee giuen to that cruell knight thy disloyall father, giuing him to vnderstand of this my troublesome death, the occasion whereof was his vnreasonable crueltie: and making an end of saying this, the miserable Queene fell downe, not hauing any more strength to sit vp, but let the letter fall out of her hand, the which her sorrowfull daughter presently tooke vp, and falling vpon her mothers brest, she replyed in this sorrowfull manner. O my sweete mother tell me not that you will dye, for it ads a torment more greeuous vnto my soule then the punishments which *Danaus* daughters feele in hell, I would rather be torne in peeces by the fury of some merciles monster, or to haue my heart parted in twaine by the handes of him that is my greatest enemie, then to remaine without your companie, sweete mother let these my youthfull yeeres, and this my greene budding beauty incourage you still to reuiue, and not to leaue me comfortles like an exile in the world, but if the gloomy fates doe triumph in your death, and abridge your breathing ayre of life, and that your soule must needes goe wander in the *Elizian* shades with *Crusas*[3] shaddowe and with *Didoes* ghost, here doe I protest by the greate and tender loue I beare you, and by the due obedience that I owe vnto your age, either to deliuer this your letter into the hands of my vnkinde father, or with these my ruthful fingers rent my heart in sunder, and before I will forget my vow, the siluer streamed *Tygris* shall forsake her course, the sea her tides, and the glistering Queene of night her vsuall changes: neither shal any forgetfulnes be an occasion to withdraw my minde from performing your dying requestes: Then this weak Queene whose power and strength was wholie decaied, and that her houre of death drew neere at hand, with a feeble voice she said. O you sacred & immortal Gods, and all you bright celestiall powers of heauen, into your deuine bosomes now do I commend my dying soule, asking no other reuengment against ye causer of my death, but that he may die like mee, for want of loue. After

---

[3] *Crusas*] *Trusas 1597*

this the dead Queene neuer spake word more, for at that instant, the cruell destinies gaue end vnto her life: but when *Rosana* perceiued her to be dead and she left to the world deuoide of comfort, shee began to teare the golden tramels from her head, and most furiouslye to beat her white and yuorie brest filling the emptie ayre with clamors of her mones, and making the skies like an eccho to resound her lamentations, and at last taking her mothers letter in her hands, washing it with flouds of teares, and putting it next vnto her naked brest, she said: heer lye thou neare adioining to my bleeding heart, neuer to be remoued vntil I haue performd my mothers dying testiment. O work and the last worke of those her white and yuorie hands: heere doe I sweare by the honor of true Uirgins, not to part it from my bleeding bosom vntil such time as loue hath rent the disloyall heart of my vnkinde father, and in speaking this shee kissed it a thousand times, breathing forth millions of sighes and straight with a blushing countenance as radient as *Auroras* glistring beames, she arose & said: what is this *Rosana*, dost thou thinke to recall thy mothers life with ceremonious complaints and not performe that which by her was commanded thee, arise, arise I say, gather vnto thy selfe strength and courage, and wander vp and downe the world till thou hast found thy disloyal Father as thy true heart hath promised to doe. These words being no sooner finished but Saint *Georges* Sonnes like men whose hearts were almost ouercome with griefe, came from the pine trees and discouered themselues to the Damsell, and curteously requested her to discourse the storie of all her passed mizeries, and as they were true christian knights they promised her (if it lay in their powers) to release her sorrows and to giue end vnto her mizeries. This *Rosana* when shee behelde these curteous and well demeanur'd knights which in her conceit caried relenting mindes and how kindly they desired to be partners in her griefes, she stood not vpon curious tearmes, nor vpon vaine exceptions, but most willingly condescended to their requests: so when they had prepared their eares to entertaine her sad and sorrowfull discourse, with a sober countenance, shee began in this manner: Lately I was (quoth she whilst fortune smild vpon me) the onely childe and daughter of this liueles Queene that you beholde heer lying dead, and she before my birth whilst heauen graunted her prosperitie was the maiden Queene of a Countrie called *Armenia*, adioyning neare vnto this vnhappie Iland: whome in her yong yeeres when her beautie began to florish, and her high renowne to mount vpon the wings of fame, she was intrapped with the golden baite of blind *Cupid*, & so intangled with the loue of a disloyall knight, cal'd the Knight of the black Castle, who after he had florisht in the spoyle of her Uirginitie, and had left his fruitful seede springing in her womb grew wearie of his loue, and most discurteously left her as a shame vnto her Countrie, and a staine vnto her kindred, and after gaue himself to such lustfull and lasciuious manner of life, that hee vnlawfullie maried a shepheards daughter in a forraine land, and likewise rauished her own sister, and after committed her most inhumane slaughter in a solitarie woode: this being done, he fortified himselfe in his blacke Castle, onely consorted with a cunning *Nigromancer*, whose skill in magick is so excellent, that al the knights in the world can neuer conquere the Castle, where euer since hee hath remained in despight of the whole earth.

But now speake I of the tragical storie of my vnhappy mother, when as I her vnfortunate babe beganne first to strugle in her womb, wherin I wold I had bene strangled: she heard newes of her knights ill demeanure, and how he had wholly giuen himself to the spoile of virginitie, and had for euer left her loue, neuer intending to returne again the grief wherof so troubled her mind, that she could not in any wise desemble it, for vpon a time being amongst her Ladies, calling to remembrance her spotted Uirginitie, and the seede of dishonor planted in her wombe, she fell into a wonderfull and strange traunce, as though she had been oppressed with sodain death, which when her Ladies and damsels beheld, they presently determined to vnbrace her rich ornaments, and to carrie her vnto her bed, but she made signes with her handes that they should depart and leaue her alone, whose commaundement they strait way obayed, not without great sorrow of them all, their loues were so deere. This afflicted Queen when she saw that she was alone, began to exclaime against her fortune, reuiiling[4] the fates with bitter exclamations, O vnconstant Queene of chance (said shee) thou that hast warped such strange webs in my kingdom, thou that gauest my honor to that tirants lust, which without al remorse hath left me comfortles, tis thou that didst constraine me to set my life to sale, & to sel my honor as it were with the crier, compelling me to do that which hath spotted my Princely estate, and stain'd my bright honor with blacke infamie: woe is me for my virginity, yᵉ which my parents gaue me charge to haue respect vnto: but I haue carelessely kept it, & smally regarded it: I will therefore so chastice my body, for thus forgetting of my selfe, and be so reuenged for the little regarde that I haue made of my honour, that it shall be an example to all noble Ladyes and Princes of high estate.

Oh miserable Queene, oh fond and vnhappy Lady: thy speeches be too too foolish, for although thy desperate hand should pull out thy dispised harte from thy bleeding brest, yet can it not make satisfaction for thy dishonour.

Oh Heauens, why do you not cast some fiery thunderbolt downe vpon my head? or why doth not the earth gape and swallowe my infamous bodye? Oh false and deceiuing Lord, I would thy louing and amourous words had neuer beene spoken: nor thy quicke sighted eyes, neuer gazde vpon my beautie: then had I florisht still with glory and renowne, and liu'd a happy Uirgin of chaste *Dianaes* traine.

With these and other like lamentations, this grieued Queene passed away the time, till at laste she felte her wombe to growe big with childe: at the which she receiued dubble paine, for that it was impossible to couer or hide it, and seeing her selfe in this case, like a woman hated and abhorred, she determined to discouer her selfe publikely vnto her subiectes, and deliuer her body vnto them to be sacrificed vnto their Gods: and with this determination, one day she caused certaine of her Nobles to be sent for, who straightway fulfilled her commaundement but when she perceiued her Lords, Knights and Gentlemen of honour came altogether before her, she couered her selfe with a rich robe and sate vpon her bed in her priuate chamber, being so pale and leane, that all them that sawe her had greate

---

[4] reuiling] reuealing *1597*

compassion vppon her sorrowe: beeing all set round about her bed and keeping silence, she reuealed to them the cause of her griefe in this manner.

My Lords (quoth she) I shame to intytle myselfe your Queene and Soueraigne, in that I haue defamed the honor of my Countrie, and little regarded the welfare of our Common wealth: my glistering crowne me thinkes is shadded with a cloude of black disgrace, and my Princely attire conuerted into vnchaste habiliments, in which I haue both lost the libertie of my heart, and withall my wonted ioy, and am now constrained to indure perpetual paine, and an euer pining death: For I haue lost my honour, and recouered shame and infamie.

To conclude, I haue forgone the liberty of a Queene, and solde my self to a slauish sinne, onely mine own is the fault, and mine owne shall be the punishment. Therfore without making any excuse, I heere surrender vp my body into your powers, for that you may (as an euill[5] queen) sacrifize me vnto our Gods: also that within my accursed wombe, for now my Lords you shall vnderstand, that I am dishonored by the knight of the black Castle: he hath planted a Uine within my fruitful garden, and sowen a seede that hath made *Armenia* infamouse: he it is that hath committed so many euils in the world: he it is that delights in virgins spoiles, and hee it is that hath bereau'd mee of my honor, but with my good will I must needes confesse, and left me for a testimonie of this my euill deed, big with child, by which my virgins glory is conuerted to a monstrous scandall: and with this she made an end of her lamentable speach: And being greeuously oppressed with the paine of her burthenous wombe, she sate her downe vpon her rich bedde, and attended their wils: but when these Earles, Lords and honorable personages that were present, had vnderstood all that the Queene had saide vnto them, like men greatly amazed, they changed their cullors from red to white, and from white to red, in signe of anger, and looking one vpon an other, without speaking any worde, but printing in their hearts the fault done by their Queen, to the great disgrace of their countrie, and so without any further consideration, they depriued her from all princely dignitie, both of her Crowne and regiment, and pronounced her perpetuall banishment from *Armenia*, like subiectes not to bee gouerned by such a defamed Prince, that hath grafted the fruit of[6] such a wicked tree within her wombe.

So at the time appointed like a woman forlorne and hated of all companies, shee stored her selfe sufficient with treasure, and betooke her selfe to her appointed banishment, after whose departure the *Armenians*, elected them selues an other Prince, and left their lawfull Queene wandring in vnknown Ilands, big with child deuoide of succour and reliefe, where insteed of her Princely bed couered with Canopies of silk, shee tooke her nightly reposes vpon the green grasse, shadoed with the sable curtaines of heauen, and the nurses that were prouided against her deliuerie were Nimphes and Faieries dauncing in the night by *Proserpines* commaundement: thus in greate griefe continued she many daies contenting her selfe with her appointed banishment, making her lamentations to the whispring winds, which seemed in her conceipt to reansweare her complaints: at length the glistering moone had ten times borrowed light of the golden *Phœbus*, and the

---

[5] (as an euill] as an (euill *1597*
[6] of] of of *1597*

nights cleare candle were now almost extinguished, by which time approached the houre of her laborsome trauell, wherein onely by the assistance of heauen shee was deliuered of me her vnhappy daughter, where euer since I haue beene nourished by the deuine powers of heauen, for many times when I came to yeeres[7] of discretion, my wofull mother would discourse vnto me this lamentable story of both our mizeries, the which I haue moste truely declared[8] vnto you.

Likwise shee told me that many times in my infancie, when she wanted milke in her brestes to nourish me, there would come a Lionesse, and sometimes a shee Beare and gently giue me sucke, and contrarie to the nature of wilde beastes, they would many times sporte with, where by she coniectured that the immortall powers had preserued me for some strange fortune: likewise at my birth, nature had pictur'd vpon my brest, directly betwixt my tender Paps, the liuely forme of a purple Rose, which as yet doth beautifie my bosome with a vermillion collour: and this was the cause that my mother named me *Rosana*, answerable to natures marke.

After this we liu'd many a yeere in great distresse, penurie and want,[9] soliciting heauen to redresse our woes, more oftner then we had liued houres: the aboundance of our teares might suffize to make a watry sea, and our sighes in number to countervaile the starres of heauen: but at last the fatal sisters listed to my mothers mones & to my great sorrow depriued her of her life, where now I am left a comfortles Orphant to the world, attending the time vntill that heauen send some curteous Knight that may conduct me to that blacke Castle where my disloyall father hath his residence, that I might there perform my mothers dying will: these wordes being finished, *Rosana* stood silent, for that her extreame griefe hindred the passage of her tongue, and her eyes rained such a shewer of pearled teares vpon the liueles body of her mother, that it constrained Saint *Georges* Sonnes to expresse the like sorrow: but after they had let fall a few salt teares down from their sad eyes, and had taken truce for a time with griefe, they tooke *Rosana* by the hand, (which before that time neuer touched the body of any man) and protested neuer to depart from her company til they had safely deliuered her into the blacke Castle.

After this when the Christian Knightes had pitifully bewailed the mizerie and vntimely death of her mother, they tooke their daggers and digged a deep graue vnder a Bay tree and buried her body, that hungry rauens might neuer seaze vpon it, or furious beasts teare it in peeces, nor rauenous Harpies deuour it: and after with the point of their daggers they in graued this Epitaph in the rinde of the Bay tree, which words were these that follow.

The Epitaph ouer the graue of the
vnfortunate Queene of Armenia.

Heere lies the body of a haples Queene,
Whose great goodwill to her, smal loue did bring:

---

[7] yeeres] yeeree *1597*
[8] declared] delared *1597*
[9] want,] want. *1597*

Her faithfull minde requited was with teene
Though she deserud for loue a regall King.
And as her corpes inclosed heere doth lye,
Her lucklesse fate, and fame shal neuer dye.

So when they had made this Epitaph and couered her graue with greene turues, they departed forward on their iorney towards the blacke Castle, where wee will leaue them in their trauels, and returne to the disloyal *Leoger*,[10] and howe hee fortified his Castle by magick arte, according to the learned skill of a cunning *Nigromancer*, and of the aduentures that hapned to Saint *George* with the other Christian Champions in the same Castle, therefore graunt you immortall powers of heauen, that my penne may be dipt in the waters of that learned fountain, where the nine sisters doe inhabite, that by the helpe of that sweet liquor my muse may haue a delightfull vaine, so that mixing the speach of *Mercury* with the prowesse of *Mars*, I may discourse of the strangest accident that euer hapned to wandring Knights.

---

[10] *Leoger*] *Leager 1597*

CHAP. VIII.

Of the preparation that the Knight of the blacke Castle made by magick arte, to withstand his enemies, and how the seuen Champions entred the same Castle, where they were inchaunted into a dead sleep, so long as seuen Lamps burned, which coulde not bee quenched but by the water of an inchaunted Fountaine.

THe wicked *Leoger* as you haue read of before, being the knight of the blacke Castle, and one that for wealth and treasure surpassed the mightiest potentate of those countries, when he grew detested and abhorred in euerie companie, as well by noble Knights, as gallant Ladies, for the spoile and murther of those three comely Damsels, whose pittifull stories you heard in the two passed Chapters, and fearing a sodaine vengeance to fall vpon his head, hee fortified himselfe strongly in his Castle, and with his treasure hyred many furious Giants to defend it: likewise if they fayled, & shold chance to be ouercome, he consorted with a wicked *Nigromancer* that with charmes and spels should worke wonders in his Castle, which magicall accomplishments we will passe ouer till a more conuenient time, because I purpose to explaine the historie in good order to the readers: first speake we of Saint *George* with the other christian knights that came in reuenge of the Shepheard and his vnfortunate daughter, who with good successe ariued vpon the shoare of the Iland, where this wicked *Leoger* and the *Magitian* had fortified their blacke Castle: In which countrie the Christian Champions, like the inuinsible followers of *Mars*, fearing no danger nor the frowns of vnconstant fortune, but betooke themselues the readiest way towards the Castle, in which iorney they were almost rauished with the pleasures of the Iland, for entring into a broad and straight lane, garnished on both sides with trees of diuers sortes, wherein they heard howe the Sommer birds recorded their pleasant melodies, and made their sweet and accustomed songes without feare of any man to molest them, in which rowe of pleasant trees that delighted them on both sides: there wanted not the green lawrel, so much exteemed of learned scholers: nor the sweet mertel tree, loued by Ladies: nor the high Cipresse so much regarded of Louers, nor the stately pine, which for his flourishing height is called the prince of trees: wherby they iudged it to be rather[1] a habitation for the Gods then any terestrial country, for that the golden Sun with his glistering beames did passe through those greene and pleasant trees without any hindrance of black cloudes: for the heauens were as cleare as tried siluer, likwise the westerne winds did softly shake the shiuering leaues, whereby it made as sweet a hermonie as the celestiall Cherubins of heauen: a thousand little streamed brookes ran vpon the inamelled grounde, making sundry fine workes by their crooked turnings, and ioyning one water with another, with a very gentle meeting, making such siluer musicke, that the Champions with the pleasure thereof were almost rauished, and smally regarded whether[2] their horses went right or no: and trauelling in this sorte, they rode forward till they came into a meruailous great

---

[1] rather] *om. 1597*
[2] whether] whither *1597*

and wide meddow, beeing of so greate fairenes, that I am not able with any pen to painte out the excellencie there of: where as were feeding both wilde and tame Hartes, adorned with great and cragged hornes: likwise the furious wild Bore, the fierce Lyon and the simple Lambes were altogether feeding with so great friendship, as to the contrary by nature they were enemies.[3]

Wherat the noble Champions were almost ouercome in their owne conceites, and amazed in their imaginations, to see so strange loue cleane contrarye vnto nature, and that there was no difference betwixt the loue of wilde beastes and tame: in this manner they trauelled, till vppon a sodaine they arriued before the buildinges of the blacke Castle: and casting their eyes towards the same, they beheld neere vnto the principall Gate, right ouer the Castle, twelue Marble Pinicles, of such an exceedinge height, that the Piramides of *Egipt*, were very lowe, in comparison of them: in such sorte, that whosoeuer would looke vpon them, was scant able with his sight to comprehend the height thereof: and they were all painted moste gorgiouslye with seuerall cullours.

Downe belowe vnder the Castle there was an Arche with a Gate, which seemed to be of Diamondes, and all was compassed about with a great moate or ditch, being of so great a depth, that they thought it to reach to the midst of the earth and it was almost two hundreth paces broad, and euery Gate had his Draw-bridge, all made of redde boordes, which seemed as though they had beene bathed all in blood.

Then the Champions rod to the other side of this goodly Castle, wondring at the curious and sumpteous workmanship, where they espyed a Piller of beautifull Iasper stone: all wrought full of precious stones of strange work, the which Piller was of great value, and was garnished with chaines of golde, that were made fast vnto it by Magicks arte, at which Piller likewise hung a very costlye siluer Trumpet, with certaine letters carued about the same, the which contayned these wordes following.

> *If any dare attempt this place to see,*
> *By sounding this, the Gate shall opened be.*
> *A Trumpet heere inchaind by magick arte*
> *To daunt with fear the proudest champions hart*
> *Looke thou for blows that entrest in this gate*
> *Returne in time, repentance comes too late.*

The which when Saint *George* beheld, and had vnderstoode the secrets of these misticall woordes, without anye more tarryinge, he sette the siluer Trumpet to his mouth, and sounded such a vehiment blaste, that it thundred in the elements, and seemed to shake the foundation of the Castle: whereat the principall Gate presently opened, and the drawe Bridge was let downe, without the helpe of any visible hand, which made the Champions to wonder, and to stand amazed at the strange accident, but yet intending not to returne like cowards daunted with a puffe of

---

[3] enemies.] enemies: *1597*

winde, they allighted from their warlike steedes, and deliuered them vnto the olde sheepheards hands, to be fed vpon the fragrant and greene grasse, till they had performed the aduenture of the Castle, the which they vowed either to accomplish or neuer to returne: so locking down their Beauers and drawing foorth their kiene edged fawchions, they entred the Gates, and beeing safely within, the champions looked round about them to see if they could espye any body, but they saw nothing but a paire of winding stayres, whereat they ascended, but they had not gone many steps therein, when as there was so great a darkenes, that scarce they could see any light, so that it rather seemed the similitude of hell, then any other worldly place, and so groping by the walles, they kept their going down those narrow and turning staires, which were very long, and of such length, that they thought they descended into the middle of the earth.

They spent a great time in descending those stayres, but in the end they came into a very faire and large Court all compassed with Iron grates like vnto a prison, or a place prouided to keep vntamed Lyons, wherein casting their eyes vp to the toppe of the Castle they behelde the wicked knight walking with the *Nigromancer* vpon a large gallerie, supported by huge pillers of brasse: likewise there was attending vpon them seuen Giants, armed in mighty Iron coates, holding in their hands bats of steele: to whom the bolde and venterous Champion of England spake with a haughty courage and lowde voyce in this manner.

Come downe thou wicked knight, thou spoyle of virginity, thou that art inuironed with those monstrous Giants, those the wondring worke of nature, whose daring lookes seemeth to scale the heauens, like vnto the pride of *Nemrod* when hee offered to builde vp *Babels* confused Tower.

Come downe I say, from thy Brazen gallery, and take to thee thy armor, thou that hast a heart to commit a Uirgins rape, for whose reuenge we come: now likewise haue a courage to make thy defence, for we vow neuer to returne out of thy Castle til we haue confounded thee and all thy forces.

At which words he held his peace, and expected an answere. But the wicked knight when hee heard these heroyicall speeches of Saint *George*, began to fret & fume like to the starued Lyon famished with hunger, or the ireful Tiger musling in humane bloud, with a great desire to satisfie his thirst: or like the wrath of dogged *Cerberus* when as he feasted with *Alcides* flesh, euen so raged *Leoger* the Knight of the blacke Castle, threatning forth furie from his sparkling eyes: and in this vile manner he reanswered the noble Champion of England: proud knight (said he) or peasant, whatsoeuer thou arte, I passe not the smallest haire of my head, for thus vpbrayding me with thy vnruly tunge, I will returne thee speechlesse into hell, for the pauements of my Castle shal all be sprinkled with thy accurssed blood, and the bones of those thy vnhappy followers shall be buried in the sinkes[4] of my channelles: if thou hadst brought the armie of inuincible *Cæsar*, that made all landes to tremble where he came; yet were they but a blast of winde vnto my forces: Seest thou not my Giants which stand like oaks vppon this brazen gallery? they at my commaundment shall take you from the places where you stand, and

---

[4] sinkes] stakes *1597*

throwe you ouer the walles of my Castle, in such sorte, that they shall make you flye into the ayre, more then tenne fathams high: and for that thou hast vpbrayded me with the disgrace doon vnto a virgin: I tell thee, if I had thy mother heere, of whome thou tookst first the ayre of life, my hand should split her womb, that thou mightst see the bed of thy creation as *Nero* did in *Rome*: or if thy wife and children were heere present before thy face, I would abridge their liues, that thy accurssed eyes might be witnesses of their bloodie murthers: so much wrath and hate now rageth in my heart, that al the blood in *Asia* cannot wash it thence.

At which words, the Giants which he had hyred to defend him from his foes, came vnto him very strongly armed with sturdie weapons in their handes, and requested him to be quiet, and to abate his vnsufferable anger, and they woulde fetche vnto his presence, all those brauing knightes that were the occasion of his disquietnesse and anger: and so without tarying for any answer, they departed downe into the Courte, and left the knight of the Castle with the Magitian, standing still vppon the gallery to beholde the following encounters:

But when the Giants approched the Champions presence, and sawe them so well proportioned and furnished, and knightes of so mighty statures, they florished about their knotty clubbes, and purposed not to spend the time in wordes but in blowes.

Then one of the fiercest and cruellest Giants of them all (which was called *Brandamond*) seeing Saint *George* to be the forwardest in the enterprize, and iudging him to be the Knight that had so braued his Lord, he began with a sterne countenance to speake vnto him in this manner: Art thou that bolde Knight (said the Giant) that with thy witlesse woordes haste so angred the mighty *Leoger* the Lord of this Castle? if thou bee, I aduise thee by submission, to seeke to appease his furious wrath before reuengement be taken vppon thy person.

Also I doe require thee (that if thou wilt remaine with thy life) that thou doost leaue thy armour, and yeilde thy selfe, with all these thy followers, with their handes fast bound behinde them, and goe and aske forgiuenes at his feete: to which Saint *George* with a smiling countenance answered, Giant (said he) thy councell I doe not like, nor his honor will I receiue, but rather we hope to send thee and all thy followers without tongues to the infernall King of fiery *Phlegethon*:[5] and for that you shall not haue any more time to speake such folly and foolishnes, eyther returne your waies from whence you came, and repent you of this which you haue said, or els prepare your selues to mortall battell.

The Giants when they heard the Champions resolutions, and how slightly they regarded theyr proffers, without any longer tariance they fell vppon Saynt *George* and his company intending with their knotty bats of steele to beate them as small as flesh vnto the pot, but the Queene of chaunce so smyled vppon the christian Champions, that the Giants smally preuailed, for betwixt them was fought a long and terrible battell, in such danger that the victory hung wauering on both sides not knowing to whome she should fall, the bats and faushions made such a noyse vpon one anothers armors, that they sounded like to the blowes of the Ciclops working

---

[5] *Phlegethon*] *Plegethon 1597*

vpon their fiery Anuils: and at euery blowe they gaue, fire flew from their steeled Corselets, like sparkles from the flaming furnaces in hell, the skies resounded backe the ecchoes of their stroakes, and the grounde shooke as though it had beene oppressed with an earth-quake: the pauements of the Court was ouerspred with an intermixed colour of bloud and sweat, and the wals of the Castle was mightily battered with the Giants clubs: but by the time that glistering *Apollo* the daies bright Candle began to declare from the top of heauen, when the Giants (wearied in fight) began for to faint: whereat the Christian Knights with more courage, beganne to increase[6] in strength and with such rigor assayled the Giants that before the golden Sunne had diued to the westerne world, all the Giants were quite discomfited and slaine,[7] some lay with their heads dismembred from their bodies weltering in purple gore, some had their braines sprinkled against the walles, some lay in the channels with their intrals trayling downe in streames of bloud, and some ioynteles with their bodies cut in peeces, so that there was not one left aliue to withstand the Christian Champions.

Whereat Saint *George* with the other sixe Knightes fell vpon their knees and thanked the immortall Rector both of heauen and earth for their victorie.

But when the knight of the blacke Castle which stood vpon the gallerie during all the time of the incounter and saw how all his Giants were slaine by the prowesse of those strang Knights, he raged against heauen and earth, wishing that the ground might gape and swallowe him, before he were deliuered into the handes of his enemies, and presently would haue caste himselfe head-long from the top of the gallery, to haue dasht his braines against the stony pauements, but that the *Nigromancer* which stoode likewise by him beholding the euent of the incounter, intercepted him in his intended drift, and promised that hee would performe by arte, what the Giants could not do by force.

So the *Nigromancer* fel to his magick spels & charms, by which the Christian Champions were mightily troubled and molested[8] and brought in danger of their liues, by a terrible and strange manner as shall bee heereafter showne.

For as they stoode after their long incounters vnbuckling their armors to take the fresh ayre and to wash theyr bloudy wounds receiued in their last conflicte: the *Magitian* caused by his arte an[9] angry spirit in the likenes of a Lady of a marualous and faire beauty, looking through an yron grate, who seemed to leane her faire face vpon her white hand very penciuely, and distilled from her christal eyes great aboundance of teares, which when the Champions saw this beautiful creature, they remained in great admiration, thinking with themselues, that by some hard misfortune she was imprisoned in those yron grates, with that this Lady did seeme to open her faire and christeline eyes, looking earnestly vpon Saint *George*, and giuing a greeuous and sorrowful sigh, she with drew her selfe from the grate, which sodaine departure caused the Christian Knights to haue a great desire to

---

[6] increase] increarse *1597*
[7] slaine] staine *1597*
[8] molested] molestled *1597*
[9] an] and *1597*

know who it should be, suspecting that by the force of some inchantment they should be ouerthrowne: and casting vp their eyes againe to see if they could see her, they could not, but they saw in the very same place a woman of a great and princely stature, who was all armed in siluer plates, with a swoord girded at her waste, sheathed in a golden scabberd, and had hanging at her necke an Iuory bowe and a gilt quiuer, this Lady was of so great beautie, that she seemed almost to excell the other, but in the same sorte as the other did, vpon a sodaine she vanished away, leauing the Champions no lesse troubled in their thoughtes then before they were.

The christian Knightes had not long time bewayled the absence of the Lady, but that without seeing any body they were stricken with such furious blowes vpon their backes, that they were constrayned to stoop with one knee vpon the ground, yet with a trice they arose againe, and looking about them to see who they were that strook them, they perswaded them to be the likenesse of certain knights which in great haste seemed to runne into a doore that was at one of the corners of the Courte, and with the great anger that the Champions receiued, seeing them selues so hardly intreated, they followed with their accustomed lightnesse after the knightes, in at the same doore: wherein they had not entred three steps, but that they fell downe into a deepe caue, which was couered ouer in such subtill sorte, that whosoeuer did tread on it, straight way fell into the caue, except he was aduertised thereof before: with in the caue it was as darke as the silent night, and no light at all apeared: but when the Champions saw themselues so trecherously betrayed in the trap, they greatly feared some further mischiefe would follow, to their vtter ouerthrowes, so with their swords drawne, they stood readye charged to make their defence, againste what soeuer should after happen, but by reason of the great darkenesse they could not see any thing, neither discouer wherein they were fallen, they determined to settle themselues against something, either poste, piller or wall: and groaping about the caue, they searched in euery place for some other doore that might bring them foorth out of that darkesome denne, which they compared to the pit of hell.

And as they went groping and feeling vp and downe, they found that they troad vpon no other thinges but dead mens bones, which caused them to stand still: and not long after, they espyed a secret windowe, at the which entred much cleerenesse, and gaue a great light into the den where they were, by which they espyed a bed moste richly furnished with curtaines of silke, and golden pendants which stoode in a secret roome of the caue, behung with rich tapestrie of a sable colour: which bed when the Champions beheld, and being somewhat weary of their long fight which they had with the Giants in the Court of the Castle, they required some rest and desired some sleepe vpon the bed, but not all at one instant: for they feared some daunger to bee at hand, and therefore Saint *George* as one most willing to be their watchman, and to keep senternell in so daungerous a place, caused the other Champions to take their reposes vppon the bed, and he would be as wakefull as the cocke against all daungerous accidents: so the sixe Christian Knights repaired to the bed, whereon they were no sooner layde, but presently they fell into a heauy and dead sleep, in such sort that they could not be awaked by any manner of violence, not all the warlike drums in *Europe* if they were sounded in their eares, nor the ratling thunder claps of heauen were sufficient to recall them from their sleeps, for indeed the bedde was inchaunted by the *Nigromancers* charmes, in such manner that whosoeuer but sate vpon the sides, or but the furniture of the bed, were presently cast into as heauy a sleepe as if they had drunke the ioyce of dwaile or the seede of Poppie, where we will leaue them for a tyme like men cast into a traunce and speake of the terrible aduenture that hapned to S. *George* in the caue, who little mistrusting of their inchantments, stoode like a carefull guard keeping the furious wolfe from the spoile of the silly sheep: but vpon a sodaine his hart began to throb, & his hayre to stand vpright vpon his head, yet hauing a heart fraught with inuinsible corage, he purposed not to awake ye other knights, but of himselfe to withstand whatsoeuer hapned, so being in his princely cogitation there appeered to him as hee thought the shape of a *Magitian* with a visage leane, pale and full of wrinckles, with lockes of blacke hayre hanging downe to his shoulders like to wreathes of inuenomed Snakes, and his body seemed to haue nothing vpon it but skin and bones, who spake vnto Saint *George* in this dispitfull manner: in an euill houre (said the *Magitian*) camst thou hether, and so shall thy lodging be, and thy entertainment worse, for now thou art in a place whereas thou shalt looke for no other thing, but to be meat vnto some furious beast, and thy surmounted strength shall not be able to make any defence.

The English Champion whose heart was oppressed with extreame wrath: answered, O false and accursed charmer (said he) whome Gods confound for thy condemned artes, and for whom the fiends hath dig'd an euerlasting tomb in hell, what furie hath incenst thee, that with thy false and deuelish charmes thou dost practise so much euill against trauelling and aduenterous Knightes, I hope to obtaine my libertie in dispight of al thy mischiefe and with my stronge arme to breake all thy bones in sunder.

All that thou dost and wilt do wil I suffer at thy hands replyed the *Nigromancer*, onely for the reuengement that I will take of thee for the slaughter of the seauen Giants, which as yet lyes murthered in the court, and that very quickly. And[10] therewithall hee went inuisibly out of the Caue: so not long after at his backe hee heard a sodaine noise, and beheld as it were a window opening by little and little, where as there appeared a cleare light, by the which Saint *George* plainely perceaued that the wals of the Caue were washt with bloud, and likewise sawe that the bones whereon they treade at their first entry into the den were of humane bodies, which appeared not to be very long since their flesh was torne off with hard and cruell teeth, but this consideration could not long endure with him, for that he heard a great rumor and looking what it should be, he saw that there was comming forth out of an other den, a mightie serpent with wings, as great in body as an Elephant, he had onely two feet which appeared out of that monstrous body but of a span length, and each foote had three clawes of three spannes in length, she came with her mouth open of so monstrous and huge a bignes,[11] and so deformed, that a whole armed Knight horse and all, might enter in thereat, she had vpon her Iawes twoo tuskes which seemed to be as sharpe as any needles, and al her body was

---

[10] And] and *1597*
[11] bignes] bigne *1597*

couered with hard scales of diuers colours, and with great fury she came with her wings all abroad, Saint *George* although he had a valiant and an vndaunted minde, yet could he not chuse but receiue some feare in seeing so monstrous a beast.

But considering with him selfe, that it was then time, and great need to haue courage, and to be expert and valliant for to make his defence, hee tooke his good cutting sword in his hand, and shrowded himselfe vnder his hard and stronge sheelde, and tarried the comming of that vgly monster.

But when the furious beast saw that there was a pray whereon she might imploy her sharpe teeth, shee stroake with her inuenomous wings, and with her pearcing clawes she griped, and layd fast hold vpon Saint *Georges* hard shield, pretending to haue swallowed whole this coragious warrier, and fastning her sharp tuskes vpon his helmet, which when she found so hard, she let goe her hold and furiously pulled at his target, with such a strenght that shee pulled it from his arme: with that the English knight stroake at her head a most mighty and strong blow with his swoord, but in no wise it could hurt her, by reason of the hard scales wherewith it was couered, and though he gaue her no wound, yet for all that shee felt the blow in such sort that it made her to recoile to the ground, and to fall vpon her long and hideous tayle, then this oppressed Knight made great hast to redouble his force to strike her another blow: but all was in vaine, for that vpon a sodaine she stretched her selfe so high, that he could not reach her head: but yet kinde Fortune so fauoured his hand, that he stroke her vpon the belly, whereas shee had no defence with scales, nor anie other thing but feathers: whereout issued such abundance of blacke blood, that it besprinkled all the denne about.

This terrible and furious Serpent, when she felt her selfe so sore wounded, stroke at Saint *George* such a terrible blow[12] with her taile, that if he had not seene it comming it had been sufficient to haue parted his bodie in peeces. The Knight to cleare himselfe from the blow, fell flat vpon the ground, for he had no time to make any other defence. But that terrible blow was no sooner passed ouer him, but straight waies he recouered his feete, at such time as the furious Serpent came towards him. Here Saint *George* hauing a great confidence in his strength, performed such a valiant exployt, that all former Aduentures that hath been euer done by anie Knight, may bee put in obliuion, and this kept in perpetuall memorie: for that he threw his sword out of his hand, and ran vnto the Serpent, and imbraced her betwixt his mightie armes, & did so squeeze her, that the furious Beast could not helpe her selfe with her sharpe clawes, but onely with her wings she beat him on euerie side. This valiant Champion and noble Warrier would neuer let her loose, but still remained holding her betwixt his armes, continuing this perillous and dangerous fight, till all his bright armour was imbrued with her bestiall blood, by which occasion shee lost a great part of her strength, and was not able long to continue.

Long indured this great and dangerous incounter, and the infernall Serpent remained fast vnto the noble and valiant breast of the English Knight, till such time as he plainly perceaued that the Monster began to wexe faint, and to loose her

---

[12] blow] a blow *1597*

strength. Likewise it could not be otherwise, but Saint *George* wexed somewhat wearie, considering the former fight he had so lately with the Giants. Notwithstanding when he saw the great weaknes of the Serpent, he did animate himselfe with courage, and hauing opportunitie by reason of the quantitie of blood that issued from her wounds, he tooke his trustie sword & thrust it into her heart with such violence, that he cloue it in two peeces: so this infernall Monster fell downe dead to the ground and carried the Christian Champion with her, for[13] that they were fast closed together, and by reason that the Serpent lacked strength, hee quickly cleered himselfe out of her clawes, and recouered his sword. But when he saw certainly that hee was cleere from the Monster, & that she had yeelded vp her detested life into yᵉ brittle aire, he kneeled downe and gaue thankes to the immortal maiestie of God for his safe deliuerie. The venome was so great that the Serpent threw out to infect the knight, that if his armour had not been of a precious vertue, hee had been impoysoned to death.

After the victorie was obtained and the Monster dead, he grew verie wearie and vnquiet, and was constrayned to sit and coole himselfe by a Well which was full of water, standing by in a corner of the Caue, from whence the monstrous Serpent first appeared and came foorth. And when he found himselfe refreshed, he repayred to the Inchaunted bed whereupon the other sixe Champions laye sleeping, dreaming of no such straunge accident that had happened to him: to whom he purposed to reueale the true discourse of all the dangers that had befalne him in that accident.

But no sooner approached he vnto that inchaunted bed and had set himselfe downe vpon the one side thereof, and thinking to begin his discourse, but he presently fell into a heauie and dead slumber.

There will we leaue them sleeping and dreaming vpon the inchaunted bed, not to be wakened by anie means, and returne to the *Nigromancer* that was busied all the time of the Serpents incounters, with *Leoger* in burying of the dead Giants: But now he knew by his arte, that the Serpent was slaine, and likewise Saint *George* oppressed with a charmed sleepe, in companie of the other Champions vpon the inchaunted bed, from whence hee purposed that they neuer more should awake, but spende their followed fortunes in eternall sleeps.

Then by his deuilish artes he caused seuen Lampes to burne continually before the entry of the Caue, the properties whereof were so strange, that so long as the Lampes continued burning, the Champions should neuer be awaked and the fiers should neuer be quenched but by the water of an inchaunted fountaine, the which he likewise by magick arte had erected in the middle of the court guarded most strongly with fearefull shapes, and the water should neuer be obtained but by a Uirgin which at her birth should haue the forme of a Rose most liuely pictured vpon her brest.

These thinges being performed by the secrets of the *Magitians* skill added suth a pleasure to *Leogers* heart, that he thought himselfe eleuated higher then towers of

---

[13] for] for for *1597*

heauen, for he accompted no ioy so pleasing vnto his soule as to see his mortall enemies captiuated in his power, and that the *Magitian* had done more by his artes, then al the Knights in *Asia* could performe by prowesse: we will not now onely leaue the Champions in their sleeps dreaming of no mishap, but also the *Magitian* with *Leoger* in the blacke Castle, spending their time securely, careles of all insuing daunger, and speake now of the olde Shepheard whome the Champions at their first entring in at the gates of the Castle, where they left him to looke vnto their warlike palfries as they fed vpon the greene grasse: but when this olde man coulde heare[14] no newes of the Champions returne, he greatly mistrusted their confusion, and that by some trecherie they were intercepted in their vowed reuengement, therefore he protested secretly with his owne soule, in that for his sake so many braue Champions had lost their liues, neuer to depart out of those fieldes, but to spend his daies in more sorrow then did the haplesse King of *Babilon*, that for seauen parching Summers, and as many freezing Winters was constrained to feede vpon the flowers of the fieldes, and to drinke the dewe of heauen, till the haires of his heade grewe so stiffe as Egles feathers, and the nailes of his fingers like vnto birds clawes, the like extremitie he vowed to indure, vntill he either reobtained a wished sight of those inuincible knights (the flowers of chiualry) or else were constrained by course of nature to yeeld vp his loathed life, to the furie of those fatall sisters: In this deepe distresse will my wearie muse likewise leaue this old shepheard mourning for the long absence of the English Champion and the other Christian Knights, and returne vnto Saint *Georges* valiant Sonnes, whome we left trauelling from the Queene of *Armenias* graue, with her vnhappy[15] daughter *Rosana*: to take reuengement for her disloyal Lord, being the Knight of this blacke Castle, of whose vilanies you haue heard so much of before.

---

[14] heare] hears *1597*
[15] vnhappy] vnvappy *1597*

CHAP. IX.

How Saint Georges three sonnes after their departure from the Queene of Armenias sepulcher, in companie of her Daughter, Rosana, met with a Wilde-man, with whom there hapned a strange Aduenture: and after how they entered the Blacke Castle, whereas they quencht the Lamps, and awakened the seauen Champions of Christendome, after they had slept seauen dayes vppon an inchaunted bedde, with other things that chanced in the same Castle.

THe budding Flowers of Chiualrie the valiant Sonnes of S. *George* to performe their Knightly promises, & to accomplish what they had protested to *Rosana* at the Queene her Mothers graue, which was to deliuer her safely into the Blacke Castle, where her vnkinde father had his residence. First they bought her a Palfray of a silke colour of Spaine traynd in that Countrey, with certaine chaines and iewells that she wore about her necke and wrestes, which steede was furnished with blacke Capparisons, in signe of her heauy and discontented minde, & his forehead beautified with a spangled plume of feathers.

Thus trauailed they day and night from the Confines of *Armenia*, with succesfull fortune, till they happily arriued vpon the Iland of the Blacke Castle: where they were constrained to rest themselues manie nights vnder the shaddowes of greene leaued trees, where the melodie of siluer tuned birds brought them to their sweete sleepes: and in steede of delicate fare, they were forced to satisfye their hungers with sweete Orenges and ripe Pomegranades, that grew verie plentifully in that Iland. But vppon a morning, when the skies appeared in theyr sightes verie cleere and pleasant, and at such time as when the Sunne began to spread his glistering beames vppon the loftie mountaines and stately Cedars, they set forward on their iourney, hoping before the cloasing in of the Dayes bright countenance, to arriue at the Blacke Castle, beeing their long wisht for hauen, and desired Port. But entering into an vnknown way and narrow path not much vsed, they were intercepted by a strange and wonderfull Aduenture. For as they trauelled in those vntroden passages, spending the time in pleasant conference, without mistrusting of anie thing that should happen to them in that pleasant Iland: vpon a sodaine (not knowing the occasion) their horses started and rose vp with their forefeet, and turned backward into the aire in such sort, that they had almost vnsadled their Masters: whereat the valiant Knights vppon a sodaine looked round about them, to see who or what it was that caused so much feare: but when they perceiued nothing, nor could coniecture what should be the occasion of such terror, they grewe wonderfullye troubled in minde. Then one began to encourage ye rest, saying: Beleeue me Brethren, I muse what should bee the cause of this alteration in our horses? hath some spirit glided by vs, or lodgeth some deuill among these bushes? Whatsoeuer it be, let vs by the power and fauour of God attempt to know, and with our warlike weapons reuenge the frighting of our horses, for our mindes are vndaunted by the powers[1] of men, nor feared with the furye of deuils.

---

[1] powers] porwes *1597*

These woordes being spoken with greate courage and maiestie, caused *Rosana* to smile with a cheerefull countenance, and to imbolden her heart against all insuing accidents: so presently they came vnto a riuer which was both cleere and deepe, the which they iudged to runne quite thorowe the middle of the Iland: and so trauelling along by the riuers side, where within a little while their horses began againe to stagger and to be wonderfully affraide, and casting about their vigilant eyes, to see if they coulde perceiue what it should be that made their horsses so timerous they espyed a terrible Monster in the shape and form of a Satyre or a wilde man, which did crosse ouerthwarte the Iland, of a wonderfull great and strange making, who was as bigge and broade as any Giant, for he was almost foure squaire: his face was three foote in length and had but one eye, & that was in his forehead, which glistred like vnto a blazing Comet or a fierye Planet: his bodye was couered all ouer with long and shagged haire, like to the impoysoned stinges of Serpents: and in his breaste, there was as though it had beene a glasse, out of the which there seemed a great and shining light to proceed.

This Monster directed his way towards certaine Rockes of stone which stood in the Iland, and by reason of the stragling and greate noyse that the horsses made, he cast his head aside and espyed the three Knightes trauelling in companie of the Lady: vpon whome he had no sooner cast his blazing eye, but with a deuilish furye he ran towards them, and in steed of a Club, he bare in his hand a mighty great and knotted Maple tree.

These valiant Knightes neuer dismaide at the sight of this deformed creature, but against his comming, they cheered vp their horsses, and pricked their sides with their golden spurres, giuing a great shoute as a signe of incouragement, and withall, drawinge foorth their sharpe cutting swords they stood attending the furie of the Monster, who came roaring like a Bull, and discharged his knotted tree amongst the magnanimous Knightes, who with light leapes cleered themselues from his violent blowes, that his club fell downe to the ground with such a terrible fall, as thogh with the violence it wold haue ouerthrowne a Castle.

With that the Knights presently alighted from theyr horses, thinking thereby more nimbler to defende themselues, and with more courage to assaile the Satyre. Manie were the blowes on both sides, and dangerous the incounter, without signe of victorie inclining vnto eyther partie.

During the Battell, *Rosana* (through the griefe and feare that she receiued) swounded vpon her palfray, & had fallen beside his back, if she had not first closed her hands about the pummell of the saddle: and being come a little vnto her selfe, she made her humble supplication vnto the Gods, soliciting heauen, that she might rather be buryed in the Monsters bowells, thereby to satisfie hys wrathe, than to see such noble Knights loose the least drop of blood, or to haue the smallest haire vpon their heads diminished: such was the loue and true zeale she bore vnto these three Knights.

But Sa. *Georges* Sonnes so manfully behaued themselues in the Encounter, bearing the prowesse of their fathers minde, that they made manie deepe wounds in the Monsters flesh, and such terrible gashes in his body, that all the greene grasse was couered with his blacke blood, and the ground all to besmeared & strewed with hys mangled flesh.

When the diuelish Monster felt himselfe wounded, and saw how his blood stood vpon the earth like coniealed gore, hee fled from them more swifter than a whirlewinde, or like vnto an arrow forced from a musket, and ran in great hast to the Rockes that stood thereby, where presently he threw himselfe into a Caue, pulling downe after him a Rocke of stone, which did close vp the entry, the which was done with so great lightnesse, that the Knights had no time to strike him, but after a while when they had blessed themselues to see such a strainge and sodaine thing they assayed by strength to remoue the Rocke, and to cleare the mouth of the Caue, the which they did without any difficultnes.

Yet for all that they coulde not finde which way they might enter in thereat, but like vnto Lyons fraughted with anger, fretting and chafing, they went searching round about the Rock to see if they could espie any entry, and at last they found a great cliffe on the one side of the Rocke, and looking in thereat, they espyed the monster, lying vpon the floare licking of his bleeding wounds with his purple tongue.

And seeing him, one of the Knights said: O thou traitor and distroyer by the high waies, O thou infernall deuill and enemy vnto the world, thou that art the deuourer of humane fleshe, and drinker of mans bloud, thinke not that this thy stronge and fast closing vp of thy selfe in this Rocke of stone shall auayle thee, or that thy deuelish body shall escape vnslaughtered out of our handes, no, no our bloudy weapons shal be sheathed in thy detested bowels, and riue thy damned heart asunder, and therewithall they thrust their weapons through the clift of the Rocke, and pearced his throat in such sorte that the monster presently dyed, the which being done they returned in tryumph like conquerers to *Rosana*, where they founde her halfe dead lying vpon her palfrie.

But when shee sawe them returne in safetie like one new risen from death, with a ioyfull and lowde voice shee said, O God how hath it pleased thy deuine maiestie, to furnish these Knights with more strength and prowesse, then any other in all the world, else coulde they not haue choosd but haue beene ouercome by this remorceles monster, which seemed to be of force to destroy kingdomes: therewithall she alighted in good state from her Palfray, and sate her downe vnder the shadow of a Pine-tree, where the three knights likewise sate downe, & laid theyr wearie heads vpon her soft lap to sleepe, vpon whose faces she fanned a coole breathing ayre, and wiped their sweaty browes with her handkercher, vsing all the meanes shee could to moue them contentment.

Long had they not reposed themselues vpon *Rosanaes* lappe, refreshing their wearie bodies with a golden sleepe, but they awaked and mounted vpon their steedes, and the next morning by breake of day, they approached the sight of the blacke Castle, before whose walles they found seauen portly steedes, feeding within a greene pasture, and by them an ancient father, bearing in his face the true picture of sorrowe, and caruing in the barke of trees the subiect of all his passed griefes: this man was the olde sheapheard which the seauen Champions of christendome (before their inchaunted sleepes in the Castle) lefte without the Gates to ouersee their horsses, as you heard before in the last Chapter.

But Saint Georges sonnes (after they had a while beheld the manner of the sheapheards silent lamentations) demaunded the causes of his griefe and wherefore he remayned so neere the danger of the Castle? to whose demaundes, the curteous olde man answered in this manner.

Braue Knightes (saide hee) for you seeme to be no lesse by your Princely demeanures, within this Castle remaineth a bloody tirant and a wicked homicide, called *Leoger*, whose tyrannie and lust hath not onely rauished but murthered two of my daughters, with whome I was honored in my yong yeares, in whose reuenge there came with me seauen christian knights of seauen seueral countries, that entred this accursed Castle about seauen daies since, appointing me to stay without the gates, & to haue a vigilent care of their horses, till I heard either newes of the Tyrants confusion, or their ouerthrowes: but neuer since by anie meanes could I learne whether good or bad were betided them.

These words strooke such a terror to their hearts, that for a time they stood speechlesse, imagining that those seauen Knightss were the seauen Champions of Christendome, in whose pursutes they had traueled so many countreyes. But at last when Saint *Georges* Sonnes had recouered their former speeches, one of them (though not intending to reueale what they imagined) sayd vnto ye olde Shepheard: that likewise they came to bee reuenged vpon that accursed Knight, for the spoyle of a beauteous and worthie Uirgine Queene, done by the said lust inflamed Tyrant.

Then the Ladie and the three Knightes alighted from their horses, and likewise committed them to the keeping of the olde Shepheard: who courteously receiued them, & earnestly prayed for their prosperous proceedings. So the three Knightes buckled close their armours, laced on their helmets, and put their shields vpon their armes, and in companie of Rosana they went to the Castle gate, the which glistered against the Sunne like burnisht golde: whereat hung a mightie Copper Ring, wherewith they beate so vehemently against the Gate, that it seemed to rattle like a violent tempestuous storme of thunder in the Element.

Then presently there appeared (looking out at a marble pillored window) the Magitian, newly risen from his bed, in a wrought shirt of blacke silke, and couered wyth a night gown of damaske veluet: and seeing the Knights with the Ladie standing before the gate, he thus discurteously greeted them.

You Knights of strange Countreys said he, for so doth it appeare by your strange demeanours: if you desire to haue the gates opened, and your bones buried in the valts of our Castle, turne backe vnto the Iasper piller behinde you, and sound the siluer Trumpet that hangs vpon it, so shall your entrie be easie, but your comming foorth miraculous. And thereupon the Magitian left the window.

Then one of the Knights went vnto the Iasper piller, and with a vehement breath sounded the inchanted trumpet as S. *George* did before, whereat the gates flew open in like manner: wherein (without anie disturbance) they entred: & comming into the same Court where ye champions had fought with the Giants, they spied the inchanted Lampes, which hung burning before the entrie of ye caue where the Champions lay vpon the inchanted bed. Under the Lampes hung a siluer tablet in an yron chaine, in it was written these words following.

> *These fatal lamps with their inchanted lights,*
> *In deaths sad sleep hath shut 7. christen knights*

Within this caue they ly with sloth confounded
Whose fame but late in eury place resounded.
Except these flaming lampes extinguisht bee,
Their golden thoughts shall sleepe eternally.
A Fountaine framde by furies raisd from hell,
About whose spring doth fear & terror dwel:
No earthly water may suffise but this
To quench the lamp where art commander is.
No wight aliue this water may procure,
But she that is a Virgin chast and pure.
For Nature at her birth did so dispose,
Vpon her breast to print a purple Rose.

These verses being perused by the three Knights, & finding them as it were contriued in the manner of a mysticall Oracle, they could not imagine what they should signifie: but *Rosana* being singularly well conceated, and of a quicke vnderstanding, presently knewe that by her the Aduenture should be finished, and therefore shee incouraged them to a forwardnes, and to seeke out the inchaunted Fountaine, that by the water thereof the lamps might be quenched, and the seauen Champions deliuered out of captiuitie.

This importunate desire of *Rosana*, caused the three yong Knights not to loose anie time, but to search in euery corner of the Castle, till they had found the place wherin the Fountaine was: for as they went towards the North side of the Court, they espied another little doore standing in the wall, and when they came to it, they sawe that it was made all of verie strong yron, with a portal of steele, and in the key hole thereof there was a brazen key, with the which they did open it, whereat presently (vnto theyr wonderfull amazements) they heard a verie sad and sorrowfull voyce breath foorth these words following.

Let no man bee so foolish hardy, as to enter here, for it is a place of terror and confusion.

Yet for all this they entered in thereat, and would not be daunted with anie ceremonious fear, but like knights of an heroycall estimation they went forward: wherein they were no sooner entred, but they saw that it was wonderfully darke, and it seemed vnto them that it should be a verie large Hall, and therein they heard verie fearefull howlings, as though there had bin a legion of helhounds, or that *Plutoes* Dogge had been vice gerent of that place. Yet for all this these valiant Knights did not loose anye of their accustomed courage, nor wold the Ladie leaue their companies for anie danger: but they entred in further, & tooke off their gauntlets from their left hands, whereon they wore meruailous great and fine Diamonds, which were set in rings, that gaue so much light, that they might plainly see all things that were in the Hall, the which was verie great and wide, and vppon the walls were painted the figures of manie furious fiends and diuells, wyth other straunge Uisions framed by Magicke arte, onely to terrefie the beholders. But looking verie circumspectlye about them on euerie side, they espied the inchanted fountaine standing directly in the middle of the Hall, towards which they went with their shieldes braced on theyr left armes, and their good swords charged in their hands, readie to withstand anie daungerous accident whatsoeuer should happen.

But comming to the Fountaine, and offering to fill their helmets with water, there appeared before them a strange and terrible Griphon, which seemed to bee all of flaming fire who stroke all the three Knights one after another in such sort, that they were forced to recoyle backe a great way: yet notwithstanding with great discretion they kept themselues vpright, & with a wonderfull lightnesse, accompanied with no lesse anger, they threw theyr shields at their backes, and taking their swordes in both their handes, they began most fiercely to assaile the Griphon with mortall and strong blowes. Then presentlye there appeared before them a whole legion of diuels with flesh-hookes in their hands, spitting forth flames of fire, & breathing from their nosthrills smoking sulphure & brimstone. In this terrible sort tormented they these three valiant Knights, whose yeres although they were but yong, yet with great wrath and redoubled force aduentred they themselues amongst this hellish crue, striking such terrible blowes, that in spite of them they came vnto ye Fountaine, and proffered to take of the water: but all in vain, for they were not onely put from it by this diuelish companie, but the water it selfe glided from their hands.

Oh in what great trauel and perplexitie these Knights remained amongst this wicked and diuellish generation, for to defend themselues that they might attaine to the finishing of this Aduenture, according to their knightlye promise.

But during the time of all these daungerous encounters, *Rosana* stood like one bereft of sense, thorough ye terror of the same: but at last remembring her selfe of ye prophecie written in the siluer tablet, the which the knights perused by the inchaunted Lampes: the signification of which was, that the quenching of the lights should be accomplished by a pure Uirgin, that had the liuely forme of a Rose naturally pictured vpon her breast: all the which *Rosana* knew most certainly to bee comprehended in her selfe.

Therefore whilst they continued in their fight, she tooke vp a helmet that was pulled from one of the Knightes heads by the furious force of the Griphon, and ranne vnto the Fountaine and filled it with water, wherewith shee quenched the inchaunted Lampes, with as much ease, as though one had dipped a waxen torch in a mightie riuer of water.

This was no sooner done and finished to *Rosanaes* cheefest contentment, when that the heauens began to waxe darke, and the cleere skies to be ouerspred with a blacke & thicke clowd, and it came with great thundrings & lightnings, and with such a terrible noyse, as though the earth would haue sunke: and the longer it indured, the more was the furie thereof, in such sort that the Griphon wyth all that deluding generation of spirits vanished away, and the Knights forsooke their incounters, and fell vpon theyr knees, and with great humilitie they desired of God to be deliuered from the furie of that exceeding and terrible tempest.

By this sodaine alteration of the heauens, the knight of the Castle knew that the Lampes were extinguished, the Champions redeemed from their inchaunted sleepes the Castle yeelded to the pleasure of the three knights, and his owne life to the furies of their swords, except hee preserued it by a sodaine flight, so presently hee departed the Castle, and secretly fled out of the Iland vnsuspected by anie one: of whose after fortunes, miseries, and death, you shall heare more hereafter in the course of the historie following.

The Nigromancer by his Arte likewise knew, that the Castle was yeelded vnto his Enemies power, & that his charmes and magicke spells nothing preuailed: therfore he caused two ayrie spirits in the likenes of two Dragons to carrie him swiftly through the ayre in an Ebonie Chariot.

Heere we leaue him in his wicked & diuelish attempts and diuelish enterprises, which shall bee discoursed heereafter more at large: because it appertaineth to our Historie now to speake of the seauen Champions of Christendome, that by the quenching of the Lampes were awakened from their inchauntments, wherein they had laine in obscuritie for the space of seauen dayes. For when they were risen from their sleepes, and had rowsed vp theyr drowsie spirits, like men newly recouered from a trance, being ashamed of that dishonorable enterprice, they long time gazed in each others faces, being not able to expresse their mindes, but by blushing lookes, beeing the silent speakers of their extreame sorrowes. But at last Saint *George* began to expresse the extremitie of his griefe in this manner.

What is become of you braue *Europes* Champions (said he) where is now your wonted valors, that hath bin so much renowmed through the world? what is become of your surmounting strengths, that hath bruzed inchaunted helmets, and quaild the power of mightie multitudes? what is become of your terrible blowes, that hath subdued mountaines, hewen in sunder diamond armours, and brought whole kingdomes[2] vnder your subiections, now I see that all is forgotten & nothing worth, for that we haue buried all our honors, dignities, and fames in slouthfull slumbers vpon a silken bed.

And there vpon hee fell vpon his knees, and said: thou holy God, thou rector of the riding racks of heauen, to thee I inuocate and call, and desire thee to help vs, and doe not permit vs to haue our fames taken away for this dishonor, but let vs meritte dignitie by our victories, and that our bright renownes may ride vpon the glorious winges of fame, whereby that babes as yet vnborne may speake of vs, and in time to come fill whole volumes with our princely atchiuements.

These and such like reasons pronounced this discontented[3] Champion, till such time as the elementes cleared, and that golden faced *Phœbus* glistred with splendant brightnes into the caue through a secret hole, which seemed in their conceits to daunce about the vale of heauen, and to reioyce at their happie deliueries.

In this ioyfull manner returned they vp into the court of the Castle, with their armors buckled fast vnto their bodies, which had not beene vnbraced in seuen dayes before, where they met with the three Knightes comming to salute them, and to giue them the curtesies of Knighthood.

But when Saint *George* saw his Sonnes whome he had not seene in twice two yeeres before he was so rauished with ioy, that he swounded in their bosomes, and

---

[2] kingdomes] kindomes *1597*
[3] discontented] disconted *1597*

not able to giue them his blessing, so great was the pleasure he tooke in their sights.

Heere I leaue the ioyfull greeting betwixt the Father and his Sons, to those that knowes the secret loue of parents to their children, and what deare affection long absence breedeth.

For when they had sufficiently ostended the integritie of their soules each to other, and had at large explained how many daungers euery Knight and Champion had passed since their departures from England, where as they begun first their intended pilgrimage to Ierusalem as you heard in the beginning of this booke, they determined to search the Castle, and to finde out *Leoger* with his assosiate the wicked inchaunter, that they might receiue dew punishments for their committed offences, but they like wylie foxes were fled from the hunters traces, and had left the emptie Castle to the spoile of the Christian Champions: But when *Rosana* sawe her selfe dismist from her purpose, and that she could not performe her mothers will, against her disloyall Father, she protested by the mightie God of heauen, neuer to close vp her carefull eyes with quiet slumbers, nor neuer rest her wearie limbes in bed of Downe, but trauell vp and downe the circled earth till she inioyd a sight of her disloiall Father whome as yet her eyes did neuer see. Therefore shee coniured the Champions by the loue and honor that knights should beare vnto Ladies in distresse, to graunt her libertie to depart and not to hinder her from her intended trauell.

The Knights considered with themselues that shee was a Lady of a deuine inspiration, borne vnto some straunge fortune, and one by the heauens appointment which had redeemed them from a wonderfull mizerie.

Therefore they condescended to her desires, and not onely gaue her leaue to depart, but furnished her with all thinges belonging to a Ladye of so braue a minde.

First they found within the Castle an armor fit for a woman, the which the inchaunter had caused to be made by magick arte of such a singuler nature that no weapon could pearce it, and so light in wearing, that it wayed no heuier then a Lions skin, it was contriued after the *Amazonian* fashion, plated before with siluer plates, like the scales of a Dolphin, and riuetted together with golden nayles: so that when she had it vppon her backe, shee seemed like to *Diana*, hunting in the Forrests of transformed *Acteon*.

Likewise they found (standing in a stable at the East side of the Castle) a lustie limbed Steed, big of stature, & of a verie good haire, because the halfe part forwards was of the colour of a Wolfe, and the other halfe was al black, sauing that here and there it was spotted with litle white spots: his feete were clouen, so that he needed not at anye time to be shod: his necke was somewhat long, hauing a little head, with great eares hanging downe like a hound: his pace was with great maiestie, and he so doubled hys necke, that his mouth touched his breast: there came out of his mouth two great tuskes like vnto an Elephant, and hee did exceede all horses in the world in lightnes, and dyd runne with an exceeding good grace. This likewise bestowed they vppon the Ladie, the which did more content her minde, than anie thing that euer her eye had seene before that time. Also the ten christian Knights gaue her at her departure ten diamond rings, continually to weare vpon her ten fingers, in perpetuall remembrance of their curtesies.

This being done, without anie longer tarriance, but thanking them for their great kindnes shewed vnto her in distresse, she leapt into the saddle without helpe of stirrop or anie other thing, and so rode speedely awaye from their sights, as a shower of raine driuen by a violent tempest.

After her departure, the Champions remembred the olde Shepheard, whom they had almost forgotten, thorough the ioy that they tooke in their happie meetings: he as yet remained without the Castle gates, carefully keeping their horses, whom now they caused to come in, and not onely gaue him the honour due vnto his age, but bestowed frankly vpon him the state and gouernment of the Castle, with store of iewels, pearles and treasure, onely to be maintained and kept for the releefe of poore Trauailers.

This being perfourmed with their generall consents, they spent the remnant of the day in banquetting and other pleasant conference of their passed Aduentures. And when that Night with her sable clowdes had ouer-spred the Dayes delightfull countenaunce, they betooke them to their rests: the seauen Champions in a chamber that had as manie windowes as there were daies in the yere, the olde Shepheard by himselfe in a rich furnished Parlour, and Saint *Georges* three Sonnes in the greatest Hall in the Castle.

CHAP. X.

How after the Christian Knightes were gone to bed in the black Castle: Saint George was awaked from his sleep in the dead time of the night, after a most fearefull manner, and likwise how he found a Knight lying vpon a tombe, that stood ouer a flaming fire, with other thynges that hapned vpon the same.

MOst sweete were the sleepes that these[1] Princely minded companies took in the Castle all the first part of the night, without molestation eyther by disquiet dreames or disturbing motions of their mindes, till such time as the glistering Queene of night had runne halfe her wearie Iorney, and had spent the better part of the night: for betwixt twelue and one, being the chiefest time of feare and terror in the night, such a strainge alteration worked in Saint *Georges* thought that he coulde not inioy the benefite of sweete sleepe, but was forced to lye broad waking like one disquieted by some sodaine feare: but as hee laye with wakefull eyes thinking vppon his passed fortunes, and numbring the minutes of the night with his cogitations, hee heard as it were a cry of night Rauens, which flew beating their fatal wings against the windows of his lodging, by which he immagined that some direfull accident were neere at hand: yet being not frighted with this fearefull noise, nor daunted with the croking of these Rauens he lay silently not reuealing it to any of the other Champions that lay in the sixe seuerall beds in the same chamber: but at last being betwixt waking and sleeping, hee heard as it were the voice of a sorrowfull Knight that constrained these bitter passions from his tormented soule, and they contayned these words following.

Oh thou inuincible knight of England, thou that art not frighted with this sorrowful dwelling, wherein thou canst see nothing but torments, rise vp I say, from thy sluggish bed & with thy vndaunted courage and stronge arme, infringe the charme of my inchauntment.

And therewithall hee seemed to giue a most terrible grone and so ceased: This vnexpected noyse caused Saint *George* (without the knowledge of any of the other Champions) to arise from his bedde, and to buckle on his armor, and to search about the Castle to see if hee might finde the place that harbored the Knight that made such sorrowfull lamentation.

So going vp and downe the by corners of the Castle, all the latter part of the night, without finding the aduenture of this strange voice, or disturbance by any other meanes but that he was hindred from his naturall and quiet sleepes, but by the breake of day, when the darke night began to withdraw her sable curtaines, and to giue *Aurora* libertie to explayne her purple brightnesse, he entred into a foure square parlor, hunge rounde about with blacke cloth, and other mournfull habiliments, where on the one side of the same he sawe a tombe all couered

---

[1] these] hese *1597*

likewise with blacke, and vppon it there lay a man with a pale colour, who at certaine times, gaue moste meruelous and greeuous sighes, caused by the burning flames that proceeded from vnder the tombe, being such that it seemed that his body therewith should bee conuerted into coales: the flame thereof was so stincking that it made Saint *George* somewhat to retyre himselfe from the place where hee sawe that horrible and fearefull spectacle.

He which lay vpon the tombe, casting his eyes aside, espied Saint *George*, and knowing him to be a humane creature, with an inflicted voyce he said: Who art thou Sir Knight that art come into this place of sorrow, where nothing is heard but clamors of feare and terror?

But tell me said Saint *George*, who art thou, that with so much griefe dost demaund of me, that which I stand in doubt to reueale to thee.

I am the King of *Babilon* (answered hee) which without all consideration, with my cruell hand did pearce through the white and dilicate brest of my beloued daughter: woe be to me and woe vnto my soule therefore: for shee at once did pay her offence by death, but I a most mizerable wretch with many tormentes doe dye lyuing.

When this worthy Champion Saint *George* was about to answere him, he saw come foorth from vnder the tombe, a damsell who had her hayre of a yellow and wan colour hanging downe about her shoulders, and by her face she seemed that she should be verie strangely afflicted with tormentes, and with a sorrowfull voyce shee said.

Oh vnfortunate Knight what doest thou seeke in this infernall lodging, where cannot be giuen thee any other pleasure, but mortall torment, and there is but one thing that can cleare thee from them, and this cannot be tolde thee by any other but by me: yet I will not expresse it except thou wilt graunt mee one thing that I will aske of thee.

The English Champion that with a sad countenaunce stood beholding of the sorrowful damsel, and being greatly amazed at the sight which he had seene, answered and said: The Gods which are gouernours of my liberty, wil doe their pleasures, but touching the graunt of thy request I neuer denied any lawfull thing to either Lady or Gentlewoman, but with all my power and strength I was ready to fulfill the same, therefore demaunde what thy pleasure is, for I am readie in all thinges that toucheth thy remedie.

And with that the damsell threw her selfe into that sepulcher, and with a greeuous voice she said. Nowe moste curteous Knight performe thy promise: strike but three stroakes vpon this fatall tombe, and thou shalt deliuer vs from a world of mizeries, and likewise make an ende of our continuall torments.

Then the inuincible knight replyed in this order, whether you be humane creatures said he, placst in this sepulcher by inchauntment, or furies raisd from fiery *Acheron* to worke my confusion or no I know not, and there is so little truth in this infernall Castle, that I stand in doubt whether I may beleeue thy words or not: but yet dicourse vnto me the truth of all your passed fortunes, and by what meanes you were brought into this place, and as I am a true Christian Knight, and one that fights in the quarrell of Christ, I vow to accomplish whatsoeuer lyeth in my power.

Then the Damsel began with a greeuous and sorrowfull lamentation, to declare as strange a tragedie as euer was told. And lying in the fatall Sepulcher, vnseene of Saint *George*, that stood leaning his backe agaynst the wall to heare her discourse and lamentable Storie: with a hollow voice like a murthered Ladie, whose bleeding soule as yet did feele the terrible stroke at her death, shee repeated this pittifull tale following.

CHAP. XI.

Of a tragicall Discourse pronounced by a Ladie in a Toombe: and how her Inchauntment was finished by saint George, with other straunge accidents that hapned to the other Christian Knights.

IN famous *Babylon* somtimes reigned a King, although a Heathen, yet adorned with noble and vertuous customes, and had onely one Daughter that was verie faire, whose name was *Angelica*, humble, wise, and chast: who was beloued of a mightie Duke, & a man[1] wonderfull cunning in the Blacke arte. This Magitian had a seuere & graue countenance, and one that for wisedome better deserued ye gouernment than anie other in the kingdome, and was verie well esteemed throughout all *Babylon*, almost equally with the king: for the which there ingendred in the kings heart a secret rancour and hatred towards him. Thys Magitian cast his loue vppon the yong Princesse *Angelica*, and it was the Gods will that shee should repaye him wyth the same affection: so that both theyr hearts beeing wounded with loue the one to the other, in such sorte that the fire kindled dayly more and more, and neither of them had any other imagination but onelye to loue: and not knowing how to manifest their griefes, they indured sundry great passions.

Then loue which continually seeketh occasions, did on a time set before this Magician a wayting maid of *Angelicaes*, named *Fidela*: the which thing seemed to be wrought by the immortall power of the Goddesse *Venus*: oh what feare this Magitian was in to discouer vnto her all his heart, and to bewray the secrets of his louesicke soule: but in the end, by the great industrie and diligence of the waighting Maid (whose name was answerable vnto her minde) there was order giuen that these two louers shuld meete together.

This faire *Angelica*, for that she could not at her ease enioy her true Louer, she did determine to leaue her own naturall Countrey and Father: and with this intention being one night with her Loue, she cast her armes about his necke and said.

Oh my sweete and welbeloued Frend, seeing that the soueraigne Gods haue been so kinde to me, as to haue my heart linked in thy breast, let me not finde in thee ingratitude, for that I cannot passe my time, except continually I enioye thy sight: and doo not muse (my Lord) at these my words, for the entyre loue that I beare to you, dooth constraine me to make it manifest. And this beleeue of a certaintie, that if thy sight be absent from mee, it will bee an occasion that my heart will lacke his vitall recreation, and my soule forsake his earthly habitation. You knowe (my Lorde) how that the King my Father dooth beare you no good will, but doth hate you from hys soule, which wil be the occasion that we cannot enioy our harts contentments: for the which I haue determined (if you thinke well thereof) to leaue both my Father and my natiue Countrey, and to goe and liue with you in a strange Land. And if you denie me this, you shall verie quickly see your

---

[1] man] man man *1597*

welbeloued Ladie without life: but I know you will not denie me it, for thereon consisteth the benefite of my welfare, and my cheefest prosperitie. And therewithall shedding a few teares from her christall eyes, she held her peace.

The Magitian (as one halfe rauished with her earnest desires) answered and said.

My Loue and sweete Mistres, wherefore haue you anie doubt that I will not fulfill and accomplish your desire in all things? therefore out of hand put all things in a readines that your pleasure is to haue done: for what more benefite and contentment can I receaue, than to enioy your sight continually, in such sort that neither of vs may depart from the others companie, till the fatall Destenies giue end vnto our liues. But if it so fall out that fortune frowne vpon vs, that wee bee espied and taken in our enterprise, and suffer death together, what more glorie can there be vnto my soule, than to dye with thee, and to leaue my life betwixt thy armes? Therefore doo not trouble your selfe my sweete Ladie and Mistres, but giue me leaue for to depart your presence, that I may prouide all things in a readines for our departures. And so wyth this conclusion they tooke leaue one of the other, and departed away with as great secrecie as might possibly bee deuised.

After this within a fewe dayes, the Magitian by hys inchauntments caused a Chariot to bee made, that was gouerned by two flying Dragons into the which without being espied by anie one, they put themselues, in companie of their trustie wayting Maid: and so in great secret they departed out of the Kings Pallace, and tooke theyr iourney towards the Countrey of *Armenia*: in the which Countrey in a short time they arriued, and came without anie misfortune vnto a place whereas deepe riuers doo continually strike vpon a mightie rocke, vpon the which stood an olde and ancient building, wherein they intended to inhabit as a most conuenient place for their dwellinges, whereas they might without all feare of beeing found, liue peacefullie in ioying in each others loue.

Not farre from that place there was a small Uillage, from whence they might haue necessarie prouision for the maintayning of their bodies: great ioy and pleasure those two Louers receiued when they founde themselues in such a place wheras they might take their ease and inioy their loues.

The Magitian delighted in no other thing but to goe a hunting with certaine Countrie dwellers that inhabited in the next Uillage, leauing his sweete *Angellica* accompanied with her trustie *Fidela* in that stronge house, so in this order they liued together foure yeares, spending their daies in great pleasure: but in the end time (who neuer resteth in one degree) did take from them their rest and repayed them with sorrow and extream mizerie. For when the King her father found her missing,[2] the sorrowe and griefe was so much that he receiued, that he kept his chamber a long time, and would not be comforted of anie bodie.

Foure yeares he passed away in great heauinesse, filling the Courte with Ecchoes of his beloued daughter, and making the skies to resound his lamentations: sorrowe was his foode, salte teares his drinke, and griefe his chiefe companion.

---

[2] missing] missiing *1597*

But at last, vppon a time as he sate in his Chayre lamenting her absence with great heauinesse, and beeing ouercharged with griefe, he chanst to fall into a troublesome dreame, for after quiet sleepe had closed vp the closets of his eyes, he dreamd that he saw his daughter standing vppon[3] a Rocke by the sea side, offring to cast her body into the waues before she would returne to *Babylon*, and that he beheld her Louer with an Armye of Satyrs and wilde men ready furnished with habiliments of warre to pull him from his Throane, and to depriue him of hys Kingdome.

Out of this vision he presently started from his chaire, as though it had been one frighted with a legion of spirits, and caused foure of the cheefest Peeres of his Land to bee sent for, to whom he committed the gouernement of hys Countrey: certefying them that he intended a voyage to the Sepulcher at *Memphis*, thereby to quallifie the furie of his Daughters ghost, whom he dreamed to be drowned in the seas, and that except he sought by true submission to appease the angrie heauens, whom hee had offended by his vnnaturall sorrowes, hee should be deposed from hys Kingdome.

None could withdraw him from this determination, though it was to the preiudice of his whole Land, therefore within twentie dayes he furnished himselfe with all necessaries as well of armour and martiall furniture, as of golde and treasure, and so departed from *Babylon* priuately and alone, not suffering anie other (though many desired it humbly, and were verie earnest) to beare hym companie.

But he trauelled not as he told his Lords after any ceremonious order, but like a bloud-hound serching Countrey after Countrey, Nation by Nation, and Kingdome by Kingdome, that after a barbarous manner hee might be reuenged vpon his Daughter for her disobedience. And as he trauelled, there was no caue, den, wood nor wildernesse, but he furiously entered, and diligently searched for his *Angelica*.

At last by strange fortune he happened into *Armenia*, neere vnto the place whereas his Daughter had her residence: where, after he had intelligence by the Commons of that Countrey, that she remained in an olde ruynated Building on the top of a rocke neere at hand, without anie more tariance hee trauelled vnto that place, at such a time as y[e] Magitian her louing Husband was gone about his accustomed hunting: where comming to the gate and finding it lockt, hee knockt thereat so furiously, that hee made the noyse to resound all the house ouer, with a redoubling Eccho.

When *Angelica* heard one knocke, she came vnto the gate and with all speed did open it. And when she thought to imbrace him, thinking it to be her Louer, she saw that it was her Father, and with a sodain alteration she gaue a great shrike, and ran with all the speed she could backe into the house.

The King her Father being somewhat angrie, like a furious Lion followed her, saying: It dooth little auayle thee *Angelica* to run away, for that thou shalt dye by thys reuengefull hand, paying me with thy death the great dishonour that my royall crowne hath now by thy flight receaued.

---

[3] vppon] vppo *1597*

So he followed her till he came to the chamber where her wayting Maid *Fidela* was, who likewise presentlye knew the King: vpon whose wrathfull countenance appeared the image of pale death, and fearing the harme that should happen vnto her Ladie, she put her selfe ouer her bodie, and gaue most terrible, lowd, and lamentable shrikes.

The King as one kindled in wrath, and forgetting the naturall loue of a Father towards his Childe, hee laid hand vppon his sword, and said: It dooth not profite thee *Angelica* to flie from thy death: for thy desert is such, that thou canst not escape from it: for heere mine owne arme shall be the killer of mine owne flesh: and I vnnaturally hate that, which Nature it selfe commaundeth me especialy[4] to loue.

Then *Angelica* with a countenaunce more red than scarlet, answered and said: Ah my Lord and Father, wil you be now as cruell vnto me, as you had wont to be kind and pittifull? appease your wrath, and withdraw your vnmercifull sword, and hearken vnto this which I saye in discharging my selfe in that you charge mee withall,[5] you shall vnderstand my Lord and father, that I was ouercome and constrained by loue for to loue, forgetting all fatherly loue and my dutie towardes your Maiestie: yet for all that, hauing power to accomplish the same, it was not to your dishonour in that I liue honorablie with my husband: then the King (with a visage fraught with terrible ire) more liker a dragon in the woods of *Hercania* then a man of meeke nature, answered and said:

Thou viperous brat, degenerate from natures kinde, thou wicked Traitor to thy generation, what reason hast thou to make this false excuse, when as thou hast committed a crime that deserues more punishment then humaine nature can inflicte? and in saying these wordes, he lift vp his sword, intending to strike her vnto the harte and to bathe his weapon in his owne daughters blood, whereat *Fidela* being present, gaue a terrible shrike and threw her selfe vpon the body of vnhappy *Angelica*, offring her tender brest to the furie of his sharpe cutting sword onely to set at libertie her deere Lady and Mistresse.

But when the furious King sawe her in this sorte make her defence, he pulled her off by the haire of the hed, offring to trample her delicate body vnder his feete, thereby to make a way that he might execute his determined[6] purpose without resistance of any.

Fidela when she sawe the King determined to kill his daughter, like vnto a Lyonesse she hung about his necke, and said: thou monstrous murtherer, more crueller then mad dogs in *Egipt*, why dost thou determine to slaughter the moste chaste and loyallest Ladye in the worlde? euen she within whose lappe vntamed Lyons will come and sleepe?

Thou arte thy selfe (I say) the occasion of all this euill, and thyne onely is the faulte, for that thy selfe wert so malicious and so full of mischiefe, that shee durst not let thee vnderstand of her sodaine loue.

---

[4] especialy] especily *1597*
[5] withall] withll *1597*
[6] determined] denermined *1597*

These wordes and teares of *Fidela* did little profite to mollifie the Kings heart, but rather like a wylde Boare in the Wildernes beeing compassed about with a companie of Dogges, doth shake his members: euen so did thys King shake himselfe, and threw *Fidela* from him in such sort, that he had almost dasht her braines against the chamber walls, and with double wrath hee did procure to execute his furie. Yet for all this, *Fidela* with terrible shrikes sought to hinder him, till such time as with his cruel hand he thrust the poynt of his sword in at her breast, so that it appeared foorth at her backe, whereby her soule was forced to leaue her terrestriall habitation, and flye into Paradice to those blessed soules, which dyed for true loues sake.

Thus this vnhappie *Angelica*, when shee was most at quiet, and content with her prosperous life, then Fortune turned her vnconstant Wheele, and cast her from a glorious delight to a sodaine death.

The yrefull King, when he beheld his daughters blood sprinkled about the chamber, and that by his own hands it was committed, he repented himselfe of the deede, and accursed the hower wherein ye first motion of such a crime entered into his minde, wishing the hand that did it euer after might be lame, and the heart that did contriue it to be plagued with more extremities, than was miserable *Oedipus*: or to be terrified with her ghastly spirit, as was the *Macedonian Alexander* with *Clitus* shadow, whom he causeles murthered.

In this manner the vnfortunate King repented hys Daughters bloodie Tragedie, with this determination, not to stay till the Magitian returned from his Hunters exercise, but to exclude himselfe from the companie of all men, & to spend the remnant of his loathsome life among vntamed beasts in some wilde wildernes. Upon this resolution he departed the chamber, and withall said: Farewell[7] thou liuelesse bodie of my *Angelica*, and may thy blood which I haue spilt, craue vengeance of the Gods against my guiltie soule, for my earthly bodie shall indure a miserable punishment. Likewise at his departure he writ vppon ye chamber wals these verses following in his daughters blood.

> *For now to hills, to dales, to rockes, to caues I goe,*
> *To spend my dayes in shameful sorrow, griefe & woe.*

Fidela (after the departure of the King) vsed such violent fury against her selfe, both by rending the golden tramelles of her hayre, and tearing her Rosie coloured face with her furious nayles, that shee rather seemed an infernall Furie subiect to wrath, than an earthly creature furnished with clemencie.

She sat ouer *Angelicaes* bodie, wiping her bleeding bosome with a damaske scarffe, which shee pulled from her waste, and bathing her dead bodie in luke-warme tears, which forcibly ranne downe from her eyes like an ouerflowing Fountaine.

In this wofull manner spent ye sorrowfull *Fidela* that vnhappie day, till bright *Phœbus* went into the westerne seas: at which time the Magitian retourned from his

---

[7] Farewell] Farwell *1597*

accustomed hunting, and finding the doore open, he entered into *Angelicaes* chamber, where when he found her bodie weltring in congealed blood, and beheld how *Fidela* sate weeping ouer her bleeding wounds, he cursed himselfe, for that he accompted his negligence ye occasion of her death, in that he had not left her in more safetie. But when *Fidela* had certefied him, how that by the hands of her owne Father she was slaughtered, he began like a franticke tyrant to rage against heauen and earth, and to fill the ayre with terrible exclamations.

Oh cruell murtherer (said he) crept from the womb of some vntamed Tyger: I wilbe so reuenged vpon thee, O vnnaturall king, that all ages shal wonder at thy misery.

And likewise thou vnhappie Uirgin, shalt indure like punishment, in that thy accursed tung hath bruted this fatall deed vnto my eares: the one for committing the crime and the other for reporting it. For I will cast such deserued vengeance vpon your heads, and place your bodies in such continuall torments, that you shall lament my Ladies death, leauing aliue the fame of her with your lamentations.

And in saying these words, he drew a Booke out of his bosome, and in reading certaine charmes and inchauntments that was therein contained, he made a great & verie blacke clowde appeare in the skies, which was broght by terrible and hastie windes, in the which he tooke them vp both, and brought them into this inchaunted Castle, where euer since they haue remained in this Tombe, cruelly tormented with vnquenchable fire: and must eternally continue in the same extremitie, except some curteous Knight will vouchsafe to giue but three blowes vpon the Tombe, and breake the inchauntment.

Thus haue you heard you magnanimious Knight,[8] the true discourse of my vnhappie fortunes. For the virgine which for the true loue she bore vnto her Ladie was committed to this torment is my selfe: and this pale body lying vpon the Tombe, is the vnhappie *Babylonian* King which vnnaturally murthered his owne Daughter: and the Magitian which committed al these villanies, is that accursed wretch, which by his charmes and diuellish Enchauntments hath so strangely withstood your valiant incounters.

These words were no sooner finished, but Sa. *George* drew out his sharpe cutting sword, and gaue three blowes vpon the inchaunted Tombe, whereat presentlye appeared the *Babylonian* King standing before him, attyred in rich robes, with an Emperiall Diadem vpon his head: & the Ladie standing by him, with a countenance more beutifull than the damaske Rose.

When Saint *George* beheld them, he was not able to speake for ioy, nor to vtter his minde, so exceeding was the pleasure that he tooke in their sights. So without anie long circumstance, he tooke them betwixt both his hands, and led them into the chamber, whereas hee found the other Knights newly risen from their beds. To whom hee reuealed the true discourse of the passed Aduenture, and by what meanes he redeemed the King and the Lady from their inchauntments: which to them was as great ioye, as before it was to Saint *George*.

---

[8] Knight] Knights *1597*

So, after they had for some sixe dayes refreshed themselues in the castle, they generaly intended to accompany the *Babilonian* King into his Countrey, and to place him againe in his Regiment.

In which trauel we wil leaue the Christian knights to the conduction of Fortune, and returne againe vnto *Rosana*, whom (as you heard before) departed from the Castle in the pursute of her disloyal father: of whose strange accidents shall be spoken in this following Chapter.

CHAP. XII.

How the Knight of the Blacke Castle after the conquest of the same by the christian champions, wandred vp and downe the world in great terror of conscience, and after how he was found in a wood by his own daughter, in whose presence he desperately slew himselfe, with other accidents that after hapned.

You doo well remember when that[1] the Christian champions had slaine the seuen Giants in the inchanted castle, and had made conquest thereof, disloyall *Leoger* being lord of the same, secretly fled: not for anie anger of the losse, but for the preseruation of his life. So in great greefe and terror of conscience he wandred like a fugitiue vp and downe ye world: sometimes remembring of his passed prosperitie, other times thinking vpon the rapes he had committed, how disloyally in former times he had left the Queene of *Armenia* big with Childe, bearing in her wombe the staine of her honour, and the confusion of his reputation. Sometime his guiltie minde imagined, that the bleeding ghosts of the two Sisters (whom he both rauished and murthered) followed him vp and downe, haunting his ghost with fearfull exclamations, and filling each corner of the earth with clamours of reuengement.

Such feare and terrour raged in his soule, that he thought all places where he trauelled, were filled with multitudes of[2] Knightes, and that the strength of Countries pursued him, to heape vengeance vpon his guiltye head for those wronged Ladyes.

Whereby hee curssed the hower of his birth, and blamed the cause of his creation, wishing the Heauens to consume his bodye with a flashe of fire, or that the earth would gape and swallowe him: In this manner trauelled he vp and downe, filling all places with Ecchoes of his sorrowes and griefe, which brought him into such a perplexitie, that many times hee would haue slaine himselfe, and haue ridde his wretched soule from a worlde of mizeries.

But it happened that one morning very early, by the first light of *Titans* golden toarch, he entred into a narow and straight path, which conducted him into a very thicke and solitarie Forrest, wherein with much sorrowe he trauelled till suche time as glistring *Phœbus* had passed the halfe parte of his iorney.

And beeing wearye with the longe waye, and the greate waighte of his Armour, hee was forced to take some rest and ease vnder certaine freshe and greene Myrtle trees, whose leaues did bathe themselues in a faire and cleare Fountaine, whose streame made a bubling murmure on the pebble.

Beeing set, he began a newe to haue in remembrance his former committed cruelty, and complaining of Fortune he published his great griefe, and although he was weary of complaining, and seeing himselfe[3] without all remidy, he resolued

---

[1] that] that that *1597*
[2] of] of of *1597*
[3] himselfe] hinselfe *1597*

like vnto the Swan to sing awhile before his death: and so thinking to giue some ease vnto his tormented heart, he warbled forth these verses following.

Mournfull Melpomine approach with speed,
and shew thy sacred face with teares besprent:
Let all thy sisters harts with sorrow bleed
To heare my plaints and rufull discontent.
And with your moanes sweet Muses all assist
My wailfull song, that doth on woe consist.

And then I may at large paint out my paine,
Within these desert groues and wildernesse:
And after I haue ended to complaine,
They may record my woes and deep distres:
Except these myrtle trees relentles bee,
They will with sobs assist the sighes of mee.

Time weares out life, it is reported so,
And so it may I will it not denie:
Yet haue I tride long time, & this do knowe,
Time giues no ende to this my miserie.
But rather fortune, time and heauens agree,
To plague my hart with woe eternally.

ye siluan nimphs that in thes wods do shroud
To you my mournfull sorrowes I declare:
You sauage satyrs let your eares be bound
to heare[4] *my woe, your sacred selues prepare:*
Trees, herbs & flowrs, in rural fields that groe,
While thus I morne, do you some silence sho.

Sweet Philomel cease thou thy songs a while
And will thy mates[5] *their melodies to leaue:*
And all at once attend my mournfull stile,
which wil of mirth yor sugred notes bereaue
If you desire the burthen of my Song:
I sigh and sob, for Ladies I did wrong.

You furious Beasts that feed on montains hye,
And restlesse run with rage your pray to find:
Drawe nere to him whose brutish crueltye
Hath cropt the bud of Virgins chaste & kind.

---

[4] *heare*] *heaare 1597*
[5] *mates*] *mate 1597*

This onely thing yet rests to comfort mee:
Repentance comes a while before I dye.

Since heauens agree for to increase my care,
What hope haue I for to enioy delight?
Sith fates and fortune do themselues prepare,
To work against my soule their full despight.
I know no meanes to yeild my hart reliefe:
But only death, which can desolue my griefe.

I muse and may my sorrowes being such,
That my poore hart can longer life sustaine:
Sith dayly I doe find my griefe so much,
As euery day I feele a dying paine.
But yet alas I liue afflicted still:
And haue no helpe to heale me of my ill.

When as I thinke vpon my pleasures past,
Now turnd to paine, it makes me rue my state
And since my ioy with woe is ouercast,
O death giue ende to my vnhappy fate.
For onely death will lasting life prouide:
Where liuing thus, I sundry deathes abide.

Wherfore all you that hear my mornful song
And tasted haue the griefe that I sustaine:
All lustfull rauishers that haue done wrong,
With teare-fild eyes assist me to complaine.
All that haue beeing, doe my beeing hate:
Crying haste, haste, this wretches dying state

This sorrowfull song being done, he laide himselfe all along vpon the greene grasse closing vp the closets of his eyes, in hope to repose him selfe in a quiet sleepe, and to abandon al discontented thoughts: in which silent contemplation we will leaue him for a while, and returne to *Rosana* the Queens daughter of *Armenia* that bolde *Amazonian* Lady, whome you remember likwise departed from the blacke Castle (clad with inchaunted armour) in the pursute of her disloyall Father, whome she neuer in her life beheld: this curteous Lady (to performe her mothers will) trauelled vp and downe strange countries, many a wearye step, yet neuer could she meet with her vnkind father, vnto whome she was commaunded to giue her mothers letter, neither could she heare in any place wheresoeuer she came, where shee might goe to seeke him: In which trauell shee met with many strange aduentures, the which with great honor to her name she finished, yet for all this she wandred ouer hils and dales: mountaines and vallies, and through many solitary woods. But at last she hapned by fortune into the wildernesse, whereas this discontented[6] knight laye sleeping vpon the greene grasse, neere to which place she likewise reposed her selfe vnder the branches of a Chesnut tree, desiring to take some rest after her long trauel.

But vpon a sodaine being betwixt waking and sleeping, she heard towardes her left hand, a verie dolorous grone, as it were of some sorrowfull knight, which was so terrible, heauie, and bitter, that it made her to giue an attentiue eare vnto the sounde, and to see if shee coulde heare and vnderstande what it shoulde be.

So with making the least noyse that shee could possibly, she arose vp and went towardes the place whereas shee might see what it was, and there shee behelde a Knight very well armed, lying vpon the greene grasse, vnder certaine fayre and greene mirtle trees, his[7] armour was all russet, and full of barres of blacke steele, which shewed to bee a very sadde, sorrowfull and heauie inamelling, agreeable to the inward sadnesse of hys heart.

Hee was somewhat of a bigge stature of bodie, and well proportioned, and there seemed by his disposition, to be in his heart great greife, where after shee had a while stood in secret beholding his sorrowfull countenaunce,[8] in a wofull manner hee tumbled his restlesse bodye vppon the greene grasse, and with a sad and heauy looke he breathed foorth this ruefull lamentation.

Oh heauye and peruersse Fortune (said he) why doost thou consent that so vilde and euill a wretch doe breathe so long vpon the earth, vpon whose wicked head the golden Sun disdaines to shine, and the glistering Elementes denyes their chearfull lightes?

Oh that some rauenous Harpey woulde welter from his denne, and make his loathsome bowelles my fatall Tombe, or that my eyes were sightles[9] like the mizerable King of *Thebes*, that I neuer might againe beholde this earth, whereon I haue long liued and committed many cruelties.

I am confounded with the cursse of heauen for wronging that Mayden Queene of *Armenia*, in the spoyle of whose Uirginitie I made a triumphant conquest.

Oh *Leoger Leoger*, what furye did induce thee to committe so great a sinne, in leauing her staind with thy lust, and dishonoured by thy disloyaltie?

Oh cruell and without faith, thou wert nurssed with the vnkindly milke of Tigers, and borne into the worlde for thine owne torment: where was thy vnderstanding when thou forsookst that gracious Princesse? who[10] not only yeilded to thee her libertie, loue and honour, but therwith a Kingdome and a golden Diademe, and therefore woe vnto mee Traytor, and more woes vppon my soule then there be hayres vpon my head, and may the sorrows of olde *Priam* be my eternall punishment.

What doth it profite me to fill the ayre with lamentations, when that the crime is already past, without all remedye or hope of comforte? this being said, he gaue a greeuous and terrible sigh and so held his peace.

---

[6] discontented] discentented *1597*

[7] his] is *1597*

[8] countenaunce] counteaunce *1597*

[9] sightles] sightes *1597*

[10] who] whome *1597*

Rosana by those heauye and sorrowfull lamentations, togeather with his reasons which shee heard, knewe him to bee her disloyall Father after whome shee had so long trauelled to finde out: but when she remembred how that his vnkindenesse was the death of her mother, her harte indured such extreame paine and sorrowe, that she was constrayned (without anye feeling) to fall downe to the ground.

But yet her couragious harte would not remaine long in that passion: but straight waies shee rose vp againe on her feete, with a desire to performe her mothers will, but yet not intending to discouer her name, nor to reueale vnto him that shee was his daughter: so with this thought and determination, shee went vnto the place where *Leoger* was, who when he heard the noyes of her comming, straightway started vpon his feete.

Then Rosana did salute him with a voyce some what heauye, and *Leoger* did returne his salutation with no lesse showe of griefe.

Then the *Amazonian* Lady tooke forth the letter from her naked breste, where as so longe time she had kept it, and in deliuering it into his handes, she said:

Is it possible that thou art that forgetfull and disloyall Knight, the which left the vnfortunate Queene of Armenia (with so great[11] paine and sorrowe) big with Childe amongste those vnmercifull Tyrantes her Countrimen, which banished her out of her Countrie in reuenge of thy committed crime, where euer since she hath bene companion with wilde beasts that in their natures hath lamented her banishment?

Leoger when he heard her to say these words began to beholde her, and although his eyes were all to be blubbered and weary of weeping, yet he most earnestly gazed in her face and answered her in this manner.

I will not denie thee gentle *Amazon* (said he) that which the high heauens doth complaine of[12] and the lowe earth doth mourne for. Thou shalt vnderstand that I am the same Knight, whom thou hast demaunded after, tell mee therefore what is thy will.

My will is said she, thou most vngrateful Knight, that thou read heere this Letter, the last worke of the white hand of the vnhappie *Armenian* Queene.

At which words, the Knight was so troubled in thoght and greeued in minde, that it was almost the occasion to dissolue his soule from his bodie: and therewithal putting forth his hand somewhat trembling, he tooke the Letter, & set him verie sorrowfully downe vpon the greene grasse: without anie power to the contrarie, his greefe so abounded the bounds of reason.

No sooner did he open the letter, but he presently knew it to be written by the hands of his wronged Ladie yᵉ Armenian Queene, who with great alteration both of hart & minde, he read the sorrowfull lines, the which contayned these words following.

---

[11] great] groat *1597*
[12] of] off *1597*

The Queene of Armenia her
Letter.

To thee thou disloyall Knight of the Blacke Castle, the vnfortunate Queene of Armenia, can neither send nor wish salutations: for hauing no health my selfe, I cannot send it vnto him, whose cruel mind hath quite forgotten my true loue, I cannot but lament continuallye and complain vnto the Gods incessantly,[13] considering that my fortune is conuerted from a crowned Queene to a miserable and banished caytiue, where the sauage beasts are my chiefe companions, & the mournfull birds my best solliciters. Oh *Leoger, Leoger*, why didst thou leaue me comfortlesse without all cause, as did *Aeneas* his vnfortunate *Dido*? what second loue hath bereaued me of thy sight, and made thee forget her, that euer shall remember thee. Oh *Leoger*, remember the day when first I saw thy face, which day bee fatall euermore, and counted for a dismal day in time to come, both heauy, blacke, and full of foule mischances, for it was vnhappie vnto me: for in giuing thee ioy, I bereaued my selfe of all, and lost the possession of my libertie and honour: althogh thou hast not esteemed nor tooke care of my sorrowfull fortunes, yet thou shouldst not haue mockt my perfect loue, and disdained the feruent affection that I haue borne thee, in that I haue yeelded to thee that precious iewell, ye which hath been denied to manie a noble King. Oh Loue, cruel and spitefull Loue, that so quickly didst make mee blinde, and depriuedst mee of the knowledge that belonged vnto my royall Highnesse.

Oh vncurteous Knight, beeing blinded with thy loue the Queene of *Armenia* denied[14] her honestie which shee ought to haue kept, and preserued it from the biting canker of disloyall loue.[15] Hadst thou pretended to mocke me, thou shouldst not haue suffred me to haue lost so much as is forgone for thy sake.

Tell me, why didst not thou suffer mee to execute my will, that I might haue opened my white brest with a pearcing swoord, and sent my soule to the shady banke of sweete *Elizium*? Then had it beene better for me to haue died, than to liue still, and dayly die.

Remember thy selfe *Leoger*, and behold the harm that will come heereof: haue thou a care vnto the pawn which thou leftst sealed in my wombe, and let it bee an occasion that thou doost (after all thy violent wronges) retourne to see me sleeping in my tombe, that my childe may not remaine fatherlesse in the power of wilde beastes, whose hearts he fraughted with nothing but with crueltie. Doe not consent that this perfecte loue which I beare thee, should be counted vaine, but rather performe the promise the which thou hast denied me.

---

[13] incessantly] incescessantly *1597*

[14] denied] stained *1616*

[15] loue.] loue? *1597; 1608; 1616*

O vnkinde *Leoger*, O cruell and heard heart, is falshoode[16] the firme loue that so fainedly[17] thou didst professe to me? what is he that hath beene more vnmercifull then thou hast beene? There is no furious beast nor lurking Lion in the deserts of *Libia*, whose vnmercifull pawes are all besmearde in bloud, that is so cruell harted as thy self, els wouldst thou not leaue me comfortles, spending my dayes in solitarie woods, where as the Tigers mourne at my distresses, and chirping birdes in their kindes, grieue at my lamentations: the vnreasonable torments and sorrowes of my soule are so many, that if my penne were made of *Lidian* steele, and my Inke the purple Ocean, yet could not I write the number of my[18] woes.

But nowe I determine to aduertise thee of my desired death, for in writing this my latest testament, the fates are cutting a sunder my thrid of life, and I can giue thee knowledge of no more. But[19] yet I desire thee by the true loue which I beare thee, that thou wilt read with some sorrow these fewe lines: and heere of the powers of heauen, I do desire that thou maist dye the like death that for thee I now dye. And so I ende.

> *By her which did yeeld vnto thee her*
> *life, Loue, Honor, Fame*
> *and Liberty.*

When this sad and heauie knight had made an end of reading this dolorous letter, hee could not restraine his eyes from distilling salte teares, so great was the griefe that his hart sustaned: *Rosana* did likewise beare him company to solemnize his heauines, with as manye teares trickling from the Conduite of her eyes.

The greate sorrowe and lamentation was such and so much in both their hartes, that in a great space the one coulde not speake vnto the other: but afterwardes, their griefes being some what appeased, *Leoger* began to say.

Oh Messenger, from her with the remembrance of whose wronge my soule is wounded, being vndeseruedly of me euill rewarded: tell me (euen by the nature of true loue) if thou dost knowe where she is? showe vnto me her abiding place, that I may goe thither and giue a discharge of this my great fault, by yeilding vnto death.

Oh cruell and without loue (answered *Rosana*) what discharge canst thou giue vnto her, that alreadye (thorow thy crueltie) is dead and buryed? onely by the occasion of such a forsworne knight.

This penitent and payned knight, when he vnderstood the certaintie of her death, with a sodaine and hastie fury he strooke him selfe on the breast with his fist, and lifting his eyes vnto the heauens, in manner of exclamation against the Gods, giuing deepe and sorrowfull sighes, he threwe him selfe to the ground, tumbling and wallowing from the one part vnto the other, without taking any ease, or hauing anye power or strength to declare his inward griefe which at that time he felt, but

---

[16] falshoode] alshoode *1597*
[17] fainedly] faindedly *1597*
[18] my] *om. 1597*
[19] But] but *1597*

with lamentations which did torment his hart, he called continually on the *Armenian* Queene, and in that deuilish furye wherein he was, drew out his dagger and lifting vp the skirt of his shirt of mail, he thrust it into his body, and giuing himself this vnhappy death (with calling vpon his wronged Lady)[20] he finished his life, and fell to the ground.

This sad and heauie Ladie when she beheld him so desperately to gorge his martiall breast, and to fall liuelesse to the earth, she greatly repented her selfe that she had not discouered her name, and reuealed to him how that shee was his vnfortunate Daughter, whose face before that time he neuer had beheld: and as a Lion (though all too late) who seeing before her eyes her yong Lionesse euil intreated of the Hunter, euen so she ran vnto her wel beloued Father, and with great speed pulled off his helme from his wounded head, and vnbraced his armour, the which was in colour according to his passion, but as strong as anie Diamond, made by Magicke arte. Also she tooke away his sheeld, which was of a russet field, and in ye middest thereof was portrayed the God of Loue with two faces, the one was verie faire, and bound about with a cloth his eyes, and the other was made meruailous fierce and furious.

This being done, with a faire linnen cloth shee wyped off the blood from his mortal face. And when she was certaine that it was him after whom she had traueled so manie wearie steps, and that he was without life, with a furious madnes she tore her attyre from her head, and all to rent her golden haire, tearing it in peeces, and then returned again and wyped that infernall face making such sorrowfull lamentation, that whosoeuer had seene her, would haue been mooued to compassion. Then shee tooke his head betwixt her hands, procuring to lift it vp, and to lay it vpon her lap, and seeing for al this that there was no moouing in him, she ioyned her face vnto his pale and dead cheekes, and with sorrowfull words, she said.

Deare Father, open thine eyes, and behold me, open them sweete Father, and looke vppon mee thy sorrowfull Daughter: if fortune be so fauourable, let me receiue some contentment whilest life remaineth. O strengthen thy selfe to looke vpon me, wherein such delight may come to me, that we may either accompany other. Oh my Lord and onely Father, seeing that in former times my vnfortunate Mothers tears were not sufficient to reclaime thee, make me satisfaction for the great trauell which hath been taken in seeking thee oute.[21] Come now in death, and ioye in the sight of thy vnhappie Daughter, and dye not without seeing her: open thine eyes, that she may gratefie thee in dying with thee.

This being said, *Rosana* began again to wipe his face, for that it was again all to be bathed in blood, and with her white hands she felt his eyes and mouth, and all hys face and head: till such time as she touched his breast, and put her hand on the mortall wound where she held it still and looked vpon him whether he mooued or no. But when she felt him without sense or feeling, she began anew to complayne, and crying out with most terrible exclamations, she said.

---

[20] Lady)] Lady, *1597*
[21] oute.] oute *1597*

Oh my haplesse Father, how manie troubles, & great trauells hath thy Daughter passed in seeking thee, watering the earth with her teares, and alwayes in vaine calling for thee? Oh how manie times in naming thy name hath she been answered with an Eccho, which was vnto her great dolour and griefe? and now that Fortune hath brought her where thou art, to reioice her selfe in thy presence, the same Fortune hath conuerted her wishes into greefe and dolor. Oh cruell and vnconstant Queene of Chaunce, hath *Rosana* deserued this, to bee most afflicted when she expected most ioy. Oh *Leoger*, if euer thou wilt open thine eyes now open them, or let the glasses of my eyes be cloased eternally.

Herewith she perceiued his dim eyes to open, and hys senses now a little gathered together: and when hee saw himselfe in her armes, and vnderstood by her words, that she was his Daughter whom hee had by the vnfortunate Queene of *Armenia*, he sodainly stroue against weaknes, and at last recouering some strength, he cast hys yeelding armes about the milke white necke of the faire *Rosana*, and they ioyned their faces the one with the other, distilling betwixt them many salte and bitter teares, in such sort that it would haue moued the wilde beasts vnto compassion: and with a feeble and weake voice, the wounded knight said:

Ah my daughter, vnfortunate by my disloyaltie, let me recreate and comforte my selfe, in enioying this thy mouth the time that I shall remaine aliue and before my sillie soule doth departe the company of my dying bodie: I do confesse that I haue beene pittilesse vnto thy mother and vnkinde to thee, in making thee to trauell with great sorrow in seeking me, and now thou hast found me I must leaue thee alone in this sorrowfull place with my dead body pale and wanne: yet before my death sweet girle giue me a thousand kisses: this onely delighte I craue, for the little time I haue to tarrie, and afterward I desire thee to intombe my body in thy mothers graue though it be far in distance from this vnluckie Country.

O my deere Lord answered she, dost thou request of me to giue thy body a Sepulcher? well I see that it is requisit, to seeke some to giue it vnto vs both, for I knowe my life can not continue longe, if the angry fates depriue me of your liuing companye: and without strength to proceed any further in speaches, she kissed his face with great sobbing and sighes, making within her selfe a terrible conflicte, tarying for the answere of her dying Father, who with no lesse paine and anguish of death, said:

Oh my Childe, how happy should I be, that thus imbracing one in the others armes, we might depart togeather? then should I be ioyfull in thy company, and account my selfe happy in my death: and here vppon I leaue thee vnto the worlde: daughter farwell, the Gods preserue thee and take me to their mercies. And when he had said these wordes, hee enclyned his necke vppon the face of *Rosana* and dyed.

When this sorrowfull Ladye sawe that the soule had got the victorie and departed from the body, she kissed his pale lippes and giuing deepe and dolorous sighes, shee beganne a meruailous and heauy lamentation, calling her selfe vnhappie and vnfortunate, and layde her selfe vpon the dead body, cursing her destinies, so that it was lamentable to heare.

O my deere father sayd she, what small benefite haue I receiued for all my trauell and paine, the which I haue suffered in seeking of thee, and nowe in the finding of thee the more is my griefe, for that I came to see thee dye? Oh most vnhappie that I am, where was my minde when I saw that fatall dagger pearce thy tender brest? whereon was my thought? wherefore did I stand still, and did not with great lightnes make resistance against that terrible blow?

If my strength would not haue serued me, yet at the least I shoulde haue borne thee companie: you furious beastes that are hid in your dens and deepe caues, where are you now? why doe you not come and take pittie vpon my griefe in taking away my life? in doing so you shewe your selues pittifull, for that I doe abhoore this dolorous life, yet she did not forget the promise that shee made him, which was to giue his body burial in her mothers tombe. This was the occasion that she did somewhat cease her lamentation, and taking vnto her selfe more courage then her sorrowfull griefe would consent vnto, she put the dead bodie vnder a mightie pine Apple tree, and couered it with leaues of greene grasse, and like wise hung his armor, vpon the bowes, in hope that the sight thereof would cause some aduenturous knight to approach her presence, that in kindenes would asist her to intombe him: heere we will leaue *Rosana* weeping ouer her fathers body, and speake of the *Nigromancer* after his flight from the black Castle.

How the Magitian found Leogers armour hanging vpon a pinetree, kept by Rosana the Queenes Daughter of Armenia, betwixte whome hapned a terrible battle: also of the desperate death of the Lady: And after how the Magitian framed by magick arte an inchaunted Sepulcher, wherin he inclosed himselfe from the sight of all humane creatures.

I Am sure you doe well remember when the Christian Knights had conquered the black Castle which was kept by inchauntment, how the furious *Nigromancer* to preserue his life fled from the same, caried by his arte through the ayre in an yron Chariot, drawne by two flying Dragons: in which charmed Chariot he crossed ouer many parts and plaines of the easterne[2] climets.

At last being wearie of his iourney, he put himself in the thickest of the forrest, wherin traueling w^t his whirling Dragons, hee neuer rested till hee came vnto a mightie and great riuer, the which seemed to bee an arme of the purple Ocean, there he alighted from his chariot for to refresh himselfe, and tooke water, with his handes, and drunke thereof, and washed his face: and as he found him selfe all alone, there came into his minde many thoughts, amongst all his passed life, and how hee was vanquished by the Christian Knights for which with great anger he gaue terrible sighes and began to curse, not onely the hower of his birth, but the whole world, and the generation of mankinde.

Likewise he remembred the great sorrowe and trauell that euer since hee endured; and what toyle trauelling knights must indure: In these variable cogitations spent he the time away till golden *Phœbus* began to withdraw himself into his accustomed lodging, and hyding his light in the occidentall parts, and therewith drew on the darke and tenebrous night, which was the occasion that his paine did the more increase: al that night he passed away with such sorrowfull lamentations for his late disgraces, that all the woods and mountaines did resounde his wofull exclamations, till that *Apollo* with his glistering beames began to couer the earth.

The which being seene by the Magitian, with a trice he arose vp, and intended to prosecute his iorney, but lifting vp his eyes towards the heauens hee did discouer hanging vpon a high and mightie pine apple tree the armour of *Leoger*.

Which was hung there in remembrance of his death by *Rosana* as you heard in the last Chapter, the armour had almost lost his bright colour and beganne to ruste through the great aboundance of raine that fell thereon.

Yet for all that it seemed of great vallew and of a wonderfull richnesse, so without any farther circumspection or regarde, hee tooke downe the most bright armor, and armed himselfe therewith, and when he lacked no more to put on but the helmet, hee heard a voice that said, bee not so hardy thou knight as to vndoe thys Trophie, except thou prepare thy selfe to winne it by thy sword.

---

[1] XII] *sic 1597*
[2] easterne] earsterne *1597*

The Magitian at this vnexpected noyse, cast his head on the one side, and espied *Rosana* newly awaked from a heauy sleep, most richly armed with a stronge inchaunted armor after the manner of the *Amazonians*, but for al that he did not let to make an ende of arming himselfe, and hauing laced on his Burgonet, hee went towardes the demaunder with his sworde ready drawne in his hand, inuiting her with mortall battell.

Rosana who saw his determination, did procure to defend her selfe, and offend her enemy.

Oh my muse that I had such learned eloquence, for to set out and declare the noble incounters of these two gallant warriors: *Rosana* although shee was but a Feminin nature, yet was she as bolde in heroycall aduentures as any Knight in the world, except the Christian Champions.

But now to returne we to our historie, the valliant *Amazonian* when her enemy came vnto her, she stroke him so terrible a blow vpon the visor of his helmet, that with the fury therof she made sparkles of fire to issue out with great aboundance, and bowe downe his head vnto hys brest.

The *Magitian* did returne vnto her his salutation, and stroake her such a blow vpon her helmet, that with the great noyse thereof, it made a sound in al the mountaines. Now began betweene them a maruelous and fearefull battell, fortune not willing to vse her most extremitie declined the foyle to neither party, nor giuing the conquest as yet to any: all the time of the conflicte, the furious *Magitian* and the valiant *Amazonian* thought on no other thing, but either of them procured to bring his aduersarie to his ouerthrow, striking at each other such terrible blowes, and with so great furie, that manie times it made either of them to loose feeling: and both seeing the great force of one another, were meruailously incensed with anger.

Then the valiant Lady threw her sheeld at her backe, that with more force she might strike and hurt her enemy: and therewithall gaue him so strong a blow vpon the burgonet, that he fell astonied to the earth without anie feeling.

But when the Magitian came againe to himselfe, he returned *Rosana* such a terrible blow, that if it had chanced to alight vpon her, it would haue clouen her head in peeces, but with great discretion she cleared her self therof in such sort, that it was stroken in vaine, and with great lightnes she retyred, and stroke the Magitian so furiously, that she made him once againe to fall to the ground, al astonied, and there appeared at the visor of his helme the abundance of blood that issued out of his mouth: but presently he reuiued, and got vp in a trice, with so great anger, that the smoke which came from his mouth, seemed like a myst before his helme, so that almost it could not be seene.

Then this furious deuill (blaspheming against his Gods) hauing his mortall sword verie fast in his hand, he ran towards his enemie, who (without anie feare of hys furie) went foorth to receaue him: and when they met together, they discharged their blowes at once, but it fortuned, that the Amazonians blow did first fasten with so great strength that for all the helmet of the Magitian, which was wrought of the strongest steele, it was not sufficient to make defence, but with the rigorous force wherwith it was charged, it bended in such sorte that it brake all to peeces: and the Magitians head was so greeuouslye wounded, that streames of blood ran downe his armour, and he was forced for want of strength, to yeeld to the mercie of the valiaunt Ladye, who quickely condesended to his requestes, vppon this condition, that hee woulde be a meane to conuaye her fathers dead body to an Iland nere adioyning to the borders of *Armenia*, and there to intomb it in her mothers graue, as shee promised when that his ayre of life fleeted from his body.

The Magition[3] for safegarde of his life, presently agreed to performe her desires, and protested to accomplish what soeuer she demaunded.

Then presently by his Arte he prepared his yron Chariot with his flying dragons in a readines, wherein they layd the murthered bodye of *Leoger* vppon a pillowe of mystle-toe, and likewise placed themselues therein, wher in they were no sooner entred, with necessaries belonging to their trauelles, but they flewe thorowe the ayre more swifter then a whirl-wind, or a shippe sayling on the seas in a stormye tempest.

The wonders that he performed by the way, be so many and miraculous, that I want an Orators eloquence to discribe them, and a Poets skil to expresse them.

But to bee shorte, when *Rosana* was desirous to eate, and that her hunger increased: by his charmes he would procure birdes (of their owne accordes) to fall out of the skyes, and yeild themselues vnto their pleasures, with all things necessary to suffice their wantes.

Thus was *Rosana* with her fathers dead body, caryed through the ayre by Magicke arte, ouer hilles and dales, mountaines and valleys, wooddes and forrestes, townes and Citties, and through many both wonderfull and strange places and countries.

And at the last, they arriued neere vnto the confines of *Armenia*, beeing the place of their long desired rest: But when they approached neere vnto the Queene of *Armenias* graue,[4] they descended from their inchaunted Chariot, and bore *Leogers* body to his burying place, the which they found (since *Rosanaes* departure) ouergrowne with mosse and wythered brambles: yet for all that they opened the Sepulcher, and layd his bodie (yet freshly bleeding) vpon his Ladies consuming carcasse: which beeing done, the Magitian couered againe the graue with earth, and laid thereon greene turues, which made it seeme as though it neuer had been opened.

All the time that the Magitian was perfourming the ceremonious Funerall, *Rosana* watered the earth wyth her teares, neuer withdrawing her eyes from looking vppon the Graue: and when it was finished, shee fell into this most sorrowfull and distresfull lamentation following.

Oh cruell Destinies (said she) sith your rigours haue bereaued me of both my Parents, & left me to the world a comfortlesse Orphane, receaue the sacrifice of my chastitie, in payment of your vengeaunce: and let my blood here shed vpon this Graue, shewe the singlenesse of my heart. And with the like solemnitie may all their hearts be broken in peeces, that seeke the downfall and dishonor of Ladies.

As she was vttering these and suchlike sorrowes, shee tooke foorth a naked sword, which she had readie for the same effect, and put the pummell to the

---

[3] Magition] Magtion *1597*
[4] graue] groue *1597*

ground, and cast her breast vpon the poynt. The which shee did with such furious violence and such exceeding hast, that the Magitian although he was there present could not succour her, nor preuent her from committing on her selfe so bloodie a fact.

This sodaine mischaunce so amazed him, and so greeued his soule, that his heart (for a time) would not consent that his tung should speake one word to expresse hys passion.

But at last, (hauing taken a truce with sorrowe, and recouering his former speach) he tooke vp the dead bodye of *Rosana*, bathed all in blood, and likewise buried her in her Parents Graue: and ouer the same he hung vp an Epitaph that did declare the occasion of all their deathes.

This being done to expresse the sorrowes of his heart for the desperat death of such a Magnaminious Lady, and the rather to exempt himselfe from the company of all humaine creatures: he erected ouer the graue (by magicke arte) a very stately Tombe, the which was in this order framed. First there was fixed foure pillors, euery one of a very fine Rubie: vpon the which was placed a Sepulcher of Cristall: within the sepulcher there seemed to be two faire Ladyes, the one hauing her breste peirced thorowe with a sword and the other with a Crowne of golde vpon her head and so leane of body that she seemed to pine away: and vpon the sepulcher there lay a knight all along with his face looking vp to the heauens, and armed with a coarselet of fine steele, of a russet enamelling: vnder the sepulcher there was spread abroad a great carpet of gold, and vpon it two pillors of the same, and vpon them lay an olde sheapheard with his sheep-hooke lying at his feete: his eyes were shut, and out of them distilled manye pearled teares: at euery pillor there was a gentlewoman without any remembrance, the one of them seemed to be murthered, and the other rauished.

And neere vnto the sepulcher there lay a terrible great beast, headed like a Lyon: his brest and body like a wolfe, and his tayle like a scorpion, which seemed to spitte continually flames of fire: the sepulcher was compassed about with a wall of yron, with foure gates for to enter in therat: the gates were after the manner and cullour of fine Diamonds, and directly ouer the top of the chiefest gate, stood a marble pillor whereon hung a table written with red letters: the contentes whereof were as followeth.

> *So long shall breath vpon this brittle earth,*
> *The framer of this stately Monument,*
> *Till that three children of a wondrous birth,*
> *Out of the Northerne climate shall be sent.*
> *They shall obscure his name as fates agree:*
> *And by his fall, the fiendes shall tamed bee.*

This Monument being no sooner framed by the assistance of *Plutos* legions, and maintained by their deuillish powers, but the Nigromancer enclosed himselfe in the walles, where he consorted chiefly with furyes and walking spirits, that continually fed vpon his blood, and left their damnable seales sticking vnto his left side, as a sure token and witnes that he had giuen both his soule and body to their gouerments after the date of his mortall life was finished.

In which inchaunted sepulcher we will leaue him for a time conferring with his damnable mates, and returne to the christian knightes, where we left them trauelling towardes *Babylon*, to place the King againe in his Kingdome.

CHAP. XIII.

How the seauen Champions of Christendome restored the Babylonian King vnto the Kingdome: and after how honourably they were receiued at Rome, where Saint George fell in loue with the Emperours Daughter, being a professed Nunne. Of the mischiefe that insued thereby, and of the desperate ende of yong Lucius Prince of Rome.

THe valiant Christian Champions hauing as you heard in the Chapter going before, perfourmed the Aduenture of the inchaunted monument, accompanied the *Babylonian* King home to his kingdom of *Assiria*, as they had all verie solemnly and faithfully promised to him.

But when they approached the Confines of *Babylon*, and made no question of peacefull and princely entertainment, there was neither signe of peace, nor likelihood of ioyfull or frendly welcome: for all the Countrey raged with intestine warre, foure seuerall Competitors vniustly striuing for what to the King properly and of right belonged.

The vnnaturall causers and stirrers vp to thys blood-deuouring controuersie, were the foure Noblemen, vnto whom the King vnaduisedly committed the gouernment of his Realme, when hee went in the tragicall pursute of his faire daughter, after his dreaming illusion that caused him so cruelly to seeke her death. And the breaking out into this hurly burly, grew first to head in this maner following.

Two yeres after the Kings departure, these Deputies gouerned the publike State in great peace, and with prudent policie, til after no tidings of the King could be heard notwithstanding so manie messengers as were in euerie quarter of the world sent to enquire of him: and then did Ambition kindle in all their hearts,[1] each striuing to wrest into his hand the sole possession of the *Babylonian* Kingdome.

To this end did they all make seuerall frends: for this had they contended in manie Fights, and now lastly they intended to set all their hopes vpon this maine chaunce of warre, intending to fight all till three fell, and one remained victor ouer the rest, whose head should bee beautifyed with a crowne.

But of traitors and treason the end is sodaine & shamefull: for no sooner had Saint *George* (placing himselfe betweene the Battells) in a breefe Oration shewed y[e] aduentures of the King, and he himselfe to the people discouered his reuerend face, but they all shouted for ioye, and haled the Usurpers presently to death, and reinstalled in his ancient dignitie, their true, lawfull and long lookt for King.

The King being thus restored married *Fidela* for her faithfulnes: and after the nuptiall Feasts, the Champions (at the earnest request of Saint *Anthonie*) departed towards *Italy*: where in *Rome* the Emperour spared no cost honourably and most sumptuously to entertaine those neuer daunted Knightes, the famous Wonders of Christendome.

---

[1] hearts] hears *1597*

At that time of the yeare when the Summers Queen had beautefied the Earth with interchaungeable ornaments, Saint *George* (in companie of the Emperour) with the rest of the Champions chanced to walke along by the side of the Riuer *Tyber*, and to delight themselues with the pleasurable meades, and beauteous prospect of the Countrey.

Before they had walked halfe a myle from the Cittie, they approached an ancient Nunnerie, which was right faire and of a stately building, and likewise incompassed about with christall streames and greene meddowes, furnished with all manner of beauteous trees, and fragrant flowers.

This Nunnerie was consecrated to *Diana* the Queene of Chastitie, and none were suffered to liue therein, but such chast Ladies and Uirgins, as had vowed themselues to a single life, and to keepe their Uirginities for euer vnspotted.

In this place the Emperours onely Daughter liued a professed Nunne, and exempted her selfe from all companie, except it were the fellowship of chast and Religious Uirgins.

This vertuous *Lucina* (for so was shee called) hauing intelligence before by the ouerseeers of the Nunnerie, how that the Emperour her Father with manie other Knights were comming to visite their religious Habitation, against their approach shee attyred her selfe in a gowne of white satten, all layd ouer with gold lace, also hauing her golden lockes of haire somewhat laid foorth: and vpon her head was knit a garland of sweete smelling flowers, which made her seeme celestiall and of a diuine creation.

Her beautie was so excellent, that it might haue quailed the heart of *Cupide*, and her brauerie exceeded the *Paphian* Queenes. Neuer could *Circe*[2] with al her cunning frame so much beautie in anie creature, as was vpon her face: nor neuer could the flattering Syrens more beguile the trauellers, then did her bright countenaunce inchant the English Champion, for at his first entrance into the Nunnerie, he was so rauished with her sight, that he was not able to withdrawe his eyes from her beauty, but stoode gazing[3] vppon her Rosie culloured cheekes, like one bewitched with *Medusaes* shadowes: but to bee shorte, her beauty seemed so Angellicall, and the burning flames of loue so fiered his heart, that he must either inioy her companye or giue ende to his life by some vntimely meanes.

Saint *George* beeing wounded thus with the darte of loue, dissembled his griefe and not reuealed it to any one, but departed with the Emperor back againe to the Cittie, leauing his heart behind him cloased in the stonye Monastery with his louely *Lucina*.

All that ensuing night he could not enioy the benifit of sleepe, but did contemplate vpon the diuine beautye of his Lady, and fraughted his minde with a thousand seuerall cogitations how hee might attaine to her loue, beeing a chaste virgin and a professed Nun.

In this manner spent hee away the night, and no sooner appeered the mornings brightnesse in at his chamber window, but he arose from his restlesse bed, and attyred him selfe in watchet veluet, to signifie his true loue, and wandred all alone

---

[2] *Circe*] Circes 1597
[3] gazing] zigag 1597

vnto the Monastery wher he reuealed his deepe affection vnto his Ladye, who was as farre from graunting to his requests, as heauen is from earth, or the deepest seas from the highest Elements: for shee protested while life remayned within her bodye, neuer to yeild her loue in the way of mariage to anye one, but to remaine a pure virgin and one of *Dianaes* traine.

No other resolution could Sa. *George* get of the chaste Nun, which caused him to departe in great discontent, intending to seeke by some other meanes to obtaine her loue, so comming to the rest of the Christian Champions, he reuealed to them the truth of all things that had hapned, who in this maner counsailed him, that hee should prouide a multitude of armed Knightes, euery one bearing in their handes a sword ready drawen, and to enter the Monastery at such a time as she little mistrusted, and first with faire promises and flattering speeches, to entice her to loue, then if she yeelded not, to fill her eares with cruell threatnings, protesting that if she will not graunt to requite his loue with like affection, he would not leaue standing one stone of that Monastery vppon an other, and likewise to make her a bloudy offering vppe to *Diana*.

This pollicy liked wel Saint *George*, though he intended not to prosecute such cruelty: so the next morning by break of day he went vnto the nunnery in company of no other but the christian champions armed in bright armour with their glistering swordes ready drawen; the which they caried vnder their side cloakes to preuent suspition.

But when they came to the Monastery, and had entered into the chamber of *Lucina* (whom they found kneeling vpon the bare ground at her ceremonious orasons) Saint George first proffered kindnes by faire promises, and afterward made knowne his vnmercifull pretended cruelty, and therewithall shaking their bright swordes against her vertuous brest, they protested (though contrary to their mindes) that except she[4] would yeeld vnto Saint *George* her vnconquered loue, they would bathe their weapons in her dearest bloud.

At which wordes the distressed Uirgin, being ouercharged with feare, sunke down presently to the ground, and lay for a time in a dead agony, but in the ende, recouering her selfe, she lifted vp her angelicall face, shrowded vnder a cloude of pale sorrow, and in this maner declared her minde.

Most renowned, and well approoued Knights said she, it is as difficult to me, to climbe vppe to the highest toppe of heauen, as to perswade my minde to yeeld to the fulfilling of your requests.

The pure and chast Goddesse *Diana* that sittes nowe crownde amongst the golden starres in heauen, will reuenge my periured promise if I yeeld to your desires, for I haue long since deepely vowed to spende my daies in this religious house, in the honour of her deity,[5] and not to yeelde the flower of my virginity to any one, which vow I will not infringe for all the Maiesty of Roome: you know braue champions, that in time the watery droppes will mollify the hardest Diamond, and time may weede out this deepe roote and impression from my heart.

---

[4] she] he *1597*

[5] deity] diety *1597*

Therfore I request of you by the honour of true knighthood, and by the loues you beare vnto your natiue countreyes, to graunt me the liberty of seauen daies, that I may at full consider with my heart, before I giue an answere to your demaunds, and to the intent that I may make some publike sacrifice as well to appease the wrath which the chast Goddesse *Diana* may conceaue against me, as to satisfie mine owne soule, for not fulfilling my vowe.

These wordes being no sooner ended, but the champions incontinently without any more delay ioyfully consented, and moreouer profered themselues to bee all present at the same sacrifice, and so departed from the Monastery with exceeding great comfort.

The champions being gone, *Lucina* called togither all the rest of the Nuns, and declared to them the whole discourse of her assailment, where after amongst this religious company, with the help of some other of their approued friends, they deuised a most strange sacrifice, which hath since been the occasion that so many inhumaine and bloudy sacrifices hath bin committed.

The next morning after sixe daies were finished, no sooner did bright *Phœbus* shew his golden beames abroad, but the Nunnes began to prepare all thinges in readines for the sacrifice: for directly before the doore of the Monestary, they hyred cunning workmen to erect a scaffold, all very richly couered with cloth of golde, and vpon the scaffold (about the middle therof) was placed a faire table couered also with a Carpet of cloth of golde, and vppon it a chafingdish of coales burning: all this beeing set in good order, the Emperor with the Christian Champions, and many other Roman knights being present to beholde the cerimonious sacrifice, who little mistrusting the dolefull tragedie that after hapned.

The assemblie beeing silent, there was straightwayes heard a sweete and hermonious sound of Clarions and Trumpets and sundrie other kind of Instrumentes: these entred first vppon the scaffolde, and next vnto them were brought seauen Rammes, all adorned with fine white woole, more softe in feeling then *Arabian* silke, with huge and mightie cragged hornes bound about with garlands of flowers: after them followed a certaine number of Nunnes attyred in blacke vestures, singing their accustomed songes in the honor of *Diana*: after them followed an auncient Matrone drawne in a Chariot by foure comly virgins, bringing in her handes the Image of *Diana*: and on either side of her two auncient Nunnes of great estimation, each of them bearing in their handes rich vessels of golde full of most precious and sweete wines: then after all this came the beautifull *Lucina* apparelled with a rich Roabe of estate, beeing of a great and inestimable value.

Thus cerimoniously they ascended the scaffold, where the Matrone placed the Image of *Diana* behinde the chafingdish of coales that was there burning: the rest of the Nunnes continued still singing their songs and drinking of the precious wines that was brought in the golden vessell: this being done, they all at once brought lowe the necks of the Rams by cutting their throates, whose bloods they sprinckled round about the scaffold, and opened their bowelles and burned their inward partes in the chafingdish of coales.

Thus with this slaughter, they made sacrifice[6] vnto the Queene of Chastitie: at the sight whereof was present, the surfetting Louer Saint *George*, with the other sixe Christian Knightes armed all in bright armor, and were all verye attentiue to this that I heere haue tolde you.

The sacrifice ended, this *Lucina* commaunded silence to be made, and when all the company were still she raysed vp her selfe vpon her feete, and with a heauie voyce distilling many salte teares: she said

O most excellent and chaste *Diana*, in whose blessed bosome we vndefiled Uirgins doe recreate our selues: vnto thy deuine excellency doe I now commende this my last sacrifice, crauing record of all the Gods, that I haue done my best to continue a spotles maiden of thy most beautiful traine.

Oh heauens shall I consent to deliuer my Uirginitie willingly to him whose soule desires to haue the vse of it, or shall I my selfe commit my vtter ruine and sorrowfull destruction, the which proceedeth onely by the meanes of my flouring beautie, the which woulde it had beene as blacke as the nightly rauens, or like to the tawny tanned Moores in the furthest mountaines of *India*.

O sacred *Diana*, thou blessed Queene of chastitie, is it possible that thou doest consent that a Uirgin descended from so royall a race as I am, should procure to spotte the worthines of her predecessors, by yeelding her Uirgins honor to the conquest of loue without respecting my beauty, or regarding my chaste vowe I haue made vnto thy deity?[7]

Well seeing it is so that I must needes violate my selfe against all humane nature, I beseech thee to receiue the solempnitie of this my death, which I offer vp in sacrifice to thy deuine excellencie, for I am heere constrained with mine own trembling hand to cut off the flourishing branches of these my dayes: for this I sweare before the Maiestie of heauen, that I had rather offer vp my soule into the societie and sacred bosome of *Diana*, than to yeeld the castle of my chastitie, to the conquest of anie Knight in the world.

And now to thee I speake thou valiant Knight of *England*, behold heere I yeeld vnto thy hands my liuelesse bodie, to vse according to thy will and pleasure, requesting onely this thing at thy hand, that as thou louedst mee lyuing, thou wilt loue me dead, and like a mercifull Champion suffer me to receaue a princely Funerall.

And last of all, to thee diuine *Diana* doo I speake, accept of this my bleeding soule, that with so much blood is offered vnto thee.

So in finishing this sorrowfull speach she drew out a faire and bright shining sword, which shee had hidden secretly vnder her gowne, and setting the hylt agaynst the Scaffold (little looked for of her Father and those y[t] were present) shee sodainly threw her selfe vppon the poynt of that Sword, in such a furious manner, that it ryued her bloodie heart in sunder, and so rendred her soule to the tuition of her, vnto whom she offered her bloodie and ruthfull sacrifice.

What shall I heere declare the lamentable sorrowes and pittifull lamentation that was there made by her father and other Roman Knights that were present at this

---

[6] sacrifice] sacifice *1597*
[7] deity] diety *1597*

vnhappie mischance? so great it was, that the walles of the Monasterie ecchoed, and their pittifull shrikes ascended to the heauens.

But none was more greeued in mind than the afflicted English Champion, who (like a man distraught of sense) in great furie rushed amongst the people, throwing them downe on euerie side, till he ascended vpon the scaffold: & approaching the dead bodie of *Lucina*, hee tooke her vp in his armes, and with a sorrowfull and passionate voyce he said. O my beloued ioy, and late my only hearts delight, is this the Sacrifice wherein (through thy desperatenes) thou hast deceiued me, who loued thee more than my selfe? is this the respite that thou requiredst for seauen dayes, wherein thou hast concluded thy own death and my vtter confusion?

Oh noble *Lucina*, and my beloued Ladie, if this were thy intent, why didst not thou first sacrifice mee thy Seruant and Loue, wholly subiected vnto thy deuine beautie? Woe be vnto mee, and woe bee vnto my vnhappie enterprise: for by it is she lost, who was made souereigne Ladie of my heart.

Oh *Diana*, accursed by this chaunce, because thou hast consented to so bloodie a tragedie, by the eternall powers of heauen, that neuer more thou shalt be worshipped, but in euerie Countrey where the English Champion commeth, *Lucina* in thy stead shall be adored. For euermore will he seek to diminish thy name, and blot it from the golroll of heauen, yea and vtterly extinguish it in eternitie: so that there shall neuer more memorie remaine of thee, for this thy bloodie Tyrannie, in suffering so lamentable a Sacrifice.

No sooner had he deliuered these speaches, but incensed with furie he drew out his sword, and parted the image of *Diana* in two peeces, protesting to ruinate the Monasterie, within whose walls the deuice of this bloodie Sacrifice was concluded.

The sorrow and extreame greefe of the Romane Emperour so exceeded for the murther of his Daughter, that he fell to the earth in a senselesse swound, and was carried halfe dead with greefe by some of his knights home to his Pallace, where he remained speechles by the space of thirtie dayes.

The Emperour had a Sonne, as valiant in armes as anie borne *Italian* except Saint *Anthonie*. This young Prince whose name was *Lucius*, seeing his sisters timeles death and by what meanes it was committed, he presently intended with a traine of a hundred armed Knightes, which continually attended vpon his person, to assaile the discontented[8] Champions, and by force of armes to reuenge his sisters death.

This resolution so incouraged the Romaine Knyghtes, but especially the Emperors sonne, that betwixt these two companies began as terrible a battle as euer was fought by any knights, the fearcenes of their blowes so exceeded the one side against the other, that they did resounde ecchoes, and they yeelded a terrible noyse in the great woods.

This battell did continue betwixt them both sharp and fierce for the space of two houres, by which time the valor of the encensed Champions so preuailed, that most of the Romaine knights were discomfited and slaine, some had their handes pared from their shoulders, some had their armes and legs lopped off, and some lay

---

[8] discontented] discontended *1597*

breathles weltring in their owne blouds, in which incounter many a Romaine Ladie lost her husband, many a widowe was bereaud of her Sonne, and many a childe was left fatherles to the great sorrow of the whole country.

But when the valiant young Prince of *Roome* sawe his knightes discomfited, and hee lefte alone to withstand so many noble Champions, he presently set spurs to his horse, and fled from them like to a heape of dust forced by a whirlewinde.

After whom the Champions would not persue, accountting it no glory to their names to triumph in the ouerthrow of a single knight, but remained still by the scaffolde, where they buried the sacrificed Uirgin, vnder a marble stone close by the monasterie wall. The which being done to their contentments, Saint *George* ingraued this Epitaph vppon the same stone with the point of his dagger, which was in this wise following.

> *Vnder this marble stone interd doth lye*
> *Luckles Lucina, of beautie bright:*
> *Who to maintaine her spotles chastitie*
> *Against the assailment of an English Knight,*
> *Vpon a blade her tender breast she cast:*
> *A bloodie offering to Diana chast.*

So when hee had written this Epitaph, the Christian Champions mounted vpon their swift foote steedes, & bad adieu to the vnhappie Confines of *Italy*, hoping to finde better fortune in other Countries. In which trauell wee will leaue them for a time, and speake of the Prince of *Rome*: who after the discomfiture of the Romane knights, fled in such hast from the furies of the warlike Champions. After which, hee like a starued Lion trauersed along by the Riuer of *Tybris*, filling all places with his melancholy passions, vntill such time as hee entred into a thicke groue, wherein he purposed to rest hys wearie limbes, and lament his misfortunes. After he had in this solitarie place vnlaced his Helmet, and hurled it scornfully against the ground, the infernal Furies began to visite him, and to sting his breast with motions of fierie reuenge. In the end he cast vp his wretched eyes vnto heauen, and said. Oh you fatall torches of the elements, why are you not clad in mournefull abiliments, to cloake my wandring steps in eternall darknes? shall I be made a scorne in *Rome* for my cowardise? or shall I return and accompanie my *Romane* frends in death? whose bloodes me thinkes I see sprinkled about the fields of *Italy*. Mee thinks I heare their bleeding soules fill each corner of the earth with my base flight: therefore will I not liue to bee tearmed a fearfull coward, but dye couragiously by mine owne hands, wherby those accursed Champions shall not obtaine the conquest of my death, nor triumph in my fall. This being said, he drew out his dagger, and ryued hys heart in sunder. The newes of whose desperate death, after it was bruted to his Fathers eares, hee interred hys bodie with his Sister *Lucinaes*, and erected ouer them a stately Chappell, wherein the Nunnes and ceremonious Monkes during all their liues sung Dirges for his Childrens soules.

After this the Emperour made proclamation through all his Dominions, that if anie Knight were so hardie as trauell in pursute after the English Champion, & by force of armes bring him backe, and deliuer his head vnto the Emperour, he should not onely be held in great estimation through the Land, but receaue the gouernment of the Empire after his decease. Which rich proffer so encouraged the mindes of diuers aduenterous Knightes, that they went from sundry Prouinces in the pursute of Saint *George*, but their attempts were all in vaine.

CHAP. XIIII.

Of the triumphs, tilts and turnaments that were solemnly held in Constantinople by the Grecian Emperour, and of the honorable aduentures that wer there atchiued by the christian champions, with other strange accidents that happened.

IN the Easterne Parts of the world the fame and valiant deedes of the Champions of Christendome was noysed, with their honourable victories, heroycall actes, and feates of armes, naming them the myrrours of nobilitie, and the types of bright honour. All Kings & Princes (to whose eares the report of their valors was bruted) desired much to behold their noble personages. But when the Emperour of *Grecia* (keeping then his Court in the Cittie of *Constantinople*) heard of their mightie and valiant deedes, he thirsted after their sights, and his minde could neuer bee satisfied with content, vntill such time as he had deuised a meane to trayne them vnto his Court, not onely in that he might enioy the benefit of their companies, but to haue his Court honoured with the presence of such renowmed Knights: & therfore in this manner it was accomplished.

The Emperour dispatched Messengers into dyuers parts of the world, giuing them in charge to publish thorough out euery Countrey and Prouince as they went, of an honourable Turnament that should bee holden in the Cittie of *Constantinople* within six months following: thereby to accomplish his intent, and to bring the Christian Champions (whose companie hee so desired) vnto hys Court.

This charge of the Grecian Emperor (as he commanded) was speedely perfourmed, with such diligence, that in a short time it came to the eares of yᵉ Christian knights, as they trauelled betwixt the Prouinces of *Asia* and *Africa*. Who at the time appointed came in great pompe and maiestie to *Constantinople*, to furnish foorth the honorable Triumphs.

At the fame whereof likewise resorted thether a great number of Knights of great valour and strength: among whom was the Prince of *Argier*, with a goodly companie of noble persons: and the prince of *Fesse*, with many well proportioned Knights. Likewise came thether the King of *Arabia* in great state, and with no lesse maiestie came the King of *Silicia* and a Brother of his, who were both Giants. Manie other braue and valiant Knights (whose names I heere omit) came thether to honour the Grecian Emperour: for that he was verie well esteemed of them all. And as they came to honor the triumphs, so likewise they came to prooue their fortitudes, and to get fame and name, & the praise that belongeth to aduentrous knights. It was supposed of all the companie, that the King of *Silicia* wold gaine by his prowesse the dignity from the rest, for that he was a Giant of verie big members, although his Brother were taken to be the more furious Knight: who determined not to iust, for that his Brother should get the honour and praise from all Knightes that came. But it fell out otherwise, as heereafter you shall vnderstand.

So when the day of turniment was come, all the Ladies and damsels put themselues in places to beholde the iusting, [1] and attired themselues in the greatest

---

[1] iusting] iesting *1597*

brauerie[2] that they could deuise, and the great court full of people[3] which came thither for to see the triumphant tourniment.

What should I say heere of the Emperours Daughter, the faire *Alcida*, who was of so great beauty that she seemed more liker a deuine substance then an earthly creature and sate glistering in her rich ornaments amongest the other Ladies like vnto *Phœbe* in the Christall firmament, and was noted of all beholders to be the fairest Princes that euer mortall eye beheld: so when the Emperour was seated vppon his imperiall throane vnder a tent of greene veluet, the Knights began to enter into the listes, and hee which was the first that entred was the King of Arabia, mounted vpon a very faire and well adorned courser, he was armed with blacke armour, all to be spotted full of siluer knobs, and brought with him fifty Knightes all apparelled with the same liuery, and thus with great Maiesty he rode rounde about the place, making great obedience vnto all the Ladies and damsels.

After him entred a Pagan Knight, who was Lorde of Siria, and armed with armour of a Lyons collour, accompanied with a hundred Knights all apparelled in veluet of the same colour, and passed rounde about the place, shewing vnto the Ladies great friendship and courtesie as the other did.

Which being done, he beheld the King of Arabia, tarrying to receaue him at the Iust: and the trumpets began to sound, giuing them to vnderstand that they must prepare themselues ready to the incounter: whereat these Knights were nothing vnwilling but spurred their coursers with great fury and closed together with couragious vallure.

The king of Arabia most strongly made his encounter, and stroke the Pagan without missing vpon the brest: but the Pagan at the next race, being heate with furie stroke him so surely with his launce, in such sort that he heaued him out of his saddle, and he fell presently to the ground, after which the Pagan Knight rode vp & downe with great pride and gladnes.

The Arabian king being thus ouerthrowne, there entered into the listes the king of Argier armed with no other furniture but with siluer male and a brestplate of bright steele before his brest, his pompe and pride exceeded all the knightes that were then present, but yet to small purpose his pride and arrogancy serued, for at the first encounter hee was ouerthrowne to the ground: in like sort did this Pagan vse fifteene other knightes of fifteene seuerall prouinces, to the great wonder and amazement of the Emperour and all the assembly.

During all these valiant encounters Saint *George* with the other christian champions stood a farre off vpon a high gallery beholding them, intending not as yet to be seene in the tilte.

But now this valiant Pagan after he had rode some sixe courses vp and downe the place, and seeing none entring the tilt yarde, he thought to beare[4] all the fame and honour away for that day.

But at that same instance there entred the noble minded Prince of Fesse, being for courage the only pride of his countrey hee was a merueilous well proportioned

---

[2] brauerie] brauere *1597*
[3] people] peoply *1597*
[4] beare] heare *1597*

knight and was armed all in white armour, wrought with excellent knottes of golde, and hee brought in his company a hundred Knightes, all attired in white satten, and riding about the place he shewed his obedience vnto the Emperour and to all the Ladies, and[5] thereupon the trumpets began to sound.

At the noyse whereof, the two Knightes spurred their coursers and made their incounter so strong and with such great furie that the proude Pagan was cast to the grounde and so departed the listes with greate dishonour.

Straight way entered the braue King of *Silicia*, who was armed in a glistering corslet of very fine steele, and was mounted vpon a mighty and rich courser, & brought in his company, two hundred knightes, all apparelled with rich cloth of gold, hauing euery one a seuerall instrument of musicke in their hands, sounding thereon most heauenly melody.

And after the *Silician* king had made his accustomed compasse and courtesie in that place, hee locked downe his beuor and put himselfe in readinesse to iust.

So when the signe was giuen by the chiefe harrolde at armes, they spurred their horses and made their encounters so valiant, that at the first race they made their launces shiuer in the aire and the pieces thereof to scatter abroade, like aspen leaues in a whirlewinde.

At the second course the young Prince of Fesse was caried ouer his horse buttockes,[6] and the saddle with him betwixt his legs, which was a great griefe vnto the Emperour, and all the company that did see him, for that he was wel beloued of them al, and held for a knight of great estimation.

The *Silician* king grewe proude at the Prince of Fesses ouerthrow, and was so incouraged and so furious that in a small time he left not a knight remaining on horsebacke in their saddles that durste attempt to iust with him, but euerie one of what Countrey and Nation soere auoyded the attempt: so that there was no question among eyther Nobles or the multitude but that vnto hym the vndoubted honour of the victory in triumph would bee attributed.

And being in this arrogant pride, hee heard a great noise in the maner of a tumult drawing neere, which was the occasion that he stoode still, and to expect some strange accident, and looking about what it should bee, he beheld Saint George entering the listes, who was armed with his rich and strong armour, all of purple, full of golden starres, and before him roade the champions of France, Italy, Spaine and Scotland, al on stately coursers, bearing in their handes foure silken streamers of foure seuerall colours.

And the champion of Wales followed him carrying his shield whereon was portraied a golden Lyon in a sable field, and the champion of Ireland likewise carried his speare being of knotty ash strongly bound about with plates of steele, all which shewed the highnesse of his discent, in that so many braue Knightes attended vppon him.

So when Saint *George* had passed by the royall seate whereon the Emperour sate, inuested in whose company was many knights of great authority, he rode along by the other side, whereas *Alcida* the Emperours faire Daughter sate amongst

---

[5] and] end *1597*
[6] buttockes] buttockea *1597*

many gallant Ladies and faire damsels richly apparelled with vestures of gold, to whom he valed his bonnet shewing them the courtesie of a knight and so passed by *Alcida*, who[7] at the sight of this noble champion could not refraine her selfe, but that with a high and bold voice she said vnto the Emperour.

Most mighty Emperour and my royall father (saide she) this is the Knight in whose power and strength, all christendome doth put their fortunes, and this is he whom the whole world admires for chiualrie.

Saint *George*, although[8] he heard very well what the louely Princesse had said, passed on, and dissembled as though he had heard nothing, and so when he came before the face of his curious aduersary, hee tooke his shield and his speare and prepared himselfe in readinesse to iust, and so being both prouided, the trumpets beganne to sounde, whereat with great fury, these two warlike knights met togither, and neither of them missed their blowes at their encounter: but yet by reason that Saint *George* had a desire to extoll his fame, and to make his name resounde thorough the worlde, hee stroke the giant such a mighty blowe vpon his brest, that he presently ouerthrewe him to the ground, and so with great state and maiesty he passed along without any shew of disdaine, whereat the people gaue a great shoute that it resounded like an eccho in the ayre: and in this maner said.

The great and mighty boaster is ouerthrown, and his furious strength hath little auailed him. After this many Princes[9] proued their aduentures against this English champion, and euery knight that were of any estimation iusted with him.

But with great ease he ouercame them al in lesse then the space of two houres: so at such time as bright *Phœbus* began to make an end of his long iourney, and the day to draw to an ende, there appeared to enter into the listes the braue and mighty giant, being brother to the *Scilician* king with a mighty great speare in his hande, whose glimmering point of steele glistered through al the court, he brought with him but onely one squire, attired in siluer male bringing in his hand another launce.

So this furious giant without any care of curtesie due vnto the Emperour or any of his knights there present entered the place, the which being done, the squire that brought his other speare, went vnto the English champion and saide. Sir Knight (quoth he) yonder braue and valiant giant, my Lord and Maister doth send vnto thee this warlike speare, and there withall he willeth thee to defend thy self to the vttermost of thy power & strength, for he hath vowed before sun set, to be either Lord of thy fortunes or a vassell to thy prowesse and likewise saith that he doth not only defie thee in the turniment, but also challenge thee to mortall battaile.

This brauing message caused Saint *George* to smile, and bred in his brest a new desire of honour, and so returned him this answere, friend go thy waies and tell the giant that sent thee, that I doe accept his demaunde, although it doth grieue my very soule to heare his arrogant defiance to the great disturbance of this royall company, and in the presence of so mighty an Emperour, but seeing his stomacke is gorged with so much pride, tell him that *George* of England is ready to make his defence, and also that shortly he shall repent him by my pledge of Knighthood.

---

[7] who] *om. 1597*

[8] *George*, although] *George* although, *1597*

[9] Princes] Princesse *1597*

In saying these words he tooke the speare from the squire, and deliuered him his gauntlet from his hand to carry to his master, and so put himselfe to the standing, awaighting for the encounter.

At that time he was very nie the place where the Emperour sate, who heard the answere which the English knight made vnto the squire, and was much displeased that the giant in such sort should defie S. *George* without any occasion.

But it was no time as then to speake but to keepe silence, and to pray vnto his Gods to take away his great pride and arrogancie.

All this time the two warriours (mounted vpon their steedes) tarried the signe to bee made by the trumpets, which being giuen, they set forward their coursers, with their speares in their restes, with so great fury and desire the one to vnhorse the other, that they both fayled in their encounter.

The giant who was very strong and proude, when he sawe that he had missed his intent, he returned against Saint *George*, carrying his speare vppon his shoulder, and comming nie vnto him, vpon a sodaine before he could cleare himselfe, he stroke him such a mighty blowe vpon his corslet, that his staffe broke in pieces, by reason of the finenesse of his armour, and made[10] the English Knight to double his body backewardes vppon his horse crupper.

But when he sawe the great villany that the giant vsed against him, his anger increased very much and so taking his speare in the same sort, he went towards the giant and saide.

Thou furious and proude beast, thou scorne of nature and enemy of true knighthood, thinkest thou for to entrap me trecherously, and to gore me at vnawares like to a sauage boare: Now as I am a christian knight, if my knotty speare haue good successe I will reuenge me of thy cruelty.

And in saying this, hee stroke him so furiously on the brest, that his speare passed through the giants body, and appeared foorth at his backe, whereby hee fell presently downe dead to the ground, and yeelded his life to the conquest of the fatall sisters.

All that were present were very much amazed thereat, and wondred greatly at the strength and force of saint *George*, accompting him the fortunatest knight that euer weelded launce, and the very patterne of true nobility.

At this time the golden sun had finished his course, hauing nothing aboue the orizon but his glistering beames, whereby the Iudges of the turniments, commanded with sound of trumpets that the Iustes should cease, and make an end of the day.

So the Emperour descended from his imperial throne into the tilting place, with all his knightes and Gentlemen at armes, for to receaue the noble champion of England, and desired him that he would go with them into his pallace, there to receaue al honors due vnto a knight of such desart: to the which he could not make any denial, but most vnwillingly consented, after this the Emperors daughter (in company of many courtly virgins) likewise descended their places, wher Alcida

---

[10] made] mado *1597*

bestowed vpon saint George hir gloue, the which he wore for her fauour many a day after in his burgonet.

The six other christian champions, although they merited no honour by this turniment, because they did not try their aduentures therein, yet obtained they such good liking among the Grecian Ladies, that euery one had his mistresse, and in their presence they long time fixed their chiefe delightes: nowe must we leaue the champions in the Emperours courte for a time surfeiting in pleasures and returne to Saint Georges sons traueiling the world, to seeke out aduentures.

CHAP. XV.

How a Knight with two heads tormented a beautifull Maiden, that had betroathed her selfe to the Emperors Sonne of Constantinople: and how she was rescued by Saint Georges Sonnes, and after how they were brought by a strange Aduenture into the companie of the Christian Champions, with other things that hapned in the same trauells.

THis renowmed Emperour (within whose Court ye Christian champions made their aboades) of late yeares had a Sonne named *Pollemus*, in all vertues and knightlye demeanours, equall with anie liuing. This young prince in the spring time of his youth, through the pearcing dartes of blinde *Cupide*, fell in loue with a Maiden of a meane parentage but in beautie and other precious gifts of Nature most excellent.

This *Dulcippa* (for so was she called) being but daughter to a Countrey Gentleman, was restrained from the Emperours Court, and denied the sight of her beloued *Pollemus*, and he forbidden to set his affection so low, vpon the displeasure of the Emperour his Father: for he being the Sonne of so mightie a Potentate, and she the daughter of so meane a Gentleman, was thought to be a match vnfit and disagreeable to the lawes of the Countrey: and therefore they could not be suffered to manifest their loues as they would, but were constrained by stealth to enioye each others most beloued and heartely desired companies.

So vpon a time these two Louers concluded to meete together in a vally betwixt two hills, in distance from the Emperours Court some three miles, wheras they might in secret (deuoyd of all suspition) vnite and tye both theyr hearts in one knot of true loue, and to preuent the determination of their Parentes, that so vnkindlye sought to crosse them.

But when the appoynted day drew on, *Dulcippa* arose from her restlesse bed, and attired her self in rich and costly apparell, as though she had been going to performe her nuptiall ceremonies.

In this manner entred she the Ualley, at such time as the Sunne began to appeare out of his golden Horizon, & to shewe himselfe vppon the face of the Earth, glistering with his bright beames vppon the siluer floating Riuers. Like wise the calmie westerne windes did verie sweetely blow vpon the greene leaues, and made a delicate harmonie: at such time as the fairest *Dulcippa* (accompanyed with high thoughts) approched the place of their appointed meeting.

But when shee found not Prince *Pollimus* present, she determined to spend ye time away till he came in trimming of her golden haire, and decking her delicate bodie, and such like delightful plesures for her contentment and recreation.

So sitting downe vpon a greene banke vnder the shaddow of a myrtle tree, she pulled a golden cawle from her head, wherein her haire was wrapped, letting it fall and disperse it selfe all abroad her backe, and taking out from her christalline breast an yuorie comb, she began to kemb her haire, her hands and fingers seeming to be of white alablaster, her face staining the beautie of roses and lyllies mixed together, and the rest of her bodie comparable to *Hyrens*, vpon whose loue and beautie *Mahomet* did sometime doate.

But now marke (gentle Reader) how frowning Fortune crossed her desires,[1] and changed her wished ioyes into vnexpected sorrowes. For as she sate in this deuine and angelicall likenes, there fortuned to come wandring by an inhumane tyrant, surnamed the Knight with 2. heads, who was a rauisher of virgins, an oppressor of infants, & an vtter enemie to vertuous Ladies, and strange trauelling Knights.

This tyrant was bodied like vnto a man, but couered all ouer with lockes of haire. Hee had two heads, two mouthes, and foure eyes, but all as red as blood. Which deformed creature presently ranne vnto the Uirgin, and caught her vp vnder his arme, and carried her away ouer the mountains into another Countrey, where hee intended to torment her, as you shall heare more at large hereafter.

But now returne we to Prince *Pollemus*, who at the time appointed likewise repaired to meete his betroathed Louer: but comming to the place, he found nothing but a silken scarffe, the which *Dulcippa* had let fall through the fearfull frighting she tooke at the sight of the three headed Knight.

No sooner found he the scarffe, but he was oppressed extreamly with sorrow, fearing *Dulcippa* was murthered by some inhumane meanes, and had left her scarffe as a token that she infringed not her promise, but perfourmed it to the losse of her owne life. Therefore taking it vp, & putting it next his heart, he breathd foorth this wofull lamentation.

Heere rest thou neere vnto my bleeding heart, thou precious token and remembraunce of my deerest Ladie, neuer to bee hence remooued, till such time as my eyes maye either behold her bodie, or my eares heare perfect newes of her vntimely death, that I may in death consort wyth her.

Frowne you accursed Lampes of heauen, that gaue first light vnto this fatall morning: for by your dismall light the pride of earthly women is dishonoured. Come, come, you wrathfull planets, descend the lucklesse Horizon, and rayne vpon my head eternal vengeance, oppresse my bodie with continuall miserie, as once you did the wofull King of *Thebes*: for by my slouthfull negligence and ouer-long tariance, this bloodie tragedie hath beene committed.

Yet for her sake I vowe to trauell through the world, as farre as euer golden *Phœbus* lendes his light, filling each corner of the earth with clamours of her name, and making the Elements resound with Ecchoes of my lamentations.

In this resolution returned he home to the Emperour his Fathers pallace, dissembling his greefe in such manner, that none did suspect his discontented sorowes, nor the strange accident that vnto beauteous *Dulcippa* had happened.

So vpon a day as he was imagining with himselfe, seeing the small comfort that he tooke in the Court, considering the want of her presence whom so much hee desired, he determined in great secret as soone as it was possible to depart the Court.

This determination he straight wayes put in practise, and tooke out of the Emperours Armourie verie secretly an exceeding good corslet, the which was all

---

[1] desires] desiros *1597*

russet, and enameled with blacke, and embrothered round about with a gilded edge verie curiously and artificially grauen and carued.

Also he tooke a sheelde of the same making, sauing that it was not grauen as the armour was, and commaunded a young Gentleman, that was Sonne vnto an ancient Knight of *Constantinople*, of a good disposition and hardy that he should keepe them safely, and gaue him to vnderstand of his determined pretence.

Although it did greeue this young man verie much, yet for all that seeing the great freendship which hee vsed towardes him, in vttring his secret vnto him before any other, without replying to the contrarie, hee verie diligently tooke the armour, and hidde it, till hee founde a conuenient time to put it into a Shippe verie secretly.

So likewise he put into the same Ship two of the best horses which the Emperour had, and foorthwith he gaue the Prince vnderstanding, that all thinges were then in a readines, and in good order. *Pollimus* dessembling with the accustomed heauines hee vsed, withdrewe himselfe into his Chamber, till such time as the darke night came.

Which when it was come he made himselfe readie with his apparell, and when all the people of the Court were at their rest, and in their deade sleepes, hee alone with his page, who was named *Mercutio*, departed ye pallace and went to the Sea side. His page did call the Marriners of the Ship, who straight way brought vnto them their boate, into the which they entred and went straight aboord.

And being therein for that the winde was verie faire, he commaunded to waigh their Anckers and to hoyse vp Sailes, and to commit themselues to the mercy of the waters: as he commaunded all was done, and so in short time, they founde themselues ingulfed in the mayne Ocean, far from the sight of any land.

But when the Emperour his Father vnderstood of his secret departure, the lamentation which hee made was verie much: and he commaunded his knights to goe vnto the sea side, to know if there were anie ship that departed that night. And when it was told them that there was a Barke that hayled anchor and hoysed sayle, they vnderstood straight way that the prince was gone awaye in her.

I cannot heere declare the great griefe and sorrowe which the Emperour felt in his wofull heart for the absence of his Sonne, which a long time he alwayes suspected and feared.

But when the departure of *Pollemus* was bruted thorough all *Constantinople*, all sports and feasts ceased, and all the vassalls of the Country were ouercome with a generall sorrow.

So *Pollemus* sayled through the deepe seas three dayes and three nightes with a verie fayre and prosperous forewinde.

The fourth day in the euening, beeing calme, and no Winde at all, the Marriners went to take their restes, some on the poope, and some in the foreship, for to ease their wearied bodies:

The prince (who sate vpon the poope of the ship) asked his page for his Lute, the which straight way was giuen him: and when he had it in his hands, he playde and sung so sweetely, that it seemed to be a most heauenly melodie, and being in this sweete musicke, he heard a verye lamentable crye, as it were of a Woman: and leauing his delicate musicke hee gaue a listening and attentiue eare to hearken, what this sorrowfull creature sayd, and by reason of the stilnes of the night, he might easely heare the voyce vtter these words.

It will little profite thee thou cruell tyrant, this thy bold hardinesse: for that I am beloued of so worthie a Knight, as will vndoubtedly reuenge this thy tirannous crueltie profered mee.

Then he heard another voyce which seemed to answere.

Now I haue thee in my power, there is no humane creature of power able enough to deliuer or redeeme thee from the tormentes, that (in my determination) I haue purposed thou shalt indure.

Pollemus could heare no more, by reason that the Bark wherein they were passed by so swiftly: but hee supposed that it was his Ladies voyce which he heard, and that she was carried by force away. So (laying downe his Lute) he began to fall into a great thought, and was verie heauie and sorrowfull, in that he knew not how to aduenture for her recouerie.

Beeing in this cogitation, hee retourned to hys page which was asleepe, and strake him with his foote, and awaked him, saying: What didst not thou heare the great lamentation which my Ladie *Dulcippa* made (as to mee it seemed) beeing in a small Barke that is passed by, and gone forwards along the seas. To the which his page *Mercutio* aunswered nothing, for that hee was still in a sound sleepe.

To[2] whome the Prince called againe, saying: arise I say, bring foorth mine armour, call vp the Marriners that they may launch their boate into the Sea, for by the omnipotent *Iupiter* I sweare that I will not bee called the Sonne of my Father, if I doe suffer such violence to bee done against my loue, and not to procure with all my strength to reuenge the same, *Mercutio* woulde haue replyed vnto him, but the furious countenance of the Prince would not giue him leaue, no, not once to looke vpon his face: so hee broughte foorth his armour and buckled it on.

In the meane time the Marriners had launched their boate into the Sea, wherein he leaped with a hastie fury, and caried with him his page, and foure of the Marriners for to towe the Barke, and he commaunded them to take their way towards the other companie that passed by them.

So they labored all the night till such time as bright *Phœbus* with his glistering beames gaue vnto them such light that they might discouer and see the other Barke, although somewhat a farre off.

So laboured they in great courage, till two partes of the day was spent, at which time they sawe come after them a Gallie which was gouerned with eyght oares vpon a side, and it made so great way, that with a trice they were with them, and hee saw that there were in her three Knightes in bright armour, to whome *Pollimus* called with a loude voyce saying. Moste curteous Knightes I request you to take me into your Gallie, that being in her I may the better accomplishe my desire.

---

[2] To] to *1597*

The Knightes of the Gallie passed by the Prince without making returne of any aunsweare, but rather shewed that they made but little accompt of him.

These three knightes were the sonnes of the English champion which departed from their father in his iourny towards Babylon, to set the King againe in his kingdome.

But now to follow our history, the Prince of Constantinople seeing the little account they made of him, with the great anger and fury that he receaued, he tooke an ore in one hand, and an other in the other hand, and with such strength he stroke the water, that he made the slothfull barke to flie, and laboured so much with his oares, that with a trice they were equall with the gally.

So leauing the oares with a light leape he put himselfe in the gally with his helme on, and his shield at his shoulder, and being within he said.

Now shall you doe that by force, which before I vsing great courtesie you would not yeeld vnto.

This being said, one of Saint *Georges* sonnes tooke the incounter in hand, thinking it a blemish to the honor of knighthoode by multitudes to assaile him, so the two braue knightes without any aduantage the one of the other made their encounters so valiantly that it was a wonder to all the beholders.

The Prince of Constantinople stroake the Englishe Knight such a furious blow that he made him to decline his head to his brest, and forced him to recoile backwards two or three steppes, but he came quickly againe to himselfe and returned him so mighty a blow vpon his helme, that he made all his teeth to chatter in his head, which was pittifull to see.

Then beganne betwixt them a merueilous and well foughten battle that al that beheld them greatly admired: with great pollicy and strength, they indured the bickering all that day, and when they saw the darke and tenebrous night came vpon them, they did procure with more courage and strength for to finish their battle.

The Prince of Constantinople, puffing and blowing like a bull[3] lifted[4] vp his sword with both his handes and discharged it so strongly vpon his enemy that perforce hee made him to fall to the ground and therewithal offered to pull his helmet from his head.

But when the English Knight sawe himselfe in that sort, he threwe his shielde from him, and very strongly caught the other about the necke and held him fast, so that betwixt them beganne a mighty and terrible wrestling tumbling and wallowing vp and downe the gally breaking their plankes and oares that it was straunge to beholde.

At this time the night began to be very darke, whereby they called for lightes, which presently were brought them by the Marriners, in the meane time these knights did somewhat breath themselues, although it was not much.

So when the Lightes were brought, they returned to their late contention with new force and strength.

---

[3] bull] bell *1597*
[4] lifted] lifting *1597*

O heauens said *Pollimus*, I cannot beleeue to the contrary but that this is *Mars* the God of war that doth contend in battle with me, and for the great enuy he beares against me, he goeth about to dishonour me.

And with these wordes they thickned their blows with great desperatenesse.

And althogh this last assault continued more then two houres, yet neither of them did faint, but at the last they both together lift vp their swoordes, and charged them together the one vpon ye others helm with so great strength that both of them fell downe vppon the hatches without any remembrance.

The rest that did looke vpon them, did beleeue verily that they were both dead, by reason of the aboundance of bloud which came foorth at their visors, but quickly it was perceaued that there was some hope of life in them.

Then presently there was an agreement made betwixt the Knightes of the gally and the Marriners of the barke that they should conioyne together and to trauell whither fortune would conduct them in this order as you haue heard carried they these two Knightes without any remembrance.

But when the Prince of *Constantinople* came to himselfe with a loude voice he said, Oh God is it possible to be true that I am ouercome in this first encounter & assault of my knighthood.

Here I curse the day of my creation and the houre when first I merited the name of a knight, hence forth Ile bury all my honours with disgrace, and spend the remnant of my life in base cowardice, and in speaking these wordes he cast his eie aside and beheld the English knight as one newly risen from a trance, who likewise breathed foorth these discontented speeches.[5] Oh vnhappy son of S. *George*, thou coward and of little valour, I know not howe thou canst name thy selfe to be the son of the mightiest Knight in the world, for that thou hast lost thy honour in this last assault.

This being said, the two weary knights concluded a peace betwixt them, and reuealed each to the other their names and liuing and wherefore they aduentured to trauell, the which when it was known they sailed forwards that way whereas the dolorous woman went, so in this sort they trauelled all the rest of the night that remained, till such time as the day began to be cleare, and straightway they descried land, to which place with great hast they rowed.

And comming a land they found no vsed way, but one narrow path, the which they kept, wherein they had not traueiled long when that they met with a poore simple countrey man, with a great hatchet in his hand, and he was going for to cut some firewood from high and mighty trees, of whom they demaunded what countrey and land it was.

This countrey (said hee) is called Armenia, but yet most curteous Knightes you must pardon me, for that I doe request you to returne againe, and proceede no farther if you doe esteeme of your liues, for in going this way there is nothing to be had but death.

---

[5] speeches] speeces *1597*

For that the Lord of this countrey is a furious monster called the two headed Knight, and he is so furious in his tyranny, that neuer any stranger as yet could escape out of his hand aliue.

And for proofe of his cruelty no longer then yesterday he brought hither a Lady prisoner, who at her first comming on shoare all to be whipt and beat her in such sorte that it would make the tyrannous tyrant to relent and pitty her distresses, swearing that euery day he would so torment her, till such time as her life and body did make their seperation.

Pollimus the Prince of Constantinople was very attentiue to the olde mans words, thinking the Lady to be his *Dulcippa*[6] after whom he so long traueiled: the griefe he receaued at this report stroke such a terrour to his hart that he fell into a sound, and was not able to go any further.

But Saint *Georges* sonnes who knew him to bee a Knight of much vallour incouraged him, and protested by the honour of their Knighthoodes neuer to forsake his company, till they saw his Lady deliuered from her torments and he safely conducted home into his owne countrey.

So traueiling with this resolution the night came on, and it was so darke, that they were constrained to seeke some place to take their restes, and laying themselues downe vnder a broad branched tree of Oake, they passed the night pondering in their mindes a thousand imaginations.

So when the morning was come and that the Diamond of heauen began to glister with his beames vpon the mountaine toppes, these martiall Knightes were not slothful, but rose vppe and followed their iourneies.

After this they had not traueiled scarce halfe a mile, when that they hearde a pittifull lamentation of a woman, who by reason of her lowde shrikes her voice was very hoarse, so they staid to heare from whence that lamentable noise should come.

And presently a farre off, they behelde a high piller of stone, out of the which there came foorth a spoute of faire and cleare water, and thereat was bounde a woman all naked, her backe fastned to the piller, her armes backeward imbracing it, with her armes fast bounde behinde her.

Her skinne was so faire[7] and white, that if it had not beene, that they heard her lamentation, they would haue iudged her to haue beene an image made artificially of allablaster ioyned vnto the piller.

These warlike Knights laced on their helmets, and came vnto the place where she was, but when the prince of Constantinople saw her, he presently[8] knewe her to be his Lady and louely mistresse.

For by reason of the coldnesse of the darke night, and with her great lamentation and weepings, she was so ful of sorrow and affliction, that she could scarce speake.

Likewise the Princes hart so yerned at the sight of his vnhappy Lady, that almost he could not looke vppon her for weeping.

---

[6] *Dulcippa*] *Dnlcippa 1597*
[7] faire] fare *1597*
[8] presently] presenly *1597*

But yet at last with a sorrowfull sigh he said, Oh cruell hands is it possible that there should remaine in you so much mischiefe, that whereas there is such great beauty and fairenes, you should vse such basenes and villany? she doth more deserue to be loued and serued, than to bee in this sort so euill intreated.

This wofull Prince with much sorrow did behold her white skin and backe all to it vppon her and couered her body, and tooke her in his armes, whilest the other knights vnlosed her.

This vnhappy Lady neuer felt nor knew what was done vnto her, till such time as shee was vnbound from those bands and in the armes of her louer.

Then giuing a terrible sigh she thought that shee had beene in the armes of the monstrous two headed knight saying, Oh *Pollimus* thou true betrothed husband where art thou now that thou comst not to succour me? and therwithall ceased her speeches.

This Prince hearing these words would haue answered her, but he was disturbed by hearing of a great noise of a horse, which seemed to be in the woods amongst the trees.

The rest of the Knights intending to see what it should be left the Lady lying vpon the greene grasse in the keeping of Prince *Pollimus* and the Marriners, and so saint *Georges* sonnes went towards the place, whereas they heard that rushing noise, and as they vigelently lookt about them they beheld the two headed monster mounted vpon a mighty and great palfrey, who returned to see if the Lady were aliue for to torment her anew.

But when he came to the piller and saw not the Lady, with an ireful looke he cast his eies, looking about him on euery side, and at last he saw the three knights, comming towards him with a reasonable and quiet pace and howe the Lady was vntied from the piller wher he left her and in the armes of another Knight making her sorrowfull complaint.

The two headed knight seeing them in this order, with great fury vpon his mighty horse he came towards them, and when he was neare them, he staid, and did behold the princely proportions, and gentle dispositions of ye knights that without my leaue hath aduentured to vntie[9] the Lady from the piller where I left her, or come you to offer vppe your blouds in sacrifice vpon my fauchion, to whom one of the three valiant brothers answered & said, we be knights of a strange countrey, that at the sorrowfull complaint[10] of this Lady arriued in this place, and seeing her to be a faire and beautifull woman, and without any desert to be thus so euill intreated, it moueth vs to put our persons in aduenture against them that will seeme farther to misuse her.

In the meane time that the knight was speaking these wordes, the deformed monster was beholding him very presizely, knitting his browes with the great anger hee receaued in hearing his speeches, and with great fury he spurred his monstrous beast, that he made him to giue so mighty a leape that he had almost fallen vppon the English knight: who with great lightnes did deliuer himselfe, and so drawing

---

[9] he staid … vntie] hee sayde fonde knightes, what wretched folly and madness hath bewitched you, that without my leaue you haue aduentured to vntie *1608*; *1616*

[10] complaint] complant *1597*

foorth his sword he would haue stroken him, but the beast passed by with so great fury that he could not reach him.

Here began as terrible a battaile betwixt the two headed knight and saint *Georges* sonnes, as euer was fought by any knights, their mighty blowes seemed to rattle in the elements like to a terrible thunder, and their swords to strike sparkling fier, in such abundance as though it had beene from a smithes anuile.

During this conflict the English Knights were so grieuously wounded, that all their bright armours were stained with a bloudy gore and their helmets brused with the terrible stroakes of the monsters fauchion, whereat they grew more inraged, and their strengthes beganne to increase in such sort that one of them stroake an ouerthwart blow with his trusty sword vpon his knee, and by reason that his armour was not very good he cut it cleane a sunder, so that legge and all fell to the ground, and the two headed knight fell on the other side to the earth, and with great roring he began to stampe and stare like a beast, and to blaspheme against the heauens for this his sodaine mishap.

The other two brothers seeing this, presently cut off his two heads, whereby he was forced to yeeld to the mercy of imperious death.

There was another knight that came with the monster, who when he sawe all that had passed, with great feare returned the way from whence he came.

These victorious conquerours, when they sawe that with so great ease they were deliuered from the tyrantes cruelty, with lowde voices they saide, oh thou God whom we christians still doe worship, we doe giue thee humble thankes, and doe acknowledge this our good successe and victory doth proceede from thee.

Therefore we doe promise and vow before thy celestiall Maiesty, that once comming to our father and the other Christian champions, generally to erect a shrine, and consecrate it to thy blessed sonne, vnder whose banner we euermore doe fight.

This being said, they departed with conquest to the Prince of Constantinople, where they left him comforting of his distressed Lady.

So when they were altogether, they commanded the marriners to prouide them somwhat to eate, for that they had great neede thereof, who presently prepared it, for that continually[11] they bore their prouision about them: of this banquet the Knights were very glad, and reioyced much at that which they had atchieued and commanded that the Lady should be very well looked vnto and healed of her harme receaued.

So at the end of three daies when the Princes[12] Lady had recouered her health, they left the countrey of Armenia and departed backe to the sea whereas they had lefte their ships lying at roade, and there tarried vntill their comming.

Wherein they were no sooner entered, but the Marriners hoysed saile, and tooke their way toward Constantinople as the Knights commanded. The windes serued them so prosperously, that within a small time they arryued in *Greece*, and landed within two dayes iourney of the Courte: which laye then at *Peru*, a myle from *Constantinople*.

---

[11] continually] continuall *1597*

[12] Princes] Princesse *1597*

Being aland, the Prince *Pollemus* consulted with S. *Georges* three Sonnes, what course were best to be taken for their proceeding to the Court. For saith he, vnlesse I may with the Emperour my Fathers consent enioye my deerest *Dulcippa*, I wyll liue vnknowen in her companie, rather than delight in the heritage of ten such Empyres.

At last they concluded, that the Ladie should bee couered in a blacke veyle for being knowen, and *Pollemus* in black armes, and the other Knights all sutable shuld ride together: which accordingly they did, and about tenne in the morning entred the Pallace: where they found the Emperour, the seuen Champions with manie other princes in the great hall: to whom one of Sa. *Georges* Sons thus spake.

Great Emperour and noble Knights, this Knight that leadeth the Lady hath long loued her, in their births there is great difference, so that their Parents crosse their affections: for him she hath indured much sorrow, for her he will and hath suffered manie hazards. His comming thus to your Court is to this end, to approoue her the onely desertfull Ladie in the world, himselfe the faithfulst Knight against all Knights whatsoeuer: which with your Emperiall leaue, he, my selfe and these two my associates will maintaine: desiring your Maiestie to giue iudgement as we shall deserue.

The Emperour condescended, and on the greene before the Pallace, those foure ouerthrew more than foure hundred Knights: so that Sa. *George* and three other of the Champions entred the lysts, and ran three violent courses against the Blacke knights, without moouing them: who neuer suffered the poynts of their speares to toutch the armour of the Champions. Which the Emperour perceiuing, gessed them to be of acquaintaunce: wherefore gyuing iudgement that the Knight should possesse his Lady, at his request they all discouered themselues.

To describe the delightfull comfort that the English Champion tooke in the presence of his Children, and the ioy that the Emperour receiued at the returne of hys lost Sonne, requires more arte and eloquence, than my tyred senses can affoord. I am therefore here forced to conclude this Part, leauing the Flowers of Chiualrie in the Cittie of *Constantinople*. Of whose following Aduentures I wil at large discourse hereafter: so that the gentle Reader (with a kinde looke and a smiling countenance) wyll curteously accept of this which is alreadie finished.

FINIS.

Notes

Bibliographical references in the notes are by author's surname, sometimes with short title; full details of these works can be found in the Bibliography (pp. 310–15 below). All references to the works of Shakespeare are to the second edition of the Arden Shakespeare, ed. Harold F. Brooks and Harold Jenkins; all references to Chaucer are to *The Riverside Chaucer*, ed. Larry D. Benson (Boston, MA: Houghton Mifflin, 1987); all references to *BH* are, unless otherwise stated, to the edition of *Syr Bevis of Hampton* printed by Thomas East (1582?); all references to classical authors are to volumes in the Loeb Classical Library. The names of classical figures are given in their Roman forms, since these are the ones with which Johnson himself was familiar. I have cited the Geneva Bible but have indicated the chapter and verse numbers in the Authorized Version where these differ.

To avoid excessive cross-reference in the notes, I have provided an index of the names or terms that occur repeatedly in *7Ch* (see pp. 308–9 below).

3	**Lord Thomas Howard**: Thomas, First Earl of Suffolk (1561–1626), son of Thomas Howard, Fourth Duke of Norfolk. In 1591 he commanded the expedition against the Spaniards in the Azores in which Sir Richard Grenville famously lost his life. There is a nice irony in the fact that both parts of *7Ch*, which takes such liberties with its 'saintly' protagonists, are dedicated to members of England's premier Roman Catholic family.

Phaiton: son of Phoebus Apollo, god of the sun, Phaeton asked to be allowed to drive his father's chariot across the heavens for one day. He lost control of the chariot, and Jove eventually hurled him from it with a thunderbolt in order to save the earth from destruction. His story, which is told in Ovid's *Metamorphoses* (I.750–II.380), came to epitomize the dangers of overweening pride and ambition.

seauen Champions ... through Europe: see p. xvi above.

mislike: displeasure.

rudiments: principles.

4	***chattering Cranes***: possibly a reference to the cranes which (according to Homer) in a literal, physical sense habitually attack the pygmies (*Iliad*, III.3–6).

Momus: the personification of blame, and one of many forces which, according to Hesiod's *Theogony*, were born of Nyx, the goddess of night, without sexual union.

passe: regard.

conceited: intelligent, clever.

factes: deeds.

Mars: the Roman god of war.

detected: brought an accusation against.

registreth: records.

5   **After the angrie Greekes ... flourish**: for the 'legendary history' that
           linked the foundation of Britain with Trojan and Roman history, see *Sir
           Gawain and the Green Knight*, lines 1–19; *FQ*, II.x.5–13; Andrew King,
           p. 182 n. 30; Barron, Le Saux and Johnson, passim. The royal houses of
           both York and Tudor claimed direct descent from Brutus.
           chiefest Cittie in *Phrigia*: Troy.
           exempted ... habitation: cf. *fato profugus* (Virgil, *Aeneid*, I.2).
           like Pilgrims: a Christianized way of emphasizing the divinely appointed
           nature of Aeneas's mission.
           happie: prosperous, well-situated. In their annotation to *Sir Gawain and
           the Green Knight*, line 13, Tolkien and Gordon point out that '*felix* was a
           conventional term for founders of cities'.
           fourth decent from *Aenæas*: the details of Brutus's descent from Aeneas
           correspond to those in Geoffrey of Monmouth's *Historia regum
           Britannie*, I.iii (cf. Layamon's *Brut*, lines 68–151); they are not found in
           FQ.
           Monsters, Gyants, and a kinde of wilde people: cf. 'hideous Giants, and
           halfe beastly men' (*FQ*, II.x.7).
           Troynouant ... London: London was supposedly so called after Lud, a
           descendant of Brutus who rebuilt the city and gave his name to Ludgate:
           cf. *FQ*, II.x.46; Geoffrey's *Historia*, I.xvii; also lines 1–18 of 'London's
           Description' in Johnson's *The Pleasant Walkes of Moore-fields*.
           deuided into Sheires and Counties: cf. *FQ*, II.ix.59 ('diuision into
           Regiments').
           Dukedomes ... mindes: presumably intended primarily as a compliment
           to the book's aristocratic dedicatee and his family.
           Couentrie: the choice of Coventry as the English birthplace of St George
           is perhaps connected with the associations between that part of
           Warwickshire and the romance hero Guy of Warwick (with whom St
           George's son Guy is identified at the end of the 1616 redaction of *7Ch*). It
           is on Dunsmore Heath (a few miles south-east of Coventry) that Guy,
           according to later tradition, is supposed to have slain the Dun Cow and
           that St George himself kills a second dragon in the 1616 *7Ch* (see
           Richmond, p. 98; p. xxiv above).
                 Caludon Castle, at Wyken near Coventry, claims the distinction of
           being St George's birthplace – presumably on the authority of *7Ch*,
           although the castle itself is not named here. Perhaps coincidentally, there
           is a connection between Caludon Castle and the Howard family, to
           members of which both parts of *7Ch* are dedicated. It fell into disrepair
           after Thomas Mowbray, Duke of Norfolk, was banished by Richard II in
           1398, but was rebuilt around 1580 by Henry, Lord Berkeley, who married
           the daughter of Henry Howard, Earl of Surrey.
           golden garter ... Kinges: St George is the patron of the Order of the
           Garter, founded by Edward III around 1348. Cf. 'A Gallant Song of the
           Garter of England' in Johnson's *The Golden Garland of Princely
           Pleasures and Delicate Delights*.

Caliope: chief among the nine classical Muses, Calliope is the Muse of heroic poetry, poetic inspiration, and eloquence.

discourse: account, narrative.

6 **Lord high steward of** *England*: Guy of Warwick's father (see note to p. 5 above) is steward to the Earl of Warwick; Bevis of Hampton, from whose story *7Ch* borrows extensively, is created the King's 'marshall' (*BH*, sig. Giv^v). The title of Earl Marshal is also a hereditary dignity pertaining to the Dukes of Norfolk (cf. notes to pp. 3 and 5 above).

yet neuer ... till now: the motif of a long-childless couple producing a child who either has anomalous physical attributes or fulfils some extraordinary destiny is common in romance and folktale, as well as in biblical narrative: see, e.g., *Chevelere Assigne*, lines 15–18; the Grimms' tales of *Rapunzel* and of *Hans My Hedgehog*; and the biblical stories of Isaac (Genesis xxi.1–5) and John the Baptist (Luke i.13–24); cf. also Johnson's *Tom Thumbe*, pp. 3–4.

calculate: prognosticate.

methought ... deaths: Alexander's mother, Olympias, dreams that she is impregnated by a dragon (*Kyng Alisaunder*, B 347–54), but the choice of that creature as emblem here is more likely to be due to its traditional association with St George. Like Hecuba's dream (see below), that of St George's mother comes true, since her son is in some sense the cause of both his parents' deaths – though, of course, without the blame attaching to Paris for the destruction of Troy.

Hecuba ... firebrand: cf. Virgil, *Aeneid*, VII.320, X.704–5; *The Seege or Batayle of Troye*, lines 239–42; *Troilus and Cressida*, II.ii.111. By stealing Menelaus's wife, Helen, Paris precipitated the Trojan War which is the subject of Homer's *Iliad* and the retrospective portions of Virgil's *Aeneid*, and to which Johnson so often alludes.

Illium: Troy.

viperous: treacherous, malignant.

a milke white Lamb: a milk-white lamb is associated with the future St George, through Una, in *FQ*, I.i.4.

So trauailing ... woodes: cf. the account of the eponymous hero's mother's visit to Merlin in Johnson's *Tom Thumbe*, p. 4. There are general correspondences also to the account of Britomart's visit to Merlin in *FQ*, III.iii.7–14.

bellowing ... monsters: cf. *FQ*, IV.x.46.

Kalyb: the name is perhaps meant to recall that of the nymph Calypso, who in the *Odyssey* charms and seduces Ulysses, keeping him as her lover as Kalyb seeks to keep St George.

brasen horne: the motif of the horn hung up for passers-by to blow is a commonplace of romance (cf., e.g., Malory, vol. II, p. 320), though it usually operates in the context of chivalric adventure as a means of issuing a challenge.

A Dragon fell: a not altogether appropriate image for Albert's saintly offspring (cf. note on Hecuba above).

7   **regarding more ... aliue**: this is not entirely consistent with the fact that
George's mother has been led by her earlier dream to believe that his birth
might not be to anyone's benefit: cf. 'viperous' (p. 6 above).

Bloody Crosse: exactly the same phrase is used to denote the traditional
emblem of St George in *FQ*, I.i.2.

three nurses: cf. *The Seven Sages of Rome*, lines 713–18.

stele the Infant: the motif of a child stolen from the cradle or in early
infancy and brought up away from the world, often by a fairy or magician,
is another romance commonplace: cf. *FQ*, I.ix.3; I.x.65 (where the child is
St George himself); II.iii.26; V.i.6; *Lancelot of the Laik*, lines 215–20.

weeping *Niobe*: wife of Amphion, King of Thebes, Niobe was the mother
of many children and boasted that she was therefore superior to the
goddess Latona, who had only two. The gods took revenge by killing all
her children, and Niobe herself was transformed into a rock which forever
streamed with water like tears (Ovid, *Metamorphoses*, VI.301–12). She is
commonly used as an image of inconsolable grief (as in *Hamlet*, I.ii.149).

why couer ... behold the sunne: such outbursts are a literary
commonplace: cf. *FQ*, I.vii.22–3; Marlowe, *The Jew of Malta*, I.ii.193–5.

Oedipus: the reference is to Oedipus's blinding of himself on learning that
he has unwittingly killed his father and married his mother. His story
would probably have been known to Johnson through Seneca's tragedy on
the subject: all Seneca's dramatic works were translated into English
during the Elizabethan period.

record: here probably 'give heed to', though the verb can also mean to
sing or tell of something.

if hee bee ... flie: the words are somewhat blasphemously reminiscent of
Psalm cxxxix.

8   **speed**: prosper, be successful.

Bohemia: a kingdom within the Holy Roman Empire dominated by the
Habsburg dynasty from 1526 to 1618, Bohemia quite often occurs as a
setting in Elizabethan fiction: e.g. in William Painter's *The Palace of
Pleasure*, II.xxvii, and in Robert Greene's *Pandosto* – whence in *The
Winter's Tale*.

twice seauen yeares: Sir Percival is raised in the woods (by his mother)
until he is fifteen; like St George, he is instinctively drawn towards
chivalric pursuits despite the attempts of his protectress to keep him from
them: see *Sir Percyvell of Gales*, lines 229–30, 315–16.

apple of her eye: a proverbial expression, ultimately biblical in origin
(Deuteronomy xxxii.10, etc.).

Satiers: satyrs are usually depicted as largely human but with some
animal attributes (most commonly goats' legs and horns). In *FQ*, they are
encountered in wild places (their natural habitat) and generally represent
the animal side of man's nature, specifically male sexual appetites. The
account of the nurture of Sir Satyrane by his satyr father in *FQ*, I.vi.21ff.
is a version of the motif common to *7Ch* and the Percival story (see

above) and may have suggested to Johnson the idea of satyrs as Kalyb's attendants.

pollicie: guile.

affect: like, love.

(Sir Knight): George is not, of course, a knight as yet.

as to mooue ... world: cf. *FQ*, III.iii.12.

Loue would make the wisest blind: proverbial. Cupid, the classical god of erotic love, is often represented as blindfolded.

Brasen Castel: perhaps suggested by the 'brasen wall' of *FQ*, III.iii.10–11.

Saint Dennis **[etc.]**: see p. xvi above.

whereof ... England: cf. *FQ*, I.x.61, where Redcrosse is likewise told of his future destiny as England's patron saint.

9   *Bayard*: the name of a horse of extraordinary powers given by Charlemagne to Renaud/Rinaldo, one of the four sons of Aymon. Johnson may have known of him from Caxton's *The Foure Sonnes of Aymon*, translated from a French Charlemagne romance, or from Sir John Harington's translation (1591) of Ariosto's *Orlando Furioso*; but Bayard had already by this time become a generic name for a horse (see, e.g., Chaucer's *Troilus and Criseyde*, I.218).

Sir Bevis of Hampton is unusual among Middle English romance heroes in having a named horse (Arundel) and sword (Morglay), and it is only in the parts of *7Ch* most heavily indebted to *BH* that the names of St George's horse and sword (see below) are mentioned again.

Ninus **the first Monarke**: called Nimrod in the Bible, Ninus was King of Assyria, founder of Nineveh, and husband of Semiramis. He is the first person to be named as a king in the Bible (Genesis x.8–12).

Lidian **steele**: Lydia (part of present-day Turkey) was a country of Asia Minor rich in natural resources and renowned for its metalwork – hence, no doubt, the legendary wealth of its last king, Croesus. According to Greek tradition, King Gyges of Lydia (687–652 BC) was the inventor of the earliest coins. Lydian steel is mentioned also in John Lyly's *Sapho and Phaon*, V.i.8.

Ascalon: the name of a Philistine city of southern Palestine mentioned (as As(h)kelon) in the Bible (e.g. 2 Samuel i.10). The reason, if there is one, for giving this name to St George's sword is not clear. Cf. the note on Bayard above.

Ciclops: the Cyclopes, the one-eyed giants of classical mythology, were armourers to the gods, forging Jove's thunderbolts and Neptune's trident. Their forges were thought to be under Mount Etna, thus accounting for its volcanic activities.

hew ... steele: King Arthur's sword, Excalibur, was also able to cut through steel (Malory, vol. I, p. 142).

such pretious vertue: such valuable power. Cf. the description of Excalibur in *FQ*, II.viii.20–1.

So the Lady … deliuery: Kalyb's imprisonment by St George recalls that of Merlin by Nimue (Malory, vol. I, p. 126), referred to in *FQ*, III.iii.11.

10–11   **CHAP. II**: the account of Kalyb's death bears certain similarities to descriptions of the death of Dr Faustus, whose story was current in English translation in the 1590s.

10   **swarmes … inhabite**: perhaps an allusion to the plagues of flying insects with which God afflicted Egypt (Exodus viii.24, x.13–15).

like a wreath … creature: the Furies, the avenging goddesses of classical mythology, are usually depicted with snakes entwined in their hair.

Magoll, Cumath, Helueza, Zontomo: the names 'Magoll, Cumath, Hellbeza' occur also in the pamphlet account of the execution of a family of witches in Germany around the end of the sixteenth century (*A Strange Report of Sixe most Notorious Witches* (London, 1601), sig. Aiii').

venite festinate inquam: 'come, hasten, I say'.

spirits … fire: cf. Marlowe, *Doctor Faustus*, I.iii.16–17.

11   **Obligation … blood**: Faustus's contract with demonic powers is likewise written with his own blood (*The History of the Damnable Life and Deserved Death of Dr John Faustus*, pp. 13–14).

sad Executors: *sad* perhaps here means 'steadfast' or 'inexorable'; *executor* can mean 'executioner' as well as 'executor' in the modern sense (either sense, or both, would be appropriate here).

Phlegethon: one of the rivers of the classical Underworld; its name means 'fiery'.

Calderne … brimstone: cf. the punishment of Almidor in Chapter XIIII below.

Acheron: the river of woe in the classical Underworld.

but all the spirits … peeces: Faustus is likewise dismembered by fiends in Marlowe's play (*Doctor Faustus*, V.iii.6–7; cf. *FQ*, III.iii.8, line 9, where the setting is similar to that in *7Ch*).

inrold: inscribed, recorded.

12   **herse**: tomb, grave.

mantles of *Flora*: flowers. Flora was the Roman goddess of flowers and the spring.

whereat … deuided: the motif of heroes setting out together in quest of adventure and going their separate ways at a crossroads is common to folktale and romance: see, e.g., the Grimms' story of *The Four Artful Brothers*; Malory, vol. II, p. 538.

happily: by chance.

Father: more probably a title denoting respect for an older man than an indication that St George takes the hermit for a man of the Church.

Burgonet: helmet.

12–15   **Dragon**: Johnson's account of St George's fight with the dragon draws on a variety of different sources: the hermit's description of Egypt's 'distresse' is reminiscent of the *Legenda aurea* and its derivatives (the Middle English *Gilte Legende*; Caxton's *Golden Legend*), though there the dragon-fight takes place in Libya and there is no offer of the princess's hand in marriage as a reward for killing the beast; the fight itself is heavily indebted to *BH*, which is often quoted verbatim, but it also betrays the influence of *FQ*; while Almidor's attempt to rob George of the glory of victory recalls both the Tristan story and *BH*. See annotation below and, further, Fellows, 'St George', pp. 37–8.

will he breath ... all thinges: in Caxton's *Golden Legend*, St George's dragon 'venomed the people with his breeth' (*Medieval Saints' Legends*, ed. Sperk, p. 119).

13   *Arabian* **silke**: Arabian silk seems to have been available in Europe since classical times: Propertius mentions it in his *Elegies* (I.i.7–8), and La Alacaicería, a market established in Granada by the Moors during the fourteenth century, was a centre for its sale.

who no sooner had a sight ... brused: the whole passage is very close, both verbally and in substance, to *BH*, sig. Fii^v (see Fellows, 'St George', pp. 49, 51–2).

with his burning winges: although dragons traditionally breathe fire (cf. *FQ*, I.xi.44–5), Johnson's dragon may be unique in having burning wings.

Orringe tree: the function performed here by the orange tree is fulfilled in *BH* (*7Ch*'s principal source for this episode) by a miraculous well which protects the hero from the dragon and heals his wounds; *FQ* (I.xi.29–30, 46–9) has both well and tree. Johnson's tree recalls the Peridexion of the bestiaries, whose shade dragons are unable to approach (see *Physiologus Latinus*, p. 116). On the association of dragons, trees and wells in a romance setting, see further Fellows, 'St George', p. 38 and notes 65–6.

13–14   **who no sooner feeling ... trunchion of a speare**: cf. *BH*, sig. Fiii^{r-v}; Fellows, 'St George', pp. 50, 52–3.

14   **purple**: an epithet frequently used for blood in *FQ* (III.i.65, etc.).

Almidor: cf. Almanzor, a name adopted by several Moslem rulers.

Sabra: the name recalls both 'Saba', a name sometimes given to the biblical Queen of Sheba, and 'Saber', the name of the hero's paternal uncle in *BH* (sig. Aiv^v, etc.).

manhood: manly virtues or, possibly, sexual attractiveness.

robbe ... victorie: in the Tristan story, the hero is attacked after his dragon-fight by a wicked steward who, like Almidor, is motivated by sexual jealousy (see *Sir Tristrem*, lines 1459–60); in *BH* (sig. Ci^r), a steward who is envious of Bevis's prowess in killing a monstrous boar waylays him with a band of foresters in an attempt to appropriate to himself the credit for Bevis's victory.

barkes at the Moone: a proverbial expression for a useless endeavour (see *ODEP*, M1143).

& by force ... three of the *Egiptian* Knights: there are many verbal parallels here to *BH* (see sig. Ci^r; Fellows, 'St George', pp. 50–1, 53–4).

15   **the Queene of chaunce**: Fortune, traditionally personified as a woman.

Ptolomie: Johnson may have known the name Ptolemy as that of an Egyptian potentate from Sir Thomas North's translation (1579) of

Plutarch's *Lives*, the principal source for Shakespeare's *Antony and Cleopatra*.

Musicke ... Angels: after his victory over the dragon, Bevis is greeted by 'priestes and clearkes' singing (*BH*, sig. Fiii^v); when Redcrosse is betrothed to Una after *his* dragon-fight, 'there was an heauenly noise ... / Like as it had bene many an Angels voice' (*FQ*, I.xii.39).

Pale: *pall*, 'robe'.

Knighthood ... spurres: the presentation of spurs was part of the investiture ceremony for a knight (see Keen, pp. 7, 65). Cf. note to p. 8 above.

***Auroraes* ... East**: Aurora, goddess of the dawn, is often described as blushing as she rises in the morning from the bed of her lover, Tithonus (e.g. *FQ*, I.xi.51).

16   **Greekish Wine**: 'Greekish wine' is referred to quite frequently in sixteenth-century texts (e.g. Marlowe, *2 Tamburlaine*, II.iii.45; Shakespeare, *Troilus and Cressida*, V.i.1). Richard Surflet's recipe, in *The Covntrey Farme* (1600 edition), p. 613, for making 'wine like vnto Greekish wine' suggests that it would have been a strong, sweet wine made from dried, or partially dried, grapes.

three droppes of blood: according to superstition, one drop of blood from the nose portends sickness; three portend something worse. Cf. the woodcut on the title-page of the 1621 edition of Johnson's *The History of Tom Thumbe*. See also Radford and Radford, p. 60.

some secret poyson: in the *Legenda aurea* and its derivatives, the Emperor Dacian's 'enchauntour' attempts to poison St George – unsuccessfully because the saint makes the sign of the Cross over the goblet (*Medieval Saints' Legends*, ed. Sperk, pp. 116, 121).

chafed: enraged. The adjective is often used in similes of wild animals brought to bay (cf. Maxwell's note to *Titus Andronicus*, IV.ii.138).

vnder a Garden wall: Johnson's principal source here is *BH* (sigs Cii^v–iii^r), where the Saracen princess Iosian woos a reluctant Bevis. In the Middle English romance of *Amis and Amiloun*, a similar episode takes place, as here, in a garden setting; later, a jealous steward betrays the lovers, Amis and Belisaunt, to the latter's father.

gordion knot: a knot which cannot be untied. Gordius, a peasant who became King of Phrygia, dedicated his cart to Jove and coupled the yoke to the beam with an ingenious knot; an oracle declared that whoever could untie it would become lord of Asia. Alexander the Great unfastened the knot by cutting through it with his sword.

vnder the cope of heauen: under the over-arching canopy or vault of Heaven. The phrase was very commonly used to denote everything in the world.

contrarie to kinde: against nature.

17   **seek to aime at higher States**: cf. 'In all the world is no man, neither King, Duke, or Soudan, / But they would haue thee to their Queene, & if they had thee once seene' (*BH*, sig. Cii^v).

great Monarcke of the East: an epithet more usually applied to Alexander the Great.

at shutting vp of *Titons* golden gates: at sunset. The name Titan is applied to the sun in Virgil and in Ovid.

deepe pretended Treason: cf. the slightly different accusation in *BH*, sig. Ciii^r: 'Beuis this same day, hath made Iosian forsake her lay. / And surely he will lye her bye ...'.

Mahomet, Apollo*, and *Termagaunt: as Mahoun(d), Appolyn and Teruagaunt, the prophet Mahomet, the classical god Apollo and the imaginary deity Termagaunt occur frequently in Middle English romances, including *BH*, as gods believed to be worshipped by Saracens.

my cosen the *Persian* Soldan: in *BH*, the hero is despatched to the court of King Bradmound, who has earlier attempted to seize Iosian by force of arms but has been defeated by King Ermine's army under the leadership of Bevis.

bigger *Asia*: the part of Asia to the east of Asia Minor.

17–18   **bearer ... death**: 'thy seruant' is here in apposition to 'death': cf. Marlowe, *1 Tamburlaine*, v.i.17.

18   **for hys pawne ... horses**: Bevis is likewise forced to leave behind his horse and sword (*BH*, sig. Ciii^v).

dismall crie ... mischance: both ravens and crickets were regarded as creatures of ill omen (cf. *Macbeth*, I.v.38–40, II.ii.15).

the walles and towers ... the light thereof: the description of the sultan's palace is heavily indebted to that of Damascus in *BH* (sig. Di^r).

inamiled: ornamented, beautified.

lattine: brass, or a metal similar to it in appearance.

streamers ... pictured: in reality, of course, Islam forbids the visual depiction of the deity.

18–19   **trampled ... succour**: cf. *BH*, sig. Di^r. *BH* may itself here be influenced by the St George legend: see Matzke (1902), p. 510.

19   **like swarmes of Bees**: cf. 'About Beuis gan they driue, as Bees do about an hiue' (*BH*, sig. Dii^r).

First ... horses: the tortures here described are typical of accounts of martyrdom in early hagiography, though none of them is usually associated with St George.

Royall blood: George's maternal grandfather is the King of England (see p. 6 above).

wrath and discontent: in *BH*, by contrast, we are told that Bradmond 'made therfore great ioy & blisse' on receiving the letter ordering Bevis's death (*BH*, sig. Di^v).

Ianasaries: the sultan's guard.

20   **Target**: shield.

blood ... ends: cf. 'al his fingers on blood out brast' (*BH*, sig. Dii^r).

plagues of *Pharo*: the plagues visited by God upon Egypt, in order to induce Pharaoh to let the Israelites depart for the Promised Land (Exodus vii–xii).

daughters rauishments: Priam's daughter Cassandra was raped by Ajax when the Greeks sacked Troy; the fates of others of his many daughters are described in Euripides' play *The Trojan Women*.

accursing his birth day: cf. 'he cursed the time y^t he was borne' (*BH*, sig. Diii^v).

soliciter: ally.

Hiperion ... **waues**: when the sun had set in the sea, and the moonlight had danced upon the waves, thirty times: i.e. when a month had passed. (The name Hyperion is often used of the sun-god; Thetis, the mother of Achilles, was a sea-goddess; Cynthia is one of the names given to the goddess of the moon.)

compleat mones: full month.

two ... Lyons: in the corresponding passage of *BH* (sig. Dii^r), Bevis encounters 'two Dragons of much might'. The lions here recall both the Middle English romance of *Richard Coer de Lion* (see below) and, less directly, the biblical story of Daniel in the lions' den (Daniel vi).

sweat blood: a common image, perhaps a literalistic distortion of Luke xxii.44.

21   **thrust ... harts**: in *Richard Coer de Lion*, the hero (likewise in prison at the time) tears the heart out of a lion sent to kill him; one of the Middle English manuscripts states: 'All in kerchese his arme was wonde' (ed. Brunner, p. 138). Cf. also lines 71–91 of 'A Princely Song of Richard Cordelion King of England' in Johnson's *The Golden Garland of Princely Pleasure and Delicate Delights*.

some monster ... Sea: perhaps the janissaries fear that St George has been sent to punish their land as the sea-monster Cetus (slain by Perseus) was sent to punish the people of Ethiopia for the boastfulness of their queen, Cassiopeia.

rats ... wormes: cf. 'Rats and Mice and such small chere [*var.* dere], was his meat that seauen yeare' (*BH*, sig. Dii^r; echoed in *King Lear*, III.iv.135–6). Earlier, Bevis's prison has been described as containing, in addition to the two dragons, 'other wormes many moe' (*BH*, sig. Diii^v).

neuer tasted ... water: cf. 'But once a day without lesse, of Wheat branne he had a messe ... / Bread of corne eate he none, but of water he had great wone' (*BH*, sig. Dii^r).

comlier ... Ceder: cf. Song of Solomon, v.15.

Paphian **Queenes**: Venus, the classical goddess of love and beauty, is said to have come to land at Paphos in Cyprus after she was born from the foam of the sea.

found: became.

map: embodiment.

mirrour: image, exemplar.

sowing ... Sampler: an oblique allusion to the classical story of Philomela, to which Johnson refers many times in *7Ch*. Having been raped by her sister's husband, Tereus, who then cut out her tongue to ensure her silence, Philomela depicted her story in needlework. She and her sister, Procne, took revenge on Tereus by serving him with the flesh of Itys, his young son, in a pie. Procne was transformed into the swallow, Tereus into the hoopoe, and Philomela into the nightingale, whose song forever mourns the wrongs done to her. Johnson would have known the story from Ovid's *Metamorphoses*, VI.424–674.

22   *Syrens*: enchantresses (sometimes described as having wings) who lured sailors to their deaths by the sweetness of their singing. Odysseus successfully resisted them by having his men tie him to the mast of his ship until the danger was past.

refused: left, departed from.

I greatly feare some treacherie: cf. 'Haddest thou neuer me forsake, but some treason did it make' (*BH*, sig. Diii^r).

Morpheus: the son of Hypnos (Sleep), Morpheus was the god of dreams in classical mythology.

Genet: jennet, a small Spanish horse.

watchet: light blue.

Barbarie: the Saracen lands of North Africa. The term is also applied to non-Christian lands more generally.

The Persian ... fire: the line is metrically defective, but neither the 1608 nor the 1616 edition emends it.

triple Crowne: perhaps a disrespectful, Protestant allusion to the triple crown of the Papacy.

23   **brittle**: insubstantial; there may also be overtones of deceptiveness and inconstancy.

Dido: in book IV of the *Aeneid*, Virgil tells of the love affair between Dido, Queen of Carthage, and Aeneas, who eventually leaves her in order to fulfil his divinely appointed destiny. In despair, Dido has a pyre built and kills herself on it with Aeneas's sword. In post-classical literature, the emphasis is increasingly on Dido as a woman wronged (as in Chaucer's *The Legend of Good Women*). Marlowe's play *Dido Queen of Carthage* was published in 1594.

wedded ... Nation: cf. '... he is gone into England. / And liueth on his heritage, he hath a wife of great parentage. / A kinges daughter wedded hath he' (*BH*, sig. Dii^v).

chaine of golde ... true virgin: in *BH* (sig. Diii^r), Iosian preserves her virginity during her marriage to King Iour by means of letters hung around her neck.

Sirrian powders: Syria was noted for the production of perfumes and incense derived from balsamic plants; Syrian perfumes are frequently mentioned in classical and later literature (e.g. Catullus, VI.8).

Tripolie ... Barbarie: Johnson, whose geography is vague at the best of times, may not have been aware that Tripoli is in Libya, not Morocco.

24   *Apollo* **with his siluer Harpe**: the classical god Apollo presided over the Muses and was patron of music and the arts. His most common attributes are his lyre and bow (the latter, according to Homer, being made of silver).

Castalian **springes**: Castalia was a spring near Delphi sacred to Apollo and the Muses.

25   *Thessalie*: a kingdom of ancient Greece; in the sixteenth century it was under Turkish rule.

till the haires ... clawes: cf. the biblical account of the madness of Nebuchadnezzar (Daniel iv.29–30; iv.32–3 in the Authorized Version).

tipe: emblem, symbol.

all you pitteous powers of heauen: an inappropriate apostrophe in the mouth of a Christian saint!

pray for dogs: the allusion is to the story of Actaeon, who angered the virgin goddess Artemis/Diana because he saw her bathing; he was transformed by her into a stag and was torn to pieces by his own hounds.

26   **recording**: singing.

at the prime of noone: in the Middle English romance of *Sir Orfeo*, it is at noon that Orfeo sees the fairy hunt (line 282). Cf. Friedman, passim.

In former times ... sensles thing: the transformation of human beings into trees occurs in Dante's description of the wood of the suicides (*Inferno*, XIII) and in *FQ*, I.ii.31ff. The punishment of Eglantine for pride is also reminiscent of that of Mirabella in *FQ*, VI.vii.28–30, though Mirabella's pride is of a somewhat different nature (but cf. the note to p. 29 below on 'proude *Eglantine*').

Nectar and Ambrosia: the food and drink of the classical gods on Mount Olympus.

28   **garden of *Hesperides***: the Hesperides were nymphs who guarded a tree bearing golden apples in a garden in the westernmost part of the world.

Fauchion: sword.

Spanish steele: Spain, and in particular Toledo, was famed for the production of swords.

29   *Daphnie ... Bay*: Daphne was in fact turned into a laurel tree by her father, the river-god Peneius, to preserve her from the lustful attentions of Apollo.

Pigmalions **Iuorie Image**: Pygmalion fell in love with a statue of his own creation; Venus took pity on him and turned it into a living woman.

an Iuorie Tower: cf. Song of Solomon, vii.4.

Mœanders **Christall streame**: the river Meander was a winding river in Phrygia; it features in Homer's *Iliad*.

Treasures of rich *America*: in 1595 (a year before the publication of the first part of *7Ch*), Sir Walter Ralegh had sailed to Guiana (present-day Venezuela) in search of gold. He published an account of his findings in *The Discoverie of Guiana* (1596).

golden Mines of higher *India*: in the Middle Ages, India was thought of as being divided into either two or three parts; the nomenclature of these divisions varied (see Roberts, passim; I am indebted to Dr Jon Coe for this reference). *Mandeville's Travels* refers both to 'Ynde the Lasse' and to 'Inde the More'/'High Ynde'. Seymour glosses the former as 'the land-mass extending from Arabia to the Indus delta', the latter as 'the Indian sub-continent and adjacent eastern lands'. Reference is also made in Mandeville (p. 115) to the diamond and gold mines of India. The 'Emperour of Inde the more' features in *Arthur of Little Britaine*, fol. 27, etc.

dominions of *Proserpine*: the classical Underworld, whither Proserpine was carried off by Pluto, thus becoming queen of the realms of the dead.

proude *Eglantine*: in Caxton's *Blanchardyn and Eglantine*, the eponymous heroine is referred to throughout as 'thorguylleuse damours' or 'the proude pucelle in amours'.

secret: sacred, solemn.

gaue her the courtesie of his countrie: greeted her in accordance with the conventions of courtesy prevailing in his country.

curious webs: skilful weaving. The reference is presumably to Indian silken goods, luxury items whose availability in Europe in the sixteenth century would have been increased by the development of trade between India and Portugal via the sea route.

royaltie: splendour.

30   **fire made of Ginniper**: fires of juniper are hot, sweet-smelling and long-burning. Their use in seventeenth-century tobacconists' shops for lighting pipes would have been because they could be kept burning more or less indefinitely. Cf. Jonson, *The Alchemist*, I.iii.31.

discouering: revealing.

31   **burning ... *Sicill***: the dragon-like, fire-breathing monster Typhon/Typhoeus was imprisoned by Zeus under Mount Etna in Sicily, thus accounting for its volcanic nature.

Capadocia: part of present-day Turkey, Cappadocia is the native land of St George in most accounts of his life (see, e.g., *Medieval Saints' Legends*, ed. Sperk, p. 119).

red seas: probably the Red Sea as we know it, though the plural is unusual.

Ierusalem: the description of Jerusalem corresponds in a general way to that of the New Jerusalem in Revelation xxi.

braue: splendid.

golden gates: in Jewish tradition, the Messiah will enter Jerusalem through the Golden Gate; for Christians it is the scene of Christ's last entry into the city: cf. 'the Gildene Gate ... be the whiche gate oure lord entrede on Palme Sonday vpon an asse' (*Mandeville's Travels*, p. 59).

Temples ... *Greece*: this is probably another example of Johnson's lack of geographical knowledge (though, according to Pausanias's *Description of Greece*, there *were* Greek pyramids, smaller than those of Egypt). Solomon's temple is linked with the Egyptian pyramids in that the architecture and geometry of both have been associated with the Knights Templar and/or the Freemasons.

rauished conceit: rapt/entranced imagination.

Adonis: a beautiful youth whom Venus loved and who was killed by a wild boar; Venus transformed him into a blood-red flower. His story is told in Ovid's *Metamorphoses*, X.300–739, and in Shakespeare's poem *Venus and Adonis*.

32   **engendred by the winde**: according to Pliny (*Historia naturalis*, VIII.lxvii), certain Portuguese mares are impregnated by the west wind – hence the swiftness of their foals. Cf. Webster, *The Duchess of Malfi*, I.ii.40.

Turkish Bowes: the Turkish bow was a composite recurved bow, made of sinew and horn. It was shorter than the English longbow and could therefore be used on horseback.

Celestine: Celestine occurs as a male (usually a papal) name in sixteenth-century texts (e.g. the anonymous play *Freewyl* (1561)); I have found no other instances of its being given to a woman before Thomas Dekker's *Satiro-mastix* (1601?). The form Celestina occurs in John Rastell's *Calisto and Melebea* (*c.* 1527), based on the Spanish novel *Celestina*, and in Barnabe Riche, *His Farewell to Militarie Profession* (1581).

Amazonian **Dames**: in classical mythology, the Amazons were a race of female warriors.

Barbarian **Steeds**: Barbary horses, the name given to a particular equine breed (cf. Ure's note to *King Richard II*, V.v.81).

Palfrayes: small saddle-horses, especially for ladies.

Nabuzaradan ... *Ierusalem*: in the Bible, the captain of Nebuchadnezzar's guard is called Nebuzaradan (2 Kings xxv.8). The name also recalls that of Nebuchadnezzar, King of Babylon, himself.

Beuer: part of the face-guard of the helmet.

the Wildernes of *Iuda*: cf. 'the wildernesse of Iudea' (Matthew iii.1)

furniture: armour.

32–3 **This Bore ... Bores head**: the account of St James's battle with the boar is heavily indebted to *BH* (sigs Biv^v–Ci^r).

33   **intestine**: internal.

cankered stomacke: malignant feelings.

wealthie *Spanish* **mines**: probably a reference to the gold and silver mines of Spanish South America.

Alphes ... *Spaine*: an egregious example of Johnson's lack of geographical knowledge.

this loue: this favour/concession.

timmerous: fearsome.

fatall sisters: the classical Fates (Clotho, Lachesis and Atropos), who control the destinies of humans and appoint when they are to die. Clotho spins the thread of a man's life, Lachesis measures it out, and Atropos cuts it at the moment of death.

entertained: perhaps 'held', though the word does not usually mean this except in a figurative sense.

34   **wash ... soule**: the metaphor is related to the Christian notion of tears of true repentance washing away the stain of sin.

Canibals: the earliest examples of this word cited in *OED* are all from mid- to late sixteenth-century accounts of the New World. Cf. Ridley's note to *Othello*, I.iii.143–5.

Scilla ... **safetie**: Scylla's father, Nisus, had a lock of red hair on which his life depended. In Ovid's account (*Metamorphoses*, VIII.6–151), Scylla fell in love with his enemy, Minos, and betrayed her father by cutting off the lock while he slept. Minos, however, was so disgusted at her treachery that he sailed away, and Scylla was drowned while swimming after his ship.

Mœdea ... **Fleece**: the daughter of Aeëtes, King of Colchis, Medea helped Jason to perform the tasks set by her father and thus to win the Golden Fleece. Medea fled with Jason from her father's anger and, when pursued by the Colchian fleet, killed her little brother, Apsyrtus, and scattered the pieces of his dismembered body on the sea to delay her pursuers. Spenser alludes to the story in *FQ*, II.xii.45.

posie: motto, inscription.

Ardeo affectione: 'I burn with love.'

35   **to continue dumbe ... onlie Champion**: in the Middle English romance of *Sir Gowther*, and in the related prose romance of *Robert the Deuyll*, the penance enjoined on the hero for his considerable sins is that he should pretend to be dumb and should eat only such food as he can snatch from dogs. He fulfils the terms of his penance at the Emperor's court and becomes the champion of the Emperor's daughter.

enuied: bore a grudge against.

Admirall: an Arabic term denoting an emir or prince under the Sultan. In *Sir Gowther*, it is the Sultan himself who demands the Emperor's daughter; in *Robert the Deuyll*, it is a seneschal with Saracen backing.

Maske: masques, originally performed in dumb show and often containing allegorical or symbolic elements, were a feature of courtly life in England during the sixteenth and seventeenth centuries. Many Elizabethan and Jacobean poets and dramatists (including Thomas Campion and George Chapman) wrote masques.

Consort of Musicke: musical ensemble.

curiously imbrothered: intricately embroidered.

Diana, Venus, **and** *Iuno*: Johnson probably intends to refer to the three goddesses who competed for the golden apple to be awarded by Paris to the most beautiful of them. However, the three are usually Juno, Venus and Minerva (like Diana, a virgin goddess).

three Graces: Euphrosyne, Thalia and Aglaea, minor goddesses who personified beauty and charm. They are often associated with the Muses and with Venus.

Morisco daunce: morris dance.

36   **shodde ... backewards**: when Mercury attempted to steal some of the cattle belonging to his half-brother, Apollo, he drove them backwards to confuse the trail; the same trick was used by Hercules when he stole the cattle of Geryon.

Ciuill: Seville. The patron saint of Spain was in fact one of Christ's apostles. He is associated with Spain because, according to legend, his body was miraculously conveyed in a boat to the coast of Spain after his death in Palestine.

37　　*Thrasia*: Thrace, a kingdom to the south-east of modern Bulgaria, with coastlines on the Aegean and Black Seas. It figures quite prominently in classical legend, being regarded by the Greeks as a cruel and barbaric land. According to Golding's translation of Ovid, its inhabitants are 'above / All measure prone to lecherie' (VI.596–7; cf. Ovid, *Metamorphoses*, VI.459–60).

38　　**mightie Oake ... necke**: cf. 'His staffe was a yong Oke' (*BH*, sig. Eiv^r).

Dimmilaunce: demi-lance, a lance with a short shaft.

Princockes: conceited youth, coxcomb.

Hercules ... **shoulders**: Hercules offered to take over the load of the giant Atlas, who held up the sky on his shoulders, if Atlas would fetch the apples of the Hesperides for him. The giant was later turned into Mount Atlas when Perseus showed him the head of the Gorgon Medusa, whose face was so terrible that it turned all who looked on it into stone.

pollicie ... ruinated: Ulysses' guile ('pollicie') was largely responsible for the sack of Troy: he stole the Palladium, the image of Athena which afforded protection to the Trojans, from her temple and devised the plan of the wooden horse in which the Greeks finally entered the city.

Xerxes ... **passed**: cf. Herodotus, VII.xxi. Herodotus is indicating the size of the army that Xerxes led when he invaded Greece.

good speede: success.

impartiall ... destenie: chance.

as small as flesh vnto the potte: cf. 'And they eat also the flesh of my people ... and chop them in pieces, as for the potte, and as flesh within the caldron' (Micah iii.3).

fat: sweaty. Cf. Dickson '"Fat"', passim.

with a fresh supplie: with renewed energy. *OED*, however, does not record any precisely corresponding sense for *supply*.

39　　**the Sunne ... Elements**: the sun was at the zenith, i.e. it was noon.

Rossalinde: the name is perhaps borrowed from Thomas Lodge's *Rosalynde* (1590), a principal source of Shakespeare's *As You Like It*.

dead: without visible signs of life.

as *Thisbe* ... *Pyrramus*: the lovers Pyramus and Thisbe met by night because their parents forbade their meeting. Arriving first at the place of assignation, Thisbe was frightened away by a lioness, dropping her veil as she fled. When Pyramus arrived, he took the veil, stained with blood from the lioness's jaws, as evidence of Thisbe's death and killed himself with his sword. Thisbe returned and, finding his body, killed herself with the same sword. The story is told in Ovid's *Metamorphoses*, IV.5–166 and in Chaucer's *The Legend of Good Women*, lines 706–923; it is also the subject of the play performed by the 'rude mechanicals' in *A Midsummer Night's Dream*.

as the Swanne ... death: the tradition that the swan sings only at the point of death goes back to classical times and is a commonplace of medieval and Renaissance literature (e.g. Chaucer, *The Parliament of Fowls*, line 343; Shakespeare, *Othello*, V.ii.248–9). The motif links Rossalinde's song to the subsequent description of her sisters' plight.

40   *Elisium*: the abode of a few blessed mortals after death. Classical authors vary as to the location they assign to it, but Virgil (*Aeneid*, VI.637–65) makes it a region of the Underworld.

     flourish: flowery.

     leaues of brasse: sheets/pages of brass. The expression derives from the use of brass in funerary monuments and denotes an enduring memorial.

41   **purple garments**: purple traditionally symbolized luxury and power.

     pampered Iades: cf. Marlowe, *2 Tamburlaine*, IV.iii.1.

     fed ... flesh: one of the labours of Hercules was to capture the man-eating horses of Diomedes. He fed them with the flesh of their own master.

     the Elements: the skies.

     clearer than quicksiluer: brighter than mercury.

     six ... neckes: in the widespread legend of the Swan Knight, which would have been familiar to English readers through the Middle English romance *Chevelere Assigne* and Caxton's prose version, *Helyas, Knight of the Swan*, a woman bears seven children at one birth, each of them with a chain around the neck. Six of them are robbed of their chains and are thereupon transformed into swans.

        Johnson's version of the story has some unusual features: all the children are female, whereas the closest analogues require that at least one should be a boy who can grow up to avenge the wrongs done to his family; and, while the transformation into swans in *Chevelere Assigne* and *Helyas* saves the children from death at the hands of their grandmother's servant, in *7Ch* it is more like an Ovidian metamorphosis in that it occurs in answer to prayer in order to save their virginity – though Johnson later calls it their 'punishments' (p. 47). Miss Elizabeth Williams has pointed out to me that the seven Pleiades were likewise changed into birds, to save them from the lust of Orion.

42   **deflowre**: violate; a Spenserian locution (e.g. *FQ*, IV.xi.42).

43   **some Noble estate**: some person of noble rank.

     sounded: swooned.

     the woful King ... streetes: when King Priam's eldest son, Hector, was killed by Achilles, the latter tied his body to his horse and dragged it round the walls of Troy.

     obsequiously: in a manner proper to funeral obsequies.

44   **the Sunne ... west**: three days had passed. (The chariot of the sun is drawn across the sky by horses; Luna is the moon.)

     dumpe: depression.

     Penelopes **compare**: Ulysses' wife, Penelope, remained faithful to her husband during his ten-year absence at the siege of Troy and throughout the period of his subsequent wanderings, successfully warding off the many suitors who hoped to marry her. Her name became synonymous with wifely fidelity.

carpet dancer ... Chamber: cf. *King Richard III*, I.i.12–13. The term 'carpet dancer' is here apparently synonymous with 'carpet-knight', a stay-at-home soldier, though *OED* does not record it in this sense.

Ninus: a mistake for Nisus (see note to p. 34 above); it is not corrected either in the 1608 or in the 1616 edition.

like *Thesius* sonnes: when Theseus's son Hippolytus was falsely accused by his young stepmother, Phaedra, of trying to rape her, Theseus cursed him and called on Neptune to kill him. Neptune sent a bull from the sea, and Hippolytus's horses threw him from his chariot in their terror; he became entangled in the reins and was dragged to his death. Spenser alludes to the story in *FQ*, I.v.37–8.

Camma ... Sinatus: the story of Camma is told in George Pettie's *A Petite Pallace of Pettie His Pleasure*; it tells how Synorix, governor of Siena, became enamoured of the beautiful Camma and had her husband, Sinnatus, murdered. In order to be revenged on him, Camma agreed to marry him but at the nuptials poisoned both him and herself.

Alsione ... Ceyx: according to Ovid (*Metamorphoses*, XI.410–748), Alcyone was the devoted wife of Ceyx, who was drowned when he sailed away to consult an oracle. Juno eventually took pity on Alcyone, who anxiously awaited her husband's return, and sent her a dream which revealed the truth to her; Alcyone hastened to the sea-shore, only to find Ceyx's body washed up there. The gods transformed them both into halcyons (kingfishers) so that they could be reunited. Chaucer tells the story in *The Book of the Duchess*, lines 62–269.

45   **like a Page**: Rossalinde's disguise as a boy suggests the possible influence of Lodge's romance (see note to p. 39 above).

sarcenet: a silken material.

list: a strip of cloth.

Turkish blade: a slightly curved, flexible scimitar.

Poniarde: dagger.

God of loue ... lap: in obedience to his mother, Venus, Cupid assumed the shape of Aeneas's little son, Ascanius; in that form he sat on Dido's lap and ensured that she would fall in love with Aeneas (Virgil, *Aeneid*, I.664–722). Chaucer recounts this episode in *The Legend of Good Women*, lines 1139–44; it is also the subject of Marlowe's *Dido Queen of Carthage*, III.1.

Ganemede: Ganymede was a beautiful Trojan youth who was snatched by Jove's eagle and carried up to Olympus, where he became the cup-bearer of the gods. This is also the name taken by Rosalynde in Lodge's romance (cf. notes to pp. 39 and 45 above).

Cockbote: small ship's boat.

46   *going fire*: moving flame.

beyond ... sunne: Homer (*Odyssey*, XI.13–22) describes the land of the Cimmerians, who live in perpetual darkness 'beyond the ocean stream'. Cf. *Mandeville's Travels*, pp. 187–8.

a kind ... one another: Mandeville describes an island called Nacumera, whose inhabitants have dogs' heads; but, far from eating each other, 'thei ben fulle resonable and of gode vnderstondynge' (*Mandeville's Travels*, p. 143); cf. *Kyng Alisaunder*, B 6356–62. The bestiaries mention *cynocephali* ('dog-headed ones'), which appear to be some kind of ape and are perhaps related to the dog-headed deities of ancient Egypt.

a vale of walking spirits: cf. the description of the Valeye Perilous in *Mandeville's Travels*, pp. 203–4.

***Ignis fatuus*, the fire of destenie**: a mistranslation, *fatuus* in fact meaning 'foolish'.

iustly: in the proper manner, in the right direction.

the guider of the night: the moon.

47   **to be rent**: in Middle English, *to* in conjunction with a past partciple is intensive in function: thus *to rent* means 'torn to bits'. The usage survives in Spenserian English (e.g. in *FQ*, IV.vii.8) but frequently seems to be misunderstood by Johnson (or his compositors).

in this order ... *Saturne*: the deities here associated with the various days of the week are the ones that give their names to those days in Romance languages such as French; likewise, the activities that Johnson describes for each day are appropriate to those deities.

Manuall professors: those who work with their hands. Saturn is supposed to have taught mankind the arts of agriculture.

48   **Bees ... birds**: bees are referred to as 'the Muses birds' in William Warner's *Albions England* (1596), II.69, in his account of the infancy of Jove; they are frequently associated with the Muses, who are said to have sent them to anoint the lips of the poet Pindar with honey. In classical and medieval texts, bees are usually classified as birds (e.g. Pliny, *Historia naturalis*, XI.xviii; Chaucer, *The Parliament of Fowls*, line 323).

chearefully: ungrudgingly.

Fountaine of Eloquence: Hippocrene, a fountain on Mount Helicon associated with the Muses, the chief among whom (Calliope) is the Muse of eloquence.

a siluer Crosse set in blue silke: cf. Herbert Maxwell's note on St Andrew's cross in *Notes and Queries*, 10th series, 9 (1908), 32–3.

49   **traced his horse**: made his way on his horse. The verb is not normally used transitively as here.

had the foyle: was defeated.

varnished: embellished, adorned.

those Giants ... linnage: probably a reference to the Titans (who ruled the earth until they were overthrown by the Olympians under Zeus), the Cyclopes, and their monstrous, hundred-handed brothers (Briareus, Cottus and Gyges).

fierie ... Anuill: such similes are commonplace in Middle English romance: cf. *Sir Ferumbras*, line 605; *Otuel and Roland*, line 492.

iustly downe: right down.

50 **Curtleaxe**: cutlass.

prophaned: blasphemous. The participial form of the adjective is unusual in this sense; it may be simply a compositor's error, though it is uncorrected in the 1608 and 1616 editions.

mornings messengers: birds, singing at daybreak; cf. Sidney, *Astrophel and Stella*, XCIX.

51 **homely**: rough.

russet: 'coarse homespun woollen cloth of a reddish-brown, grey or neutral colour, formerly used for the dress of peasants and country-folk' (*OED*).

mourning cloth: the use of black or purple cloth to drape rooms or buildings as a sign of mourning has persisted until modern times: cf. accounts of reaction to the death of President J. F. Kennedy. The practice perhaps gave rise to Shakespeare's image 'Hung be the heavens with black' (*1 Henry VI*, I.i.1).

52 **the Ile ... Turkes**: Willkomm (p. 67) describes as 'a pious fiction' (*eine fromme Fiktion*) Johnson's account of the recovery of Rhodes. In fact the island was captured from the Knights Hospitaller by the Ottoman Turks in 1522 and, though it remained a scene of conflict between Western and Turkish forces (cf. *Othello*, I.i.28), remained in their hands until it was taken by Italy in 1912.

a maze ... Gardner: the maze was introduced into England as a garden feature in the fourteenth century, but became particularly popular during the Elizabethan period.

balefull misselto: the same phrase occurs in *Titus Andronicus*, II.iii.95. The plant probably acquired its sinister reputation because it was with a dart of mistletoe that the Norse god Balder was slain by his blind brother, Hoder. According to one tradition, Christ's cross was made of mistletoe, which is also associated with the Druids and thereby with human sacrifice.

52–3 **hauling by the hayre**: cf. *FQ*, II.iv.3.

53 **euery one ... trees**: cf. note to p. 38 above.

so mightely ... farewell: cf. note to p. 13 above; *FQ*, VI.v.18.

Most redeemed: clearly, a line or so of text has been accidentally left out between these two words – hence the omission of the rest of the paragraph from subsequent editions.

55 *Moroco* **Steede**: probably synonymous with 'Barbary horse' (cf. note to p. 32 above).

wrought ... Indian women: cf. note to p. 29 above.

golden ... blew: the arms here described are actually those of the Montagu family (*Boutell's Heraldry*, p. 81).

Countie *Palatine*: a count with quasi-royal jurisdiction over a particular area.

timeles: untimely.

abashed: confounded, horrified.

56   **bace blood**: person of humble birth (not necessarily one born out of wedlock).

precious ... Sonne: the phraseology recalls that of the Book of Common Prayer (in the order of service for Holy Communion) to the point of blasphemy.

the dreadfull ... followe: cf. note to p. 10 above. In Aeschylus's *Oresteia*, Orestes is thus pursued by the Furies after he has killed his mother, Clytemnestra, and her lover, Aegisthus, to avenge their murder of his father, Agamemnon.

mercie ... minde: cf. Chaucer, *The Canterbury Tales*, I.1761; Shakespeare, *The Merchant of Venice*, IV.i.180–93.

considerate: careful, considered.

57   **labors of *Hercules***: when Hercules, in a fit of madness, killed his wife and children, he consulted the oracle at Delphi as to how he might expiate his sin. The oracle bade him serve King Eurystheus, who imposed on him twelve seemingly impossible labours.

enterprise ... Fleece: at the behest of King Pelias, Jason undertook a journey fraught with perils on the ship *Argo* in order to recover the Golden Fleece from Colchis, where it was guarded by a dragon which never slept.

Macedonian ... world: it was in Babylon that Alexander the Great died. *Angels* is almost certainly an error for *Angles* (cf. *FQ*, III.ix); it remains uncorrected in the 1608 edition, though the 1616 edition reads: 'when he had conquered part of the world'.

Inchaunted Garden: Ormondine's enclosed garden, with the threats to chivalric prowess posed by its soporific charms, recalls not only the island of the Sirens (cf. note to p. 22 above) but also the garden of Gatholonabes in *Mandeville's Travels* (pp. 200–2), the magic garden described in *Gesta Romanorum*, XXIV (pp. 55–6), and Acrasia's Bower of Bliss (*FQ*, II.xii).

incompassed ... briers: cf. the Grimms' story of *Brier Rose* (the Sleeping Beauty story).

blazing Commets: comets were commonly seen as portents of disaster (as was Halley's comet in 1066).

patterne: image.

at hys conceit: to his imagination.

In which Rock ... sworde: the motif inevitably recalls the sword that Arthur must draw out of the stone in order to prove his right to the throne. Cf. also *Arthur of Little Britaine*, fol. 81ʳ.

58   **conceited**: fantastic, mistaken.

a sodayne & heauie sleepe: the motif of an enchanted sleep occurs also in Malory's 'The Tale of Sir Launcelot du Lake' (vol. I, pp. 256–7).

Culuers: doves.

conceited: ingeniously devised.

Arions **Harpe**: Arion, a Greek poet and singer, was a historical figure around whom fictitious traditions grew up. According to legend, the crew of a Corinthian ship plotted to throw him overboard and steal the money that he had earned by his music in Italy and Sicily. However, they granted his dying wish to sing one last song, and a dolphin, charmed by his music, bore him safely on its back to land. The story is told by Herodotus (I.xxiv).

Orpheus ... **notes**: the story of Orpheus's descent to the Underworld, where his music charmed all who heard it and persuaded Pluto and Proserpine to let him take his wife, Eurydice, back with him to the world above, is told in Ovid's *Metamorphoses*, X.1–85. The terms 'hell' and 'diuelles' suggest a Christianized view of the pagan Underworld as a place of punishment. For the effect of Orpheus's music on inanimate nature, see Ovid, *Metamorphoses*, XI.44–8; and cf. Shakespeare, *The Two Gentleman of Verona*, III.ii.77–80; *The Merchant of Venice*, V.i.79–80; *King Henry VIII*, III.i.3–14.

60   **Ladie** *Ver*: a personification of spring.

cursed the day of his creation: cf. 'he cursed the time y^t he was borne' (*BH*, sig. Diii^v).

Many times ... dayes: cf. 'out of my life I would I wore ... / Now giue me grace heauen to winne, and out of prison that I am in' (*BH*, sig. Diii^v).

a certaine Iron Engin ... ground: in *BH* (sigs Diii^v–Div^r), Bevis tricks his gaolers into descending into his dungeon; he kills them and, with divine help, is able to leap out of the dungeon.

60–1   **At last ... escape**: *7Ch*'s dependence on *BH* (sig. Div^r) in this passage has given rise to narrative inconsistency in that St George has not 'murdered his warders' (cf. previous note).

61   **purple spotted**: i.e. dappled or streaked with red.

Grecia: in *BH* (sig. Div^v), we are not told precisely where Bevis's encounter with the giant takes place, but we *are* told that he has crossed the sea since escaping from his prison in Damascus. Cf., however, note to p. 75 below.

if I were now ... browne bread: cf. 'if I were king of Armony, / I would giue it without read, for one shiuer of browne bread' (*BH*, sig. Div^v).

distressed Ladie: although this whole episode is based closely on *BH*, there is nothing there to suggest that the giant's lady is any sense a damsel in distress.

Queenes of *Troy*: Hecuba's.

62   **one meales meate**: a direct quotation of *BH* (sig. Div^v).

curst: angry.

Sir Knight ... commixt: cf. *BH*, sigs Div^v–Ei^v, which Johnson here follows closely.

first gaue ... consisted: there is no parallel to this pious act of thanksgiving in *BH*.

So trauailed ... *Tartarie*: probably Johnson was unaware of the location of these countries in relation to one another and did not realize that he has made his hero travel thousands of miles back eastwards. But cf. note to p. 75 below.

63   **by a thred of vntwisted silke**: i.e. by a single strand of silk.

Armour ... mad: after the death of Achilles, Ajax and Ulysses both laid claim to the dead hero's armour. It was awarded to Ulysses, and the furious Ajax decided to kill the Greek leaders in revenge. However, Athena sent him mad, with the result that Ajax killed the Greek livestock instead. When he recovered his sanity and realized what he had done, he killed himself.

sprung ... *Troian* **warriours**: cf. note to p. 5 above.

that thou take to wife a pure maide: this injunction is given to Bevis by the Patriarch of Jerusalem (*BH*, sig. Ei^v).

64   *Scythia*: an ancient country of central Asia, with a reputation for cruelty and barbarity (cf. *King Lear*, I.i.115; *Titus Andronicus*, I.i.131).

attractiue Adamants: lodestones, magnets.

Armenia: Armenia features prominently in *BH*; it is the native land of Bevis's future bride, Iosian.

laying dishonour in her dish: accusing her of dishonour; assigning the blame to her.

65   **chamberloue**: apparently, secret love unsanctified by marriage; there are also connotations of wantonness and unmanliness (cf. *OED*, s.v. chamber, sb, III).

like *Priams* **sonne ... wife**: like Paris before Helen.

goe sing ... birdes: probably an allusion to the Procne legend (cf. note to p. 21 above).

Caue ... Uirginitie: Castria's words (inappropriately) recall those of Jephthah's daughter (Judges xi.37).

maske: perform a masque.

blaze: torch.

66   *Hymens* **holy rites**: marriage, Hymen being the classical god of marriage.

vse: custom.

Court table: a small, movable table.

burne blew: an evil omen or a sign of ghostly presence (cf. Shakespeare, *King Richard III*, V.iii.181). See also *Præterita: the Autobiography of John Ruskin*, p. 454.

Caule: a close-fitting cap, or a net for the hair.

67   **in company ... lakes**: the Styx, one of the rivers of the classical Underworld, is sometimes said to be that over which the ferryman Charon carries the dead to their final dwelling-place. According to Virgil (*Aeneid*, VI.327–8), Charon will not ferry those whose bodies are unburied. It may be that Castria – who, as a suicide, would be excluded from Christian burial – is conflating classical and Christian beliefs and envisages herself as wandering for ever along the shores of the Styx, unable to cross.

regiment: kingdom.

Danaus **daughters**: when the fifty daughters of Danaus were married against their will, their father secretly gave each of them a dagger with which to kill her husband on the wedding-night. Forty-nine of them obeyed him and, in punishment, were forced to spend the afterlife putting water into leaking vessels.

68   *Crusas* **shadow**: Creusa, Aeneas's wife, was killed when Troy was sacked by the Greeks. Her ghost appeared to Aeneas, urging him to leave Troy and fulfil his divinely appointed destiny. Aeneas tried to embrace her, but the apparition faded away (*Aeneid*, II.738–94).

Didos **Ghost**: when Aeneas descended into the Underworld, he encountered the ghost of Dido (though not in the Elysian Fields). He addressed her, seeking to excuse his desertion of her, but she turned silently away and went back to her husband, Sychaeus (*Aeneid*, VI.450–76).

Ghost: spirit, life.

wordes vaine: a biblical locution (e.g. Exodus v.9; Ephesians v.6).

fatall twist: the thread of life spun, measured and cut by the three Fates.

Tartar gulfes: Tartarus was the nethermost part of the classical Underworld, and the place where evil-doers were punished (*Aeneid*, VI.577–627).

burning lakes: Johnson is probably referring to Acheron, which is sometimes described as a marshy lake rather than a river, and which he himself often calls 'burning'.

Cossitus: Cocytus, the river of wailing in the classical Underworld.

gape, gape, sweete earth: cf. Shakespeare, *1 Henry VI*, I.i.161; also Hammond's note to *King Richard III*, I.ii.65.

flying musicke: swiftly travelling report.

69   **famine … wicked**: cf. the account of the Four Horsemen of the Apocalypse in Revelation vi.

warie: fearsome? The 1616 edition reads *wanny*.

Auerna: Avernus, a lake near Naples, was thought to be one of the entrances to the Underworld. The name was also applied (as here) to the Underworld itself (cf. *Aeneid*, VI.126–9).

that inticed … whole world: a variation on the Faustian pact, where the soul is traded in exchange for worldly wealth and power.

confusion: overthrow, dissolution.

70   **Chalkey cliffes**: the white cliffs of Dover.

top of a huge mountaine: cf. *FQ*, I.x.53–7, where the future St George views the New Jerusalem from the top of a high mountain.

71   **Tragedy**: downfall.

Graue father … finished: the passage corresponds closely to *BH* (sig. Eiiʳ), though there the exchange is between Bevis and a knight whom he meets by chance as he travels towards Armenia.

exchaunge thy clothing: Bevis (*BH*, sig. Eiiʳ) similarly exchanges clothing with a palmer.

in boote with: in addition to.

72–7   **My deare brethren … which in this order was dressed**: the entire episode of George and Sabra's reunion and their flight from Almidor's court relies heavily on *BH* (sigs Eii^r–Eiii^r), though Johnson elaborates the narrative with Sabra's song and omits the details of the ruse by means of which Bevis and Iosian get the latter's husband out of the way. Johnson's dependence on *BH*, indeed, betrays him into inconsistency, since George hears Sabra sing '*I liue and die a maide*' but later, in a passage which corresponds closely to *BH*, questions her virginity.

72   *abandon*: dispel.

73   **Then ... annoy**: 'Then sorrowful lamentations shall end, together with profound suffering.'

     wed me to their will: made me marry as they wished.

     beneuolence: i.e. the benevolence to be shown towards him and the other palmers by Sabra.

     Polixena ... sacrifice: the Trojan princess Polyxena was sacrificed by the Greeks on the grave of Achilles.

     ouerchanged ... siluer: there is no parallel in *BH* to this passage, which is untypical of romance – though Sabra almost immediately becomes 'beauteous *Sabra*' again. Cf. Johnson's description of the hero's mother, Angellica, in *Tom a Lincolne*, pp. 66–7.

     sometimes: at one time.

74   **bruted**: rumoured, reported.

     approued: trusty, loyal.

     Bucephalus: the horse of Alexander the Great.

     seale vp the quittance of our former loues: this appears from the context to mean 'fulfil the vows of love that we made before', although *quittance* normally denotes release or discharge from a debt or promise.

75   **an Euenuke**: in *BH* (sig. Eiii^r), it is Boniface, Iosian's 'Chamberlaine' (sig. Cii^v), who advises the lovers and accompanies them in their flight.

     alwaies kneeled downe: remained kneeling.

     they looked ... Græcia: either this is a further instance of Johnson's confused geography, or he perhaps means by '*Græcia*' what we would call Asia Minor.

     Melpomine: Melpomene, whose name means 'singer', was the Muse of tragedy.

76   **there appeared ... maidens lappe**: the episode of the lions is borrowed from *BH*, though with some modifications. In *BH* (sig. Eiv^r), Iosian offers to hold one of the lions while Bevis kills the other, but he angrily rejects her suggestion ('What maistry is it them to slo, in handes when ye hold them so?'); the ensuing battle between man and lions is 'strong and perilous'.

     The belief that a lion will not harm one of royal blood is a commonplace of medieval and Renaissance literature (e.g. *Torrent of Portyngale*, lines 283–8; *FQ*, I.iii.5–6; cf. Humphreys's note to *1 Henry IV*, II.iv.267–8). In *BH*, and therefore in *7Ch*, the lions combine with this property that of the unicorn, which can only be subdued by a virgin, in whose lap the creature will lay its head.

77   **pocket**: bag, pouch.

fire-locke: the term is recorded in *OED* only as denoting that part of the mechanism of a firearm which produces a spark in order to ignite the priming. Here, however, it seems to mean a tinder-box.

they generally ariued: they arrived all together.

78 **To speake ... Homer**: the *Iliad* (II.484–877) gives a long catalogue of the troops mustered by the Greeks for the assault on Troy.

a golden penne: i.e. a pen fit to record the most noble and illustrious deeds.

bearing ... Armes: the ancient French royal arms had an azure field powdered with golden fleur-de-lis; Edward III quartered the French arms on his Great Seal in 1340. The number of fleur-de-lis was later reduced to three in both France and England (*Boutell's Heraldry*, pp. 35, 86).

79 **deuices**: i.e. heraldic devices.

after the Barbarian manner: this probably denotes armour lighter than the full metal suit of armour.

a golden ... Rome: the heraldry of *7Ch* seems to be largely Johnson's own invention, though the eagle here may possibly recall the standard borne by Roman legionaries.

the King of Sycils Daughter: Rossalinde has previously been described as the King of Thrace's daughter (see p. 39 above).

Tritons: minor sea-gods, the retinue of Neptune.

a corner Crosse ... Armes: these are not, of course, the arms of Scotland (cf. note to p. 48 above). The term 'corner Crosse' possibly denotes a saltire, whose upper arms extend to the top corners of the shield; the expression is not recorded in *OED*.

Portegues: the portague or crusado was a gold Portuguese coin current in the sixteenth century and ranging in value from £3 5s. to £5 10s.

Hobbie: a small, ambling horse or pony, usually referred to as being of Irish breed.

siluane Knights: such figures were a feature of masques and pageants (e.g. Thomas Campion's *A Maske Presented in Honour of the Lord Hay's Marriage*).

80 **approue**: put to the test.

a siluer Griffon ... Brittaine: 'Brittaine' here appears to denote Wales, though lions and dragons are the creatures usually associated with Welsh arms (*Boutell's Heraldry*, p. 218).

siluer Table ... scarfe: probably a woven picture (*table* meaning 'picture', and damask being a rich silken material often woven with elaborate designs in a variety of colours).

ioyntles Elephants: according to the bestiaries, the elephant has no joints in its legs and so is unable to rise if it falls down; it sleeps leaning against a tree. In order to capture an elephant, therefore, the canny hunter saws partway through the tree's trunk. The elephant thus symbolizes sinful man, since it was through a tree, in the Garden of Eden, that Adam and Eve fell. Appropriately enough, the elephant figures in the arms of St George's birthplace, Coventry.

inuincible tamer … throne: possibly a reference to Typhon/Typhoeus, a many-headed monster who challenged the power of Jove (cf. note to p. 31 above); he was overcome by Jove himself.

81   *Phrigian* … **Maske**: I have been unable to identify this allusion; the 'Paragon of *Asia*' is presumably Helen.

& when shee daunst … for loue: the whole passage reads like barely prosified verse, but I have been unable to identify the source, if there is one. The phrase '*Thetis* tripping on the siluer sandes' has an exact parallel in Arthur Warren's poem *Poverties Patience* (1605); it may be an image for the 'dancing' of waves on the sea-shore, since Thetis (the mother of Achilles) was a sea goddess (cf. the description of Perdita's dancing in *The Winter's Tale*, IV.iv.140–1). It was in fact Jove who fell in love with her, but she rejected his advances out of loyalty to his wife, Juno, who had raised her. Cf. p. xxii above.

82   *Prester Iohns* **Dominions**: Prester John was a legendary Christian emperor. In Marco Polo's *Travels*, he is lord of the Tartars; in *Mandeville's Travels*, he is called 'the grete emperour of Ynde' (p. 194).

bay of *Portingale*: the Bay of Biscay. Willkomm (p. 66) relates this reference to the international political climate of the later sixteenth century, when 'die Augen Englands nach der iberischen Halbinsel gerichtet waren', and in particular to the Battle of Alcazar in 1578. Cf. also Hirsch's note to *Tom a Lincolne*, p. 16, line 17.

sequell: ensuing part.

83   **as the** *Græcians* … **Troy**: Agamemnon, the brother of Helen's husband, Menelaus, was the leader of the Greek troops when they besieged Troy.

colours: heraldic devices.

83–4   **sanguine … Lyon**: a golden lion bearing a banner with a red cross, and representing England, is one of the supporters in the Scottish arms (see *Boutell's Heraldry*, plate VI).

84   **whose conquering … earth**: in *Toxophilvs* (1545), Roger Ascham prescribes the use of goose feathers for fletching arrows (B, fols 16–18). English armies in the medieval and early modern periods used large numbers of archers. The longbow, invariably made of yew (see below), was less powerful than the crossbow but could be reloaded more quickly; it was an effective weapon against enemy cavalry.

Arrowes … heads: cf. Ascham, *Toxophilvs* (B, fols 13, 19).

Mandillians: a mandilion is a loose coat or cassock worn by soldiers.

headdy: determined, stalwart?

Caliuer: a light firearm, or a soldier armed with such.

smaller timbred: more lightly built.

Aunsients: ensigns, banners.

Pioners: foot soldiers who clear the way for the advance of the main body of an army.

Sconses: small earthworks.

as worthy *Hanniball* … *Spaine*: in 218 BC the Carthaginian general Hannibal led an army across the Alps into Italy to attack Rome.

their colours ... Wales: cf. note to p. 80 above.

an Armie ... steele: the kerns, Irish foot soldiers drawn from the poorer classes, were commonly armed with darts or javelins made of ash and tipped with steel or iron. The gallowglasses (see below) wore armour made in part of strong leather, and their wooden shields were sometimes covered with animal skins.

85   **Gallowayes**: men from Galloway in south-west Scotland; the name is also given to a breed of small, strong horse (cf. Humphreys's note to *2 Henry IV*, II.iv.186–7). Johnson may, however, have meant 'gallowglasses', Scottish or Irish heavy infantry (cf. *Macbeth*, I.ii.13; *2 Henry VI*, IV.ix.26). *Orcadie*: Orkney.

    Callidonians: the earliest example cited in *OED* of the occurrence of the noun *Caledonian*, meaning a native of Scotland, dates from 1768.

    footeman: infantry soldier.

86   **Israels annoynted**: in the Bible, such a term would most usually be applied to a king or priest. Here it clearly refers to Christ, whose name (from Greek *Christos*) means 'anointed'.

    to climbe ... former times: the reference is to the building of the tower of Babel, often ascribed to Nimrod, although the Bible does not explicitly state that he built it (cf. Genesis x.8–10, xi.1–9).

88   **though *Hungarie* ... through the *Campe***: the implication is that Hungary is a pagan land in Asia. Firmly ensconced in Europe, however, it has been Christian since the eleventh century.

    Parthians: natives of Parthia, an ancient kingdom of western Asia.

89   **Prouinces of *Prester Iohn***: these were supposedly Christian (cf. note to p. 82 above).

    cost more ... *Ierusalem*: Johnson is referring to the fall of Jerusalem to the Romans under Titus, son of Vespasian, in AD 70. In fictionalized form, this was the subject of the Middle English romances *The Seege of Jerusalem* and *Titus and Vespasian*.

    tryed siluer: purified/refined silver.

90   **lake of obliuion**: Lethe, whose waters bring oblivion to those who drink them, is a river (not a lake) of the classical Underworld.

    The Armie ... *Barberie*: cf. *BH*, sig. Giv^{r-v}, where the troops of Bevis's stepfather, Murdure, likewise attempt to flee when their leader is captured; many of them are slain by Bevis's men.

    First ... Brimstone: Bevis's stepfather is punished in the same manner (*BH*, sig. Giv^v).

91   **the burning Ouen at *Babilon***: the 'burning fiery furnace' in which Shadrach, Meshach and Abednego were condemned to be cast for refusing to honour Nebuchadnezzar's gods (Daniel iii.15ff.).

    before him ... destenie: the wheel of Fortune is a commonplace of medieval and Renaissance iconography and literary imagery. The fall of kings or potentates is invariably depicted. Cf. Walter's note to *Henry V*, III.iv.27–39.

proffering ... Pilgrimage: cf. the ransom offered by King Iour to Bevis (*BH*, sig. Hiv^v) in exchange for his life.

Argases: trading vessels.

Lapidistes: the earliest occurrence recorded in *OED* of the word *lapidist*, denoting someone who cuts, polishes or engraves precious stones, dates from 1647.

drawe ... Charriot: cf. Marlowe, *2 Tamburlaine*, IV.iii, where Tamburlaine is drawn in a chariot by the conquered Kings of Trebizon and Soria.

91–2   **for seauen yeares ... dungeon**: cf. *BH*, sig. Dii^r.

92   *Barbary, Moroco & India*: Willkomm (pp. 65–6) points out that Tamburlaine likewise wins three crowns. Presumably the reference here is to 'Ynde the Lasse' (cf. note to p. 29 above).

by whose mightines ... power: cf. the boast of Tamburlaine: 'I hold the Fates bound fast in iron chains, / And with my hand turn Fortune's wheel about' (*1 Tamburlaine*, I.ii.174–5).

ofspringes of *Cayne*: Cain was cursed by God after he killed his brother, Abel, and condemned to a life of labour and vagrancy (Genesis iv.11–16).

generations of *Iesmaell*: Ishmael was the son of Abraham by Hagar, the handmaid of his wife, Sarah. Hagar was driven out by Sarah before the birth of her son, so that Ishmael's name (like Cain's) became synonymous with 'outcast' (Genesis xvi). Moslems claim descent from Ishmael.

seede of Uipers: cf. 'generation of vipers' (Matthew iii.7, etc.).

gates of mightie *Mahomet*: Mahomet is here regarded as a deity, like Jove (cf. note to p. 17 above).

famine of *Ierusalem*: a reference to the siege of Jerusalem under the Roman Emperor Vespasian (cf. note to p. 89 above).

93   **fell downe and broake their neckes**: in *BH* (sig. Giv^v), Bevis's mother throws herself from a high tower and breaks her neck when her husband dies in the same manner as Almidor.

imperious Pall: imperial robe.

chiefeest poynt ... Christendome: on the chivalric oath to fight in the cause of the Christian faith, see Barber, ch. 2; Keen, pp. 71–7).

canckered ease: depraved/unhealthy idleness.

94   **leastall**: laystall, i.e. refuse tip or burial place.

sillie: innocent, helpless.

95   **children may be gotten agayne**: cf. the egregiously unpaternal sentiment uttered in *Amis and Amiloun*, lines 2324–5: 'Jhesu, when it is his wille, / May sende me childer mo.'

caused seauen Pies ... Parents: the episode again recalls the story of Tereus (cf. note to p. 21 above); the detail of the pies, and the fact that more than one child is killed, suggests the influence of *Titus Andronicus* (V.iii.60–1) also. Willkomm (p. 67) draws attention to a possible relationship to an item entered in the Stationers' Register in September 1600: *The first parte of the widowe of England and her Seven sonnes who for the faythe of Jesus Christe were all most straungelie tormented to*

Deathe by the Turkes in Barbary. While this work would clearly have been too late to have influenced *7Ch*, its author and Johnson may well have drawn on a common source.

Nero ... opened: the tradition that Nero killed his mother, Agrippina, so that he could 'beholde the place of hys creation' seems to have been well known in sixteenth-century England (cf., e.g., Shakespeare, *King John*, V.ii.152–3).

96   **bid**: offer.

97   **courage**: spirit.

     Lawrell wreathes: traditional emblems of victory or success.

     my Commons blood ... hands: I shall be held accountable for the deaths of my subjects; reparation will be demanded of me.

98   **whips of wier**: cf. Marlowe, *2 Tamburlaine*, III.v.104.

     Tantalus: a Lydian king who offended the gods and was punished in the Underworld by having fruit and water enticingly near but forever just out of his reach.

     vouchsafed ... Christ Iesus: Bevis likewise forgives Iosian's father on condition that he embraces Christianity (*BH*, sig. Hiv^r).

     couered ... rooffe: cf. the description of the temple of Arsinoë in Pliny, *Historia naturalis*, XXXIV.xli.

99   **she is iudged ... Couentrie**: the episode of the attempted seduction of Sabra and her arrest for murder is loosely based on *BH* (sigs Gi^r–Gii^v), where Iosian is coerced into marriage with Earl Miles during Bevis's absence, and hangs her husband on their wedding-night. Like Sabra, she is rescued in the nick of time from burning at the stake.

100   **the Chayne ... blood**: cf. note to p. 16 above.

     the greatest Piere in all England: during the period 1483–1572 this would have been the Duke of Norfolk (cf. notes to pp. 3, 5 and 6 above). However, when the Fourth Duke was attainted for high treason in 1572 the title lapsed until 1660.

101   *Sabra* **is beautefull ... woone**: cf. *Titus Andronicus*, II.i.82–4; also *ODEP*, W681.

     her Minnions: her darling's, i.e. Mars's. The reference is apposite, in that Mars was Venus's lover despite the fact that she was married to Vulcan (as Sabra is married to St George).

     glyding shadowe: transient illusion.

     Camphire Tapors: camphor was also burned for its aromatherapeutic properties.

     began the Tapors to burne blue: cf. note to p. 66 above.

102   **the Queene of *Cipresse***: Venus (see note to p. 21 above).

     Prophetesse of *Troy*: Priam's daughter Cassandra, who was doomed to prophesy truly without ever being believed.

     Caranta: coranto, a dance in triple time characterized by a gliding step (cf. Sir John Davies, *Orchestra*, lxix).

     silence ... consentment: a proverbial saying deriving from a Latin legal maxim, *Qui tacet consentire videtur*.

Mauors: another name for Mars.

Hyren ... Mahomet: Johnson may have known the story of Mohammed the Great (sultan of Turkey from 1451 to 1481) and his love for the Greek slave Hyren/Hyrenee from William Painter's *The Palace of Pleasure*, I, xxxix, or from a lost play by Robert Greene (see Humphreys's note to *2 Henry IV*, IV.ii.156–7). Samuel Johnson's play *Irene* (1736) is based on the same story, which he took from Richard Knolles's *The Generall Historie of the Turkes* ... (1603), pp. 350–3. The story tells how the sultan incurred the criticism of his subjects because of his infatuation with Hyren, which caused him to neglect affairs of state, and therefore publicly decapitated her in order to prove that he did not place his private affections above his royal duties.

Cressida ... Troylus: Shakespeare's play about the ill-fated Trojan lovers probably postdates *7Ch*, but the story was already well known in England. It is, of course, the subject of Chaucer's *Troilus and Criseyde*. The comparison of Sabra to Cressida is hardly flattering, since Cressida's name was a byword for fickleness in love.

103 **fond**: foolish.

like to the Turtle Doue: the turtle dove is a commonplace symbol of faithful, monogamous love (cf., e.g., Chaucer, *The Parliament of Fowls*, line 355).

Ile haue thee clad ... Steedes: cf. Marlowe, *1 Tamburlaine*, I.ii.92–101, where Tamburlaine offers comparable inducements to Zenocrate.

purple Pallace ... bed: Hyperion is another name for the god of the sun. Aurora is more usually described as *rising* blushing from her bed (cf. note to p. 15 above).

104 **wanting**: lacking, needing.

pretended: there appears to be a certain amount of confusion as to whether or not the Earl really means to kill himself for love of Sabra.

106 **First will I wrappe ... disgrace**: in this echo of the Tereus and Philomela story, the influence of *Titus Andronicus* is again apparent: when Titus's daughter, Lavinia, is raped, she has not only her tongue but her hands cut off, so that she cannot (like Philomela) tell her story in needlework.

Wolfe ... Lambe: cf. Shakespeare, *The Rape of Lucrece*, line 677.

Tygers of *Hercania*: Hyrcania is the region around the Caspian Sea. On the tigers associated with it, see Cairncross's note to *3 Henry VI*, I.iv.155.

conuerted ... eyes: in the Middle English *Bevis* (though not in the text as it is found in the printed editions), Iosian disfigures herself by means of a herb so that her husband, King Yuor, will feel no physical desire for her (Auchinleck text, ed. Kölbing, lines 3671–3700). Her appearance becomes that of a 'foule mesel'.

106–7 *Romaine Lucresiaes* **Rape**: the Roman matron Lucretia was raped by Sextus Tarquinius, son of the King of Rome. After revealing to her father and her husband what had happened, she killed herself. As a result, the Tarquinii were expelled from Rome, and republican government was established. Shakespeare's poem on the subject was published in 1594.

107　　**But as women ... wittes**: proverbial; cf. Whiting, W531.
109　　**stand still ... heauen**: cf. Marlowe, *Doctor Faustus*, V.ii.129.

　　　those Dames ... blood: the Furies.

　　　King *Priams* Queene ... gore: Johnson is perhaps thinking of the episode where Hecuba tears out the eyes of Polymestor in revenge for the death of her last surviving son, Polydorus (Ovid, *Metamorphoses*, XIII.549–64).

　　　the more shee washed ... it is done: cf. *Macbeth*, V.i, which suggests the influence of the tradition that murderers cannot cleanse their hands of their victims' blood. A comparable motif occurs in the Grimms' story *Fowler's Fowl*, a version of the Bluebeard story.

　　　stroken ... Plannet: cf. *Titus Andronicus*, II.v.14.

　　　turned ... blood: the notion that the blood of a murdered man will make water run red presumably lies behind *Macbeth*, II.ii.59–62.

　　　it is the nature ... any dead man: the tradition that the robin will cover a dead body with leaves is best known from the story of the Babes in the Wood. Cf. also Webster, *The White Devil*, V.iv.96–9.

110　　**yet because ... Knight**: Johnson appears to have forgotten that Sabra is the wife of the King's own grandson.

111　　***Phœbus***: the sun.

　　　Zodiacke of heauen: i.e. the region of the heavens in which the apparent motion of the sun is seen.

　　　conceited: extreme?

　　　pummells: ornamental knobs.

112　　**Rone coloured Steede**: a horse where the prevailing colour is intermixed with another.

113　　**portly**: imposing *or* stalwart.

115　　**Country of the *Amazonians***: this was supposedly located somewhere to the east or north-east of Greece.

　　　on the toppe ... gold: cf. the description of the fairy Tryamour's pavilion in the Middle English romance of *Syr Launfal*, lines 265–73.

　　　monument ... twelue wonders: the tomb of Mausolus, King of Caria, at Halicarnassus was one of the wonders of the ancient world. Johnson is not quite alone in speaking of twelve wonders of the world (cf. Davies, *Poems*, p. 225), though Spenser alludes to the usual seven (*FQ*, IV.x.30).

　　　gallant: fine, gorgeous.

　　　browes small and proper: eyebrows slender and pleasing in appearance; cf. *Arthur of Little Britaine*, fol. 80ᵛ, where exactly the same phrase occurs.

　　　plaine: perhaps 'regular' (in the sense in which that word might be used of facial features) or, possibly, 'unembellished'. Cf. *Arthur of Little Britaine*, fol. 80ᵛ.

116　　**Kertle**: gown, over-garment.

　　　Osmond: a common anglicization of Osman, the name of the founder of the Ottoman Empire.

　　　damned Charmes: i.e. diabolical powers which will bring his soul to eternal damnation.

morter ... virgins blood: in a general way, this recalls the Castle of Maidens and the death of Perceval's sister in Malory, vol. II, pp. 887–90, 1002–4. Cf. also Golder, 'Browning's *Childe Roland*', p. 971 n. 25, for parallels in *Arthur of Little Britaine*.

117   **Griffons ... horse and all**: cf. *FQ*, I.xi.18. A griffin is a lion with the head, legs and wings of an eagle.

    talents: talons.

118   **To which ... exstreamitie**: cf. *BH*, sig. Fi^r, where Bevis defeats the giant Ascapart, who does him homage and promises to serve him.

    wicket: a small door or gate within or beside a larger one.

    Urchens: hedgehog's.

119   **great Images ... steele**: cf. *Arthur of Little Britaine*, fol. 75^v; Munday, *Amadis de Gaule*, II, i. The motif also recalls Artegall's companion in Book V of *The Faerie Queene*: 'His name was *Talus*, made of yron mould, / Immoueable, resistlesse, without end. / Who in his hand an yron flale did hould' (*FQ*, V.i.12).

    I kisse your golden spurre: I swear fealty to you.

120   **Tike**: mattress.

    Mædian: Media was an ancient country of north-west Persia.

    which Cittie ... against the Sun: cf. the description of Damascus in *BH*, sig. Di^r.

121   **rauished ... bowels**: cf. *FQ*, IV.vii.12–13., where Æmylia's plight is similar to Sabra's in that she has seen seven maidens ravished and devoured by a giant.

    an vglie toade ... feature: cf. note to p. 105 above. The toad was commonly believed to be poisonous (cf. *As You Like It*, II.i.13).

122   **Toombe of *Angelica***: the name Angelica occurs quite frequently in Renaissance literature, most famously in Ariosto's *Orlando Furioso*, which was translated into English by Sir John Harington in 1591. Johnson himself uses the name in Chapter XI of Part II of *7Ch*, and again in *Tom a Lincolne* (cf. note to p. 73 above). However, I have been unable to find any Angelica with a noteworthy tomb.

    Here is the chaine ... my deare Ladie: comparable narrative motifs occur in *FQ*, III.viii.49, where Florimel's golden girdle is found 'Distaynd with durt and bloud', and in the story of Pyramus and Thisbe (cf. note to p. 39 above).

    Melmerophon ... Sillera: I have been unable to identify this allusion.

124   *How Saint George ... boies*: the episode of the birth of Sabra's children in the forest is directly based on *BH*, sig. Hii^r. On further analogues, see Fellows, 'St George', pp. 39–41.

    Graund *Belgor*: probably Belgrade, which was captured by the sultan Suleiman the Magnificent in 1521. Given Johnson's imperfect command of geography, it should not surprise us that he situates it in Persia.

    the Inhabitantes ... Queene: Johnson's Proserpine is similar to Shakespeare's Titania, at least as regards her entourage. (*A Midsummer Night's Dream* can probably be dated to 1594–6: see Brooks's edition,

p. lv.) 'Proserpina Queene of the Fairies' features in *Arthur of Little Britaine*, fol. 79ᵛ, etc. On the tendency of classical goddesses and nymphs to become fairies in Renaissance literature, see Purkiss, p. 177.

drawne ... daunces: though susceptible of a scientific explanation, the darker circles often found in areas of grass were popularly associated with the dancing of fairies (cf. *The Tempest*, V.1.36–8).

125   **yelling of Caues**: perhaps echoes created by the sound of the wind or of wild animals?

three times ... light: cf. *FQ*, III.iii.16.

a bower of Uine braunches: in *BH* (sig. Hiiʳ), Bevis and his companion Terry make 'a lodge' for Iosian with their swords.

therefore depart ... such a case: cf. 'for Gods loue go hence away ... / shall neuer womans priuitie, to man be shewed for me' (*BH*, sig. Hiiʳ). On the common belief that it was indecent for a man to witness a woman's delivery, see *Bevis*, ed. Kölbing, note to A3630f. (p. 335).

like the Noble Queene of Fraunce: in *Valentine and Orson*, a French prose romance translated into English by H. Watson *c*. 1502 and reprinted many times, Bellyssant (empress of Constantinople and sister to King Pepin) gives birth to the eponymous heroes in the forest. Valentine is raised by his royal uncle, and Orson by a bear.

126   **both hearbes ... complayned**: cf. *FQ*, III.iv.35.

At last ... into the world: in the French analogues discussed in Fellows, 'St George', pp. 39–41, the Virgin Mary acts as a midwife; in *BH* (sig. Hiiʳ), she is invoked for spiritual aid.

winged Satier: this figure recalls Puck in *A Midsummer Night's Dream*, II.i.175–6.

for thereon ... perfectly wrought: cf. the wonderful cloth described in the Middle English romance of *Emaré*, lines 97–168.

brauerie: splendour.

127   **like *Pallas* ... heauen**: cf. note to p. 35.

shadowes: illusions.

immortall *Ioue*: Jove seems here to be synonymous with the Christian God.

128   **staine ... hue**: *staine* here means 'deprive of colour'; *her* refers to Iris, the goddess of the rainbow.

marble: dappled, variegated in colour.

her wisedome ... *Lucinaes*: Apollo was god of (among other things) prophecy and divination; Pallas Athene was goddess of wisdom; Lucina presided over childbirth.

franckly: generously.

***Iason* ... *Medeas* loue**: it was, rather, Medea who risked dangers for Jason's sake (cf. note to p. 34 above).

Conquest of rich *Babilon*: the conquest of Babylon was achieved by Cyrus the Great.

129   ***Hercules* ... *Dianaria***: Hercules won Deianeira by wrestling with the river god Achelous.

Turnus: when the Trojans under Aeneas arrived in Italy, Turnus stirred up battle against them. He was finally killed by Aeneas in single combat.

which tooke ... Caues: the motif of children being separated from one or both of their parents, often by animal agency, in a wild place such as a forest occurs frequently both in folk-tale and in romance (e.g. *Sir Eglamour of Artois*, lines 841–3; *Sir Isumbras*, lines 179–86; *Valentine and Orson*, pp. 32–4; cf. also *FQ*, III.vi.26–8); it is particularly characteristic of stories of the 'St Eustace type'. See, further, Gerould, p. 338; Fellows, 'St George', pp. 39–42 and n. 78.

130 **vnkindly**: unnatural.

of which frute ... sleepe: this recalls the stratagem by which Jason subdued the dragon that guarded the Golden Fleece. On Medea's advice, he administered to it soporific drugs concealed in honey-cakes.

Remus ... **Wolfe**: when the Vestal Virgin Rhea Silva became pregnant by Mars, she was imprisoned by her uncle, in an attempt to avert a prophecy; her twin sons, Romulus and Remus, were to be thrown into the River Tiber. However, they floated to the shore and were suckled by a she-wolf. They were responsible for the founding of Rome.

Persian ... **Bitch:** Herodotus (I.cxxii) alludes to a tradition that Cyrus the Great, having been exposed as an infant, was suckled by a bitch.

131 *Guy ... Dauid*: one of Bevis's twin sons, born under similar circumstances, is called Guy after Bevis's own father. (It is not until later editions of *7Ch* that St George's son Guy is identified with Guy of Warwick: see note to p. 5 above.) Alexander is presumably named for Alexander the Great, and David for the champion of Wales, who in *7Ch* is second in prowess only to George himself.

Uniuersity of *Wittenberge*: celebrated for its famous alumni Dr Faustus and Martin Luther.

Element: sky.

133 **graund Cayer**: Cairo, the capital of Egypt; so called to distinguish it from Old Cairo.

Churches ... Religion: this is barely consistent with the fact that, according to Johnson's account, Egypt only became Christian on the conversion of Sabra's father, King Ptolemy (see p. 98 above).

Royaltie ... conquest: probably a reference to Julius Caesar's return to Rome after his defeat of Pompey in 48 BC.

solemnitie: pomp, ceremony.

curiositie: elaborateness.

Ceres: the classical goddess of corn and fruitfulness, and the mother of Proserpine.

134 **for therein ... in the earth**: magic mirrors, in which the viewer can see distant scenes, occur also in Chaucer's Squire's Tale (*Canterbury Tales*, v.132–43) and in *FQ*, III.ii.22–4.

yᵉ maner of Elizium ... thrones: Jove and Juno were enthroned on Olympus, not in Elysium, but Johnson tends to equate both Olympus and Elysium with the Christian Heaven.

how all the gods ... Parliament: _The Parliament of the Gods_ (_Deorum concilium_) is the title of a work by the second-century Greek satirist Lucian, whose works were well known in sixteenth-century England, especially in Humanist circles.

admired: such as to inspire wonder.

middle earth: the world, situated between Heaven and Hell.

cates: sweetmeats.

conseruatiues of yᵉ Muses hony: cf. note to p. 48 above.

135   **breuiat**: cut short.

137   **to drinke vp riuers as wee marched**: cf. note to p. 38 above.

blacke-faste: black-faced (cf. Shakespeare, _Venus and Adonis_, line 773; _King Richard III_, I.ii.162.) The Furies were commonly portrayed as dressed in black.

wise _Medea_ ... fathers state: Johnson appears to be a little confused here: far from safeguarding 'her fathers state', Medea betrayed it for love of Jason (cf. note to p. 34 above); she did not invoke supernatural warriors to protect her homeland but, on the contrary, taught Jason to combat those that sprang up when he sowed dragons' teeth in accordance with her father's instructions (cf. Ovid, _Metamorphoses_, VII.1–73).

138   **the wealthie Riuer _Ganges_**: cf. the description in _Mandeville's Travels_, p. 220, of the Ganges, 'in the whiche ryuere ben manye preciouse stones ... and moche grauelle of golde'.

Pactulus ... wish away: when Midas regretted having wished that everything he touched might turn into gold, he begged the god Bacchus, who had granted him that wish, to relieve him of it. Bacchus bade him wash it away in the River Pactolus, which ever since has had golden sand.

in his studie: to his thoughts.

Courts of gard: watchmen; the phrase is perhaps influenced by the French _corps de garde_.

139   **wade ... in bloud**: hyperbole of this kind is a commonplace of Middle English romance: cf., e.g., _The Sege of Melayne_, lines 1202–3.

Stand still ... heauen: cf. note to p. 108 above.

great _Dæmon_: either Demogorgon, who is mentioned by Spenser in connection with the three Fates (_FQ_, IV.ii.47), or Satan himself.

140   **God of loue**: Cupid, the son of Venus and her lover, Mars.

as though _Medusaes_ shaddowes ... faces: as though they had been turned to stone at sight of them. The face of the Gorgon Medusa was so terrible that anyone who looked at it was, literally, petrified. In order to kill her, therefore, Perseus could only look at her reflection in his shield.

141   **poysoned dregs ... drunkennes**: according to various versions of the Alexander legend (including _Kyng Alisaunder_, lines 7833–56), Alexander the Great died from drinking poison sent to him by the Macedonian justice Antipater; it is usually said to have been administered to him by his own cupbearer. Plutarch (LXXVII.1–3) alludes to this tradition.

yᵉ iuyce ... ring: rather than submit to capture by the Romans, Hannibal took poison contained in a ring that he wore.

142   **the Doues ... for loue**: see p. xxii above.

with his sword ... peeces: St George's destruction of the enchanted tent and its seductive charms is reminiscent of Guyon's destruction of Acrasia's Bower of Bliss in *FQ*, II.xii.83.

apparantly beheld: clearly saw.

a blocke of steele: cf. the description of 'great *Dæmon*' at p. 139 above.

the teares of Crocodiles: proverbially, crocodiles lure travellers to them by feigned sobs and then shed hypocritical tears as they devour them: cf. *FQ*, I.v.18; *1 Henry VI*, III.i.226–7.

143   **Porthers**: I can find no sense for this word that fits the context; it seems also to have been problematic for the compositors of the 1616 edition, which reads *thornes*.

Haue I had power ... charmes: see p. xxii above.

all you Schollers: Johnson undoubtedly has Dr Faustus, of the University of Wittenberg, in mind.

Beldames: witches, crones.

besides a number ... themselues: cf. the Chetham text of *Bevis*, ed. Kölbing, line 3967 (p. 199).

144   **sufficing ... water**: cf. p. 21 above.

caractred: portrayed, recorded.

144–5 **his martiall exployts ... the world**: Johnson's meaning here is unclear. It is hard to see how the exploits of a Christian saint can be celebrated by heathen poets – unless by 'heathen' he means adherents of the Eastern Church. St George is certainly not among the usual nine 'worthies of the world'.

145   *Darius*: Darius III, the last ruler of the Persian Empire, strove unsuccessfully to combat the growing power of Alexander the Great. According to legend, Alexander had great respect for him, punishing his murderers (cf. *Kyng Alisaunder*, lines 4639–4715).

raging Seas: we have only just been told that 'the waues couched as smooth as Chrystall yce, and the windes blewe such gentle gale, as though the sea-gods had beene the directors of their fleete'.

Pharao ... Legions: when the Israelites fled from Egypt, the waters of the Red Sea parted so that they could cross in safety but 'returned and covered the charets and the horsemen, euen all the hoste of Pharaoh that came into the Sea after them' (Exodus xiv.28).

King of Iuda: not a biblical appellation for the deity. Cf., however, Matthew ii.6.

acceptable in thy sight: cf. Psalms xix.14.

vollew: outpouring.

incontinently: immediately.

eloquence of *Cicero*: the works of the Roman statesman and orator Marcus Tullius Cicero were highly regarded in sixteenth-century England and would have become familiar to many as school texts.

145–6 **the second part ... renowned Champions**: since the end of the 1596 edition of *7Ch* is missing, we cannot know whether Johnson always intended to write a second part or whether he was prompted to do so by the popularity of Part I (though cf. p. 149 below). Although the second (1608) edition of Part I, which is here used to supply the chapters missing from the first, was published together with Part II, it is not in fact until the 1616 edition that Johnson adds to his account of the Seven Champions' lives 'the true manner of their deaths, being seauen famous tragedies'.

149 **Lorde William Howard**: the third son of Thomas Howard, Fourth Duke of Norfolk, and brother of the dedicatee of the first part of *7Ch* (see note to p. 3 above). In many ways he is a more appropriate choice of patron than his brother: according to *DNB*, he was a friend of Sir Robert Cotton and William Camden, the latter describing him as 'a singular lover of valuable antiquity and learned withal'. On the other hand, he appears to have remained more faithful to the Roman Catholic Church than did his brother, and therefore to have been more likely to be offended by some of the subject-matter of *7Ch* (especially Part II, Chapter XIII).

being thertoo ... first part: cf. p. 145–6 above.

And accept it: if you accept it.

151 *Grecian* **Queenes ... snares of loue**: the reference seems to be to Helen, though the plural 'Queenes' is puzzling.

barbed: armed.

champion fields: fields of battle.

152 **beautefied with tapestrie**: just as black or purple hangings were used to denote mourning (see note to p. 51 above), so brightly coloured cloths and tapestries might be displayed on more festive occasions (cf. *Syr Launfal*, lines 904–6).

Arcadie: a region of the Peleponnese which was supposedly the abode of the god Pan and which became associated (through Theocritus, Virgil and, later, Sir Philip Sidney) with an idealized notion of the pastoral life.

stratagem: a 'deed of blood or violence' (*OED*).

153 **mistrusted**: suspected, foresaw.

ceremonies: portents (cf. *Julius Caesar*, II.i.197; II.ii.13).

proffering: attempting.

154 **sight-killing cockatrices**: the cockatrice, or basilisk, was supposedly hatched from a cock's (*sic*) egg and able to kill with one look from its eyes (cf. *FQ*, IV.vii.37)

gaberdines: here, loose garments as worn by almsmen or beggars.

155 **Queene ... Fountaine**: cf. note to p. 25 above.

Hellicon **or** *Pernassus* **Hill**: Helicon was a part of Parnassus, a mountain near Delphi; one of the two summits of Parnassus was consecrated to Apollo and the Muses.

156 **the pikes ... steele**: such staves would not have been part of the normal equipment of a pilgrim; but cf. the Middle English *Bevis*, where Saber sets out with knights disguised as pilgrims and armed with 'longe pikes of wel gode stel' (Auchinleck text, ed. Kölbing, line 3856).

Dolphins ... iourney: dolphins are associated with calm seas.

158 **seuerall**: separate.

cunning Inchauntresse ... Cittie: cf. the account of Kalyb at p. 6 above.

Campheere, Bisse, or Amber-greece: all aromatic substances.

the Inchauntresse ... serpents: cf. p. 10 above.

160   **bred ...** *Sardinia*: Sardinian-bred saddle-horses were famous for their hardiness and stamina.

      Ginets ... *Spaine*: cf. notes to pp. 32 and 33 above.

      Cæsars **steedes**: on Julius Caesar's horsemanship, see Suetonius, I.lvii, lxi.

161   **beaten passages**: well-trodden roads.

      Lusitania: Portugal.

162   **Moores**: at this date, a rather vague term denoting Moslems or Blacks.

162–3   *Neroes ...* **vnholie furie**: cf. note to p. 95 above. Nero was believed to have been responsible for the fire that destroyed a great part of Rome in AD 64, and to have played his lyre (or 'fiddled') while it burned.

165   *Damasco ...* **deuice**: cf. note to p. 18 above; Johnson should have been aware from *BH* that Damascus is a city, not a country.

      curteous Iew: although there are precedents for sympathetic literary portrayal of Jews (in Boccaccio, for instance), it is somewhat surprising to find Johnson going against the generally anti-Semitic tenor of the 1590s. This is the decade that saw the first performances of *The Jew of Malta* (1592) and *The Merchant of Venice* (1596–8); in 1594 Queen Elizabeth's physician, a Sephardic Jew called Lopez, had been burned at the stake for allegedly attempting to poison the Queen.

      quarries of blewstones: the precise sense here is unclear. *OED* does not record for either noun any meaning appropriate to this context.

      as many windows ... world began: cf. p. 41 above.

      Phœbus ... **bed**: cf. note to p. 103 above.

      foure ages of the World: the Four Ages (Golden, Silver, Bronze and Iron) are described in Ovid, *Metamorphoses*, I.89–150.

166   **dame nature**: the Neoplatonic personification of Nature as the beneficent vicegerent of God, presiding over the processes of procreation, can be traced back to the work of Alain de Lille in the twelfth century. In English it is best known from Chaucer's *The Parliament of Fowls*, where Nature is described as 'the vicaire of the almyghty Lord' (line 379); cf. Spenser's *Mutabilitie Cantos* (*FQ*, VII.vii.5). It is a literary commonplace to describe someone as the finest of Nature's works (e.g. *The Canterbury Tales*, VI.9–31).

167   *Hercules ...* **twaine**: Cerberus was the three-headed dog who guarded the entrance to Hades. The last of the twelve labours that Hercules performed for Eurystheus was to bring Cerberus up from the Underworld.

      Sonne of *Ioue*: Hercules, the son of Jove and Alcmene. Cf. note to p. 38 above.

      admiration: wonder, amazement.

168   **conuenient**: fitting, (morally) appropriate.

170   **Flemish Mares**: Flanders was noted for breeding heavy, powerful war-horses.

Hector: the eldest son of King Priam, and the leader of the Trojan forces.

171   **golden pledge of knighthood**: probably a reference to the Order of the Garter (cf. note to p. 7 above).

172   *Vaspasian*: the triumph of Vespasian and his son Titus (cf. note to p. 89 above) is described in Josephus, VII.v.2–7. It is said to have included the display of treasures taken from the Temple of Jerusalem.
        Sonnets: sung verses.

173   **holy Hill ... Rocke**: cf. the descriptions of the Holy Sepulchre, of 'the temple of oure lord' and of Mount Sion in *Mandeville's Travels*, pp. 55, 60, 66–8; Johnson seems to have conflated elements from each in his account of Christ's sepulchre.
        always ... *Iudea*: the twelve virgins correspond to the four (or six) Vestal Virgins who tended the sacred fire in the temple of Vesta, goddess of the hearth, in Rome.

174   **hearbes**: grass.

175   **maskte ... shapes**: went around the world disguised as humans.
        plaine: flat.

176   **treauet**: trivet.

177   **cipresse**: a wood traditionally associated with death and mourning (cf. *Twelfth Night*, II.iv.52).

181   **christall Towers of Heauen**: cf. Revelation xxi.11, describing the New Jerusalem.
        christeline: white, radiant?

182   **wherein ... thyself?**: though the general meaning here is clear, the precise sense is not. The reading remains unaltered in subsequent editions.

183   **remained**: dwelt.

184   **saddest**: darkest.

185   **why didst thou not ... childhood**: in various stories of the 'Man Tried by Fate' kind, the protagonist is offered the choice between suffering in youth or in later life; invariably (as in the Middle English romance of *Sir Isumbras*), the former is chosen.
        lustfull heauens: this apostrophe – appropriate to the classical gods of Olympus rather than to the Christian deity – has been omitted from the 1616 edition.

188   **cut my thrid of life**: cf. note to p. 33 above.
        defusedly: diffusely.
        figure: image.

189   **were the induction of**: were leading up to.
        ruthful: expressing grief (or, perhaps, penitence for having failed to deliver the letter).
        Tygris: a river in present-day Iraq; according to the Bible (where it is called Hiddekel), one of the four rivers that flowed out of Eden (Genesis ii.10–14).

191   **warped such strange webs**: wove such strange tapestries.
        to be sacrificed vnto their Gods: the punishment for Vestal Virgins guilty of unchastity was to be buried alive in an underground chamber.

192   **nurses ... commaundement**: this recalls the delivery of Sabra in Part I, Chapter XVII above.

193   **there would come ... wilde beastes**: cf. note to p. 129 above.

         rauenous Harpies: winged female creatures which snatch or defile food (cf. Virgil, *Aeneid*, III.225–8).

         teene: pain, injury.

194   **learned fountain**: Hippocrene (cf. note to p. 48 above).

         speach of *Mercury*: Mercury was the god of scholarship and learning.

195   **mertel tree ... prince of trees**: the catalogue of trees belongs to a tradition which goes back to Ovid, *Metamorphoses*, X.90–105; cf. also Chaucer, *The Parliament of Fowls*, lines 176–82; *FQ*, I.i.8–9. In *Amadis de Gaule*, II, i, a 'man made of copper' (cf. note to p. 119 above) is placed 'at the entrie of an Orchard (planted with diuerse sorts of trees)'.

196   **where as were feeding ... enemies**: this idyllic scene, unexpected in such close proximity to the Black Castle, recalls the 'holy mountain' described in Isaiah xi.6–9.

         Piramides of *Egipt*: cf. note to p. 31 above. Johnson reverts to speaking of 'Grecian Piramides' in *Tom a Lincolne*, I, VI (p. 41).

         siluer Trumpet: cf. note to p. 6 above.

197   **bats of steele**: cf. note to p. 119 above.

         Cerberus **... flesh**: when Hercules (Alcides) descended to the Underworld to capture Cerberus (cf. note to p. 167 above), he was bitten by the dog's serpent tail.

         sinkes of my channelles: probably 'the depths of my sewers'.

198   *Brandamond*: Bradmound is the name of a character in *BH* (cf. note to p. 17 above).

         without tongues: so that they cannot speak any more 'such folly and foolishnes'.

200   **without seeing ... backes**: cf. the adventure of the Forbidden Chamber in Munday, *Amadis de Gaule*, II, ii: 'Then ... hee marched right towardes the forbidden place. But he went not farre forward, when he felt himselfe layd at so sore, and so often ouercharged with the stroakes of Launces and swords, as hee verily beleeued that no man was able long to suffer them: notwithstanding ... he marched forward, laying about him heere and there, but knewe not vpon whom.'

         so hardly intreated: so hard pressed.

         troad ... bones: Willkomm (p. 75) compares the story of Jack the Giant-Killer (cf. Opie and Opie, p. 54).

201   **dwaile**: a soporific drink, perhaps made from belladonna.

         seede of Poppie: opium (cf. Ridley's note to *Othello*, III.iii.335).

         he had ... open: Johnson seems somewhat undecided as to the serpent's sex, though the pronouns are usually feminine; however, *he* remains uncorrected in later editions. Python, the dragon slain by Apollo at Delphi, was also female and also associated with a well (see below).

twoo tuskes: in the Middle English *Bevis*, though not in the printed text, the dragon of Cologne is described as having tusks (Auchinleck text, ed. Kölbing, line 2663).

202   **cutting sword**: a sharp sword for cutting, as opposed to a heavier thrusting sword.

feathers: a very unusual, if not a unique, feature in such an antagonist. However, this two-legged 'serpent' can only be visualized as birdlike in the way it moves.

imbraced ... squeeze her: this was the way in which Hercules overcame Cerberus, Pluto having granted him permission to fight the dog only on condition that he used no weapons.

204   **the haplesse King of *Babilon***: Nebuchadnezzar (cf. note to p. 25 above).

205   **silke colour of Spaine**: 'silke colour' perhaps denotes a glossy silver-grey; for Spanish horses, see p. 32 above.

206   **but one eye ... proceed**: the monster's single eye relates him to the Cyclopes of classical mythology, but I know of no parallel to the glass in his breast.

207   **musket**: the term is sometimes used to denote the matchlock, which had become a principal weapon in European warfare by the mid-sixteenth century, supplanting the crossbow.

209   *art*: i.e. magic arts.

forwardnes: daring.

Plutoes **Dogge**: Cerberus.

Diamonds ... Hall: it was believed in the Middle Ages that precious stones shone with a light of their own (cf. Heather, pp. 237–43).

210   **glided from their hands**: water similarly withdrew itself from the hands of Tantalus (cf. note to p. 97 above).

211   **two ayrie spirits ... Chariot**: after killing her own children, Medea escaped in a chariot drawn by two dragons (cf. Ovid, *Metamorphoses*, VII.350–1).

riding racks: floating clouds.

212   **traces**: pursuit.

Steed: I have been unable to identify the species of this curious beast; except in its colouring, it seems to be largely a mixture of elephant and camel.

213   **without helpe of stirrop**: commonly regarded as the sign of an accomplished rider (cf. the Auchinleck text of *Bevis*, ed. Kölbing, lines 1945–6).

214   *infringe*: break, destroy.

explayne: display.

215   **inflicted**: afflicted.

I neuer denied ... the same: it would have been part of St George's duty as a knight to afford protection and help to the 'weaker sex' (see Barber, pp. 39–40).

217   **bewray**: reveal.

his vitall ... his earthly: the pronouns are unusual here. The Latin *cor* 'heart' is neuter in grammatical gender; the soul can be either feminine (*anima*) or masculine (*animus*) but is usually referred to in English as 'she'.

218   **out of hand**: immediately.

         Chariot ... Dragons: cf. note to p. 211 above.

219   **Sepulcher ... *Memphis***: probably a reference to the tomb of Alexander the Great, whose body is supposed to have been transported in a lead sarcophagus first to Memphis and then to Alexandria.

220   **discharging ... withall**: clearing myself of the charges that you bring against me.

         within whose lappe ... sleepe: cf. note to p. 76 above.

221   *Clitus*: in a fit of drunkenness, Alexander killed Cleitus, who was his friend and the brother of his foster-mother, with a spear (cf. Walter's note to *Henry V*, IV.vii.40–1); he bitterly regretted this act.

224   **straight**: narrow

225   *doth on woe consist*: has its existence based on sorrow.

         sacred selues: the satyrs were the attendants of the god Bacchus and were sometimes seen as minor deities in their own right.

         desire the burthen: wish to know the meaning.

226   *Sith*: since.

227   **agreeable**: corresponding.

         his loathsome bowelles: the Harpies were in fact female (cf. note to p. 193 above).

         King of *Thebes*: Oedipus.

229   **and preserued it**: i.e. she ought to have preserved it.

         wilde beastes ... crueltie: this is inconsistent with p. 193 above.

230   **purple**: cf. Greek *oinops* 'wine-coloured', 'wine-dark' as applied to the sea by Homer.

         desire: request.

232   **sillie**: deserving of pity *or* helpless.

235   **let**: desist, forbear.

         declined the foyle to neither party: did not allow either party to be defeated.

         astonied: stunned (literally).

236   **(yet freshly bleeding)**: the significance of this is uncertain. It may be that this detail is supposed to indicate the speed of Rosana and the magician's journey with Leoger's body. On the other hand, it seems clear from the state of Leoger's armour before they set out (p. 233 above) that he has already been dead for some time at that point. The body of a dead person was supposed to bleed in the presence of that person's murderer; perhaps in this case Leoger's body continues to do so until it has been laid in its final resting-place.

237   **Sepulcher of Cristall**: *Sepulcher* here seems to denote some sort of memorial tableau, though the exact meaning – and the distinction between *graue*, *Tombe* and *Sepulcher* – are not altogether clear.

spirits ... side: these spirits seem to be succubi, demons to whom the necromancer has sold his soul in return for his magical powers. The left side is always associated with the Devil and forces of evil.

239	**made no question of**: had no doubt that they would get.

intestine warre: civil war.

did they all make seuerall frends: they all made separate alliances.

But of traitors ... shamefull: cf. 'It is true without lesing, of falsehood commeth no good ending' (*BH*, sig. Jii^v). This is a romance commonplace: see Kölbing's note to *Bevis*, E 4313^200 (p. 357). Cf. also Johnson's work *A Lanterne-light for Loyall Subiects*, described above (p. x).

240	*Circe*: an enchantress, encountered by Ulysses on his way home from Troy, who was capable of transforming humans into a variety of forms – though she usually chose to change them into animals such as pigs.

watchet ... loue: in medieval and Renaissance colour symbolism, blue represented fidelity.

241	**in time ... Diamond**: proverbial (cf. *ODEP*, D618).

242	**which hath ... committed**: possibly a reference to the practice described in the note to p. 191 above, but Johnson's meaning here is not clear.

243	**surfetting Louer**: i.e. one who loved immoderately.

tuition: protection.

244	**golroll**: no such word – or, indeed, any term like it – is recorded in *OED*, though it must be related to *roll* in the sense of 'muster' or 'list'.

deuice: scheme.

Lucius: Johnson's choice of this name for the Roman prince may have been influenced by his reading of Arthurian romance, in which the Emperor Lucius of Rome demands tribute of the young King Arthur (e.g. Malory, vol. I, pp. 185–247).

247	*Grecia ... Constantinople*: cf. note to p. 75 above.

Argier: Algiers.

Fesse: Fez.

Silicia: Cilicia, a region of southern Anatolia, and in the sixteenth century part of the Ottoman Empire.

iust: joust.

248	*Alcida*: the name also occurs in Jorge de Montemayor's *Diana*, an Arcadian romance written in Spanish *c.* 1559. An English translation by Bartholomew Yonge was published in 1598.

Phœbe: the moon.

race: course (in the tournament).

249	**golden Lyon ... field**: probably the heraldry here is Johnson's own invention (cf. note to p. 79 above), but a golden lion did figure in the arms of the Tudors (*Boutell's Heraldry*, p. 211).

knotty: rough, gnarled.

250	**valed his bonnet**: took off his mail cap.

curious: skilful.

252   **yet obtained ... delightes**: of the Seven Champions' wives/mistresses, only Sabra has been conveniently disposed of, but this does not seem to pose any obstacle to these further liaisons.

253   *Dulcippa*: Johnson uses the name again in *Tom a Lincolne* (pp. 30, etc.); there too it is used for a woman of humbler birth than her princely lover.

254   **No sooner ... owne life**: cf. note to p. 122 above.

255   **artificially**: ingeniously, artistically.

       determined pretence: planned ruse.

       Mercutio: the name may well have been borrowed from Shakespeare's *Romeo and Juliet*, which was probably written around 1595, although it was not published until 1597. It also occurs in Shakespeare's source, Arthur Brooke's *The Tragicall Historye of Romeus and Juliet* (1562).

       forewinde: a favourable wind, blowing the ship forwards on its course.

256   **in great courage**: with great determination.

       Gallie: a low, single-decked vessel propelled with sails and oars.

261   **lying at roade**: riding at anchor.

       Peru: it is pointless to speculate whether Johnson intended some other, similarly named place or whether he simply borrowed the name for its exotic flavour without regard to its actual location. On his situation of Constantinople in Greece, see note to p. 75 above.

262   **maintaine**: uphold in battle.

       Of whose ... hereafter: it may be that Johnson himself intended at this stage to write a third part of *7Ch*. Although he did not do so (Part III first appearing nearly a century later), he did add seven further chapters in the 1616 edition; these, however, are concerned almost entirely with the deaths of the seven champions. Cf. pp. xxiii–xxiv above.

       so that: provided that.

Index to Notes

This is an index to names or terms that occur repeatedly in the text of *7Ch* and indicates at what point they are annotated. It is *not* an index to the contents of the notes themselves.

Bibliography

Primary Sources

Amadis de Gaule: *see* Munday, Anthony.

Amis and Amiloun: *see* Fellows, Jennifer (ed.), *Of Love and Chivalry*, pp. 73–145 *Arthur of Little Britaine. The History of the Most Noble and valyant Knight, Arthur of little Britaine, translated out of French into English by the noble Iohn Bourgcher Knight, Lord Barners* [*sic*] (London: printed by Thomas East, [1582]) Ascham, Roger. *Toxophilvs, 1545* (Menston, IL: Scolar Press, 1971).

Barclay, Alexander. *The Life of St George*, ed. William Nelson, EETS 230 (London: Oxford University Press for the EETS, 1955).

Barnicle, Mary Elizabeth (ed.). *The Seege or Batayle of Troye: a Middle English Metrical Romance*, EETS OS 172 (London: Oxford University Press for the EETS, 1927).

Brunner, Karl (ed.). *Der mittelenglische Versroman über Richard Löwenherz*, Wiener Beiträge zur englischen Philologie 42 (Vienna and Leipzig: Braumüller, 1913).

—— (ed.). *The Seven Sages of Rome (Southern Version)*, EETS OS 191 (London: Oxford University Press for the EETS, 1933).

Bunyan, John. *The Entire Works of John Bunyan*, ed. Henry Stebbing, vol. I (London: Virtue, 1859).

—— *'Life and Death of Mr Badman' and 'The Holy War'*, ed. John Brown, Cambridge English Classics (Cambridge: Cambridge University Press, 1905).

Carmody, Francis J. (ed.). *Physiologus Latinus Versio Y*, University of California Publications in Classical Philology 12:7 (Berkeley and Los Angeles, CA: University of California Press, 1941).

Caxton, William. *Caxton's Blanchardyn and Eglantine c. 1489*, ed. Leon Kellner, EETS ES 58 (London: Trübner for the EETS, 1890).

Chevelere Assigne: *see* Speed, Diane (ed.), *Medieval English Romances*, pp. 150–70.

Davies, Sir John. *The Poems of Sir John Davies*, ed. Robert Krueger (Oxford: Clarendon Press, 1975).

Dickson, Arthur (ed.). *Valentine and Orson, translated from the French by Henry Watson*, EETS OS 204 (London: Oxford University Press for the EETS, 1937).

Emaré: *see* Mills, Maldwyn (ed.), *Six Middle English Romances*, pp. 46–74.

Fellows, Jennifer (ed.). *Of Love and Chivalry: an Anthology of Middle English Romance* (London: Dent; Rutland, VT: Tuttle, 1993).

Geoffrey of Monmouth. *The History of the Kings of Britain*, trans. Lewis Thorpe (Harmondsworth: Penguin, 1966).

Gesta Romanorum: *see* Swan, Charles.

Golding, Arthur. *Ovid's Metamorphoses: the Arthur Golding Translation 1567*, ed. John Frederick Nims; with a new essay, *Shakespeare's Ovid*, by Jonathan Bate (Philadelphia, PA: Dry, 2000).

Grimms' Tales for Young and Old: the Complete Stories, trans. Ralph Manheim (London: Gollancz, 1978).

Helyas, Knight of the Swan: *see* Thoms, William J. (ed.), *A Collection of Early Prose Romances*, vol. III.

Herrtage, S. J. (ed.). *Sir Ferumbras*, The English Charlemagne Romances 1, EETS ES 34 (London: Kegan Paul, Trench, Trübner & Co. for the EETS, 1879).

History of the Damnable Life and Deserved Death of Dr John Faustus, The: see Thoms, William J. (ed.), *A Collection of Early Prose Romances*, vol. III.

Johnson, Richard. *R.I., The History of Tom Thumbe*, ed. Curt F. Bühler (Evanston, IL: Northwestern University Press for the Renaissance English Text Society, 1965).

—— *The Most Pleasant History of Tom a Lincolne*, ed. Richard S. M. Hirsch (Columbia, SC: University of South Carolina Press, 1978).

Jonson, Ben. *Three Comedies*, ed. Michael Jamieson (Harmondsworth: Penguin, 1966).

Kölbing, Eugen (ed.). *The Romance of Sir Beues of Hampton*, EETS 46, 48 65 (London: Kegan Paul, Trench, Trübner & Co. for the EETS, 1885–94).

—— (ed.). *Sir Tristrem*, Die nordische und die englische Version der Tristan-Sage 2 (Heilbronn, 1882).

Kyng Alisaunder: see Smithers, G. V.

Lancelot of the Laik: see Skeat, W. W.

Layamon. *Brut*, ed. G. L. Brook and R. F. Leslie, EETS 250, 277 (London: Oxford University Press for the EETS, 1963–78).

Lodge, Thomas. *Lodge's 'Rosalynde', being the original of Shakespeare's 'As You Like It'*, ed. W. W. Greg (New York: Duffield, 1907).

Lyly, John. *The Complete Works of John Lyly*, ed. R. Warwick Bond, 3 vols (Oxford: Clarendon Press, 1967).

Malory, Sir Thomas. *The Works of Sir Thomas Malory*, ed. Eugène Vinaver, 2nd edn, 3 vols (Oxford: Clarendon Press, 1967).

Mandeville's Travels: see Seymour, M. C.

Marlowe, Christopher. *The Plays of Christopher Marlowe*, ed. Roma Gill (London: Oxford University Press, 1971).

Mills, Maldwyn (ed.). *Six Middle English Romances* (London: Dent, 1973).

—— (ed.). *Ywain and Gawain, Sir Percyvell of Gales, The Anturs of Arther*, Everyman's Library (London: Dent; Rutland, VT: Tuttle, 1992).

Munday, Anthony. *The Avncient, Famovs and Honourable History of Amadis de Gaule ...* (London: Nicholas Okes, 1619).

O'Sullivan, Mary Isabelle (ed.). *Firumbras and Otuel and Roland*, EETS OS 198 (London: Oxford University Press for the EETS, 1935).

Otuel and Roland: see O'Sullivan, Mary Isabelle.

Painter, William. *The Palace of Pleasure*, ed. Joseph Jacobs, 3 vols (1890; repr. Hildesheim: Olms, 1968).

Pettie, George. *A petite Pallace of Pettie his pleasure ...* (London: printed for R.W., [1576]).

Physiologus Latinus: see Carmody, Francis J.

Richard Coer de Lion: see Brunner, Karl.

Richardson, Frances E. (ed.). *Sir Eglamour of Artois*, EETS 256 (London: Oxford University Press for the EETS, 1965).

Robert the Deuyll: see Thoms, William J. (ed.), *A Collection of Early Prose Romances*, vol. I.

Ruskin, John. *Præterita: the Autobiography of John Ruskin* (Oxford: Oxford University Press, 1978)

Seege or Batayle of Troye, The: see Barnicle, Mary Elizabeth

Sege of Melayne, The: see Mills, Maldwyn (ed.), *Six Middle English Romances*, pp. 1–45

Seven Sages of Rome, The: see Brunner, Karl

Seymour, M. C. (ed.). *Mandeville's Travels* (Oxford: Clarendon Press, 1967).

Sidney, Sir Philip. *The Poems of Sir Philip Sidney*, ed. William A. Ringler, Jr (Oxford: Clarendon Press, 1962.

Simons, John (ed.). *'Guy of Warwick' and Other Chapbook Romances: Six Tales from the Popular Literature of Pre-Industrial England* (Exeter: University of Exeter Press, 1998).

Sir Eglamour of Artois: see Richardson, Frances E.

Sir Ferumbras: see Herrtage, S. J.

Sir Gawain and the Green Knight: see Tolkien, J. R. R., and E. V. Gordon

Sir Gowther: see Mills, Maldwyn (ed.), *Six Middle English Romances*, pp. 148–68.

Sir Isumbras: see Mills, Maldwyn (ed.), *Six Middle English Romances*, pp. 125–47.

Sir Percyvell of Gales: see Mills, Maldwyn (ed.), *Ywain and Gawain [etc.]*, pp. 103–60.

Sir Tristrem: see Kölbing, Eugen.

Skeat, W. W. (ed.). *Lancelot of the Laik: a Scottish Metrical Romance (about 1490–1500 A.D.)*, 2nd edn (London: Oxford University Press for the EETS, 1870).

Smithers, G. V. (ed.). *Kyng Alisaunder*, EETS 227, 237 (London: Oxford University Press for the EETS, 1952–7).

Speed, Diane (ed.). *Medieval English Romances*, 2nd edn, 2 vols (Sydney: Department of English, University of Sydney, 1989).

Spenser, Edmund. *The Faerie Qveene*, ed. A. C. Hamilton, Longman Annotated English Poets (London and New York: Longman, 1977).

Sperk, Klaus (ed.). *Medieval English Saints' Legends*, English Texts (Tübingen: Niemeyer, 1970).

Subrenat, Jean (ed.). *Le Roman d'Auberon: prologue de 'Huon de Bourdeaux'*, Textes littéraires français 202 (Paris and Geneva: Droz, 1973).

Swan, Charles (trans.). *Gesta Romanorum*, rev. Wynnard Hooper (London: Bell, 1905).

Syr Bevis of Hampton (London: printed by Thomas East, [1582?]).

—— *see* Kölbing, Eugen.

Syr Launfal: see Fellows, Jennifer (ed.), *Of Love and Chivalry*, pp. 199–229.

Thoms, William J. (ed.). *A Collection of Early Prose Romances*, 3 vols (London: Pickering, 1827–8).

Tolkien, J. R. R., and E. V. Gordon (eds). *Sir Gawain and the Green Knight*, 2nd edn, rev. Norman Davis (Oxford: Clarendon Press, 1967).

Valentine and Orson: see Dickson, Arthur.

Warner, William. *Albions England* [facsimile] (Hildesheim and New York: Olms, 1971).

Webster, John. *The Selected Plays of John Webster*, ed. Jonathan Dollimore and Alan Sinfield, Plays by Renaissance and Restoration Dramatists (Cambridge: Cambridge University Press, 1983).

Secondary Sources

Avery, Gillian. 'Books for the first enterers', *Signal*, 75 (1994), 194–208.

Baker, Ernest A. *The History of the English Novel: the Elizabethan Age and After* (London: Witherby, 1929).

Baldwin, Peter. *Toy Theatres of the World* (London: Zwemmer, 1992).

Barber, Richard. *The Knight and Chivalry* (London: Cardinal, 1974).

Barron, W. R. J., Françoise Le Saux and Lesley Johnson, 'Dynastic chronicles', in W. R. J. Barron (ed.), *The Arthur of the English: the Arthurian Legend in Medieval Life and Literature* (Cardiff: University of Wales Press, 1999), pp. 11–46.

Bengtson, Jonathan. 'St George and the formation of English nationalism', *Journal of Medieval and Early Modern Studies*, 27 (1997), 317–40.

Boutell's Heraldry, rev. J. P. Brooke-Little (London and New York: Warne, 1973).

Brody, Alan. *The English Mummers and Their Plays: Traces of Ancient Mystery* (London: Routledge & Kegan Paul, [1970]).

Bryant, Jerry H. 'Richard Johnson's *Musarum Plangores*', *Renaissance News*, 16:1 (1963), 94–8.

Chambers, Sir Edmund. *The English Folk-Play* (Oxford: Clarendon Press, 1933).

Chester, Allan G. 'Richard Johnson's *Golden Garland*', *Modern Language Quarterly*, 10 (1949), 61–7.

Childress, Diana T. 'Between romance and legend: "secular hagiography" in Middle English literature', *Philological Quarterly*, 57 (1978), 311–22.

Collier, J. Payne. *A Bibliographical and Critical Account of the Rarest Books in the English Language* ..., vol. II (London: Lilly, 1865).

Crane, Ronald S. 'The vogue of *Guy of Warwick* from the close of the Middle Ages to the Romantic revival', *PMLA*, 30 (1915), 125–94.

—— *The Vogue of Medieval Chivalric Romance during the English Renaissance* (Menasha, WI: University of Wisconsin Press, 1919).

Darton, F. J. Harvey. *Children's Books in England: Five Centuries of Social Life*, 3rd edn, rev. Brian Alderson (Cambridge: Cambridge University Press, 1982).

de Laborderie, O. 'Richard the Lionheart and the birth of a national cult of St George in England: origins and development of a legend', *Nottingham Medieval Studies*, 39 (1995), 37–53.

Dickson, Arthur. '"Fat" (*Hamlet*, v.ii.298)', *Shakespeare Quarterly*, 2 (1951), 171–2.

Dodge, R. E. Neil. 'The Well of Life and the Tree of Life (*The Faery Queen*, Bk. I, c. xi.)', *Modern Philology*, 6 (1908), 1–6.

Duffy, Eamon. *The Stripping of the Altars: Traditional Religion in England c.1400–c.1580* (New Haven, CT and London: Yale University Press, 1992).

Falke, Anne. '"The work well done that pleaseth all": Emmanuel Forde and the seventeenth-century popular chivalric romance', *Studies in Philology*, 78 (1981), 241–54.

Farmer, David Hugh. *The Oxford Dictionary of Saints* (Oxford: Clarendon Press, 1978).

Fellows, Jennifer. '*Bevis redivivus*: the printed editions of *Sir Bevis of Hampton*', in *Romance Reading on the Book: Essays on Medieval Narrative presented to Maldwyn Mills*, ed. Jennifer Fellows, Rosalind Field, Gillian Rogers and Judith Weiss (Cardiff: University of Wales Press, 1996), pp. 251–68.

—— 'On the iconography of a carving in King's College Chapel, Cambridge', *Journal of the Warburg and Courtauld Institutes*, 39 (1976), 262.

—— 'St George as romance hero', *Reading Medieval Studies*, 19 (1993), 27–54.

—— (ed.). '*Sir Beves of Hampton*: Study and Edition', 5 vols (unpub. Ph.D. dissertation, University of Cambridge, 1980).

Field, Rosalind. 'Romance as history, history as romance', in *Romance in Medieval England*, ed. Maldwyn Mills, Jennifer Fellows and Carol M. Meale (Woodbridge: Brewer, 1991).

Friedman, John Block. 'Eurydice, Heurodis, and the noon-day demon', *Speculum*, 41 (1966), 22–9.

Gerould, Gordon Hall. *Saints' Lives*, Types of English Literature (Boston, MA and New York: Houghton Mifflin, 1916).

Gerritsen, Willem P., and Anthony G. van Melle (eds). *A Dictionary of Medieval Heroes: Characters in Medieval Narrative Traditions and Their Afterlife in Literature, Theatre and the Visual Arts*, trans. Tanis Guest (Woodbridge: Boydell Press, 1998).

Girouard, Mark. *The Return to Camelot: Chivalry and the English Gentleman* (New Haven, CT and London: Yale University Press, 1981).

Golder, Harold. 'Browning's *Childe Roland*', *PMLA*, 39 (1924), 963–78.

—— 'Bunyan and Spenser', *PMLA*, 45 (1930), 216–37.

—— 'Bunyan's Valley of the Shadow', *Modern Philology*, 27 (1929), 55–72.

Graf, A. *I complementi della chanson d'Huon de Bordeaux*, I: *Auberon* (Halle: Niemeyer, 1878).

Hamilton, A. C. 'Elizabethan romance: the example of prose fiction', *ELH*, 49 (1982), 287–99.

Harper, Carrie Anna. *The Sources of the British Chronicle History in Spenser's 'Faerie Queene'* (1910; repr. New York: Haskell House, 1964).

Heather, P. J. 'Precious stones in the Middle-English verse of the fourteenth century', *Folk-Lore*, 42 (1931), 217–64, 345–404.

Heath-Stubbs, John. 'The hero as saint: St George', in *The Hero in Tradition and Folklore: Papers read at a Conference of the Folklore Society held at Dyffryn House, Cardiff, July 1982*, ed. H. R. E. Davidson, Mistletoe Series 19 (London: Folklore Society, 1984)

Helgerson, Richard. *Forms of Nationhood: the Elizabethan Writing of England* (Chicago, IL and London: University of Chicago Press, 1992).

Helm, Alex. *The English Mummers' Play*, Mistletoe Series 14 (Woodbridge: Brewer for the Folklore Society, 1980).

Hirsch, Richard S. M. 'The source of Richard Johnson's *Look on Me London*', *English Language Notes*, 13 (1975), 107–13.

Hole, Christina. *Saints in Folklore* (London: Bell, 1966).

Horton, Adey. 'The real St George', *Sunday Times Magazine*, 20 Apr. 1975, pp. 34–43

Hulst, Cornelia Steketee. *St George of Cappadocia in Legend and History* (London: Nutt, 1909).

Hurley, Margaret. 'Saints' lives and romance again: secularization of structure and motif', *Genre*, 8 (1975), 60–73.

Jackson, W. A., F. S. Ferguson and K. A. Pantzer (eds). *A Short-Title Catalogue of Books Printed in England, Scotland, & Ireland, and of English Books Printed Abroad, 1475–1640*, rev. edn, 3 vols (London: Bibliographical Society, 1976–91).

James, M. R. 'The sculptures in the Lady Chapel at Ely', *Archaeological Journal*, 49 (1892), 345–62.

Johnston, Arthur. *Enchanted Ground: the Study of Medieval Romance in the Eighteenth Century* (London: Athlone Press, 1964).

Keen, Maurice. *Chivalry* (New Haven, CT and London: Yale University Press, 1984).

King, Andrew. *'The Faerie Queene' and Middle English Romance: the Matter of Just Memory*, Oxford English Monographs (Oxford: Clarendon Press, 2000).

King, John N. *English Reformation Literature: the Tudor Origins of the Protestant Tradition* (Princeton, NJ: Princeton University Press, 1982).

Lieber, Naomi C. 'Elizabethan pul fiction: the example of Richard Johnson', *Critical Survey*, 12:2 (2000), 71–87.

Luckett, Richard. 'The Legend of St Cecilia in English Literature: a Study' (unpub. Ph.D. diss., University of Cambridge, 1972).

McCoy, Richard C. *The Rites of Knighthood: the Literature and Politics of Elizabethan Chivalry* (Berkeley, CA and London: University of California Press, 1989).

Mahl, Mary R. 'Richard Johnson in England's Helicon', *Notes and Queries*, 7 (1960), 52.

Mallette, Richard. *Spenser and the Discourses of Reformation England* (Lincoln, NB and London: University of Nebraska Press, 1997).

Marcus, G. J. *Saint George of England* (London: Williams & Norgate, 1929).

Matzke, John E. 'Contributions to the history of the legend of Saint George, with special reference to the sources of the French, German and Anglo-Saxon metrical versions', *PMLA*, 17 (1902), 464–535; 18 (1903), 99–171.

—— 'The legend of Saint George: its development into a *roman d'aventure*', *PMLA*, 19 (1904), 449–78.

Merchant, Paul. 'Thomas Heywood's hand in *The Seven Champions of Christendom*', *Library*, 3rd series, 33:3 (1978), 226–30.

Murray, Alan V. 'Reinbot von Durne's *Der heilige Georg* as crusading literature', *Forum for Modern Language Studies*, 22 (1986), 172–83.

O'Connor, John J. *'Amadis de Gaule' and Its Influence on Elizabethan Literature* (New Brunswick, NJ: Rutgers University Press, 1970).

Opie, Iona and Peter. *The Classic Fairy Tales* (London: Book Club Associates, 1974).

Padelford, F. M., and Matthew O'Connor. 'Spenser's use of the St George legend', *Studies in Philology*, 23 (1926), 142–56.

Plett, Heinrich F. 'An Elizabethan best seller: Richard Johnson's *The Seven Champions of Christendom* (1596)', in *Modes of Narrative: Approaches to American, Canadian and British Fiction presented to Helmut Bonheim*, ed. Reingard M. Nischik and Barbara Korte (Würzburg: Königshausen & Neumann, 1990), pp. 234–51.

Proudfoot, Richard. 'Richard Johnson's *Tom a Lincoln* dramatized: a Jacobean play in MS Add. 61745', in *New Ways of Looking at Old Texts: Papers of the Renaissance English Text Society, 1985–1991*, ed. W. Speed Hill, Medieval & Renaissance Texts & Studies 107 (Binghamton, NY: Renaissance English Text Society, 1993), pp. 75–101.

Purkiss, Diane. *Troublesome Things: a History of Fairies and Fairy Stories* (London: Allen Lane/Penguin Press, 2000).

Radford, E. and M. A. *Encyclopaedia of Superstitions*, ed. and rev. Christina Hole (London: Hutchinson, 1961).

Riches, Samantha. *St George: Hero, Martyr and Myth* (Thrupp, Stroud: Sutton, 2000).

Richmond, Velma Bourgeois. *The Legend of Guy of Warwick*, Garland Studies in Medieval Literature 14; Garland Reference Library of the Humanities 1929 (New York and London: Garland, 1996).

Roberts, Brynley F. 'Yr India Fawr a'r India Fechan', *Llên Cymru*, 13:3/4 (1980–1), 281–3

Salzman, Paul. *English Prose Fiction 1558–1700* (Oxford: Clarendon Press, 1985).

Simons, John. 'Medievalism as cultural process in pre-industrial popular literature', *Studies in Medievalism*, 7 (1995), 5–21.

—— 'Robert Parry's *Moderatus*: a study in Elizabethan romance', in *Romance Reading on the Book: Essays on Medieval Narrative presented to Maldwyn Mills*, ed. Jennifer Fellows, Rosalind Field, Gillian Rogers and Judith Weiss (Cardiff: University of Wales Press, 1996), pp. 237–50.

Speed, Diane. 'The construction of the nation in medieval English romance', in *Readings in Medieval English Romance*, ed. Carol M. Meale (Woodbridge: Brewer, 1994), pp. 135–57.

Spufford, Margaret. *Small Books and Pleasant Histories: Popular Fiction and Its Readership in Seventeenth-Century England* (London: Methuen, 1981).

Stephen, Sir Leslie, *et al.* (eds). *The Dictionary of National Biography* (London: Smith, Elder & Co., 1885–).

Tiddy, R. J. E. *The Mummers' Play* (1923; repr. Chicheley: Minet, 1972).

Wahlgren, E. G. 'Renseignements sur quelques manuscrits français de la Bibliothèque nationale de Turin, *Studier i Modern Språkvetenskap*, 12 (1934), 79–124.

Watt, Tessa. *Cheap Print and Popular Piety 1550–1640*, Cambridge Studies in Early Modern British History (Cambridge: Cambridge University Press, 1991).

Weatherby, Harold L. 'The true Saint George', *ELR*, 17 (1987), 119–41.

Wells, Whitney. 'Spenser's dragon', *Modern Language Notes*, 41 (1926), 143–57.

White, Helen C. *Tudor Books of Saints and Martyrs* (Madison, WI: University of Wisconsin Press, 1963).

Whiting, Bartlett Jere. *Proverbs, Sentences and Proverbial Phrases from English Writings mainly before 1500* (Cambridge, MA and London, 1968).

Williams, Franklin B., Jr. 'Richard Johnson's borrowed tears', *Studies in Philology*, 34 (1937), 186–90.

Willkomm, H. W. *Über Richard Johnsons 'Seven Champions of Christendom' (1596)* (Berlin: Mayer & Müller, 1911).

Wilson, F. P. (ed.). *Oxford Dictionary of English Proverbs*, 3rd edn (Oxford: Clarendon Press, 1970).

Wilson, T. H. 'Saint George in Tudor and Stuart England' (unpub. M.Phil. dissertation, University of London, 1976).

Wing, Donald G. (ed.). *Short-Title Catalogue of Books Printed in England, Scotland, Ireland, Wales, and British America and of English Books Printed in Other Countries 1641–1700*, 3 vols (New York: Columbia University Press for the Index Society, 1948–51).

Wright, Louis B. *Middle-Class Culture in Elizabethan England* (Chapel Hill, NC: University of North Carolina Press, 1935).